The Challenge of
Anthropology

Other Books by Robin Fox

The Keresan Bridge: A Problem in Pueblo Ethnology
Kinship and Marriage: An Anthropological Perspective
The Imperial Animal (with Lionel Tiger)
Encounter with Anthropology
Biosocial Anthropology (editor)
The Tory Islanders: A People of the Celtic Fringe
The Red Lamp of Incest: A Study in the Origins of Mind and Society
Neonate Cognition: Beyond the Blooming Buzzing Confusion
(edited with Jacques Mehler)
The Violent Imagination
The Search for Society: Quest for a Biosocial Science and Morality
Reproduction and Succession: Studies in Anthropology, Law and Society

ROBIN FOX

The Challenge of Anthropology

Old Encounters and New Excursions

Transaction Publishers
New Brunswick (U.S.A.) and London (U.K.)

Library of Congress Catalog Number: 93-15532
ISBN: 1-56000-119-4
Printed in the United States of America

Library of Congress Cataloging-in-Publication Data

Fox, Robin, 1934-
    The challenge of anthropology : old encounters and new excursions / by
Robin Fox.
        p.   cm.
    Includes bibliographical references (p.   ) and indexes.
    ISBN 1-56000-119-4
    1. Anthropology. 2. Ethnology. I. Title.
    GN 29.F69 193
301--dc20   93-15532
                                                                    CIP

To the memory of

MASON WELCH GROSS

1911-1977

Sixteenth President of Rutgers University

Magna vir sapientia

* * *

Contents

vii

Prologue

Encounter with Anthropology (1973) was a remarkable success, not in huge sales necessarily (although they were good) but in staying steadily before the public for fifteen years in paperback. The kill rate with books these days is so rapid that such a long run is unusual. Only *Kinship and Marriage* did better — still perfect after 26 years! What is more, no other of my books has evoked such a steady and pleasant response from the lay public and from students, many of whom were drawn into anthropology from reading it — a bit odd perhaps in a book that was highly critical of the state of affairs in anthropology at the time. But the criticism was of what was happening to a subject I believed in, and I tried to illustrate the basis of the belief. I think this came through.

The personal and autobiographical line taken (why and how did you become an anthropologist and what happened then?) also seemed to help involve the readers and get them to share some of the excitement of discovery that this unique discipline presents. As I have explained, this autobiographical line was not initially of my choosing but the result of urgings from my editor, Steven Aronson, and the encouragement of Mr. Jovanovich of the firm that bears his name (along with those of Messrs. Harcourt and Brace). This was after all a trade book, and they wanted a selling point that would make it different from the usual stuffiness of "collected essays." The paperback version took the story up to the publication and reception of *The Imperial Animal* (1971), which I wrote with Lionel Tiger, and which caused its little flap and gave us our allotted Whorholian fifteen minutes of fame. (I later coined the word "quindecimalite," meaning "one who has had his fifteen minutes." It is now officially recognized — see Jack Hitt, ed., *In a Word: A*

Dictionary of Words That Don't Exist but Ought To (New York: Dell, 1992) — along with "sheeit," "engynocize," and "yankeephilia").

So I was pleased when, the book having finally gone out of print, Irving Louis Horowitz asked to reissue it in 1991 under the imprint of Transaction Publishers. (He does these wonderful rescue jobs on social science out-of-printers.) I had been thinking of doing another collection along the same lines, since a lot of essays had piled up in the meantime, published and unpublished. I had even sketched out a new introduction to pick up the story and carry it up to the present. Faced with the new Transaction edition, however, I decided to use the new introduction as a final chapter — a "post-epilogue" — to give a finishing touch to the reissue. I called it "From Science to Survival: Twenty Years On." I had by then decided *not* to bring out another book of essays anyway. It is harder work than one might imagine if done right, and I was into other things. ILH, however, can be very persuasive, and after putting together four long pieces for him, which became *Reproduction and Succession: Studies in Anthropology, Law and Society* (1992), I was persuaded again to make the effort to bring together a representative sample of what I had been doing from 1973 to 1993. So here it is.

This leaves me in a quandary about an introduction to the work in front of us. In effect, the conclusion to the Transaction reissue of what we might call from now on *Encounter 1, is* the introduction to the present book since that was its original purpose. What to do, what to do? Somehow it didn't seem right to reprint it here. It had served its purpose as a conclusion to the reprint, and many who read this book will have read the reprint anyway. I can only slyly suggest that those who have not read it might do so, since (honestly) the two books are in a sense one, and anyone reading the first should, to get the whole story, also read the second. If so, that odd bitextual conclusion/introduction will be the bridge between them, and that is just fine.

But, one must admit, all this flurry of post hoc justification does leave at a bit of a loss the reader who has picked up this fat little fellow and is not about to rush out and court its older sister. So, skipping the play-by-play details of intellectual autobiography, let me at least try some color commentary about the state of the game: In the "post-epilogue" previously mentioned, I contrasted the passion and indignation of Fox 1 (who wrote *Encounter 1*) with the cynicism of Fox 2. The latter, in the calmer hormonal state that characterizes the mid-fifties, had failed to appreciate the ardor of his youthful self, and preferred to watch with detached amusement as the parade of fads, fashions, nonsense, and blather went noisily by. He could, he reckons, gently nudge them from time to time in a better direction, or even make enough fun of them that they will see their own foolishness.

Some hope. Satire never works. If it did, the world would now be a perfect place. The satirist — like Pope or Swift or Hogarth for example, or even the

Marquis de Sade or George Orwell — is always a pessimist. He doesn't write the satire because he thinks it will reform people, but because he wants to punish them. His satire is an end in itself. So Fox 2 does his little numbers, not hoping for some Savonarola-like influence on morals and behavior, but to let them know that they can't get away with it scott free. Little brother is watching, and little brother will tell.

Get away with what? With the dismemberment of anthropology and the dissolution of the social contract on which all science and democracy and objective enquiry rest. The two — anthropology and the social contract — are connected. Anthropology, as part of the enterprise of rational social self-enquiry started by the Greeks and picked up again in the Renaissance (not forgetting in the meantime Ibn Khaldun, the great sociologist of Islamic society in the fourteenth century, whom Christian Europe was not to match until Machiavelli), reflects the social order of which it is part. And the current fragmentation of anthropology, about which Fox 2 for all his pretense at indifference continues to protest, is a reflection of the fragmentation of society: the failure of the center to hold and the loosing of mere anarchy upon the world.

There. Savonarola couldn't have done better; but he didn't have Yeats to quote from. The Bonfire of the Vanities is lit, and the dull beast slouches toward Bethlehem to be born. And Fox 2 goes back to contemplating the Epistles (echoing Isaiah): "All flesh is as grass and all the glory of man as the flower of grass; the grass withereth and the flower thereof fadeth away" (from memory, so don't trust it). Or Jeremiah (which he looked up): "The prophets prophesy falsely, and the priests bear rule by their means; and my people love to have it so: and what will ye do in the end thereof?" Aye, what indeed? Nothing much, probably. Except what we try to do here as we did in *Encounter 1* : give an honest and goodly account of what we have tried to do to earn grace in thy sight, O Science of Man, and to hope that others will profit from seeing how the life and work of one anthropologist might serve to illustrate the strengths and beauties of your service and your calling, and the possibilities they open up to a mankind that is both your delight and your frustration.

What follows then is my continuation of encounters, and it shows strong continuities with *Encounter 1* — sex and evolution, aggression and violence, kinship and marriage, myth and monkeys, rules and language, Pueblo Indians and Donegal Islanders — as well as some new ventures (with old roots): food and warfare, archaeology and Marxism, cognition and prejudice, ideology and primatology (real primatology, that is, as opposed to assessments of other people's monkey research, which I have been doing all along). And the "message" (lord help us) is the same: the unity of anthropology, its uniqueness among the social sciences, lies in its devotion to the study of the human species as a product of evolution. This does not mean, as it seems to mean to some contemporary sociobiologists, that all and every piece of human behavior must be explained on the principles of Darwinian natural selection (as seen by these contemporary sociobiologists). Most of the time, as I have always said, anthropologists operate several removes from this theory. We do not need to be always looking over our shoulders for Darwinian explanations. Even mainstream Darwinian biologists don't do this. We can go on collecting our data and finding our connections and explaining these at a more proximate level. All I am saying is that in the end, the master paradigm that holds all this effort together must be the theory of natural selection and must connect us to our evolutionary past via the theory of the evolution of social behavior, or what we are doing will not be anthropology but some branch of some other discipline masquerading as such.

We are of course always a branch of evolutionary biology, but that's all right. The species we have to deal with is so complicated and displays such peculiarities (mind, culture, consciousness, conscience — whatever) that it needs very special handling, and the branch rapidly becomes a trunk. There are plenty of other ways to approach the peculiarities of this species, so we must pay careful attention to what it is that justifies our distinguishing our science as *the* science of mankind. That distinction does not come, for example, simply from our concern with "primitive society" as such — it is the reasons for such a concern that matter. Art historians could be concerned with "primitive society," but that wouldn't make them anthropologists. And we have always been concerned as well with very advanced and complicated societies, such as India and China. But at the same time we have been concerned with our remote past, our evolutionary origins, our physical types, and the archaeological record.

I have written at tedious length about the "split mind" of anthropology which, since the nineteenth-century paradigm of "social evolution" was lost, has not known what to do with its disparate concerns with the archaeological and evolutionary past, on the one hand, and the sociological present — including "primitive" tribes — on the other. What I have tried to argue for is a new way of putting Humpty Dumpty back together again without recreating the misshapen egg of nineteenth-century evolutionism. What I seem to have created is an omelette. But before this metaphor gets out of hand, let me repeat that the various efforts to incorporate ethology, neuroscience, and sociobiology into social anthropology proper (what I christened *Biosocial Anthropology* in 1975) are all attempts to preserve the uniqueness of anthropology as the evolutionary study of mankind.

This route to a viable future for the discipline seems to me so obvious that I am getting more and more curmudgeonly with those who do not see it. If they want to be humanists or ecologists or hermeneuticists or sociologists or historians or poeticists or critical theorists or God knows what, then let them be such and good luck to them. But let them not claim to be anthropologists. Let them enter into the lands of the heathen and go whoring after strange gods, and let them become as the heathen, strange in their ways (too much Jeremiah). But let them not claim to be any longer of the house of anthropology, and let them draw their wages from other treasuries. There is much naughtiness in their hearts (Samuel?), and they flirt with the heathen and with their gods, and this is great fun because it is indeed fun to be naughty. But they had better figure on knocking it off, and soon at that, or there will be no anthropology, and they will be floating around in a purgatory of their own making, with nowhere to go and nothing to do but wait for the judgement day when all rubbish shall be cast up on the farthest shore and those who kept alive the torch shall be led into eternal light. (OK. Enough, Old Prophet of Doom.)

I have tried by precept and example to keep all of this to the forefront of anthropological thinking. I have been told by earnest colleagues that it is not evolution but the study of culture that is the distinguishing feature of anthropology (as though culture were divorced from the process of evolution, and as though other disciplines did not study culture). Now some of those same people call me in alarm because newly constituted "Cultural Studies Departments" (manned largely by renegades from Eng. and Comp. Lit.) are stealing their concepts, their students, and their funds. Well, they should have seen it coming. They invited in the heathen and exalted their ways. They embraced relativism and antiscientism and denied their brethren who clung to the old gods of evolution and science. Now the heathen have taken away their temples, and they are become as slaves and handmaidens in their own house. (Sorry. It's very catching once you get the hang of it.)

Yes, reader, so many anthropologists have shot themselves in the foot over this one, and I'm running out of sympathy (and clichés). But there ain't no way that "Cultural Studies" can claim my lily-white body for its own. There is a firm line drawn in the sand: one side says "evolution and science," the other says "relativism and culturalism." And while my side can easily cope with anything on theirs, their side cannot but deny all validity to mine and continue with its intellectual tail chasing. For more details, read this book, especially the bit on the Teddy Bears' Picnic.

But most of this book is not about these issues at all, you will be relieved to hear. It is about getting on with the various jobs that constitute traditional anthropology. But right now I am doing the color commentary — the background against which we are playing out the current ideological drama. In *Encounter 1*, I complained of cultural anthropology's "outmoded ideology" of cultural relativism and cultural determinism, linked (wrongly) to progress, democracy, utopian social dreaming, and the pleasures of reform.

This has now come home to roost in the current intellectual crisis. But the fragmentation of which I also complained has compounded the problems of the outmoded ideology, since there is no longer, either intellectually or organizationally, any center to anthropology — only a plethora of competing special interest groups (again mirroring society at large). Anthropology no longer has any central rituals or core of beliefs (even the cultural determinists are, insofar as they still claim to be "scientific," increasingly beleaguered). Nor is there even a unity of practice provided by a commitment to "fieldwork" and the "primitive." (This latter has been thoroughly "deconstructed," of course.)

Myth

The loggers and the miners have been invited into the forest, and the tribe is breaking up. Its members are now found in straggling bands along the roadsides, peddling their pathetic wares to any takers, in sad competition with each other. Many have drifted off to join other tribes or to live in the ideological shantytowns of Feminísta and Ermenútica. They remember but a little of their language, and speak in various creolized, pidjin tongues. The scraps of tribal culture to which they cling make less and less sense to them as they drift with the human tide toward eventual homogenization in the intellectual slum at the edge of the seductive city of Novalor-Averitas, where the hard forest discipline of thinking is not encouraged, and mental handouts keep the mouths working, the minds at rest. But in what is left of the home forest, the heart of the tribe still beats. The drums sound firmly, and while the warriors may be quarrelsome and quick to faction — as they always were — they are also true to the old ways: to the hunt and the rituals of the hunt for the elusive prey of fact; to the gods and customs that made their tribe unique in the world. They will stay true, and stay quarrelsome, and stay half-hidden, while the glamour of the new gods dazzles their drifting comrades. And they will fiercely continue to speak the true language; to keep it alive for those who wish to return and those who must be raised to carry it on.

Many of the ragged demitribesmen, failing to recognize the peril of their own position, will not thank the warriors for maintaining tribal traditions. On the contrary, they will tell them that the strangers are to be welcomed, for they bring progress and emancipation. But the forest dwellers know that these things spell death if they are not integrated into the tribal culture in a way determined by the tribe itself. So the warriors will ride out the scorn and the pressure and continue to improve their skills until the day when the wicked city crumbles upon its rotten foundations, and the loggers and the miners flee back to Parisía and Francafuérta whence they came, and the forest returns to claim its own. Then shall the warriors be lords of the forest again, and the drums shall sound as confidently as they once did, only sweeter and surer, and the songs shall be more harmonious, and the dancers shall be more beautiful than before for having been sanctified by their lonely sojourn with the god of truth.

* * *

So it doesn't altogether work as a myth. But what's the point of being a mythographer if one doesn't try one's hand sometimes? And the point is still there. The current "ideological quagmire" adds a new dimension to the situation deplored in *Encounter 1*. There, it was two (or more) competing versions of truth and even science *within anthropology* that were at issue. Now, both science and truth in general are under attack. This is a time to stand up and be counted, and this book, both by direct argument and implicitly by its content, is staking a claim both for truth and science in general, and an anthropological version of these in particular. In only a few places does it preach — which is why I have felt it OK to do so a bit in this prologue — to get a few things off my chest. But the reader should come out the other end of it with a feeling one way or the other. Either what is done here by example makes sense as an endeavor and should be kept up, or let's dissolve the whole enterprise and all go our separate ways, without too many squabbles over who gets custody of the better ideas.

Part of my satirical program — to keep my colleagues guessing as to where the next blow will fall — has been to don their disguises and appear among them as one of them, then to revert back to my true appearance and tell it like it is. Trickster — in his role as shape-changer — has had a big influence (see chap. 15). Thus, in *The Tory Islanders* (1978) I appeared as a solemnly correct social anthropologist of an almost endearingly old-fashioned kind. One reviewer said the book bore most relation to Edmund Leach's classic, *Pul Eliya* — so it worked. But I couldn't resist, in the preface, insisting that *The Tory Islanders* was a work of primatology (which is technically correct, after all). Then, in *The Red Lamp of Incest* (1983), I set out to "rewrite *Totem and Taboo* with half a century of hindsight" and explore, through the lens of evolution, "The Origins of Mind and Society." This had the social anthropologists floundering and Leach fuming, since it was obviously a bad case of apostasy. In the book I coedited with Jacques Mehler, *Neonate Cognition: Beyond the Blooming Buzzing Confusion* (1985), I appeared as a sponsor of the new cognitive psychology, which makes great sense to anyone who's really following, but again left the critics flopping about. Then, in *The Violent Imagination* (1989) I popped up as a neoformalist poet with a nonlinear, multimedia metalogical mystification in a mixture of prose, dialogue, drama, verse, and some things in between, but laying claim to be taken seriously as a commentator on the human condition. And by golly I was. The persona worked. The editor of *Current Anthropology* wrote to say how amazed he was that I had "gone postmodern" on them. (Many preach it; few do it.) And the ultimate accolade came from the *American Anthropologist* itself, whose reviewer said that "if ever there was a book to show that there is more than one way to 'say' anthropology, this is it." (I don't know if it was sincere flattery or independent invention, but André Singer, usually known for his ethnographic films, did a film on "The Trial of George Washington" — part two of my book — which, while not pinching my specific ideas, at least imitated the overall scheme.) Then, in *The Search for Society* (1989), I bounced back up with a series of stern essays on, as the subtitle told it, a "Quest for a Biosocial Science and Morality." (To be fair to the whole enterprise, reader, you should get this one too, since many of the crucial essays in the ongoing series are included in it, and hence didn't make it into this book.) I then took a half-step backward — into law, anthropology, Greek tragedy, and the avunculate — in *Reproduction and Succession* (1993). Now comes this one, with its holistic-anthropology message. And the next may well be a reprise in the manner of *Violent Imagination*, but in the form of an "intellectual autobiography" (or "selflifewriting") of an offbeat kind suitable for an offbeat life. The present book is sufficiently varied so that there will certainly be something for everyone to disagree with. This makes life much easier for unimaginative but career-greedy reviewers. Go to it.

But I don't want any of what I say here to have to be apologized for in the next book. So this is all the intellectual autobiography I am going to give out at this stage. There is plenty more in some of the chapters here, from my encounters with Virgil, Frazer, and the Unitarian Church, through my flirtations with the law, to the profound influence of Paul Robeson. Life, art, and science are at best when they are a unity. If the united soul isn't quite there in fact, we can at least yearn for it or try to play with it in myth. And the congregations of naughty men (Psalms?) will seek after my soul in vain. They (and the naughty women too for that matter) know who they are, and I know where they live.

Part One

Sex and Food

Introduction to Part One

Sex is obviously the starting point. Replication is what "life" is about, and sexual reproduction is our way of replicating. Anthropologists were traditionally right to make kinship the central focus of their discipline: right both for good sociological and, as it turns out, good biological reasons. The whole thrust of modern evolutionary biology has been to recognize kinship, in its avatars of "inclusive fitness," "nepotism," "kin selection," "parental investment," and the like, as the main evolutionary force in carrying out the mandates of natural selection. The central notion of "fitness" measured in "reproductive success" says it all. The first commandment really is Be Fruitful and Multiply! Where I slightly part company with all this is with the idea that we are actually directly motivated to "maximize reproductive success," to use one of the mantras of the movement. I think we are motivated to perform a whole slew of activities: have sex, like kids, collect resources, fill our bellies, defend mates and property, enjoy companionship, strive for success, etc., etc. If we get all these right, then "maximization of reproductive success" will take care of itself. In the days before contraception, wives had one kid a year (at least) anyway, although most of them died. Perhaps only a few of the very rich and powerful males in polygynous societies consciously aimed at the production of limitless offspring as an end in itself. Must of us just plowed ahead with our proximately motivated behaviors, regardless of the end product.

The "maximization of reproductive success" is something to do with the long term — it can only be measured after several generations, and we are rarely concerned with the long term, because, as Lord Keynes reminded us, we are dead then. We have a lot of sex because we like sex even if we don't have *any* children, and even if the point (evolutionary) of our liking sex is to get us to have children. But we do have to have them and raise them or we cease to be an issue (pun intended). As a species, we are spectacularly successful in this respect (but only over the last few thousand years), and as we know, this is a success that is in danger of backfiring. So it is a root obligation of anthropology, as a science of the possible human future as well as the actual human past, to examine the nature of this ebullient sexuality.

The first essay here deals in a general way with the evolution of sexuality. It was written, at the invitation of André Béjin and Philippe Ariès, as an introduction to a book on Western sexuality that was to do with the historical period only and boasted such contributors as Michel Foucault, Paul Veyne, and Jean-Louis Flandrin. But they wanted to put this discussion into its "contexte naturel" — in a grand French Enlightenment flourish. So I tried to oblige. I was, admittedly, a bit sceptical about how the historians would take it, but Peter Laslett — a social historian who surely has everyone's admiration — in his introduction found it "astonishingly informative and perceptive," so I was definitely encouraged. In a review, however, Lawrence Stone snidely quoted a sentence completely out of context and dismissed the whole thing. So there you are with the historians.

I believe this was the first appearance of the Law of the Dispensable Male — at least deliberately described as such. This gave the editors a hard time, since I wrote *mâle disponible,* which means either "disposable" or "available" and hence is ambiguous, unlike its English counterpart. Béjin cleverly suggested *mâle facultatif* — which means "optional" — and we went with that. This is still one of my favorite "laws," if only because it is one the feminists don't seem inclined to quibble with. Why is that?

The third essay, on the incest taboo, was written for an Italian encyclopedia and suffers from the limitations of an encyclopedia entry (written to fixed format, etc.). But it was a chance for me to make a concise summary of a lifetime's thinking on the subject, which, contrary to the current sociobiological orthodoxy, cannot be dismissed as a mere matter of preventing inbreeding — practically all sexually reproducing species do that. And, contrary to the prevailing anthropological orthodoxy, it is not the crucial breakthrough from Nature to Culture.

This all harks back to a paper I wrote for Maurice Freedman as an undergraduate at the London School of Economics (LSE) (about 1956), elaborated for Robert Bales and John Whiting at Harvard (about 1958), and eventually published in the *British Journal of Sociology* in 1962 as "Sibling

Incest." Westermarck's hypothesis was completely disregarded in those days, and I singlehandedly (with the encouragement of old teacher Donald Macrae, editor of the *BJS* and a Westermarck fan himself) revived it and tried to reconcile it with the prevailing Freudian orthodoxy. This drew two other scientists into the net: Arthur Wolf from Stanford, who was working on Taiwanese marriage (through Maurice Freedman and the China connection) and came to spend a year at the LSE, and Joseph Shepher from Israel, who came to Rutgers, when I moved there, to complete his Ph.D. on marriage and sex in the kibbutzim.

The "Westermarck effect" and "Westermarck hypothesis" were thus put right back into the center of the incest issue. Much-hyped "histories" of neo-Darwinian social science completely miss this. Thus, Carl N. Degler (*In Search of Human Nature: The Decline and Revival of Darwinism in American Social Thought* [New York: Oxford University Press, 1991]) has a whole chapter on the incest issue that treats my contribution as dating from 1980 when *The Red Lamp of Incest* came out, and what is more, that treats it simply as a kind of Freudian apologetic! Despite my book's long appendix on the "Sources of the Text," which tells the whole story, he completely missed these connections. I suspect he got the whole tale on five-by-three cards from the numerous research assistants he thanks, and who surely worked diligently, but who failed to look beyond publication dates and to bother finding out the true sequence, even though the documentation was under their noses. I sometimes wonder about historians. I really do.

But recent anthropological contributions by the whiz kids who want in on the debate are no better. One cites *The Red Lamp* as part of the "continuing debate" on the "Westermarck effect" — failing to note that the "Sibling Incest" paper (which became chapter 2: "Between Brother and Sister") actually coined this phrase and set the terms of the later debate. In my younger days we were in less of a hurry, and the tighter peer control — or rather control of our elders — meant we paid great respect to scholarship and the historical development of ideas. No one cares much now, it seems. And many youngsters seem caught between the "scientific" style, which is not concerned with establishing precedence, and the "scholarly" style, which is. Still, I cite all this for the record, as we used to say. The chapter here is useful because it concentrates directly on the incest taboo issue and does not use this simply as a way into "The Origins of Mind and Society" as with *Red Lamp*. This is the concentrated rather than diluted version.

Just recently, a colleague, Alex Walter, pointed out to me that *Red Lamp* could be read as almost a point-by-point refutation of Malinowski's famous *Sex and Repression in Savage Society* (London: Routledge, 1929), and wondered why I had not been explicit about this. A very good point. I briefly mention the "Malinowski-Jones" debate but insist I don't want to get sidetracked into it. I concentrate on rehabilitating *Totem and Taboo* rather that on demolishing *Sex and Repression*, which was itself, of course, a demolition of Freud's opus. I had not thought about it, but of course I could have gone the route Walter suggested just as easily (in some ways more easily). Perhaps it was that Malinowski was only one of a chorus of people saying that Freud was so obviously wrong, and I was concerned to rehabilitate Freud's hypothesis about the primal horde rather than take on all his critics. But, of course, as a student at the LSE reared on the reverence (if critical reverence) of Malinowski, I might well have been subconsciously reluctant to use my book to demolish point-by-point one of his, providing there was another less painful and more positive route to the same destructive goal. We all like to think we are in charge of our lives and decisions. What rot. These subterranean motives rule us all. The Greeks thought that no man's virtue could be assessed until he was dead. The same is true of his motives. But then only his biographers can make the connections; for the victim, the understanding comes too late. There is, however, an easy M.A. "library" thesis in this for a willing student who likes the history of ideas. It is, after all, the business of one generation of academics to make enough mistakes, or at least create enough mysteries, to keep the next one employed. Lord knows I've tried.

The female orgasm continues to produce its plethora of explanations, none of which seems very satisfactory. Its chapter raises the whole issue of "adaptational" explanations — a current hot one. I don't know if my "explanation" will stick, but it is a nonadaptationist attempt to cut through the "just-so stories," and has some novel data.

Which brings us to food. After sex, this is the most important thing, and yet is little considered in anthropology except by ecologists and a few "symbolists" like Mary Douglas and Lévi-Strauss (*The Raw and the Cooked* and *The Origin of Table Manners* are two volumes of his *Mythologiques*). We must eat to live and breed; sex, hunger and aggression are on the same circuit of the brain: the limbic system. Language is virtually unconnected to these and stuck off in the left cerebral hemisphere.

The little essay on food reproduced here, while making the anthropological points, was not written for an anthropological audience. My eldest daughter (Kate) was helping to bring out a book on "Lifestyle" for a largely popular (and largely British) audience, and the editors lacked a vital section on Food to complement those on Cars, Houses, Gardens, etc. She talked me into this effort with a transatlantic phone call, and of course she needed it yesterday. So I wrote it off the top of my head and faxed it — amazed at the mass of information I had somehow acquired largely by osmosis and a lifelong fascination with food, wine, cooking, and eating out. For the book, they used my essay as "source material" and rewrote it to make for a "uniform style." Here I reproduce the original, with a few corrections and additions (like the bit on Joe Alsop and calorie counting). It is my own very idiosyncratic account, and has obviously an occidental bias. I invite the readers to fill in from their own experiences and cultures. Food is the great communicator; perhaps more so than music. I know hundreds of people who love Indian food and yet can't stand sitar playing — even the exquisite "Dawn Raga" by Ravi Shankar. ("Sounds like somebody endlessly tuning a banjo," my father used to say — a man who lived a large part of his life in India and loved its food.) Food crosses cultural and even temporal boundaries and unites us at our very centers: our digestions. If we indeed are what we eat, then multiculturalism is literally a melting pot, but, like a good *pot au feu*, one where each ingredient keeps its distinct taste while producing a unique gustatory combination. Stop talking: start eating.

1

The Conditions of Sexual Evolution

There are various levels of approach to the evolution of sexual behavior: from that of all sexually reproducing organisms (including plants) to that of a particular species or subspecies. The problems of the latter cannot ignore the more general problems of sexual reproduction, in particular the problem of why there should be sexual reproduction at all. Theoretically, in any competitive situation, sexually reproducing organisms should lose in competition with asexual. Assuming the original situation to be asexual, it remains a constant theoretical problem how sexual reproduction can have arisen, since any favorable mutation in an asexually reproducing organism can be immediately and rapidly replicated, while its sexual competitor must dilute the next-generation effect through breeding. Even inbreeding will not help for sexual competitors, since it is bound to be slower than in the asexual, and also will produce lethal homozygotes.

The only conclusion is that the one advantage of sexual reproduction — increased genetic variation — must have been of such overwhelming advantage in some circumstances that it had a slight competitive edge and became the dominant partner in an evolutionarily stable strategy. This still raises theoretical difficulties, but it can be seen that recombination might just win out over simple mutation and mitosis under marginal conditions. A "very rapidly changing environment" is often invoked (although this too is vague), as is sibling conflict in offspring and resistance to parasites (sexually reproducing organisms will produce enough genetic variation to stay ahead of their parasites).

However started, sexual reproduction, at whatever level, sets certain conditions. Some are minimal. The two sexes must have sufficient contact to exchange genetic material — this is perhaps the only basic requirement. The more complicated this exchange becomes, the more complicated the relations between the sexes. Hermaphroditic species solve the problem by having both sexes in the same organism. In some primitive organisms there is no definite sex distinction. The faster-moving organism of any two by definition becomes "male" because its slightly greater speed implants material in the slower one. But it is relative. In higher organisms this becomes fixed. But the basics are not lost: sperm is faster than ovum, even if it is the ovum that in fact does the "selecting."

Not only does exchange have to take place, it then becomes the responsibility of one "sex" to undertake gestation. After that, one or both or neither undertake nurturance, depending on the evolutionary path the organism has taken. Usually, the "female" undertakes gestation, and either the female alone, the female in consort with other females, the female and the inseminating male, or groups of males and females — and other combinations — undertake a variety of forms of gestation and nurturance. There is no need here to elaborate the many forms this can take throughout sexually reproducing species — this would simply stress their variety.

When we come to the mammals, we also find much variety, but it is restricted by the very characteristics of mammalian adaptation: warm blood, live birth, suckled young, internal gestation, etc. A great deal that can be said about human sexuality can be disposed of as the sexual behavior to be expected of a large-bodied, large-brained, slow-breeding, omnivorous mammal with moderate sexual dimorphism and a lack of seasonal breeding. This does not mean that only one pattern of sexual behavior is to be expected; it simply sets the limits within which variation will occur. We can best understand this variation by asking what the variables are, and this is difficult since it is all too easy to beg the question by the way it is posed. Rather than take cultural categories of dubious universality, like "nuclear family" and "marriage," it is better to take as a starting point an objective unit that is, by definition, universal in the mammals and thus not contaminated by cultural categories. The obvious unit is the mother and her dependent offspring.

It is basic to the definition of a mammal that the young are born live and suckled by the mother. What varies is (a) the amount of investment the mother herself puts into the offspring beyond the necessary minimum, and (b) the degree and nature of the attachment of a male or males to this basic unit (and the relations of the units to each other).

One interesting result of the human development of culture is that we reproduce within our own species almost all the variation found across the mammalian orders — but we shall return to that. For the moment, let us consider some mammalian extremes by way of illustration. The hamster lives in solitary burrows, and the contact of males and females is limited to a brief encounter during a brief mating season when a male enters a female's burrow and copulates. The female has a short gestation period and suckles the young for a few weeks, after which they disperse and make their own burrows. This is about the lower limit of mating organization in mammals. Consider, then, certain ungulates such as gazelles, zebra, deer, etc. They differ considerably in their herd organization, but basically the permanent herd is one of females and young. The males are either solitary for most of the year or rove in all-male bands. During the breeding season (autumn) the males compete, and the winners mate with the herds of females, then depart. The females give birth (in the spring) to precocial young who are soon able to follow and suckle. After one year the males disperse. Finally, consider a band of hunting dogs, or hyenas. The males and females are together all year round, whether or not there is a breeding season. There is a complex hierarchy of mating. The females give birth to slow-maturing young, and both males and females care for the offspring in various ways, including the regurgitation of food from kills, etc.

Thus we move from virtually no male-female contact, save for the necessary ninety seconds, through seasonal contact, to permanent year-round contact. We also move from absolutely minimal parental care, through care from the mother and the herd females, to care by all the males and females of a complexly organized pack. There are many variations on these themes, including monogamous territorial pair-bonding (gibbons, for example) and large male-female troops (howler monkeys) — but the variables we are looking at are what is important. In each case, the crucial variables we have mentioned earlier are affected by circumstances of adaptation to involve the males more or less in the affairs of the females and young. Basically, the males are dispensable. If the female has no need of the male over and above his procreative function, then he is usually dispensed with. The more complex the life of the animal, however, the more likely it is that the male will serve some other function: largely that of defense, but in some carnivores also that of providing meat for the relatively slow-developing young, and even of "teaching" them (if only through imitation) the arts of hunting. The females will also differ in the degree to which they need each other. Female hamsters are solitary, female gibbons live only with their mates, ungulate females congregate in herds, and so on.

One thing is relatively certain: When females congregate to their mutual advantage, they are likely to be related. The same *may* be true of males, but it is less likely. To understand this, and consequently to understand the human variant that we call "systems of kinship and marriage," it is necessary to look at the process Darwin christened "sexual selection," and its subsidiary process, which has recently found a name as "kin selection."

Basically, sexual selection is a variant of natural selection, but one where the struggle is not so much against what Darwin called "the hostile forces of nature" as it is the struggle of the sexes for reproductive advantage. This involves the *competition* between animals of one sex — usually the males — for mates from the other, and the *choice* by the other sex — usually the females — of mates from the successful competitors.

We can see this arising from the adaptational exigencies discussed earlier: The females need the males for at least insemination, but also for protection and food perhaps, and therefore they select among them the most able as demonstrated by success in competition. This competition can take many forms, and Darwin was chiefly interested in it as a process that explained extraordinary anatomical developments such as the antlers of the stag, or the huge claw of the fiddler crab. But of course the developments can be purely behavioral and involve "ritualized" fighting displays, for example. What is demanded of the males will differ according to the species. In the ungulates and sea mammals, for example, where the male-female association is purely seasonal and for breeding, displays of superior strength are sufficient. Where the males and females are permanently together, other qualities may be more important — the ability to rise in the male hierarchy, for example, which may involve far more than just strength.

The point about sexual selection, however, is that *whatever* criterion is used (strength, speed, territory, display, etc.), the result is that only a minority of the males gets to breed, while all the females usually succeed in breeding at least once. The reason why it should be this way is easy to see: A male can breed successfully with a large number of females, while a female, once pregnant, is committed to the foetus for anything up to a year, and in many cases well beyond that in suckling and rearing the infant. The "strategies" of the two sexes therefore are bound to differ markedly. It is to the male's reproductive advantage to mate with as many females as possible, while the female must try — since she has only one chance a year — to obtain the "best" genes for herself. The point about "kin selection" in this context is that she is often better off doing this in collaboration with related females — and we must explore why.

But first we should note that the above "strategies" will be severely restricted once it is in the male's reproductive interest to invest in his offspring. Where there is no such advantage — as with most ungulates and sea mammals — then the out-and-out competition we have discussed seems to prevail. Where the males must invest in their offspring to ensure their survival, then competition still exists but becomes more subtle and complicated, and the male must pay more attention to fewer females. This becomes more important with the primates, the social carnivores, and in particular with man. It results, for example, in much less extreme sexual dimorphism and a lack of those highly specialized anatomical features that first led Darwin to enquire into this mode of selection.

We must return to the question of relatedness or kinship since this concerns genes and this is where selection is in fact at work. And here, if I speak of the "strategies" of the genes, or of the animals, it should be needless to point out that conscious strategies are not implied. (People who are otherwise well educated still seem to miss this point.) It is just sometimes easier to speak metaphorically of "intentions" than to spell out the whole argument in correct "selection" language. Strictly speaking, the only goal of the genes is to produce replicas of themselves. Organisms are their agents. However, identical genes are not confined to one organism, but are shared by related organisms in declining proportion as the degree of relatedness becomes more distant. There is always, therefore, a group of closely related organisms sharing a large number of identical gene replicas: a kind of small gene pool. Parents and children are the closest in relatedness, together with groups of siblings. Now, the "groups of females" that we have been discussing above are almost always mother-daughter extended families: groups of female kin, closely related. If we view these, then, as a small pool of identical genes seeking to replicate themselves, we can see how, under certain evolutionary circumstances, they will do better if they act in concert than alone, and better still if they can choose "superior" male genes to combine with their own to produce a new generation.

In earlier studies of sexual selection, the emphasis was heavily on the male competition, and indeed selection does seem to work most spectacularly here. But it has more recently been seen that *female choice* may well be the ultimate determinant of the route selection will take. The males, as it were, exhaust themselves on competition; then the female groups pick out the winners as studs. Once it is realized that there can thus be considerable difference in reproductive success between the different female groups, the full dynamics of the system can be understood.

The females' strategy has to be to pick the "best" male, whatever the criteria. If a group of females can become inseminated by superior male genes, not only do their female offspring get the immediate advantages, but the chance that their "sons" will inseminate many groups of females itself increases. Thus, the genes of the original female kin group will spread in the total population more successfully than those of rival groups. If we paraphrase Samuel Butler's famous statement (that a chicken is the egg's way of making another egg) and say that a male is the females' way of making more females (or that a male is the female kin group's way of making another female kin group) then we are getting close to the heart of the sexual selection process. But we have to see it, ultimately, as the strategy of the genes to produce replicas of themselves.

We cannot here go into all the conditions that produce such "kin-coalition" behavior and its consequent interesting mode of sexual selection — indeed, they are not all known, although the most plausible candidate is advantages in foraging. It is enough that they *are* produced, and very important to us because the primates, our own order, show strong tendencies in this direction in many species, including our own. The primates, however, unlike the ungulates we have been discussing, live in groups where there is year-round contact between males and females. This factor — shared for example by the social carnivores — exercises a profound influence. It does not stop the processes of either sexual selection or kin selection, but modifies them, and this modification is the first step on the road to human sexual behavior.

It is as if the ungulate females, instead of meeting briefly with the successful males in the mating season, had decided to incorporate them permanently into the group and, what is more, to amalgamate several female kin groups into a larger group. The reasons why this occurs in some species (like the primates) are variable, with foraging success, the need for the defense of the females, and, with the carnivores, the need for provisioning the relatively slow-maturing young by the males, as leading contenders. The higher primates are vegetarian (baboons and chimpanzees hunt only sporadically) and do *not* provision their young, who must find their own food once weaned. Protection therefore seems the most likely reason. Now, the number and combination of males incorporated, and the resulting modes of social organization, are very varied across species, and we can here give only a highly summary sketch of some very general features.

At one extreme, there will only be one male incorporated into one group of females; at the other there will be many males incorporated into an equally large number of female families. Monogamous pairs — as with the gibbon — can be seen as a limiting case where, for ecological reasons, a territory will only support one female and one male. With the orangutan, females establish ranges, and males attempt to monopolize several of these females without staying permanently with any one. With chimpanzees, groups of males on the one hand, and groups of females on the other, form a forest "band," a separate "block" of the social system. With common baboons and macaques, female families, hierarchically arranged, are arrayed against a hierarchy of individual males. With hamadryas baboons, and geladas, herds are composed of "harems," each under the control of one male. Gorillas live in bands with one dominant male, some younger males, and females with young.

The "law of the dispensable male" operates here. Under extreme conditions, for example, macaque groups "shed" males until there is only one, while under lush conditions there may be a large number. Those species, characterized by "one-male groups," or harems, are most like the ungulates: Males compete in various ways and only some get harems. In the "multimale groups" it is different: The competition between the males is there, but since they stay together, they must settle it by arranging themselves in a hierarchy. Similarly, the female families are hierarchically organized, with the higher-ranking families tending to mate more frequently with high-ranked males. The "sons" of these families in turn are more likely than others to become high ranking and thus perpetuate the process. Thus, we can see how the ungulate "seasonal" pattern has been, as it were, "collapsed" here into a hierarchically organized year-round collaboration of males and female families.

The major modification this produces in the sexual selection process is in the criteria for "best genes" in the male. The one-male group species are most like the ungulates, with, for example, greater sexual dimorphism and special anatomical features for the male (the mane and "cape" of the hamadryas, for example). The multimale species show less sexual dimorphism and specialization, and capacities for group living and organization are obviously being selected for over mere strength, endurance, or display. High-ranking female groups, for example, will often not tolerate males who are too aggressive and competitive; these leave the group and become solitaries.

Is there, however, a basic primate pattern in this wide range of breeding/social systems? It is important to establish if there is, since it would be the pattern that characterized our own ancestors before the "transition to humanity" took place. It would be the raw material of hominid society: the breeding system that became the "social system." I think there is a panprimate pattern in the group-living primates that involves the dynamics of relationship, or what we have called "strategies," that exist between the three major "blocks" or interest groups of the system: (a) the established males, (b) the females and young, and (c) the peripheral or aspirant males. The "established" males are those who have access to the breeding females by virtue of having obtained harems, moved up in the hierarchy, maintained territories, and whatever else is demanded. Against them are arranged the (usually younger) males who aspire to breeding status. The females are between these two groups, "supplying" young males to the peripheral groups and seeking the "best genes" from the mature males. The possible combinations are large, but the basic pattern is there. It is not all that different from the basic pattern of the other group-living mammals, with the exception that the males are permanently incorporated, and we have seen that this itself strongly influences the criteria for "best male."

If this then is the basic pattern of the vegetarian primate, we have next to ask ourselves what the crucial change was that produced the hominid line and finally ourselves. Our ancestors would have been vegetarian primates following some variant of the pattern — most likely, given the close genetic relationship with the chimpanzee and the similarity of ecological adaptation to the common baboon/macaque, some version of the "multimale group with female kin group" system. What is incontestable now in view of the East African evidence is that somewhere between 2 and 3 million years ago this ancestor took up hunting and scavenging on a large scale. It was already bipedal, but the change from sporadic meat eating to a diet incorporating more than 50 percent meat means a radical change in the relations between the sexes and between the old and the young males. It is these changes that *created* man as we know him, for by the advent of *Homo erectus* the irreversible change had taken place — as measured by stature and brain size. And this is the crucial fact: the unprecedented rapidity of the evolution of the hominid brain (a threefold increase inside 2 million years) occurred exactly during the period when the scale of hunting increased — and increased in proportion. That is, exactly as the size and scale of prey increased, so did the size and complexity of the brain.

The causal factors are not too difficult to see here, but the consequences for the internal process of sexual selection are harder to spell out. Let us take it from the male point of view. In the "winner-take-all" type of competition, sheer strength is what counts; in the primate "hierarchical" competition, it is more control and timing; in the hunting situation, it is obviously the ability to provide meat — to provision the females and children. But it is much more complex than this: strength, control, and hunting ability cumulate in importance, but many other qualities must accrue to a successful dominant male in a cooperative hunting society. Leadership, organizational ability, and even such burgeoning talent as eloquence, shamanistic skills, etc. eventually come to characterize "dominance" and hence breeding advantage. All this is of particular importance in hominid evolution since the evolving hominids did not have millions of years of carnivorous experience in their genes, as do the social carnivores. They could not, for example, use their natural weapons in hunting but had to invent weapons; they could not regurgitate food for the young but had to carry it back to the home base — bipedalism and the freeing of the hands are of great importance here. But the major point for the males is that they had to develop intelligent solutions to the hunting challenge in all its facets; there was therefore a premium on intelligence over and above other skills.

From the female point of view, the essential change lay in the division of labor forced on them by the new, hunting way of life. Essentially, hominid females were the producers of vegetable food; for meat they depended on the males. Equally, the males depended on the females for two essential services that did not exist in the primate "baseline" situation: gathering and preparation of vegetable food, and care and provision for the more slowly maturing young. (The young were maturing more slowly because of progressive neoteny that was a consequence of bipedalism, fetal birth, and the requirements of the larger brain to grow outside the mother's body.)

The requirement that the males "invest" more heavily in their young is underlined here — as opposed to the primate situation where the weaned young fend for themselves. The strategy of the foraging female kin groups therefore must have been not only to acquire the "best genes" (which now meant "best hunters"), but to hold on to the males in order to continue having the infants provisioned with the now necessary meat.

Overall, what happened to the hominid breeding/social system in the period between two and a half and one million years ago, was that the relations between the three "blocks" of the system were revolutionized, although building on the old base. We *must* understand that a new creature was being forged here in the crucible of natural and sexual selection: a hunting ape-man. And in evolutionary terms it was a rapid change. The tensions therefore between the basic pattern and the new demands made upon it by the new creature are at the heart of the current human condition. The three blocks still had to accommodate each other and make demands on each other, but this was under ever-changing conditions. The major change, as we have seen, was in the origin of the division of labor between the sexes, which revolutionized not only the relations between the two sexes, but also the relations within the sexual groups.

The burden of this clearly fell — as is always the case in sexual selection — on the young or peripheral males. The conditions whereby they could rise in the hierarchy and become effective breeders were constantly made more complex. In turn, the older, established males found themselves faced by well-armed and capable youngsters. Thus, the struggle within the male sex between established and aspirant males must have intensified at the same time as the females were making demands for permanent provisioning from the males.

The revolutionary response to this, judging from the end product — that is, the social/breeding system of *Homo sapiens* — was the dual invention of initiation and alliance. There was no way, once the status of *Homo* was achieved, that the free-for-all competition of the males could continue. On the other hand, the rapidity of brain evolution could not have occurred without a highly assortative mating system in which only selected male genes were transferred to successive generations. The consequence was the evolution of a system geared to the control of the young males' access to the breeding system and the control of the allocation of mates by the older males.

The role of systems of initiation is easy to see in this. They are direct systems of constraint and selection, and have the psychological function of "identification with the aggressor" (Freud), ensuring that the young males will identify with the older males. Since access to the breeding system is usually delayed until after initiation — and even service as a warrior — this ensures a "pool" of young females for the old polygynists. The young males will of course try to circumvent this with illicit sexual liaisons. The higher the marriage age of males is driven, and the younger the age at which females are betrothed, the greater the chances of polygyny flourishing. The most widespread marriage pattern in human society is "the polygyny of the powerful" (75 percent of human societies), and even in those either officially or "ecologically" monogamous, the powerful usually enjoy sexual access to young females, or at least a monopoly of them for marriage purposes.

What is not so easily seen is that human kinship systems — again building on the already existing kin-selection tendencies — are equally a response to the control of younger males by the older and/or more powerful males. (Originally this would have been a pure gerontocracy. With the advent of rank and class society, it was power rather than *simply* age that counted, although within classes the young-old clash continued.) It was obviously impossible for the old "winner-take-all" system of mating to endure under the changed conditions of sexual division of labor and cooperative hunting. Freud's vision of a parricidal (and possibly fratricidal) primal horde is probably near the truth. Mitigation already existed in the selective influence of the female kin groups, and this must have been further modified by the need of the males to form alliances both within and across bands, and of the females to enjoy some security of tenure with selected males. Among the primates, both alliance, in the sense of permanent mating, and kinship, in the sense of groups based on common descent, existed — but not in the same system. The human innovation was to combine these in one system, by using the definition of relatedness to define the possibilities of alliance. (It was *not* the incest taboo. Humans, like most sexually reproducing species, avoid an excess of close inbreeding anyway. The taboo is simply confirmation of this, with certain uniquely human ingredients.)

Thus, systems of "kinship and marriage" arose to redefine the relationships and strategies between the three blocks. The major innovation was that kinship not only *linked* the members of the three blocks together, but it was used to define the mode of *allocation* of spouses: that is, effectively, the distribution of young females among males. It is then exogamy — rightly seen by Lévi-Strauss as a positive system of exchange — that is the truly human innovation. What is not usually perceived is that kinship systems do not simply ensure the exchange of spouses, but that they are "rigged" to ensure that the choice of mates open to the younger generation of males is made dependent on choices made by the older generation, thus controlling their access to the mating system through the rules themselves. The onus of control is therefore thrown onto the collectivity, and collective representations assume their role as "constraints" on the behavior of the young. (See part 4 for the details of such systems.) Where the kinship system does not do this through its rules, the older (and more powerful) males have to intervene directly in the marriage choices and opportunities of the young.

I have stressed the males, but of course the cooperative female kin groups are not silent in this matter of with whom their members mate, and often exercise considerable influence — as the basic pattern would predict — although this is highly variable. Very rarely do the interests of these groups coincide, and the ensuing struggle is what lies behind the dynamics and high degree of variability of human mating and social systems. Many other factors — of ecology, economics, politics, class, power, ideology, and technology (e.g., the pill) — intervene to present new challenges to the basic pattern. But as long as assortative mating must take place to ensure the production of future generations, the basic pattern must be respected and the new conditions come to terms with it. The much vaunted "nuclear family," for example, is simply one possible kind of accommodation that occurs, predictably, in certain societies. It is certainly not the basic pattern itself, despite what has often been stated by social scientists.

In this evolutionary perspective, therefore, we are able to take a new look at historical developments in the relations between the sexes, and one of the most important lessons is that we must view this always as a triangular relationship: established males — females and young — aspirant males. As a result of the pill, young females currently are exercising more free choice than ever before; the old have lost considerable control. It will be interesting to see to what extent the basic pattern can reassert itself. I believe it shows signs of doing so, and that many things — such as teenage pregnancy rates, divorce rates, female solidarity movements, etc. — are probably signs of a reassertion of the pattern rather than either pathologies or results of raised consciousness. They are only one or other of these if one takes the "nuclear family" as a starting point, which it is not, but rather one possible outcome.

It will be interesting for historians and anthropologists to look again at their data, which I believe can be reconciled in this framework. The work, for example, of Lévi-Strauss and Ariès makes good sense within this framework of analysis; both are dealing with aspects of the basic pattern. This is not to say that the basic scheme can never be surrendered — but it is the cause of our present behavior; it is what produced us and, as Freud saw, what we are fated to reproduce. Our brains, physiology, and behavior are the living memory of its evolution, our societies the various outcomes of the possibilities it leaves open to us. We could depart totally from it — and we show great danger of so doing. But it would then be doubtful if what remained could still be considered "human society" — or whether it would last.

2

The Female Orgasm:
Adaptation or Accident?

The female orgasm has been discussed and analyzed to death (or at least to *la petite mort*) and it may well appear that there is nothing new to say. But the debate remains in a curiously unsatisfactory state. In its early stages, inspired by the massive research of Kinsey and his associates (1953), it centered on the issue of vaginal versus clitoral sources of orgasm, coming down in favor of the latter and thus against the orthodox Freudian view. The later massive work of Masters and Johnson (1966) confirmed the clitoral theory and also pointed out the female capacity for "multiple orgasm," which in turn spawned another industry of research and argument (complicated by the supposed discovery of the contentious "G Spot"). For the sex therapy lobby, the issue was what constituted "normal orgasm" as opposed to "orgasmic dysfunction" and the like. The adaptationists weighed in with theories about the "functions" of the orgasm in females. In a sense, Freud's "vaginal" theory could be seen as one of the earliest of these, since the evolutionary "reward" of orgasmic pleasure should be associated with action designed to further reproduction. Clitoral stimulation will not do this. Therefore, in a functional sense, the reward must come from vaginal penetration.

Another popular adaptationist theory was that orgasmic contractions helped to speed the sperm on their way. Later, Desmond Morris (1967) suggested it served to keep the female lying down after intercourse and hence allowed the sperm time to swim up the fallopian tubes. And this was one of the least fanciful just-so stories paraded to "explain" the phenomenon. They all suffered the same defect: It was impossible to prove any of them, and impossible to choose between them. They were all plausible, but we had no way to know if they were true or false, or if indeed adaptation was involved at all.

This whole mode of argument had been anticipated by Lucretius (99-55 B.C.) in his remarkable epic *De Rerum Natura*, when discussing the problem of why whores moved while wives kept still during intercourse. He came to the conclusion that lying still allowed the sperm to move up to the womb, while strenuous movement prevented it. Hence the difference. Presumably too violent an orgasm would, for Lucretius, be unadaptive — at least for wives — insofar as it would help to *prevent* conception. But he does insist that "pleasure is for both" and, what is more, that "women's passion is not always feigned." In case there is a sceptic who doesn't believe me — about Lucretius — see *De Rerum Natura*, book 4, lines 1192-1277, for this and other fascinating items. (Who says a classical education has no value?)

It is noticeable that no one involved in this argument seemed much interested in the male orgasm, which is clearly so direct a pleasurable reward for sexual activity that it more or less explains itself. It was the more elusive female variety that caused the trouble for the theorists and investigators and therapists. The female orgasm presents a paradox, for while it is much more difficult to achieve than the male, it appears, when it is achieved, to be capable of giving repeated pleasure to the female in a manner denied to the male: the so-called multiple orgasm. Why, in any adaptational argument, should this be? Why should not the female pleasure be as direct and as immediately rewarding as the male? (There is of course much individual variation; we are speaking here of the general trend.)

Such puzzles have led some observers, like Stephen J. Gould (1987), to deny that there are any adaptational questions here at all. He likens the question, What is the adaptational significance of the female orgasm? to the question, What is the adaptational significance of male nipples? The answer to the latter question is, None at all. All fetuses are equipped to be either male or female, only taking the ordained direction when, as a result of having the right combination of chromosomes, hormones kick in to develop testicles and penis on the one hand or womb and vagina on the other. The male is left therefore with a pair of nipples that serve no purpose and are not intended to. They were simply there in the general package that we all share at conception whatever sex we become during fetal development.

The same, says Gould, is true of the clitoris. This is simply a female analogue of the male nipples: It is the rudimentary penis that never developed, in the same way as the labia are the testicles that never were. They serve no function. And the pleasure the female gets from their stimulation is a by-product. It is a version of the male's orgasm, just as the mildly pleasurable sensation men can get from stimulation of the nipples is a vestige of the intense pleasure females can get from such stimulation.

Moderate adaptationists like Melvin Konner (1990), while agreeing that the clitoris is "vestigial," like the male nipple, are still unhappy to think that the intense, if more elusive, pleasure the female can achieve is also merely vestigial. Just because the organ originated as a vestige of the androgynous state of the embryo, says Konner, doesn't mean it cannot have evolved purposes of its own. He harks back to the Darwinian theory of sexual selection and the development of this into the modern theory of differential sexual strategies between males and females. Males might have been selected for a "quick fix" kind of reward because this is the kind of sex it is advantageous for them to practice: spread the genes around as much as possible.

The female, on the other hand, with her much greater metabolic investment in pregnancy, has always to be more choosy, more selective. It is she who does the selecting in sexual selection. She should therefore, he argues, be slower in achieving pleasure so she doesn't just fall for every Don Juan out for his quick fix. She should take her time and give herself time for a more thorough survey of mates. That the pleasure can be best achieved for her with much foreplay and consideration by a partner, and yet be immensely rewarding when it happens, he suggests, fits with the basic female strategy: the "slow fix" if you like, as opposed to the male thrusting away "blind as a worm," as Yeats so graphically put it.

Konner's argument (which I have somewhat elaborated for him, I hope he will forgive me) is very persuasive, but as with all the adaptationist arguments, it raises the problem of how we prove its truth. Female primates, for example, and indeed all mammalian females, do their share of sexual selecting on the basis described, but it is hard to find the real equivalent of human female orgasms in any of them. I have watched thousands of monkey and ape copulations and would be pretty hard to convince that any of the behaviors that follow the few minutes' thrusting by the male really constitute orgasm. (For a survey, see Hrdy 1981.) What we find generally in animals is pretty tame stuff compared with the best that the females of our own species can achieve when properly stimulated.

So if all the other sexually reproducing species get by without, why should we be different? Perhaps it is only that we can use our intelligence and imagination to see that pleasure *can* be obtained this way, and so we go for it; not that the pleasure is an evolved *necessity* for selective behavior to be successful. And indeed all ethnographic surveys have found that there is enormous variability in the experience of female orgasm across cultures:

varying from practically zero to elaborate and extensive. But they all get the reproductive job done, and often with spectacular success precisely where orgasm is the least often experienced. So it is hard to argue that female multiple ecstasies are an evolutionary necessity.

But perhaps there is something that both Gould and Konner have missed? Let us agree that the clitoris is an analog of the male nipples. But then let us look at the pleasure derived by the male from the stimulation of the nipples. It exists, and certain homosexuals cultivate it, but it is not the full-blown pleasure the mature female is capable of (some women can achieve orgasm by nipple stimulation alone), nor is it intimately connected in men with something so central as the production of oxytocin in adult women (Campbell and Peterson, 1953; Newton 1973; Rossi 1977). It is essentially then exactly like the pleasure that a prepubescent girl might achieve by nipple stimulation.

Follow this line of reasoning: Yes, the clitoris is the female equivalent of the penis, but the penis of a *prepubescent boy*. The clitoris shares this major feature with the boy's penis: There is no ejaculation from it. There will be vaginal secretions at orgasm, but they do not come from the clitoris itself. What then if we complete the equation and say that the pleasure a woman gets with clitoral stimulation is comparable to the pleasure a prepubescent boy gets with stimulation of his nonejaculating penis? Logically this should be the case. If it is, then Gould's "vestigial" formula would work, with the important correction of locating the nipples and the clitoris in this prepubertal state, not in the fully adult condition.

Konner cites the sexual practices of Tantric yoga, where men are "contemptuous of orgasm" and where they use "various stratagems to maintain for hours on end the blissful vertiginous state that immediately precedes it." But he fails to note two things: (a) that Tantric adepts are not in fact contemptuous of *orgasm* but of *ejaculation*, and indeed by postponing ejaculation can have many orgasms *without ejaculating*; and (b) that the blissful state described is precisely the condition of prepubescent masturbatory pleasure in boys, where the lack of ejaculation means that if the "blissful vertiginous" state can be achieved, it too can be maintained, if not for hours on end, at least for a long time. The Tantric Buddhists may well be trying to relive in adult life a kind of pleasure that was lost when puberty, with its vast increase in testosterone production, brought on the quick-fix ejaculatory orgasm that would send them off looking everywhere and anywhere for mates.

One thing that holds us up in deciding this once and for all is of course the lack of information on boyhood masturbation. Masters and Johnson could use consenting adults for their sexual explorations, including nurses for female masturbation, but no one can do the same thing with prepubescent boys and stay out of jail. Nor is it very easy, given both the prevailing taboos on the subject and the problem of parental consent, even to ask them about it. I have therefore been driven, in pursuing this line of research, to depend first on personal experience and second on questioning those adult males who were willing to talk about, and who remembered, their boyhood experiences. On both counts this is a delicate topic. I am encouraged however by the success that my friend and colleague Lionel Tiger had in describing his own first masturbatory experience (in the bath while babysitting) in *The Pursuit of Pleasure*. Everyone seemed to think this quite charming and to the point, so perhaps there is a different climate for such discussion than the one I grew up in, where it would have been impossible.

Naturally my own experience confirms my theory. Indeed, it was reflections on my own experience that led to its formulation. Prepubescent masturbation could be lengthy and blissfully pleasurable, often ending through sheer exhaustion and sometimes with a fairly violent "orgasmic experience," like a series of body-shaking shudders. Descriptions of the blissful states reached by Tantric practices have always sounded to me like descriptions of these prepubertal endeavors. The onset of puberty, while bringing ejaculation and the "major" shudder of male orgasm, was also, for me, a disappointment: It meant the loss of the dreamy state of tension and indescribable pleasure that had previously been possible. Now the pleasure came all too soon and was virtually impossible to sustain. Much later in life, having read of and learned the Tantric practices (or at least my own adaptation of them, for the right female partner for such prolonged enterprises has to have special needs and capacities herself and is hard to find and train), I was able to recreate the premature bliss and know I was not misremembering something from never-never land. I was also able, by observing the reactions of female partners, to see that the prolonged pleasure a female was capable of from clitoral stimulation was indeed close in quality to what the boy experiences. Of course, we do not need to be reminded that there are wide variations in individual experiences, so a sample of one (or in the case of the females a respectable but not record-breaking number) is not enough. Hence the sample.

The way I gathered my "sample" is best described by the charming statistical term of a "random walk." It consisted of 100 men chosen on the basis of their willingness to discuss their childhood masturbatory experiences. I collected examples until I reached 100 since that gives a nice round number and one can quote accurate percentages without the tedium of calculation. It has taken me some fifteen years to compile this information. Obviously, one cannot just ask the men next to one in a bar for such information about their lives; and one learns to be leery of those who volunteer it. These had to be people I knew well enough to ask and who knew that their identities would be strictly concealed. Some were very open, others very secretive, but in all cases I have no reason to believe they were telling anything but the truth, and they had no idea what the nature of my enquiry was, simply that I studied sexual behavior and felt this (boyhood masturbation) to be a neglected area. I deliberately did not choose academic and research colleagues because their answers might be contaminated by their knowledge of the issues.

It has taken a lot of patience to get this far. (Actually, the sample was gathered mostly between 1974 and 1989). I concentrated on younger men, since they would be most likely to remember their boyhoods accurately. Obviously these were "unstructured" interviews, and mostly I simply asked them to recall in their own words what their experience had been like. They differed in their ability to put it into words, of course, and varied in the details of their memories. I usually asked what the onset of puberty had meant for them and how the postpubescent experience was different. The sample was biased toward white Western males, but included in addition to the United States (20 whites, 6 blacks, 4 Asians, 5 American Indians) and most of the European countries (25), 6 from India, 5 from the Middle East, 8 Africans (nonwhite), 2 Chinese (Taiwanese), 6 Australians (white), 2 white South Africans, 4 South Americans, 2 Mexicans, 4 East Europeans, and 1 Russian. It was to get this cross-cultural flavor that I took so much time and used the random walk. I do not trust studies using samples composed of college freshmen or respondents to newspaper advertisements, which then parade their results as "orgasmic experience of the human female" or something such. I did my best to get a widely based sample of "human males." It was interesting that I did not find the details of the answers to be correlated in any way with the ethnic or racial background of the respondents. Thus I think I can claim to have tapped a "human male experience."

This is not the place for detailed quotations, and indeed I have none, since in only a few cases was I able to write down or record the answers in detail. What I think matters was the finding that 82 percent of the sample described prepubescent masturbatory experiences that matched my own. They differed only in intensity, longevity, frequency, etc. Some respondents claimed to have had the experience at a much earlier age than I did: for example, as early as three, as opposed to my six. Some claimed far longer periods of "blissful" intensity, some much less, the whole falling on a more or less normal curve from brief at one end to prolonged at the other, with most falling between fifteen minutes and half an hour. Some reported intense "climaxes"; others did not, or at least not always. This was highly variable. Some reported "ripples" of continuous smaller climaxes preceding the major ending or quiet cessation of the activity — matching my own experience. Others missed this sensation but reported interesting variations (to be reported elsewhere). Again I stress that there was no correlation with race or nationality. The black African group, for example, differed among itself as much as the white

American or East European. Experiences matched up regardless of demographic categories.

What of the 18 percent who differed markedly? They were a mixed bunch, but the major characteristic of them was that they found the prepubertal experience disappointing and lacking in sensation. They were the "nonecstatic" minority. The degree and nature of disappointment differed, with several of them reporting much effort to no avail, and others reporting little effort because "nothing happened." It is interesting that this latter "extreme minority," at approximately 11 percent, is probably about the same figure as we find of so-called "anorgasmic" females, or at least females who have difficulty achieving orgasm even with continual clitoral stimulation. In both sexes, it seems, some are just plain out of luck. And here again this minority was spread across the categories. An even tinier minority were the "precocious" ones, who obviously had advanced glandular development and were able to have orgasms with ejaculation — of fluid if not semen — at an unusually early age.

Of the 82 (percent) who had the boyhood bliss experience in some form or other, from intense to mild, 63 reported a sense of disappointment at the loss of their earlier prepubertal pleasures and orgasms. The other 17 reported that postpubertal sex and orgasms were definitely better (as did most of those who announced disappointment with prepubertal experience). With both groups it is fair to say that they interpreted this change differently. Among the majority, some, like me, saw it as a definite loss of something precious (about 40); the rest varied but mostly saw it as a passing stage which would be righted with more experience. This was particularly true of educated males of whatever background. They knew about "premature ejaculation" and how experience would cure it, and they saw their own experience in this light. These mostly declared themselves satisfied with the progress they made, and did not see their developing ability to prolong intercourse as "restoring" the lost gift of boyhood, but as a progressive maturing process in which premature ejaculation was gradually "corrected."

Those 40 who remembered a sharp disappointment and frustration with the onset of ejaculatory masturbation also varied in their ultimate response to it; but what is significant for me is that they did indeed remember it as such and reported it as such without any prompting. It is hard to say how many of the minority group here might indeed have experienced such a loss but forgotten it fairly quickly under the pressures to "mature." Also, although my questioning on this was not systematic enough for definite results, those with the keenest sense of disappointment appear to be those whose continued sexual release after puberty was masturbation for at least three or four years. The ones who expressed the least sense of loss were those who moved quickly on to sexual intercourse (with either male or female partners or both) or who had started intercourse before puberty. Things might be different today when access to sexual partners is earlier and easier than formerly. Thus, it could be that a quick transition to heterosexual activity masks the reality of the change for many males, and concentrates their attention and sensations on full sexual performance with a partner.

There are many more fascinating details about the sample, but we are not interested in details for their own sake but for how they bear on the hypothesis here advanced about the likeness of the mature female orgasmic experience to that of the masturbatory experience of prepubescent boys. My judgement, both from personal experience again and from reading the literature on female orgasmic experience, suggests that there are strong parallels. The major difference might be that mature females are capable of experiencing much stronger climaxes than boys, and this may be accounted for by the addition of labial and vaginal sensations to the clitoral, and the increase of oxytocin at puberty. But the "plateau" state of prolonged but "unclimaxed" sensation so valued in the female experience, and so difficult to attain for the non-Tantric male, together with the "rippling" effect of multiple orgasm, seems to be a direct analogy with the majority of prepubescent male masturbatory sensations.

This would indeed make the clitoris, as Gould says, the female analog of male nipples, but with the hugely important proviso that the analogy in each case is with the *prepubescent* state, not the fully mature state. And, by extension, female sexual pleasure stemming from clitoral stimulation will be an analogy (and in some sense a homology) of the same pleasure experienced in the penis by prepubescent males. We must also recognize that female experience changes at puberty too, but I suspect somewhat differently. The oxytocin factor renders females capable of more powerful and "volcanic" orgasms after puberty, as with the testosterone-infected males. But at the same time females do not lose the "plateau" and "ripple" or multiple-orgasm effects of prepubertal masturbation. These seem to be incorporated into the experience of female orgasm precisely because they are clitoral. The male, on the other hand, because of the onset of ejaculation, loses these functions unless they are elaborately relearned later.

I doubt this is the last word; but it is the latest word, and the eager world of sex research can take it from here.

3

The Evolution of Incest Inhibition

Definition: Taboo and Avoidance

Incest is defined by the *Oxford English Dictionary* as "sexual congress of near kindred." This, like most similar definitions, leaves open the question of how near the relevant kin have to be to be included in the definition. Societies usually indicate the degree of nearness through negative sanctions on intercourse, and this varies considerably from society to society. All that is certain is that all societies forbid intercourse with some near kin. It is well known that brother-sister marriages, for example, have been commonly allowed, and even enjoined, in some cultures such as Ptolemaic Egypt and Persia (Hopkins, 1980; de Heusch 1958; Goggin and Sturtevant 1964), and that father-daughter intercourse has been allowed or enjoined in several others (Middleton 1962). Mother-son intercourse, however, is nowhere known to have been prescribed, even if it was not always punished. Outside this narrow range of primary kin, restrictions are entirely variable, with, for example, various forms of first-cousin marriage being prescribed in many cultures, and all forms of cousin marriage being forbidden in others (Huth 1877). In the social sciences, interest has usually focused on the explanation and supposed universality of the taboo on sexual intercourse with near kin. While not universal, the taboo is widespread, and even in the absence of a specific taboo, incestuous liaisons seem only to account for a very small percentage of acts of intercourse. It is therefore perhaps more accurate to say that incest is universally avoided, even though it does occur (Murdock 1949).

Incest and Exogamy

We have mentioned that brothers and sisters are sometimes allowed to marry, which of course implies that intercourse between them is not forbidden. Even so, it is necessary to keep clear the distinction between sexual intercourse between near kin (incest) and marriage between near kin. The latter, when allowed, is termed endogamy, and when forbidden, exogamy. Exogamy — the proscription of marriage with kin (however defined) — can of course be isomorphic with incest prohibitions, but it need not. In many societies people are forbidden as marriage partners between whom sexual intercourse is not a crime. Also, when it comes to the important task of explaining the prohibitions it has to be noted that explanations of exogamy do not necessarily cover incest: there may be many reasons for not marrying near kin which are not good explanations for forbidding sexual intercourse with them (Fox 1980, chap. 1).

Incest and Inbreeding

One explanation which covers both is that incest is biologically dangerous because it raises the probabilities of deleterious homozygosity in any population (Livingstone 1969). Thus, neither casual sexual intercourse nor long-term marriage should be allowed, since either will lead to offspring whose chances of viability are low, ultimately endangering the survival of the population (Lindzey 1967). While the deleterious results of close inbreeding are certainly established (Seemanova 1971; Gowen 1964), the problem with this as an explanation of human taboos is that it does not convincingly link the possible outcome with human motivation. While the breeding of monsters is often given as a reason by human cultures for banning intercourse of close kin, it is as often not given and some other explanation proffered. A response to this is that it does not matter what reason is given, since natural selection will have favored those groups or individuals who banned such intercourse, whatever the overt rationalizations. This would also take care of the fact that in many human groups observations on animal breeding would lead to the opposite conclusion: that close inbreeding had desirable results. However, it is not clear that the avoidance of malformed offspring is the biological basis — however it gets translated into human action — for human incest avoidance.

Another candidate is the biological basis of sexual reproduction itself. Thus, the evolutionary origin of sexual reproduction must lie in some adaptive advantage it had over asexual reproduction, which is on the surface more efficient at preserving favorable mutations (Williams 1975). The only secure advantage is variation: Sexual reproduction produces a higher level of genetic variation, which may be advantageous in a changing environment. If the very purpose of sexual reproduction then is variation, one would expect tendencies to evolve that would cause organisms to outbreed, since inbreeding systematically reduces such variation (Bischof 1975). Only in cases where a constant environment is encountered would we expect systematic inbreeding in sexually reproducing organisms (Hamilton 1967). This does not mean that any species would necessarily avoid all incestuous mating, but that it would reduce the amount of such mating below the level leading to a dangerous inbreeding load and consequent reduction of variation.

The sharp fall-off in genetic relatedness with cousins (.50 for siblings, .25 for nieces and nephews, .125 for first cousins, .0625 for second cousins) means that, despite a slightly heightened probability of homozygosity, cousin mating can be consistently practiced without deleterious results and without increasing the inbreeding load beyond a tolerable level (Bodmer & Cavalli-Sforza 1976). Studies of animal and even plant populations have shown that (a) close inbreeding on a heavy scale is avoided, and (b) inbreeding with organisms in the close-cousin range is often preferred. The latter indeed maximizes the benefits of concentrating related genes while reducing the dangers of too-close inbreeding. It thus perfectly solves the problem posed by sexual reproduction in the first place (Bateson 1983).

Incest in *Homo Sapiens*

Extrapolating from this latter argument, we would expect to find in humans (a) an avoidance of incestuous mating on a large scale, although some will occur, and (b) a general preference for marriage within the close-cousin range. Taking human history as a whole, before the advent of huge modern populations, this was indeed the pattern. Whatever the rules of marriage in small communities, even if they did not specify marriage with cousins, there would have been no alternative to it. Indeed, in European communities marriage was often expressly forbidden with first and second cousins by the Church, and the prohibition even extended further. But in any small community this would have meant that the only people available as spouses were within the third-cousin range anyway. The phenomenon of "pedigree collapse" means that most people for most of history were marrying people related to them with some degree of cousinship, and in most places still are (Shoumatoff 1985). It would appear then that there is nothing left to say about human incest avoidance: We avoid incest and mate with cousins like most other sexually reproducing organisms. What this account does not explain, however, are the specific proximate mechanisms that cause us to avoid close inbreeding. All it says for any species is that such inbreeding will be by and large avoided, but each species differs in the manner in which this avoidance is motivated.

Mechanisms of Avoidance

One of the simplest methods is dispersion, where the young at sexual maturity or before are ejected or leave the natal group. This does not require a specific motivation for inbreeding avoidance since the related animals are not likely ever to meet and mate. The combination of mate competition and harems, as among ungulates and sea mammals, has a similar effect in that only the successful male mates, and this cuts down on the inbreeding possibilities (Bischof 1975). Problems arise when, as in humans, the sexually mature young remain in the group or available to each other and their parents. For most of human history the rate of possible incest must in effect have remained low, given late puberty, short life span, high infant mortality, wide birth spacing, and considerable differential age at marriage, with females marrying at puberty (Slater 1959). With the change in circumstances brought about by the Neolithic revolution, however, availability would have increased and, with it, opportunity. Very few human communities, however, opted for institutionalization of incest in the form of incestuous marriages.

Nature versus Culture

Until recently, social and behavioral science, and philosophy, assumed that this near-universal taboo on incest was a particularly human intrusion into a natural situation which would have been promiscuous and incestuous (see, e.g., Lévi-Strauss 1949). But, as we have seen, the situation in nature is the opposite of what was supposed: Mating is ordered and incest is avoided. Thus, with humans, it is not the case that incest avoidance is an intrusion of culture into nature. But, of course, an incest taboo is. This is, however, simply because only humans have language and self-awareness and so are able to impose explicit sanctions against actions. The universal taboo against murder is likewise different from the animal ritualization of aggression against conspecifics. The question remains: Why, when the opportunity and demographic circumstances make it possible, do humans insist, with few exceptions, on nonincestuous mating? It has been plausibly argued that the few instances of prescribed incestuous marriage in humans are in fact what constitutes the intrusion of culture into nature, which is otherwise averse to such close inbreeding (Arens 1986).

Theories of Taboo and Exogamy

Because it has often been assumed that the banning of incestuous marriages is the essence of the issue, much confusion has ensued. Arguments concerning the benefits of banning marriage with close relatives do not necessarily tell us what the motivations of the parties are. These arguments for exogamy are many and various, but they have in common that they spell out some benefit to human groups for practicing exogamy (reduce conflict in the family, make for wider social ties, promote organic solidarity), or some dire consequence for not practicing it (confusion of family relationships, failure of socialization process, etc.). All these may be true (although some are contradictory), but they do not necessarily tell us why humans avoid incestuous mating without the help of some subargument (Fox 1967, chap. 2).

Thus, it might be argued that humans consciously see the benefits proposed (or the disasters that might follow) and so ban sex with the relatives concerned. Many people, indeed, put forward arguments quite like the observers' to the effect that no man would want to marry his sister since this would deprive him of a brother-in-law, and so on. But this would not necessarily rule out sex with the sister. The test case would be one where sisters were allowed as sexual partners. We could then see whether siblings would voluntarily choose each other. But even where sex with the sister (or mother or daughter) would not upset the rules of exogamy (in wife-lending societies, for example), it does not seem to occur. There seems, therefore, to be a prima facie case for examining a proximate mechanism or motivation for avoiding sex with close relatives separate from any social benefits accruing from exogamous marriages.

Freud and Westermarck

Two theories have dominated Western social science with regard to this possible mechanism. A third theory, that there is an inbuilt aversion — an instinct — against incest has generally been dismissed on the grounds that it requires a sure identification of genetic relatedness which we are not known as a species to possess. Indeed, most species operate not on such recognition but on rules of thumb like "animals I grew up with are likely to be related" or "animals with the same smell are relatives." Putting aside the instinct theory, then, we are left with interactions during socialization. The two theories on the effects of these seem to be diametrically opposed. Sigmund Freud proposed that, for children, parents and then siblings were indeed the first "love objects" and elicited a strong desire, but that this desire was "repressed" with the coming of the genital stage of sexual development and the maturing of the superego (Freud 1922). In response to the question of why, if we have such strong desires we do not simply act on them, Freud's ultimate answer was an evolutionary scenario in which a patricidal band of brothers "renounced" their mothers and sisters as a result of deferred guilt over the killing of their fathers (Freud 1913). While this phylogenetic theory has been dismissed, Freud's point that if we do not have a strong desire to commit incest, then we should not have such fierce sanctions against it, has been generally accepted.

In opposition to this view stands that of Edward Westermarck, who observed that people who had been raised in close proximity seemed to lack strong sexual desires for each other (Westermarck 1926). Since they did not like to see others doing what they felt to be wrong, they instituted sanctions against incest. Freud, James Frazer, and Claude Lévi-Strauss, among others, insisted that stern prohibitions against incest pointed to strong desire for it, the argument being that we would not bother to forbid something to which we were averse anyway — we would simply not do it. It is hard to resolve such an argument in terms of sanctions since we have not always a good idea as to what motivates people to impose them. Either argument is plausible, but it is better to look directly at evidence for avoidance motivations.

There is evidence from animal experiments and observations, particularly on our close relatives the great apes, which suggests such avoidance mechanisms may exist. Siblings, in particular, who have been raised closely together, seem to be unwilling mates. Mother-son mating seems very rare in animals, particularly primates, but father-daughter matings occur with some frequency (Pusey 1980; Sade 1968). This seems to hold across many species, and the figures we have suggest that the same is true of our own. The findings are compatible with both theories. Freud would assume that the taboos are primarily directed at the young male, and that he would therefore as a result of both paternal power and inherited guilt be kept from sister and mother, while as "father" he would have less compunction. Freud, however, downplayed the possibility of father-daughter incest, attributing it to patient fantasies. The facts also fit the Westermarck hypothesis: Son and mother would always be in close contact through suckling; brother and sister would be socialized together but with varying degrees of closeness; father and daughter would usually have least contact of all.

In an attempt to reconcile the theories, Fox (1962; 1980) proposed that they might be referring to different socialization processes. Thus, siblings, for example, would be reared with differing degrees of closeness, sometimes with intimate physical contact, sometimes in close proximity but with no contact. If we assume that physical contact is a necessary element in developing the aversion, then in the one case the aversion would develop and in the other not. But in the second case (the Freudian prototype) the sibling of the opposite sex would be an object of desire at puberty. At least with siblings, then, the theories seem reconcilable. A survey of ethnographic examples revealed a continuum from complete childhood interaction, producing aversion to sex between cosocialized children at puberty, to complete separation, leading to intense desire at puberty as evidenced by dreams, myths, projective behavior, etc. Two particularly telling cases are the Israeli Kibbutzim (Shepher 1983), where children raised in close physical contact before six years of age refuse to marry even when their elders encourage and expect it, and Taiwan, where young girls are adopted into families as potential brides for the sons and raised closely together with them. The marriages are generally failures and there is great unwillingness to consummate them (Wolf and Huang 1980). (In the Kibbutz case all the children are not siblings to each other, but real siblings will be among those so raised, so the effect will be to avoid incest. But see the criticism of Shepher's methods in Hartung 1985.)

The question posed by Freud, etc. is still asked, namely, if people in fact do not wish to have intercourse with near kin, why do they impose sanctions on those who do? The questioners sense an inconsistency, but the answer was there in Westermarck: we often impose sanctions against behavior we do not wish to indulge in precisely because of our distaste for such behavior. If we truly do not want to do it ourselves, we do not sympathize with those who, for whatever reason, do wish to; hence we ban the behavior in question. It can always be assumed that there will be a minority of people who are different, and these are usually persecuted by the majority. Thus it is with incest. It is forbidden precisely because the majority of us do not wish to do it. This would be the Westermarckian answer.

To sum up the modern version of the Westermarck theory, Fox proposed the following general law: The intensity of heterosexual attraction between cosocialized children after puberty is inversely related to the intensity of physical interaction between them before puberty.

It is still not known what produces the aversion effect. Shepher proposes "negative imprinting." Fox has proposed "aversive conditioning." But neither of these is altogether satisfactory. And neither accounts for avoidance between children and parents.

Parental Incest

Mother-son and father-daughter incest stand in sharp contrast: the former is extremely rare; the latter seems to occur with some frequency in most societies. If we refer again to the demographic circumstances prevailing before the rise of medical science and hygiene, when life expectancy was short and puberty late, then we can see that the possibilities for each type are different enough to decide trends. By the time sons matured, mothers would be close to death, but fathers would have at least a chance of incest with older daughters. It makes little breeding sense for sons to mate with women at the end of their childbearing years anyway, while men, of course, can continue to breed as long as they live.

But apart from opportunity, there is the added feature of power. As Freud saw, females are usually under the control of older males, and especially the mother and sisters under the control of the father. Thus, the young male is in a poor position to put into effect any incestuous desires he may have. This situation is probably one of long standing in human evolution given that we are a species with a competitive breeding pattern in which a long association of mates is required for the raising of young to viability. This is the pattern among our nearest primate relatives, and must have characterized our original hominid ancestors. Indeed, it has been argued that the rapid evolution of the hominid line, and especially of its neocortex, could not have taken place outside a hierarchical mating system (Chance 1962).

Such a system required not only that older males wield reproductive power over younger, but that the younger males develop methods of inhibition of their sexual and aggressive drives. Particularly with the advent of bipedalism and even crude weapons, unrestricted warfare over the females would have been a disaster for the species. The growing neocortex provided exactly this mechanism, being capable of both inhibiting actions of the limbic system (sex, hunger, aggression, rage) and selectively scanning for appropriate behavior (planning and foresight). If such a scenario is correct, then the creature it produced would be strongly motivated by the archaic drives, but actually primed to inhibit them and channel them into socially appropriate (i.e., nonlethal) behaviors (see Fox 1980, chaps. 5 & 6).

If we apply this to incest, we can see that the older males ("fathers") would be motivated to monopolize females for reproductive purposes, while the younger males ("sons"), similarly motivated, would be inhibiting and redirecting their drives. Thus, when a "son" comes to puberty, he has a long history of inhibition as regards "mother" and "sister." He will therefore be unlikely to pursue sexual relations with them. The father and daughter situation has no such direct inhibitions, but the father nevertheless is still subject to strong inhibitory restrictions on his behavior since the daughter is marked as a wife for some other man, a potential ally.

It is often asked why the women in these circumstances do not initiate sexual activity, in particular the mothers with their sons. One answer, contained in the above account, is that they are usually under the direction and control of more powerful males. But mothers also have a particular relationship with sons through the suckling and socialization experience. Although the mechanisms are not known, this could well affect their motivations regarding adult sexuality with their sons, and vice versa (Count

1967). Certainly, in circumstances where they could carry out any incestuous wishes, they do not seem to do so on any large scale.

Breakdown of Avoidance Mechanisms

None of these human motivations for ensuring close inbreeding avoidance are 100 percent secure. As in the animal world, they can break down and do. We have only recently begun to uncover the real frequencies for such intercourse, and even now we can never be sure, since the majority of instances are probably not reported. But, as would be predicted by the foregoing theory, father-daughter incest turns out to be the most common and reaches quite high levels, if figures are to be trusted (Herman 1981). This is always the most vulnerable dyad, since the mechanisms of automatic avoidance or inbuilt inhibition are weakest here. In many such cases reported, the mother is either missing or inadequate, and the daughter steps into her place — in some cases without guilt until discovery and social ostracization produce this (Weinberg 1955). In other cases, the father is obviously exploitative and the mother afraid to intervene. We must understand that the mechanisms proposed for avoiding incest are subject to variation, like any others. The majority of men have intact and functioning inhibitory mechanisms, and are also capable of appreciating the positive values of a nonsexual, loving relationship. Some men, however, even a sizable minority, lack such strong controls, particularly if alcoholism is involved. Alcoholism can indeed be traced to a genetic source and may well involve a specific weakness of inhibitory capacity in the neocortex. Such males will be less able to control their impulses if sexually aroused by their children — or any children. It remains, however, a minority affair, and the vast majority of males and females continue, in the absence of direct coercion, to avoid sexual intercourse with immediate kin.

Conclusion

The human avoidance of intercourse with near kin has direct animal counterparts and is part of a general avoidance pattern among mammals and sexually reproducing organisms. Its specific mechanisms, however, can be traced to the particularities of hominid evolution, with the development in particular of the inhibitory capacities of the neocortex, an evolutionary development itself derived from the need to control sexuality and aggression. Modern *Homo sapiens*, then, is innately equipped, not with an "anti-incest instinct," but with the means for easily developing through socialization a set of inhibitory behaviors. These are not foolproof, and incestuous matings do occur, particularly between father and daughter, but these are a small minority of total matings. While some modern countries (e.g., Sweden) appear to be taking a more relaxed attitude to the possibilities of incestuous marriages (at least brother-sister), most of the modern world continues to observe the overt legal and social taboos which human consciousness uses to reinforce the natural tendencies.

4

Food and Eating Out

(With a Note on Shopping Malls)

The Myth of Nutrition

We have to eat; we like to eat; eating makes us feel good; it is more important than sex. To ensure genetic survival the sex urge need only be satisfied a few times in a lifetime; the hunger urge must be satisfied every day. It is also a profoundly social urge. Food is almost always shared; people eat together; mealtimes are events when the whole family or settlement or village comes together. Food is also an occasion for sharing, for distributing and giving, for the expression of altruism, whether from parents to children, children to in-laws, or anyone to visitors and strangers. Food is the most important thing a mother gives a child; it is the substance of her own body, and in most parts of the world mother's milk is still the only safe food for infants. Thus food becomes not just a symbol of, but the reality of, love and security. All animals eat, but we are the only animal that cooks. So cooking becomes more than a necessity, it is the symbol of our humanity, what marks us off from the rest of nature. And because eating is almost always a group event (as opposed to sex), food becomes a focus of symbolic activity about sociality and our place in our society.

The body needs fuel. But this need could be served by a rough diet of small game, roots, and berries, as it was for several million years. Or, even more extreme, pills could be synthesized to give us all we need (except bulk). But our "tastes" have never been governed solely by nutrition. Modern nutritionists chant the litany of the "four food types" (vegetables, grains, dairy products, meats) from which we are supposed to take more or less equal amounts daily. But grains and cereals, particularly processed, and dairy and domestic meat fats, particularly saturated, can be killers. (A new "food pyramid" — equally misleading, is now being touted.) In fact, nutrition plays only a small part in our food choices. Adele Davis, whose bossy opinions on food were to a whole generation as authoritative as Dr. Spock's on childrearing (she recommended a diet of liver and yogurt), held that European history was determined by food habits. The French ate white bread and drank wine and strong coffee, she said, and this was about as nutritionally disastrous as possible; the Germans, on the other hand, ate dark bread and drank beer — both nutritionally sound. Was it any wonder, she asked, that the Germans kept beating the French? But even if both nations were to accept this interesting hypothesis as sound, do we believe they would change their food preferences?

Nor are these preferences solely governed by what is available. All cultures go to considerable lengths to obtain preferred foods, and often ignore valuable food sources close at hand. The English do not eat horse and dog; Mohammedans refuse pork; Jews have a whole litany of forbidden foods (see Leviticus); Americans despise offal; Hindus taboo beef — and so on. People will not just eat anything, whatever the circumstances. In fact, omnivorousness is often treated as a joke. The Chinese are indeed thought by their more fastidious neighbors to eat anything. The Vietnamese used to say that the best way to get rid of the Americans would be to invite in the Chinese, who would surely find them good to eat.

You Eat What You Are

Since everyone must eat, what we eat becomes a most powerful symbol of who we are. To set yourself apart from others by what you will and will not eat is a social barrier almost as powerful as the incest taboo, which tells us with whom we may or may not have sex. Some cultures equate the two taboos. Margaret Mead quotes a New Guinea proverb that goes, "Your own mother, your own sister, your own pigs, your own yams which you have piled up, you may not eat." Own food, like related women, is for exchange, for gift giving, for social generosity, for forging alliances, but not for personal consumption. The obverse of this is that you identify yourself with others by eating the same things in the same way. To achieve such identification, people will struggle to eat things they loath, and avoid perfectly tasty food that is on the forbidden list. In the process of social climbing people have to learn to like caviar, artichokes, snails, and asparagus, and scorn dumplings, fish and chips, and meat and potato pie — all more nutritious, but fatally tainted with lower-class associations.

There are as many kinds of food identification as there are the same in fashion, speech, music, manners and the like. The obvious ones are ethnic, religious, and class identifications. Ethnic food preferences only become identity markers in the presence of gustatory "foreigners," such as when one goes abroad, or when the foreigners visit the home shores. The insecure will cling desperately to home food habits: English housewives on the continent even break open tea bags to make a "proper" cup of tea (the taste is identical). Popular songs attest to the food difficulties of interethnic marriages' "bangers and mash vs. macaroni." When various ethnic groups are forcibly thrown together, there is both an intensifying of food identity and a growing mishmash. The American melting pot is almost literally that: the food preferences of dozens of nations are put side by side, and there cannot help but be overlap and mixing. The most startling example is the popularity of the Chinese kosher restaurant, and it is not uncommon to find a restaurant advertising itself as "Chinese-Italian-American" along with the proud boast "All Our Wines Are Chilled." The ubiquitous "diner" with its vast menu served twenty-four hours a day is a microcosm of the melting pot, having Greek salad, Italian pasta, German rye bread, Polish kielbasi, Chinese chow mein, Belgian waffles, French quiche, Hungarian goulash, Irish stew, Jewish gefilte fish, Russian blintzes, English muffins, Austrian pastries, Swiss cheese, Mexican enchiladas, Spanish gazpacho, Canadian bacon, Japanese teriyaki, German sausages, Norwegian herring, Lebanese pita, Nova Scotia salmon, and Virginia ham.

Tables and Table Manners

Not knowing how to eat "properly" is universally a sign of outsider status. Proper eating includes the kind of food used, the way of preparing it, the manner of serving it, and the way of eating it. The intricacies of the tea ceremony are known only to experienced Japanese; social climbers in the West can be spotted immediately by their inability to master the details of place settings; "using the wrong fork" is an offense as grave as spitting in public. Since anyone wishing to integrate himself into a group must eat with it, there is no surer way of marking off those who are in and those out than by food etiquette. Dipping with hands into a communal dish is de rigeur in some cultures, abhorrent in others. Shoveling food into the mouth with a fork would be seen as the height of indelicacy by some; the absence of forks as the height of barbarity by others. Fingers may have been made before forks, but ever since Catherine (and Marie) de Medici brought these essential tools for noodle eating from northern Italy to France, the perfectly useful finger has been socially out, except for fruit and cheese. It took the elaborate dining habits of the upper classes to refine the use of multiple forks (as well as knives, spoons, and glasses).

The timing of eating shows up class differences. In the past, as in the novels of Jane Austen, for example, the upper classes breakfasted late (about 10 o'clock), as befitted their leisure status. (This distinguished them from the lower orders, who eat very early before going off to work.) They had perhaps an informal lunch of cold meats, but the next main meal was dinner, which was eaten anywhere between five and seven, depending on the pretensions of the family. A light supper might be served before bedtime. The lower orders, meanwhile, would be eating a light midday meal and then a hearty "tea" after the day's work was done, with again a supper before bed.

The importance of "lunch" as a main meal came later from the business community, and "dinner" was pushed back into the evening, with supper more or less abolished. The lower orders continued to make midday "dinner" and "high tea" major meals, and since dinner was pushed later for the middle classes, "tea" became an institution around four o'clock. There is no nutritional sense to the timing of eating. It could be done differently. The late breakfast was primarily a sign of status and nothing else; Jane Austen's characters always had to kill time in some way before breakfasting, and these were good hours in which to advance the plot. In France, the enormous midday meal, with its postprandial siesta, is what the day revolves around. The entire country comes to a stop and wakes up again between three and four. In effect, the healthiest way of eating would be to have a heavy protein meal in the morning, light lunch and tea, and a heavier carbohydrate meal (e.g., pasta) in the evening.

The order in which foods are eaten, which really does not matter, becomes highly ritualistic: Soup, fish, poultry, meat, dessert (which echoes the process of evolution) becomes a standard. Sweet should not be eaten before savory, and rarely (in France never) with. The French eat salad after the main dish, the Americans rigidly before; the English, to the disgust of both, put it on the same plate as the (cold) meat. In the East, it is more common to serve all the food together, often in communal dishes, and allow a wide sampling of different items. In the more individualistic West, place settings are rigidly set of from each other, and so are "courses." The serving of wine with food becomes even more rigidly a matter of protocol, and operates to mark off differences of status within classes: those who "know" wine and those who do not. Classes in "corporate health" in the United States now include sessions on "How to Read a Wine Label." The rationale is that without such knowledge corporate executives may be subject to "stress," which would impair their performance.

Foreign foods tend to be shunned by the working classes, but among the upper-middle and upper they become items of prestige. A knowledge of foreign food indicates the eater's urbanity and cosmopolitanism. Until recently, being conversant with foreign food was a privilege of those who could afford to travel, but now the knowledge has been democratized by cheap travel and television. Julia Child taught the aspiring middle classes how to be "French" cooks, and now TV abounds with every kind of cooking course. Publishers often find their cooking list to be their most lucrative, and cookbooks of all nations now crowd the bookstore shelves. When *Joy of Sex* was written, it deliberately took its title from the hugely successful *Joy of Cooking* — which tells us something. While a lot of this can perhaps be attributed to a genuine pleasure in new tastes, a lot more can probably be accounted for by the aura of sophistication that surrounds the food "expert." The very word "gourmet" has become a title of respect like "guru" or "mahatma." Vast changes have occurred, for example, in English eating habits, with extended travel in Europe. Ethnic identifications in food have not by any means disappeared, and the French do not, by and large, eat fish and chips; the English have not taken wholeheartedly to escargot or octopus. But spaghetti no longer comes exclusively in cans for the English. Even so, a relative conservatism of food habits persists in all countries, particularly with the lower-middle and working classes.

Conspicuous Digestion: Eating on Ceremony

The conspicuous consumption of food has always been important as an indicator of status, from three thousand pigs at a New Guinea feast to mountains of caviar and truffles at little Max Spielberg's fourth birthday party. Lavish food entertainment is part of the ancient tradition of food hospitality used mainly to impress strangers. This can vary from the inevitable putting on of the kettle to make tea in British and Irish homes, through the bringing of bread and salt in Russia, to the gargantuan hospitality of the Near East where if the guest does not finish the enormous dish of sheep's eyes in aspic the host is mortally affronted. We are not only what we eat, but how well we eat. Next to showing off military hardware, showing off food is the best way to impress the "outsider." The twenty-one-gun salute — fired with blanks — reminds the visitor that we can, but will not, hurt him; the twenty-one-course meal serves to show him our good will and to impress him with our prosperity. Here again, the manner of serving becomes important. Whether entertaining the in-laws at home or royalty at the palace, formality and lavishness are the key. Mrs. Beeton's recipes astonish us today ("take thirty-two eggs and five pounds of butter..."), but she was in charge of entertaining at Ascot, and impressing royalty and business moguls was the name of the game. (Her magnificent *Household Management* is not only the definitive English cookbook, but what it says — a detailed and fascinating directive for young wives on everything from how to manage a large household staff to how to judge, hire, and address a second footman or upstairs chambermaid — indispensable reading for all social historians or "Upstairs Downstairs" buffs.)

The French anthropologist Claude Lévi-Strauss, like all his countrymen attuned to the niceties of food customs, notes how we reserve "rich" food for the grandest occasions. The ordinary daily menu is not served, he says, and cites saumon mayonaise, turbot sauce mousseline, aspics de foie gras, together with fine wines. "These are some of the delicacies which one would not buy and consume alone without a vague feeling of guilt," he maintains. And this "rich food" has nothing much to do with "the mere satisfaction of physiological needs." It is food meant to be shared, and to be shared with those we wish to impress. To feed someone is one of the most direct and intimate ways to convey something of ourselves to the impressee. We are never just saying, "see how we can satisfy your hunger." We are saying more like "see how lavish and hospitable and knowledgeable we are." Of the most basic things in our behavioral repertoire, eating is the most accessible and effective for conveying our messages to others. We can, of course, offer sex and violence, and sometimes we do, but food, along with superior accommodations, is on the whole easier and safer.

Eating In: Dining Settings and Styles

Every meal is a message, and where we eat is as important as what we eat in getting the message across. Why do we not eat all our meals in the dining room? Its name would suggest that this is its purpose. But the very fact that we call it the "dining" room and not the "eating" room, tells its own story. The dining room is usually reserved for "ceremonial" meals: those involving extended families on special occasions — older relatives, in-laws, and important guests to be impressed. It is probably the most absurdly underused room in the house, and a conspicuous waste of space. Despite the modern trend to more informal dining, recent surveys have shown an overwhelming majority of home buyers requesting a dining room. When asked for what purpose it was needed, they usually replied, "to entertain the boss and his wife" — something that might happen at best once a year. This suggests that the fourteen-by-twelve-foot room with its dignified and dedicated furnishings is more a shrine to ambition and hope than a functioning part of the home.

The whole idea of separating the dining room from the kitchen was, of course, part of the general middle-class attempt to ape the upper class. The latter wished to sever their seating experience from the dirty, noisy, and smelly process that produced it. This often meant that food had to travel literally miles from kitchen to banqueting hall. On a smaller scale, the ambitious middle class imitated this practice.

Perhaps it was because servants were relegated to the kitchen and entered the dining room only as menials, that the progressive, egalitarian members of the middle class in the 1950s and 1960s consciously revolted against the tradition of separate dining. An orgy of wall destruction ensued which erased the distinction between the kitchen and dining room. This became a popular trend and influenced new-house design, where dining rooms gave way to "eating areas" and dinner parties to informal buffets. Of course, this was done in the name of efficiency rather than ideology, but we often disguise our ideological preferences this way, even to ourselves. And it was not a universally recognized efficiency: the dining-room crowd hung in there, and with a swing back to a more conservative ideology, there has been a swing back to more formal dining.

Despite this, entertaining at home has in general become more informal, less predictable, and more fun. There is no longer a rigid formula for "perfect entertaining," and media advice reflects this trend. There is much more room for spontaneity; more of what the hostess (or often the host) is into at the time. We no longer need to impress with the solemn procession of courses: soup, fish, meat, dessert, etc. (a system of eating that originated in Russia and was brought west by the Frenchman Carème). We can present a mixture of Japanese, Regional Italian, Vegetarian Gourmet, and Cuisine Minceur. The basic rule now seems to be: do what pleases you and is fun. The main requirement is: be innovative and surprise people. And this does not require elaborate and impressive preparation. Indeed, there is a premium on elegant simplicity: the original and unusual combination of simple elements. Thus, entertaining has become livelier, more expressive of personal style and flair, more creative, and undoubtedly more enjoyable.

Compare two different entertaining menus: one a formal dinner party of 1953, served in the dining room, with perhaps coffee and liqueurs in the sitting room; the other an informal evening buffet of 1993, served in the kitchen/dining area, with the guests ranging over the "reception" rooms of the house to eat. Both menus recognize the importance of the occasion — entertaining important guests, for example.

Despite the informality of menu 2, there are still some distinctions that are strictly observed. The essence of entertaining is still the display of concern and effort for the welfare of the guests. Despite the enormous popularity of frozen and convenience food, and of ready-made "take-out" meals, these would *never* be served to guests. The foods served on these ceremonial occasions have to be "special" — to demonstrate thoughtfulness and care on the part of the hosts, even if they no longer need to demonstrate the conspicuous consumption of time, money, servants, and energy. The food on the 1993 menu can all be made in advance, but it is all hand prepared and requires thought and effort. The mode of preparation fits the lifestyle of the new working couple, and the new kitchen technology — particularly the food processor and the microwave oven. No one expects beef Wellington any more, but the quality, style, and flair of the chili con carne (with fresh cilantro sprinkled on top for the little extra touch) will be just as critically appraised and warmly appreciated. The content may change, but the message remains the same: You are important guests and we have taken care and trouble on your behalf.

Dinner Party circa 1953

Mulligatawny Soup	Amontillado
Sole Meunière	Chablis
Beef Wellington	Burgundy
Brussels Sprouts	
Potatoes au gratin	
Artichoke hearts	
Salade Verte	
Tarte aux framboises	Sauternes
Assorted cheeses	Port/Claret
Fruit	
Coffee	Brandy/Liqueurs

Dinner Buffet circa 1993

Quiche Lorraine	Beaujolais Nouveau
Spinach Quiche	Australian Chardonnay
Broccoli and Ham Quiche	
Pasta Salad	Decaffeinated Coffee
Bean Salad	Fruit Juices/Perrier
Chile con Carne	
Ginger Chicken Pieces/Snow Peas	
Melon Balls with Prosciutto	
Warm Wheel of Brie with Almonds	
French Bread/Rolls	
Fresh Fruit	

Food as Fashion

The myth of nutrition is shown up by rapid changes in food fashions. Availability is of course important. As waves of different foods hit Europe, eating habits changed. At first these "foreign" foods, particularly spices, like foreign fashions were a privilege of the rich, but they soon percolated down. Günter Grass wrote a novel (*The Flounder*) in which each section is based on a food that changed eating habits in Eastern Europe; turnips, pepper, and potatoes loom large.

But once foods become plentiful and varied, fashion takes over, and the lure of novelty — the trendy — is often disguised as concern for nutrition. Thus vegetarian diets and nouvelle cuisine, high fiber diets and cuisine minceur, all masquerade as "healthy." In fact, they all are nutritionally suspicious, but are used like any other fashion: to show how with-it we are. Just as clothes indicate our trendiness, so does food. When grande cuisine French cooking was in, it too was extolled as "healthy." Now sushi is a fad, raw fish is praised as a "high-protein, low-fat" source, ignoring the high rates of stomach cancer in Japan. When cheeseburgers were shown to produce enzymes that might inhibit cancer, a whole generation of food faddists was thrown into turmoil since the cheeseburger was decidedly out. Food snobbism has now become as refined as wine snobbism. Not knowing about kiwi fruit tart or fresh coriander or how to prepare a ristafel or couscous in the authentic fashion, marks one as a social failure. One has not kept up with the latest in food fashion. As with all fashion industries, food fashion thrives on change; it demands it. The vast industry can only survive if people's tastes are constantly induced to change. The tremendous bombardment of food books and food programs leads educated and literate middle-class readers to feel guilty if they don't "keep up."

This is a considerable change from the days of servants, when how to get the best cook or chef was the issue. The upper and upper-middle classes did not do their own cooking, and at the very top even any knowledge of it was unthinkable. The middle-class housewife would have to know about it, but was not likely to practice it. She would most likely go by Mrs. Beeton and simply give instructions on menus to the cook. Since servants have almost disappeared, and madame (and monsieur) has moved into the kitchen, the snobbery of preparing something trendy and exotic with relative ease has moved with them.

Along with this has gone a reverse snobbery — a deliberate cultivation of proletarian tastes as long as they are romantic: chili con carne, huevos rancheros, pancakes — all cowboy foods and heavy with the romanticization of the Old West. Or take the tremendous popularity of Cajun cooking — essentially a peasant cuisine but "Louisiana French," and hence romantic.

Tex-Mex is another peasant style that has taken. All this goes along with the "rediscovery" of ethnic roots after several generations of denying them, and the lure of the "regional" and quaint. But very little of this would be so organized and spread so quickly if it were not for the demands of the food-fashion industry to find novelty. "New American" cuisine is a way simply to take the homely and make it seem exotic so as to generate yet another "new" food trend. The food-writing industry dominates magazines and the "living" sections of newspapers, and it succeeds because it is available to everyone. We may not all be able to be with-it by buying into the latest ludicrously expensive fashion trends, but we can all whip up a ratatouille, or a green chili stew, or a spinach quiche, or stir-fried shrimp, or blackened redfish, serve it with a trendy "blush" wine, and feel right up there with the new wave.

One remarkable feature of the "proletarian chic" style of cooking is the wide popularity of the "cookout" or "barbecue," using rich spicy sauces to baste large cuts of meat. ("Barbe et queue"? The OED says it's from the Haitian "barbacoa" — a crate on posts. Do we believe that?) This is, in the USA, another appropriation of cowboy cooking by the middle class — which has spread beyond America (the Australians will invite you to "put another shrimp on the barbie," if the ads are to be believed). Why, we might ask, does the man have to do the cooking outdoors and the woman indoors? Because the myths have it that cooking with fire is dangerous and should be left to the men. Again, this is probably a hangover from the romanticization of the cowboy and a way for men to feel macho while wearing aprons and preparing food. This may explain why the working class, which usually lags in the food fad business, is right on top of the cookout. Usually the workers have neither the time nor the means to be faddists. Quantity and "tastiness" (smoked or pickled) continue to dominate their diets. The quantity is not necessary and is even positively harmful. Other workers — Chinese peasants, for example — eat sparingly. It reflects a late trickle-down effect: The conspicuous consumption of large quantities of food used to be an upper-class privilege, as did obesity. This is now reversed. The upper classes consume expensive and exotic food, but in relatively small quantities. Stoutness, once a striking advertisement for one's well-fed status, is no longer socially acceptable. Joe Alsop, in his charming autobiography *I've Seen the Best of It* (New York: Norton, 1992) records what is probably the turning point here in his account of "dining out" in Washington, D.C., in the 1930s. Following delightedly the gargantuan eating customs of the capital, he achieved, through assiduous dining and scorn of exercise, a weight of over 200 lbs. and a threatening heart condition. The connection was by then obvious, and he was one of the first patients at the famous Johns Hopkins clinic of Dr. John Eager Howard, the genius who invented calorie counting combined with exercise, and thus the "Johns Hopkins Diet" — the granddaddy of them all. (The exercises were based on those used for polio victims.) When I knew the older and wiser Joe in the 1970s he was the thin and dapper dandy of his later famous years. But his book soulfully reflects his nostalgia for those great days of conspicuous calorie consumption (especially the terrapin stew, which smelled like feet but tasted like heaven).

The Quest for the Holy Quail

This goes along with the modern obsession with diets. Previously, diets were only for health reasons, rarely to do with weight and appearance as such. Now they are mainly concerned with weight reduction, significantly referred to as "slimming," the slim figure rather than the healthy body being the aim despite pious claims to the contrary. They are a major part of the food-fashion industry. In fact, none of them work. If any one did, then there would not be so many and we would not be faced almost weekly with the announcement of a new and infallible one. They come in quick succession: the Scarsdale Diet, Nathan Pritikin's Maximum Weight Loss Diet, the Palm Beach Diet, the Rotation Diet, the Beverly Hills Diet, Dr. Atkin's Diet Revolution, the Banana-Milk Diet, the I Love New York Diet, Kempner's Rice Diet, the Magic Mayo Diet, Dr. Stillman's Quick Inches Off Diet, and numerous others. (Note the use of "classy" names to attract the diet snobs. It's amazing that we haven't had the Harvard Diet yet — the Princeton Diet has arrived. The magic of California as diet heaven has given us the UCLA Diet, or the California Slim, as it is popularly known.)

In fact, in order to lose weight (and this is only "healthy" in extreme cases), the only useful diet is to exercise and eat much less food, as Dr. Howard fully understood. But the business of how not to eat too much food has paradoxically turned into one of the biggest food industries. It has become the science of what to eat and not gain weight — more or less impossible with any reasonable calorific regime. Studies have shown that diets more often than not lead to weight gain! Because the body does not know the difference between dieting and starving, once a severe dietary regime is concluded it will voraciously store food as fat as a protection against further unreasonable onslaughts. But it is with diets that fashion and fads play their largest part. Diets have replaced the weather as the basic item of polite conversation.

This is all part of a general utopianism that characterizes Western society: the search for the perfect life comes to embrace the search for the perfect food (the Quest of our section heading). And, like other utopianisms, this easily tips over into fanaticism. With the zeal of religious sectarians, people organize to hunt down restaurants that offend against the latest dietary fads. The *New York Daily News* has a full-time food reporter whose job is to make surprise visits to restaurants to test the cholesterol levels in their foods, and to award a special symbol — a heart crossed with a knife and fork — to those combining low levels with "gourmet"-quality food. In fact, there is no scientific evidence that dietary cholesterol on its own is harmful; it only becomes so when it interacts with saturated fat. But that gets too complicated for the tabloids dedicated to protecting us from the wickedness of non-cholesterol-conscious cooks. In the pursuit of perfection, to be on a diet illustrates that you are a worthy and serious person, not a slob. It is the Puritan Ethic applied to food. It has also spawned the monstrosity known as (of course) "nouvelle cuisine" in which infant-sized portions are arranged with cubist sensitivity and pastel-colored sauces, and which drive normal adults to consume huge numbers of dinner rolls to avoid a feeling of starvation.

Obesity has become for our present age what adultery was for our Victorian forebears. The real modern descent into sin and wickedness is a dieter who goes on a junk food binge. And hunting down offenders against food purity joins the list of popular witch hunts along with smokers, polluters, and people who use sexist pronouns. The State of New Jersey, in one of those frightening flashes of "Big Brother Knows Best" that frequently overtake governments, passed a law that forbad the serving in restaurants of fried eggs "sunny side up" because of the danger (slender) of salmonella poisoning. Public outcry caused it to repeal this food fascism in short order, which restores one's faith in the vox populi — a bit.

Food as Seduction

Feeding has always been closely linked with courtship. In nature this is not without its dangers. In several species of insect (the praying mantis, for example) the female devours the male after mating: he has done his job and so becomes a source of nutrition for the now expectant mother. Many species tone this down by having the male offer little packages of food to the female, who eats them and leaves him alone. The males and females of all species, including our own, seem to be involved in this mating gamble with food as the bait. Even if the male is not himself the food, he universally seems to have to make some show of feeding to be acceptable. With humans this works two ways since we are the only animals who cook: the bride is usually appraised for her cooking ability. ("Can she bake a cherry pie, Billy boy, Billy boy?") In some cultures this is far more important than her virginity.

But food and sex are generally closely linked. They are physically linked in the limbic system of the brain, which controls emotional activity generally. It is not surprising that we not only link them but do so emotionally. Good food = good sex. It is this sensuality of eating that spurs the puritan and ascetic rejection of food pleasures. But the link makes sense. To reproduce effectively, a female needs not only insemination but also provisioning. Particularly in species such as ours, where she is relatively dependent during the suckling period, she needs a male to provide food. Thus, a male's willingness to provide food becomes an important index of his suitability as a mate. Above all, it suggests his willingness to "invest" in the female's offspring. Studies of mate preferences in many cultures reveal that while men universally go for looks (actually a fair indicator of fertility), women go for provisioning: a male with resources is preferred to one without, regardless of his attractivity. Studies of Western females show that one of the most "attractive" features of a male is his willingness to "pick up the tab" for a meal. This may be an appeal to deep and atavistic survival motives in the female, but unscrupulous seducers can use it to their advantage. Courtship etiquette today seems to demand the offer of a meal by the male as part of foreplay; and the female is then supposed to cook breakfast to complete her part of the bargain. (Some modern cynic defined a contemporary "moral dilemma" as whether or not to go to bed with a man after only a cheeseburger.)

The choice of setting for food and courtship is as important as the food itself. There is a tendency to move gradually (or swiftly as the case may be) from the public to the private. For modern urban couples, "dates" usually begin in a crowded public place such as a bar or disco. On the crucial "second date," they may move to a restaurant, where the male is able to demonstrate his "resource accrual ability" by paying the bill. This stage may be prolonged, but at some time the "your place or mine" issue will arise, with, researchers have found, her place being generally preferred. At this stage she is supposed to supply a meal — usually a "romantic" candlelight dinner — thus demonstrating her abilities as a cook and hostess. Breakfast follows the consummation, again usually cooked by the female since it's her kitchen. But it is in order at this point for the male at least to offer to make breakfast, thus demonstrating his egalitarian and cooperative nature.

If the relationship gets serious, then the next important ceremonial meal is likely to be with her family. Again the meal is used as a "bridge" to mark the importance of the event and as an icebreaker and demonstration of the family's good will. The prospective mate joins her family at its most familial: eating the family meal. He can be scrutinized in this setting; his manners, speech, and behavior can be assessed. He in turn gets to see his prospective in-laws close up, in a setting which both offers information and lubricates the difficult mechanism of social interaction.

Sex and eating have perhaps never been so brilliantly brought together as in the film *Tom Jones*, where the marvelously sensual meal becomes both a prelude to, and an analogue of, intercourse. The Romantic Dinner is the form of therapy most recommended for jaded couples. Again the equation of good food, good sex, and emotional security taps very deep motives lodged in the basic mammalian search for reproductive success.

Eating Out

Most food has been made and consumed domestically throughout Western history. Eating out was for travelers, in inns and taverns where the customers were served more or less what would have been on the domestic table anyway. Regular eating out, and eating out for status with special foods reserved for the occasion, is a predominantly French institution of the Industrial Revolution. Our words for eating out are all French or translations — hotel, restaurant, café, menu, entrée, chef (chef de cuisine), wine list (carte des vins), cover charge (couvert), maitre d'hôtel, restaurateur, hors d'oeuvres, hostess (hôtesse) — only with waiter (and waitress) do we remain stubbornly Anglo-Saxon, "boy" sounding a bit strange in the context. Essentially at first an upper and upper-middle perversion, and to do with the desire to move conspicuous eating and spending into the public arena, eating out has become vastly democratized with technology, affluence, and overemployment — leaving less time for preparation at home. The great chefs, who previously cooked in the great houses, moved out to the great restaurants. The French upper classes had previously made a great public show of attending court or church. When both these institutions declined in importance after the Revolution, attendance at great restaurants became a substitute. The "great codifier" Auguste Escoffier laid down elaborate and rigid rules of cooking procedure like a pope: cuisine became "haute," and chefs ruled hierarchically organized vast kitchens like tyrannical cardinals. The great restaurants came to resemble renaissance palaces or cathedrals. The very word "restaurant" comes from the verb "to restore" and has more than practical overtones. (The original restaurants were in fact legally "health food stores.") From these grand beginnings, eating out came to be imitated by the bourgeoisie, ever anxious to give themselves upper-class airs, and finally became general in the culture and in all Western countries.

If the rituals of eating out have become less grand for the mass of people, it still retains its aura as an "event." The grand aspects are retained in expeditions to restaurants offensively overpriced but ritzy (after the Polish-French founders of the greatest of the great establishments). We spend not so much for the food as for the entertainment value and the naughty thrill of being (we hope) treated like royalty in an otherwise drab democratic environment. Even lesser expeditions still have the air of an event. The family outing to the local burger joint still has an air of preparation and difference; it can still be used to coax youngsters to eat, and provide a mild enough air of difference from routine to be "restorative." Even the necessary lunch for workers who cannot eat at home has been made into a ritual event by the relatively affluent among them.

"Doing lunch" in the business world is regarded as a kind of sacred operation where, the mythology has it, the most important deals are made. A puritanical campaign against the "three-martini lunch" by the then President Carter (Southern Baptist), had Americans as roused and angry as they had been over the tax on tea that sent their ancestors to their muskets. The business-meal tax deduction was fought for with passion, and the best the government could do was to reduce its value by 20 percent. There may not be a free lunch, but it sure as hell is deductible. Very little of this has to do with business, of course, and everything to do with status. Just to be having business lunches at all marks one down as a success in the world of business, for only "executives" (the new order of aristocracy) can have them.

At the other end of the scale, reverse snobbery asserts itself in the positive embrace of "junk food," otherwise condemned as non-nutritious, vulgar, or even dangerous to one's health. (In fact, cheeseburgers are no more dangerous to health than strict and specialized vegetarian diets.) Junk food can be socially acceptable if indulged in as part of a nostalgia for childhood: the time when we were allowed such indulgences as "treats." So giant ice cream sundaes with five different scoops of ice cream, maraschino cherries, pecans, chocolate sauce, and whipped cream; sloppy joes with french fries and gravy; malted milk shakes and root beer floats; hot dogs with mustard, ketchup, and relish — all these are still OK if treated as a kind of eating joke. Hot dogs at football games, or ice cream at the shore (seaside) are more or less de rigeur. The settings in which these are eaten vary from the simple outdoors to elaborate ice cream parlors with bright plastic furniture and a battery of machines for producing the right combinations of fat, sugar, and starch. Ostensibly these are for children, but adults eat there with no self-consciousness and without the excuse of accompanying children. But for adults, as for children, these places are for "treats," and so always remain outside the normal rules of nutrition and moderation.

We continue to make eating out special when we can. Romantic dinners, birthday dinners, anniversary dinners, retirement dinners, and all such celebrations are taken out of the home or the workplace and into the arena of public ritual. Only the snootiest restaurants will not provide a cake and singing waiters for the birthday boy. The family outing is specially catered for by special establishments — "Mom's Friendly Family Restaurant" can be found in every small American town (although the wise saying has it that we should never eat at a place called Mom's). But even in the hustle and bustle of these family establishments the individuality of the family is still rigidly maintained. No family will share a table with another. This is very different to the eating out of the still communalistic East. Lionel Tiger, in his fascinating description of Chinese eating, describes how people are crowded together in restaurants — strangers at the same table all eating from communal dishes. And far from having a reservation system, restaurants encourage a free-for-all in which those waiting in line look over the diners to find those close to finishing, then crowd behind their tables and urge them on.

The democratization of eating out is reflected in the incredible burgeoning of fast food joints and their spread beyond the United States. McDonald's is the fastest-growing franchise in Japan, and has extended its operations to China. When it opened its first franchise in Beijing, it sold so many burgers so fast that the cash registers burned out. Kentucky Fried Chicken has now opened in Beijing, and has become the chic place to eat in Berlin. These are humble foods — a ground meat patty that may or may not have originated in Hamburg; a sausage of dubious content only loosely connected to Frankfurt; deep fried chicken that was a food of the rural American South; a cheese and tomato pie that probably came from Naples. But they have taken the world by storm in one of the greatest eating revolutions since the discovery of the potato. In a curious twist, two indigenous foods of the East are rapidly turning into the fast food specials of the yuppies who would not be seen dead eating the proletarian hamburger: the Japanese raw-fish sushi, and the Chinese dim sum (small items bought by the plate) lunch. It is the oriental revenge for the McDonald's invasion.

The proletariat has evolved its own forms of eating out. The transport café in Britain with its huge portions of bacon and eggs; the French bistro, which was a working-class phenomenon before reverse snobbery turned it into bourgeois chic, with its wonderful casseroles and bifstekpommefrit; the Italian trattoria with its cheap seafood, again gentrified in foreign settings; the incomparable diner in America; the grand fish-and-chip warehouse in the north of England; the beer-and-sausage halls of Germany; the open-air food markets in all the warm countries. If we could do a speeded-up film of social change in the last fifty years we would see a grand ballet in which eating moved out of the home and into the public arena on a scale which makes rural depopulation look like a trickle. Sociologists, as usual, have still even to figure out that it is happening, much less come up with an explanation.

Dining out became a paradise for ethnic immigrants in the huge migrations from country to country that have characterized the twentieth century. What started as cooking for each other has burgeoned into a huge industry of ethnic eateries. The Chinese led the way, usually in ports and bigger cities. Chinatowns were exotic, and it became fashionable to eat there in San Francisco and New York. Chinese cooking with its marvelous variety and use of virtually everything eatable became the rage. The quick-cook method with small pieces of food had been a necessity in China because the use of human excrement as manure meant that thorough cooking was essential, and the lack of fuel meant it had to be done quickly. But this was a wonder to the Euro-American palate jaded with overcooking and heavy sauces. Chinese cooking spread like wildfire, and Chinese families branched out endlessly to open cafes in the most remote places.

What is more, the food was amazingly cheap. It was the first "foreign" food to capture both the gourmet market and the populace at the same time. Although the compromise "Cantonese," or chow mein, version remains popular with the masses, the gourmets pursue the Hunan and Sezchuan refined versions. Status differences assert themselves in short order in the West. If we are all going to go Chinese, then there has to be a form of Chinese that is more high class than the rest. Conveniently, northern Chinese cooking stepped into the gap. Now the cognoscenti can laugh at the vulgarity of sweet and sour pork and moo goo gai pen, while extolling the virtues of Mongolian beef with scallions and Colonel T'so's chicken. The world remains safe for snobbery.

What started with the Chinese has spread to a wide variety of immigrant cuisines. Even small towns in Europe and America now have a huge variety of worldwide ethnic establishments. Drink has followed food, and sake and retsina, espresso and green tea, guava juice and tequila, are available everywhere. In all this eating out, food reflects the internationalizing trends in fashion generally. It gives us all a chance to show off our cosmopolitanism in a world that values it more and more. It is astonishing when we think of it. In any one month we may order food in ten or more different languages, none of which we speak, and which can be as different as Urdu, Thai, Cantonese, Italian, Arabic, Armenian, and Hungarian. There is now an industry of critics and restaurant writers as large and as attentively followed as the theater, sports, and fashion critics. To be literate in the world of eating out — to be even ahead of the trends (knowing that fantastic little Portuguese bistro that no one has discovered) — is to demonstrate that one is on top of the complex cosmopolitan civilization of which eating out has come to be a metaphor.

Eating Out: Styles and Settings

Apart from travelers, for whom eating out was first invented, few people eat out from necessity. Even more than in the home, eating out is a ceremonial event and must be considered as such. There are basically two types of eating out: entertaining oneself and entertaining others. In what sense is the family's taking itself out to dinner ceremonial? Just as much as the family's having the grandparents round to formal Sunday tea in the dining room. It is a special occasion marked by special dress and behavior. At its lowest level it can depart little from eating informally at home: a visit to the local burger or fish and chip joint for a quick meal, for example. But even these places usually do not allow one in half dressed. You cannot lounge around the local pizza parlor in a dressing gown or underwear. To go out in the street at all one must put on footwear. It all requires an effort that does not go into the informal home eating. Then there is the matter of choice, usually conspicuously lacking on the home menu. Even the humblest "eat out" place has some choice, and this alone can provide an excitement that the home meal lacks. Also, however lax the standards of the eat-out joint, most of the behavior tolerated at home will not be tolerated there. Some considerable restraint is required, particularly from the young, and this again serves to mark it as special. It becomes an important socialization experience for young children, where they learn the basic etiquette of eating in public, although not fast enough to please most of the adults around. But they must learn to sit still, to keep their voices down, to wait patiently, to eat in an orderly manner and not throw their food about. Of course, they learn these things at home, but the pressures are much greater when eating out.

For the parents, or even a childless married couple, eating out is usually marked by even more ceremonial behavior. Except for the very affluent, it is usually regarded as a special event, and people prepare for it in a way that they would not do for the regular home meal. In particular, they will weigh carefully the type of setting as much as the type of food. If eating out were only about food then the setting would not matter. And of course there is again a reverse snobbery which pretends to despise the concern with setting and to praise the brilliance of the storefront operation that produces such wondrous and authentic Indian food — and so on. But if it is an event — and all eating out is expensive relative to eating in — then people usually pay great attention to setting. This is often not more articulated than a request for somewhere "nice," but the slightest pushing on details will reveal the niceties of the distinctions. One place is too big and too garish and has noisy waiters; another is too small and crowded and the service is too slow; another is too brightly lit and there is no sense of privacy; another is so dimly lit that one cannot see the food. In the great days of the great restaurants they had to be brightly lit and large, with every table in sight of every other so that the essential business of showing off could be accomplished. The alternative was the small and exclusive restaurant which need not be super smart but which accomplished the showing off without further ado. Today the latter is preferred, but grand dining is by no means out.

When entertaining others out, setting has to be considered carefully with reference to purpose. The main purposes of eating out with others are the same as their home counterparts: to impress on the one hand, and to be different on the other — to make a change. At home we do this by departing from the normal routine in dress, setting, and cuisine. When we go out, the latter two can be taken care of for us, and we have much more choice as far as style, setting, and expense are concerned. There are relative degrees of intimacy involved. It is usual to entertain the grandparents and in-laws at home; it would be a real treat to take them out somewhere impressive, a treat we would reserve for a special occasion. On the other hand, it would be more normal to go out to eat with the boss and his wife first, and then, once intimacy had been established, to invite them to the house.

In all of this, it is the setting rather than the food itself that is considered. Of course the food has to be "good," but the type and kind are less important than the aura surrounding the service. There used to be, in the 1950s, two Indian restaurants in London off the Charing Cross Road, in an area catering to Indian students. One was called the Agra, the other the Agra de Luxe. The same kitchen served both and the food was identical. But in the Agra students clustered around communal long tables, which were covered with oilcloth. The food was cheap and casually served, and the Indian music (recorded at local Indian films) was loud. In the Agra de Luxe there were curtains and carpets, there was a liquor license and good wine was served, there was quiet sitar music in the background, the tables had immaculate white linen, and there were uniformed, attentive waiters. The food, as we have seen, was exactly the same as in the humble next-door café, but it was four times the price. It was every male student's aim to make it in the world so that he could take his girlfriend or mother to the Agra de Luxe.

Setting is all. The perfect business lunch requires a bright setting: papers have to be exchanged perhaps, and the faces of the parties have to be clearly visible so that moods and intentions can be read. But the tables should be relatively well spaced so that conversations do not overly intrude on each other. The romantic meal, however, is more suitably placed in the evening (closer to bedtime and hence suggestive?) and in a quiet and dimly lit candlelight atmosphere conducive to quiet, intimate conversation, and even, with its dim light, thick carpets, heavy drapes, and brocade furniture, somewhat reminiscent of a bedroom. The casual lunch with a friend, however, can well be in a fairly informal, wicker-furniture-with-ferns-and-plants kind of setting, conducive to colorful salads and bright gossip. If we do not think setting (as opposed to food per se) is important, imagine a man promising his date a romantic dinner and taking her to the local ice cream parlor for a hot dog and sundae, or for fish and chips wrapped in newspaper. This can only work if she has a good sense of humor and is willing to invoke reverse snobbery again.

The point here is that it almost does not matter what food is eaten. That can be a matter of personal preference. It is usual to serve more elaborate meals in the evening, but these are often not that different from the lunch menus except in size and number of courses. There are certainly restaurants that serve the same food at dinner as at lunch, except that at dinner they double the prices, light the candles, dress up the waiters, and have live entertainment. This tactic, which again has little to do with the content of the food, is based on the shrewd observation that not much business is done in the evenings; people come for entertainment and are willing to pay for it as for any other entertainment. They come to be cosseted, spoiled, smoothed down after the business of the day, made to feel like royalty, allowed to indulge themselves in a leisurely fashion, and generally to feel as far removed from eating at home as is possible.

Purists will object that there are many people who seek out restaurants purely for the food. This is doubtful. It would be possible to do an experiment in which such a purist's favorite food was transferred from the plain little bistro with ambiance where he usually gets it, to a completely alien setting (a stand-up stall in a fish market perhaps, or the lobby of a grand hotel at ten times the price) and judge his reactions. The little bistro will turn out to be as important to his enjoyment as the authentic *brandade de morue* he so prizes. Of course the food is important, but when entertainment or even business is the issue, it takes second place to setting. Simenon's Inspector Maigret certainly searched out fine cheap food in nondescript cafes that happened to have devoted and brilliant cooks; but he would never have taken Madame Maigret to them for dinner.

At least in Paris, wherever he ate, he would have had good waiter service. His waiter would have been trained, expert, and, what is more, professional and proud of it. This used to be true throughout Europe, but especially in France and Switzerland. All the European capitals certainly had professional waiters. And these were particularly important to the setting — to the feeling of being catered to, spoiled, and made special. The idea of waiting as a profession came, of course, with the high standards of the great establishments, but it percolated down. To be a waiter in a good establishment was to be a proud member of a proud profession. It required skills and patience — customers were notoriously difficult, but always right. It was much much more than just carrying food from the kitchen to the table. It was a combination of knowledge and social work and a canny judgement of character. And the pay-off was a big tip. There was no sense among these men of being in a menial job; quite the contrary. The aim of most of them was to save enough to open their own establishments, and many of them were very successful at it.

In England and America, however, outside the grand establishments in the larger cities which more often than not employed Frenchmen, there was no such tradition. Waitresses were more common than waiters since they were cheaper labor. But by the same token they rarely regarded their jobs as a career, and usually saw them as temporary. If they were permanent, like men in the same position, they were usually disgruntled at being in a menial, dead-end job. They often took this resentment out on the customers, and the surly waiter or unpleasant waitress became something of a cliché. Today, more than ever, the job is transient, and more and more young people take it on as part-time work between school and job or between other "worthwhile" jobs. New York restaurants seem to be staffed with out-of-work actors, dancers, and musicians, or non-English-speaking immigrants. There is never the same feeling about such a restaurant as there is about one staffed with real professional waiters, but the change seems permanent, and one of the great paradoxes of the eating-out revolution is its failure to persuade anyone that to be a waiter or waitress is a worthwhile career. And until, in the Anglo-Saxon (or for that matter the Slavic) countries, waiting tables is treated as more than a menial, low-grade job, it will remain a blot on the gastronomic landscape.

The Holy Meal

Because of its centrality in our lives, food becomes a perfect vehicle for ritual, and food rituals become central to most religions; food taboos mark off one sect or denomination from another. There has been much study of the psychology of food taboos. Perhaps the most startling theory is Freud's concerning the ban on eating the totem animal among primitive tribes. This, he suggested, was a memorial to the primeval sin of killing and eating the father. The totem animal came to represent the father, and so could not be killed and eaten, except once a year when it was killed and eaten ceremoniously by the descendants of the original criminals.

Modern anthropology tends to stress the usefulness of food as a marker of social boundaries. As the late Meyer Fortes said, it is not so much that food is "good to eat" as that it is "good to forbid." Catholics, for example, could find a bond between each other and a mark of difference from Protestants by substituting fish for meat on Fridays. It was probably a mistake for the Catholic Church to end the ban on meat; it had helped make Catholics feel special, and many continue to observe it voluntarily.

Freud's theory of the "sacred meal" may appear somewhat bizarre, but his concern with it was not misplaced. The sacred meal is of crucial importance in many religions, including the "advanced" ones. We are all familiar with Seder and Holy Communion. The latter derives from an actual meal — the Last Supper — but has much older roots. It goes back to the idea of sharing a meal with God, which some scholars see as the root idea of sacrifice. This develops further into the idea of eating the god to gain his strength and virtue. The Aztecs made huge loaves in the shape of the gods, and these were thrown down the temple steps to be devoured by the multitude. Human sacrifice and cannibalism come to linked again in the idea of the sacred meal, with the supreme food being used — human flesh.

There are various versions of the eating of the ancestors. South American Indians grind up the ashes and bones of dead parents and mix them in a soup which all their relatives share. This is another version of incorporating the ancestor or god into one's own body. Our funeral feasts are a pale reflection of some of these more extreme types of sacred meal. But the idea of a memorial to the dead through eating is still there, and at Irish wakes the dead body often joins in the merriment. While such feasts, like wedding feasts, serve a practical purpose in feeding the guests, they also serve the ritual purpose of uniting the celebrants in the common act of eating, with all its rich, symbolic associations.

Grace before meat is a declining civility — Charles Lamb was already deploring its decline in the early nineteenth century. But religious ideas still cling to the act of eating — or of denying food. Frugality, in some religions and secular derivatives of them, is holiness. The Calvinist ascetic version of life equates "plain food" and the "good life." Elements of this are still there in health food faddism. The antihedonism ethic aims at food and drink as much as sex. Gluttony, after all, is one of the seven deadly sins. "Carnival" in the Latin tradition is a wonderful example of a gluttonous exception to food asceticism. The fasting of Lent is violently contrasted to the excesses of Carnival. Once again, food (and drink) is used (either in its use or its denial) to mark the passage into or out of a ritual state. The Latins tend to be more tolerant of bodily demands, and consistent food puritanism seems to be a northern and Protestant proclivity. But, as G. K. Chesterton so aptly put it:

> Water is on the Bishop's board,
>   and the higher thinker's shrine;
> But I don't care where the water goes
>   if it doesn't get into the wine.

(See also his marvelous "Song Against Grocers.")

There is, however, a counterbalancing epicurean tradition (of whom Chesterton was the bard) which does not see high living as incompatible with the good life, especially where the good life consists of high thinking. One of the oddities of English life is the tradition of the Inns of Court (which are so called because they started out as real inns where lawyers stayed while on the circuit) whereby eating a certain number of dinners "in hall" is a requirement for becoming a barrister. Similar communal dining requirements apply (in college) to those who would qualify for a master's degree at Oxford and Cambridge. High table in an Oxbridge college is a paradigm for the correlation of high living and high thinking. Commentators have noted the massive discrepancy between the cost of the Dons' meals and those of the undergraduates. Here the difference is used as an inducement or initiation procedure. The novitiates are deprived, but are reminded of the alimentary rewards of superior performance. But whether we are conspicuously eating well, or conspicuously depriving ourselves and others, we mark ourselves off — either as having more than anyone else, or less; and either is made a virtue. By their food shall ye know them.

The use of food as ritual is often not so obvious, but when we think of our linking of food with occasions and festivals, and often limiting it to these, it becomes clearer. Thus, elaborate fruit puddings and cakes are made and eaten by the English only at Christmas, and goose is rarely eaten at any other time; pancakes are made only on Shrove Tuesday and thrown about with great ceremony; Americans used only to eat turkey at Thanksgiving, and even now it is rare to cook the whole bird except at this family ceremonial; eggnog seems to be drunk only at Christmas in the States. Cooking the whole animal seems to be reserved for ceremonial and festive occasions. Suckling pig is only roasted whole in China for weddings and the like; whole oxen or pigs in Europe are only spit roasted at festivals. The animals could be cut up and cooked more conveniently, but there seems to be a conscious archaism involved in the spit roasting that underlines the special nature of the event. Numerous cakes, puddings, pies, and pastries are reserved throughout Europe for special occasions (gingerbread men and parkin pigs on Guy Fawkes' Day in England, and pumpkins at Halloween in the United States, for example). In all these cases, the special food serves to mark the special occasion and bring home to us its significance.

The Future of Food

Will anything stay the same in the whirligig of food faddism and ever-rapid changes in eating habits? Some things we can be certain of because evolution has built in certain prejudices to our digestive systems that will be hard to buck. Gluttony will remain with us. We are natural binge eaters, and, as the hopelessness of diets shows, only strict discipline can keep us from gorging. This probably stems from our uncertain past when food was not in steady supply, so we stocked up when it was there, never knowing when the next mammoth might happen along. Why then did we not all die of heart disease and become extinct? Because the meat had very little saturated fat on it, and we worked off the binges with a lot of exercise. But we still crave fat (which the body needs) and tend to stuff ourselves if the food is available and we are not stopped by outside pressures or the promptings of conscience.

We shall also continue, to the detriment of our systems and in particular our teeth, to crave sweet things. Again, our bodies need a certain amount of glucose for energy, and they get this by breaking down carbohydrates into sugar. But if we can get the sugar directly, this provides an immediate and less costly energy kick. It would make sense that we should be programmed to seek out these rare sources (honey was a major one) by implanting a craving. As long as they were indeed scarce, this was a fine motivator. The problem arises when human ingenuity makes them plentiful; we have no means of stopping the craving except by satisfying it. Add to this our need for salt, and it is safe to predict that we will snack eternally on pretzels and candy bars or their equivalents, and greedily consume that other producer of instant (if deceptive) energy based on sugar: alcohol.

More sinister is the vulnerability of the brain to certain addictive substances. Addiction is probably an evolutionary offshoot of the brain's own mechanism for absorbing its self-produced endorphins — the chemical substances that make us "feel good." But evolution never anticipated such substances as alcohol, opium, nicotine, morphine, cocaine, or caffeine. These lock into the receptors intended for beneficial substances because they do momentarily make us feel good and so fool the system. But once locked in they set up a craving that nature never intended. Thus can evolution backfire, and we can predict that despite all efforts to the contrary the power of feeling good will keep a fair number of us enslaved to dangerous but seductive opiates.

Apart from the physiological prediction, we can be sure that eating as display — as a code of messages about selves and status, role and religion, race and nation — will persist in an animal that lives by symbolic communication. And as the world grows smaller and communication more immediate, we can perhaps look toward a greater homogenization of food habits. We are perhaps at the moment very lucky to be at the stage where ethnic identity is not yet blurred and the world is in an exciting state of mixing and mingling and transferring of tastes. It may not last. And always the other side of the food-as-pleasure coin looms: the possibility of mass starvation as population outstrips resources. Soon, sheer physiological necessity may overtake the refined communicative value of food, and the only thing that will matter is whether we can get it or not. In Somalia they don't stand on ceremony: they kill you for a handful of rice.

Shopping Malls: The New Village Green

The creation of suburbs on a vast scale in post-WWII USA created a new kind of human community: one without a center. There was no plaza or piazza, no tribal dancing ground, no market or fairground, no ceremonial center common to all the inhabitants, and no common area for trading, gossiping, and just hanging out. For all these purposes the suburbanites — often living in what had been wilderness until the huge tracts were laid down — had still to trek into the nearest towns. But the towns became more and more run-down and dangerous, and, above all, parking was a nightmare. The people of the burbs were wholly dependent on their cars, for there was no public transport; the burbs were premised on the universal use of the car.

Enterprising businessmen saw a chance to usurp the role of the dying towns as market and entertainment centers, and began to build mammoth shopping malls with acres of parking in the still unclaimed wilderness areas near the burbs. As the towns continued to decline, these malls — growing ever larger and more elaborate — became the new shopping centers, and even the city dwellers preferred to drive out to them rather than shop on the high street. (In an attempt to revive downtowns, city malls have been built. But these are necessarily on a smaller scale, and there is still the parking problem.)

The malls were conceived as consumer paradises, with everything meant to entice and pamper the shopper. They became totally enclosed and climate controlled, with wide arcades, piazzas with trees, fountains and plants, and gentle escalators to upper floors. Modern technology enabled them to be large, light, and airy, with easy movement for prams so as to encourage family shopping. Every type and kind of shop was represented, but there was no major food-shopping area (the malls were smart enough not to try to compete with the already successful supermarkets). To cater to the hungry shopper, fast food shops early made an appearance — pizza, hamburgers, fish and chips, etc. These made sense. People often came considerable distances and needed to eat, but at the same time the eateries encouraged people to stay longer and spend more. What is more, they were the kind of places where the whole family could go, and this encouraged "family expeditions" to the malls. Soon more ambitious eateries moved in, and now some malls have a whole range of them: from sit-down specialist restaurants to the ubiquitous pizza parlor, with pubs and gourmet health food in between.

There is no mall built nowadays without a cinema, usually showing two to six films concurrently. But the idea behind the cinemas was not simply to provide entertainment: they were intended as a dumping ground for youngsters while the parents got on with the serious business of spending the family income. Only PG films are shown — no "adult" stuff here. The malls in fact catered essentially to the affluent adults.

But a strange (or was it?) thing happened on the way to the mall. What had started out as a purely commercial venture rapidly became subverted to social uses that have little to do with trading. For a start, the encouragement of "family shopping" — the whole family spending the better part of the day there — turned the malls into family meeting places. It became the weekend thing just to "spend the day" in the mall — shopping or not. Often very little shopping was done. People window shopped, tried the different eateries, bought from a choice of literally hundreds of kinds of ice cream, sent the kids to a movie while they had a "nice" meal by themselves, wheeled the prams around the wide arcades, and let the little ones play around the benches and tubs. In short, the mall began to look very like the fair on the village green.

More significantly, the teenagers, tired of playing around the suburban streets or the schoolyard, began to take over the mall. Teenagers need somewhere to hang out, and the burbs were notoriously lacking in the equivalent of the high-street drug store. There was no high street in the burbs. The mall became the new high street, the new town center, the new village green. The mall was usable in all weathers, there was no entrance fee, there was no harassment. It was all very public and, hence, safe for girls. And malls are colorful and exciting social places. The bustle and the movement, the tremendous variety of things and places, the food teenagers love, and even movies. But most of all, just hanging out, meeting friends, making friends, drinking coke, gossiping, joking, making dates. And all in a concentrated space — not stretched out over thousands of acres of suburb.

There are not that many shops dedicated to teenagers. A few sell jeans and tee shirts and they are popular, and of course the record stores do a brisk trade. But teenagers do not spend that much time actually shopping, to the chagrin of the owners. They mostly spend on the fast food, ice cream, and cinemas. No. They are not there to shop, they are there to be there: in their own words, to hang out. After some initial resistance and concern, the owners seem reconciled to this turn of events. It keeps the parents happy, and the parents spend there. The teenagers have very little record of crime or even disturbance in the malls. They are happy there; unsupervised and unharrassed by adults, they cruise, socialize, and munch endlessly.

As an age group, they seem largely to be between eleven and sixteen. Older teenagers tend to regard "malling" as a phase to be grown out of for more sophisticated things, but the younger ones have created a whole lifestyle around the mall, with customs and clothing peculiar to its environment. They create "looks" and styles in mixing and matching clothing items that have the originality of haute couture and certainly as much care and concern. They invent rules of behavior — no making out in public, for example — that seem to be kept without policing. They are almost never violent or vandalistic (the owners soon noticed this), for they have to share the space with a majority of adults, and everything is in public view. But their intentions are the opposite of random violence. They are obsessed with the social contacts and the parade and display. The whole atmosphere of the mall — the commercial bustle, the elegant facades and shops, the hygienic atmosphere and furnishings, the trees and seats, the family at spend and play — all contribute to an air of calm and peaceful activity in which any kind of even rowdiness would be so out of place it would deeply embarrass those provoking it. And no teenager likes to be embarrassed before peers. Rowdiness in the mall would be like shouting in the library.

The original intentions of the builders then — to make a pleasant and convenient place to shop for the suburbanites — have been subverted to another and obviously more important social use: providing a new village green/town center for the otherwise amorphous burbs. The owners and the communities have come to accept this fully. Social events now take place in the malls. "Live" entertainment, from string quartets to rock groups, is arranged there. Motor shows take up the large spaces, and local artists put up booths in the arcades. There are always stalls collecting signatures for petitions, or selling clothes for good causes. Santa Claus and the Easter Bunny make their regular appearances. Carolers come at Xmas, politicians come to press flesh, and the teenagers wander through it all with their own agendas intact. The malls have even received their ultimate accolade: a role in the universal U.S. folklore of weekly sitcom. An edition of the endlessly charming "Wonder Years" turned on the agony that our young hero, Kevin, went through when his ghastly elder brother got a driving license, thus preempting the car in which mom usually dropped Kevin off at the mall. Kevin even had to be nice to and gang up with the hated sibling or lose his ride to the one place above all he wanted to be for eating pizza, going to the movies, and meeting the pretty blonde girl of his dreams: the mall.

When "Murder She Wrote" has an episode on "The Shopping Mall Murders," we'll know that the malls have moved into the realm of the sacred: special places like market fairs and churches, which nurture the soul and the society, not just the body and the economy. They are a monument to social vitality rather than to mammon. They serve the economic end, surely, but in their untutored wisdom the families and the kids have made them serve the difficult end of being human places for human beings. Perhaps there's hope for the affluent society yet.

P.S. After this was written, the American penchant for gigantism at all costs took over the mall business, and outside Minneapolis the "Mall of America" was built. The scale of the thing is unbelievable, and up to 6 million "visitors" a year are expected in this cross between Park Avenue, Coney Island, and Disney World. This is not the friendly "local" mall but a kind of grotesque satire on consumption and entertainment. I would dearly like it to fail, except that my pension company has invested heavily in it. The moral dilemmas of our times!

Part Two

Aggression and Violence

Introduction to Part Two

These essays need little introduction since they largely speak for themselves (which means, of course, that I am going to go on at length about them). Aggression and sex are closely linked. The "firing" of one in the limbic circuit easily causes the firing or the arousal of the other, and this makes great evolutionary sense. It also may help to explain the seemingly indissoluable link between the two that informs most popular culture and a lot of sexual practices, despite the official puritanical deploring of such things as pornography, heavy metal, and vampire movies. Much of the discussion of aggression and violence, however, has been vitiated by an insistence on dichotomies of nature vs. nurture, innate goodness vs. innate depravity, instinct vs. learning, and the like. The first two essays here are both attempts to show how this is a false set of dichotomies: that aggression properly understood is part of the normal functioning of the organism, and that under normal conditions it does its appointed evolutionary job with appropriate constraints. One of our problems nowadays is that "conditions" are not "normal." This is the point of the second half of the first essay, where the "conscious out of context" theme is introduced that was the culmination of my *Search for Society* (1989). Also, I have included here some material on inhibition from a piece contributed to a *festschrift* for my old friend and neighbor Ashley Montagu, who has merrily disputed with me on this issue for nearly twenty-five years. This is my attempt at a reconciliation of ideas between those of us (whom I call the sinners) who regard aggression as normal, and those who favor the view of the perfectibility of man (whom I thought of calling the angels, but ended by calling the perfectionists).

These latter are to the fore in the third essay which, while unquestionably on the subject of aggression/violence, is really about ideology and the rash of "political correctness" and thought policing that has hit the academies lately. But I see a connection with warfare that is brought out at the end: that fanaticism (like that displayed in the Seville Statement) causes wars, not aggression, and that we could well learn from this example (see "The Violent Imagination," in P. Marsh and A. Campbell, eds., *Aggression and Violence*, Basil Blackwell, 1982).

The final essay doubts that we can, however. It was written in reply to another rash of optimism from the "war is dead" movement so currently fashionable. I think this optimism (with its "end of history" corollary) is more dangerous than a conservative scepticism about our ability to avoid wars. The conclusion of this essay neatly leads us back to the concerns of the first, and there is, in effect, a fairly tight unity of concern between these four pieces.

The first essay was written for the twentieth anniversary, in 1989, of the original Smithsonian Institution Man and Beast conference (Washington, D.C.) resulting in a book of that name, and was a grand reunion of some of the original conferees: Bill Hamilton, Michael Robinson, Lionel Tiger, and Ed Wilson. Alas, Margaret Mead was no longer with us. One of my very special memories of her was our walking side by side in a crocodile procession across the Mall, in the borrowed and billowing robes of Supreme Court justices, and I in a borrowed mortar board three sizes too big which kept swiveling round in the high wind like some demented propeller. Between grabbing the robes to prevent being carried into the air, and grabbing the hat to prevent its going likewise — all to the derisive accompaniment of a fully accoutered Scottish piper hired to lead us into the lecture hall — I reduced Maggie to a heap of uncontrollable giggles and myself to a flustered mess. Poor Wilton Dillon, who so brilliantly organized both meetings, had tried so hard to give the occasion some pomp and dignity. But, as Maggie and I recollected later in a martini-fed tranquillity, perhaps she and I had demonstrated more of the essential difference between Man and Beast than the attempted solemnity had. A new definition was born: *Homo ludicrus* — Man is the only animal that can make a complete fool of itself. (My other striking memory from that conference is not any of the academic stuff, but the daily appearance at the public lectures of Alice Roosevelt Longworth, impeccably dressed and groomed, with a bevy of nieces and great nieces and little cousins, equally impeccably turned out, who were shepherded into a row of seats and sat, gloved hands in laps, to get their minds expanded, while aunt Alice looked on to see that there was no nonsense. "I can't," Teddy Roosevelt had said, "both run the country and control Alice." Boy, would he have been proud of her then.)

The second essay was a talk given to an unusual audience which had come to hear about pub violence and licensing hours at a meeting in Oxford, England. The only reason I had an audience at all was that a "sensational" announcement was anticipated concerning recommendations on pub licensing hours, and publicans, policemen, brewers, temperance associations, and the media were there in force. I suspect that the academics who had been invited to fill in the morning session were there just to build up the tension toward the announcement. But it was an attentive and interested audience, and it seemed to be intrigued by the antics of macaque monkeys and the implied comparison with behavior in pubs; it found the idea not at all outrageous. (These are the same Bermudan macaques that crop up in chapter 16, so this account will serve as an introduction. This will also help explain the references to pubs and publicans at the end of the second essay, otherwise mysterious in this context.) The announcement? As I remember, the excellent MCM Research team proved without a doubt that it was restrictive licensing hours that caused drunkenness, and that experiments with their abolition had shown a definite drop-off in drunken violence. The brewers and the police seemed equally pleased with this conclusion.

As one who inhabits a country where one may drink twenty-four hours a day, the whole issue appeared academic. But I had grown up under the restrictive conditions in question, and distinctly remembered the desperate guzzling of pints once "time" and "last orders" had been called by the publican. There was, I think, ten minutes "drinking-up time," and we made the best of it. No one left sober. It was a system calculated to produce drunken and loutish behavior, and we obliged. I hope they do abolish it. And perhaps my monkeys can claim some credit for being involved in a bit of necessary social reform.

The other two essays are different in that they were written not as speeches but as pieces to be read in serious journals of opinion. What they have in common is that both were requested pieces (actually, I rarely write things that have not been asked for) which were intended by the respective editors to counter some perceived trendy notion that had caught the reading public's attention. Hence, both are a bit truculent since both have an ax to grind and I was determined to get a sharp edge. It fits the curmudgeonly persona, so I suppose I'll have to get used to it.

5

Aggression: Then and Now

The title of this essay was assigned to me by the organizers of the Man and Beast Revisited symposium, and my first task is to interpret its intent. "Then" presumably means the time of the first Smithsonian Man and Beast symposium, circa 1969 A.D., and I shall indeed look at the state of the art "then" and "now." But I shall take advantage of the title's vagueness to suggest another chronological contrast, to be brought out later. For the moment, however, I shall not reveal the "then" or the "now." What I shall do is disavow any attempt at a survey of research on aggression (and/or violence) over these nearly two decades. I have been involved in much of it both directly and as a sponsor, but such a survey is more appropriate to a technical journal. What is needed here, and what will be more in the spirit of the undertaking, is an assessment of the meaning of all this research. Where do we stand now? What do we know and what can we say about human aggression and its beastly counterpart?

One position on this might be that we still know pitifully little; that we need to conduct even more expensive and more elaborate research before we can evaluate, much less recommend, ameliorative measures; that looking for a "cure" for aggression is infinitely more difficult than looking for a cure for cancer and equally massive funds should be expended on the search for it. Such a position obviously suits those engaged in either the conduct or sponsorship of such research. But I beg to differ. I cannot see what we gain from further research other than marginal increments in knowledge. The increments are not without interest, but they will not affect any fundamental issue. The word is in on aggression.

There was only ever a "problem" because of the way we phrased the questions and formulated the issues. The "problem" stems from our very human capacity to create problems, not from anything about aggression per se. I worked for twelve years for a foundation dedicated to the hopeless premise that if we collected enough scientific information on the subject we would eventually be able to lessen violence and stop wars. I finally parted company with these well-meaning people because (among other things) I wanted to diversify and investigate a wide range of topics only loosely connected to aggression proper. There was no future that I could see in pouring resources into "aggression research" with this pious end in mind. Let me elaborate on this with reference to "then and now."

"Then," the issue was variously phrased, but predominantly it was a quarrel between the "original sin" mafia and the "perfectibility of man" crew (henceforward the "sinners" and the "perfectionists"). The latter were dedicated to the liberal-environmentalist position: man was basically either without instincts at all, and hence by definition without aggressive ones, or he was innately good and cooperative. In either case, aggression was "caused" by external forces that knocked him off his neutral or kindly balance. "Frustration" was popular as an external cause, and "crowding" rapidly gained ground as a favorite. The resurgence of Marxism (*soi disant*) made "exploitation" and "alienation" strong candidates. Much energy was expended in looking for "causes" of aggression and war, and again the assumption was that in the absence of such causes man would not be aggressive or warlike.

It is perhaps hard "now" to imagine that such views were seriously promulgated, but they were, and versions of them are still around and kicking (see chaps. 7 and 8). I have linked them to the ultimate premise of "the perfectibility of man," and indeed they were solidly in that Enlightenment tradition, with its nineteenth-century counterpart of inevitable progress. This Rousseauian tradition has a remarkably strong grip on the post-Renaissance occidental imagination. It is feared that without it we shall be prey to reactionary persuasions by assorted villains from Social Darwinists to eugenicists, fascists, and new-right neoconservatives. To fend off this villainy, the argument goes, we must assert that man is either innately neutral (tabula rasa) or innately good, and that bad circumstances are what make him behave wickedly. Ergo: remove the bad circumstances and human perfectibility is possible.

It is only by understanding the power of this paradigm (which I analyze at length in *The Search for Society*) that we can understand the hysterical reaction of its promulgators (in all the behavioral sciences, as well as philosophy, history, and some — but not all — life sciences) to the "original sin" movement. This was basically neo-Darwinian. Its premises had been around since Darwin, but they had been eclipsed with the decline of instinct theory and the triumph of behaviorism and environmentalism. Ironically, their resurgence after World War II was greeted with cries of welcome from Christian theologians (man was indeed a fallen creature), which was a stark contrast to the church's original reaction to Darwin himself. It did not help, in the eyes of the perfectionists, that the strongest scientific claims of this movement came out of Germany, since this was where genetic theories had been distorted in the service of precisely the kind of regime the liberals feared most. But it was not exclusively German and ethological, even if Konrad Lorenz was its leading popular exponent; it was equally South African (which didn't help with the liberals either) and anthropological, with Raymond Dart as its main scientist and Robert Ardrey as his prophet. (Its roots went back, of course, to Darwin himself, and its best previous exponent was Carveth Read in England from 1916 on. But "then," that is, in 1969, it was Lorenz and Ardrey who were the chief whipping boys of the liberals; the earlier contributions had been all but forgotten.)

What it said that was so heretical was somewhat as follows: Natural selection has programmed man to be aggressive, in part a heritage from his animal (primate) ancestry, and in part a special development of his own evolutionary history as a weapon-using hunter. This aggression is intimately linked with reproductive success (the basic Darwinian process) and hence with dominance and territory, and serves constructive and adaptational functions rather than purely destructive ones. Indeed, it is hard to see how natural selection could have worked without it. It is mitigated and constructively channeled by the tendency to "ritualize" (this was a central idea) and hence substitute displays, threats, and ceremonies for the real thing. It gets out of hand and destructive when such ritualization cannot work, as for example with weapons and killing at a distance, or in cases of crowding, where organisms cannot exhibit normal spacing behavior.

Looking back from the "now" vantage point, with the proverbial 20/20 hindsight, it is hard to see what all the fuss was about. The two positions were not all that different. Both acknowledged that external conditions could aggravate aggression and violence. They differed only in that the perfectionists did not want to admit any aggressive content to human nature, while the sinners insisted that there must be at least an aggressive potential. Otherwise, how come aggression at all?

There was, I suppose, a real difference at one level of argument. I can only summarize it thus: even if the perfectionists were willing to admit an aggressive potential, it was an essentially passive potential that had to be hit from the outside to be activated; the sinners, on the other hand, saw an appetitive quality to aggression that made it, like sex or hunger, a drive seeking satisfaction. What is more, the drive had a low threshold of activation: it didn't take much to set it in motion. The analogy with sex was obvious. People obviously have a sex drive, and while this does not mean that everyone all the time is running around looking for sex, they nevertheless are easily aroused by the appropriate erotic stimuli (external) or hormonal conditions (internal) or a combination of the two. Clearly it is of great adaptive advantage to have these drives (hunger, sex, aggression) in a state of readiness just "below the surface" so that they can easily be brought into play to serve the organism's reproductive interests. But equally important is the fact that they can easily be inhibited (sublimated, ritualized). Timing is everything in comedy and evolution; organisms must avoid "inappropriate" surges of eating, copulating, and violence, or risk expulsion from the gene pool.

I have found it necessary (although it shouldn't be) to repeat the caution that these "potentials for aggressivity" are not uniformly but normally distributed in any population. Thus, in any naturally occurring population, only about 1 percent of the individuals will be hyperaggressive. To anticipate a future argument, let me say that this presents few problems for a small group. In a primate group, such individuals will as often as not be driven out. In the small human groups in which we evolved (fifty or so members), only one or two members might be hyperaggressive. They would again either be driven out or found some useful role in fighting against other groups. Even if the group rose to five thousand (the outer limits of the Paleolithic "linguistic tribe"), fifty or so individuals do not raise a very large problem, and the small, tight social system could either constrain or channel their hyperagressivity without difficulty, as ethnographies testify. But when we come to large, heterogeneous societies of 50 million or more, then we are speaking of five hundred thousand individuals loose in a relatively anonymous setting without the inbuilt constraints of the small group. The amount of damage that half a million hyperaggressive people can do in a society of 50 million is way out of proportion to that done by fifty people in a society of five thousand. While the only change is in the absolute numbers (nothing about the organisms has changed), this alone can cause such a violent change in the conditions of violence that we can have a new "problem" of gigantic proportions. The important thing to note, however, is that it is not the "innate violence" that has "caused" the problem — that was always there. The cause of the problem is the new numbers game.

How typical it is that people only look for "causes" of things they don't like. They look, for example, for the "causes" of divorce, but never think of asking for the "causes" of marriage. Similarly, they will look for the "causes" of destructiveness, but seldom for the "causes" of creativity and creative enjoyment. Creativity is simply assumed to be spontaneous and somehow self-rewarding for "normal" individuals. Why cannot destructiveness (which in the case of people like Alexander or Napoleon is hard to separate from creativity) be also looked at as spontaneous and self-rewarding? Because it frightens us to think this way, that's why. We ask what sinister thing it is that causes people to find enjoyment in bullfighting, but we assume that the enjoyment of great music is natural, normal, and self-rewarding. Our comfortable, civilized bourgeois prejudices have a lot to do with the way we pose, and hence beg, these "scientific" questions. And they lead us to a convenient avoidance of the paradox that if we remove the stimuli to aggression we may very well end up removing the stimuli to creativity and much other human action. This is a hard paradox to live with, but one we should face, not explain away.

Nevertheless, if we put all this together, we come up with a very plausible picture of aggression that fits our common sense and systematic observations of aggressive behavior in humans and other animals, as well as the accumulation of scientific evidence on the internal states associated with aggression and violence. I stress "common sense" here, meaning observations not clouded by one of the intense ideological positions on the topic. To deeply committed liberal-perfectionist-environmentalists — and they are still with us — any suggestion of innate content in human nature is abhorrent. That such suggestions came at a time when the perfectionists were engaged in furious (and often very aggressive!) combat with forces of militarism and racial oppression (Vietnam and civil rights) made the ideological battle all the more irrational. That their intellectual opponents largely shared their position on these issues should have told them something. But they were obsessed with the fear that had haunted Locke, Mill, Hobhouse, and the liberal-reformist tradition: that to admit innate content to human nature was to give aid and comfort to political reaction.

Again, "now" we can see that this is simply not true. It does not follow from the sinners' view of aggression that I have outlined, that anyone should feel impelled to support any particular status quo, or become a raving militarist. Quite the contrary. In the same way that one can provoke high or low levels of sexual arousal by controlling the external stimuli to sex, so one can provoke high or low levels of aggression. Take away the stimuli of glory, excitement, gain, immortality, xenophobia, or whatever, and one will surely lower levels of aggression and violence. That the church regarded sin as innate and ineradicable did not mean it did not actively campaign against it and against those things that would lead us into temptation. Calvin Coolidge, that man of few words, was asked on returning from church about the subject of the sermon. "Sin," he replied. When asked further about the preacher's message on the subject, he said: "He was agin' it." (I heard this anecdote from Ashley Montagu.)

But this cautionary tale does point up a basic difference between the perfectionists and the sinners. If we lower levels of external sexual stimulation, we will still get sexual behavior because the internal stimuli, plus the inevitable existence of the two sexes, will move the organism to appetitive satisfaction. If aggression is analogous (and this is compatible with physiological findings), then we will always get some aggressive behavior no matter what we do with the environment. The internal potential is there, and there will always be enough frustration, rivalry, greed, gain, etc., no matter what the social system. And, as we have seen, there will always be a low proportion of individuals with a very low threshold of aggressive arousal who can cause problems out of all proportion to their numbers. Consequently, it is pie-in-the-sky to wish to abolish aggression. Those societies paraded as examples of such abolition always return to embarrass the paraders (for example, Pueblo Indians, Eskimos, Bushmen: all with high levels of personal aggression). On this argument, it would be as personally and socially damaging (not to say impossible) to abolish aggression as to abolish sex.

Here there is a real difference between the two views. But note that none of the perfectionists ever proposed abolishing sex. Despite their principles, their common sense would have told them this was impossible. But they did seriously propose trying to abolish aggression: remove the stimuli and it will go away. They never did adequately answer the objection (which goes back at least to George Bernard Shaw's *Fabian Tract 45* on "The Impossibilities of Anarchism," 1893) that such an argument fails to explain how we get the aggressive response in the first place. You cannot stimulate aggression if there are not internal mechanisms already in place to be stimulated.

We "now" know what these internal mechanisms are, and the tabula rasa theory is no longer even minimally respectable here, any more than it is in linguistics or cognition, for example. It can only be understood or sympathized with if one first understands its tenacious (if false) premises in the history of ideas and ideologies, and how desperately essential these appeared to be in combating reactionary, racist, and militarist evils. To this list were eventually added "sexist" evils, and the same tedious argument ensued over sex differences with the same nonissues preponderant.

Calmer times bring calmer minds. But even so, some hangover from the great debate is still with us in an age of terrorism, soccer violence, sectarian killings, and crime in the streets. Here we can perhaps turn to the second implication of "then and now." But before that, let us note something positive that emerges — a convergence of views — from the debate: Whichever position you espouse, if a lessening of violence is at issue, as opposed to its abolition, then the conclusion is that a lowering of the intensity of the stimuli to violence will be effective. But, paradoxically, the original sin position offers something more, namely, the effectiveness of ritualization or sublimation (*pace* Freud) of aggressive drives. If ritualization, for example, is as innate as aggression itself, then we have a powerful related drive, already geared to the control of aggression, to call upon. This was Lorenz's great hope, and the much-maligned Robert Ardrey firmly agreed. He used to hand out little desk plaques engraved with a quotation from his own work: "If there is hope for men, it is because they are animals." Our wonderful intelligences may not save us, but our animal propensity to ritualize just might.

Behind this propensity to ritualize, especially in *Homo sapiens*, lies the innate ability to *inhibit* our basic limbic emotional drives. Perhaps part of the confusion between the two positions (perfectionists and sinners) lies in the fact that I have argued this position regarding inhibition more consistently with the evolution of incest inhibition than in the inhibition of aggression per se. But in, for example, *The Red Lamp of Incest*, I tried to make it clear that the evolution of the capacity to inhibit — a primary function of the burgeoning neocortex — and the consequent capacity for delayed gratification, applied to all the limbic functions, including aggression. Indeed, the "incest inhibition" included the ability to inhibit "sexual and aggressive drives." The sexual drive toward the females under senior male control had to be inhibited, but so did the aggressive drive toward the senior males themselves. Michael Chance was the first to see this in an ethological context and point out its importance for the evolution of the higher primate brain. I pushed the logic of this further into the sex-aggression linkage as it related to incest inhibition.

But what clearly emerged was a picture of an animal whose evolving brain was as concerned with the *inhibition* as with the *facilitation* of aggression, and perhaps even more so. It was not that "animal aggression" was absent; it was still very much in evidence. It was that in man the aggression was constantly being monitored by consideration of delayed gratification: *aggression postponed was dominance gained*. The aggression still had to be there and easily "turned on" for the dominance struggle to be effective. But it had to be just as easily "turned off" so that the animal did not make foolish moves and spoil its chances (as is the case with the hyperaggressive animals who end up wounded, dead, or exiled). If, therefore, we could understand these "innate mechanisms" we could learn how to encourage inhibition and ritualization at the expense of aggression. We did not need to wish away our obvious aggressive impulses with appeals to a shaky *tabula rasa* theory, but could more realistically plan to achieve a better balance between facilitation and inhibition. Herein lies the reconciliation, I believe, between the sinners and the perfectionists, and an eventual end to the polemical — and in this view pointless — debate which held up progress both intellectual and practical for nearly three hundred years.

Which leads us back to the second chronological contrast and its implications. "Aggression now," that is to say in the twentieth century, is something very different from aggression in the context of our Environment of Evolutionary Adaptedness (E.E.A.) — "aggression then." The E.E.A. of any species is easily determined as that environment in which the major adaptations leading to its distinctiveness as a species occurred. For *Homo sapiens/erectus,* this is the preagricultural hunting, gathering, and scavenging environment that included 99 percent of our history and culminated in the truly astonishing cultural achievements of the Upper Paleolithic. (See the stone-tool industries, the carvings, and the cave paintings of Altamira, Lascaux, etc.) "Now" in this context is really the period after the Neolithic revolution, circa 10,000 B.P. (Before Present). In what way is "now" different from "then" regarding aggression? The organism is not different. Only some minor changes (mainly in teeth) have occurred. Hence, the basic aggressive and ritualizing mechanisms are still in place. What is different is this: These mechanisms were the result of the slow molding of ancestral primate mechanisms to the E.E.A. of the genus *Homo,* and in this environment they worked.

Thus aggression was able to perform its "constructive" functions, and ritualization was equally able to contain the aggressive inclinations. Aggression was no more a problem in this context than it is in the context of a primate group with its dominance and breeding hierarchies, or a bird colony with its breeding territories, or a lion pride with its competing males, or whatever. It was a perfectly natural extension of primate aggression, mediated by the evolving human capacities for language and symbolic expression which served both to facilitate and inhibit aggression in the newly emerging "human" context. There was aggression, there was violence, there was ritualization; but there was no "problem" unless one wishfully imagined that there should not be any such drives in *Homo.* Aggression performed the same services here, even if "culturalized" with weapons, war paint, martial songs, magic, and myths, as it did for other species: territorial spacing, formation of breeding hierarchies, distribution of resources, sexual selection, etc.

Within communities, violence was ritualized in many forms (law, customs, kinship, dueling) and even between communities. When ritualization (treaties, truces, trading, single and ceremonial combat, ceremonial cooperation, competitive sports, intermarriage) failed, the sanguinary consequences were limited by the crudity of weapons and the relatively small numbers involved. Not only was the species not threatened by all this aggressivity, it might well have benefited from the selection pressures for intelligence, foresight, strength, courage, cooperation, altruism, comradeship, and sociality that this organized, intercommunal violent activity involved.

This is not a happy picture for committed pacifists. But neither are the goings-on in a primate group. It cannot be helped. This is the way things are. It was fashionable in the late 1960s and 1970s for the perfectionists to use the "friendly and amiable" chimpanzees as a model for protohuman behavior, as against the "aggressive and irascible" baboons favored by the sinners. But more and more recent research has shown "our friends the wild chimpanzees" to be irascible, sexist, territorial, hierarchical, carnivorous, predatory, cannibalistic, and given to extreme intergroup violence to the point of genocide. It may well be that *Homo sapiens sapiens* (us) was only carrying on the traditions of its closest primate relatives when it exterminated its hominid cousins *Homo sapiens neanderthalensis* (them). This is much disputed. But they did disappear, and we're still around. However, we must realize that this happened toward the beginning of the end of our period in the E.E.A. Population expansion was already leading to serious competition for hunting territories and the destruction of the mammalian megafauna. And thereby hangs the tale.

The "population explosion" of the early Neolithic, following the shift from hunting to domestication, was of the order 1.5 million to 100 million within a millennium. One hundred million is not, in absolute terms, very large. But relatively, and in the restricted areas where it occurred (Fertile Crescent, Ganges, Indus, Yellow River), it was an enormous leap entailing a drastic change of "environment." Let us recapitulate: the basic organism was almost totally unchanged — certainly the deeply programmed systems of sex and aggression were not changed. But heretofore these had been "unproblematical." From 10,000 B.P. on, however, they had to operate in an ever more radically changing context for which they had not evolved. *It was what the changed context did to the essentially unproblematic basic mechanisms that began to constitute the "problem of violence."*

Thus, the "problem" was not aggression per se any more than it was sex per se. The problem was with the development of cities, states, slavery, castes and classes, bureaucracy, armies, universalistic religions, ideologies, nationalism, science, economic exploitation, increasingly sophisticated weaponry, and above all, sheer increase in numbers. And all of this occurred in a fraction of 1 percent of the time we have existed as a distinct genus.

Those then who hold that the "causes" of war and large-scale violence lie in class antagonism, xenophobia, ideological fanaticism, or any other "external factor" are quite correct. They are only incorrect when they insist that this in turn "causes" human aggressivity. The human aggressivity is there to start with. These external factors simply bring it into play in unprecedented ways. The "external cause" argument, as we have seen, was advanced to counter the equally erroneous argument that the innate aggressivity "caused" the wars and violence! If the reader can now see how my argument takes neither of these positions, then we have come a long way to understanding my original statement that as far as aggression is concerned there is nothing to find out; there is no problem.

The problem, to repeat at risk of being tedious, is a problem of social organization and change, not of human nature. It is not clear, therefore, how further investigations of mechanisms of human or animal aggression will help with the "problem" — interesting as they may be as additions to human knowledge. Nor is it clear how massive sociological or social psychological research will help either. We know what the triggers for aggression and violence are. We have seen them over and over again throughout history. What more do we need to know? Once we have grasped that our problems are conceptual rather than real, perhaps we can begin to talk sense on the subject.

Thus, if Marxists maintain that the abolition of class society and the withering away of the state will lead to an absence of violence, they are probably wrong. These are only two of the stimuli to violence, and before they existed there was violence anyway. But their absence would certainly remove two occasions for (I prefer this to "causes of") large-scale violence. If overcrowding and economic exploitation are associated with (again better than "causes of") violence, then their removal will add to the list of defunct triggers. But this will only reduce the incidence, not abolish the phenomenon. Why is this not enough? I was asked by the President's Commission on Violence (1968) if gun control laws would mean less violence. I said probably not, but they might mean fewer people would shoot each other, which was surely a worthy result in any case.

One of the problems in interpreting the so-called "causes" of violence and wars is the shortsightedness of the social, behavioral, and even historical sciences. They are trapped in the "now" — that is, post-10,000 B.P. And one of the main things to grasp about the "now" is that in the perspective of the species' evolution, it is a peculiar, aberrant, violent, unnatural time. Despite the triumph of various relativisms since Nietzsche, we cannot seem to shake off our Enlightenment/Victorian notions of "progress." Thus, for almost all theorists, "human behavior" means post-Neolithic behavior; before this was savagery: "the primitive." It is emotionally inconceivable that the pre-Neolithic could be essentially the "normal" equilibrium time of human behavior, and all that goes under the heading of "civilization" an aberration: an inhuman and inhumane state of frenetic change and violent deviation from a "human" norm. (And this is not a revamping of Freud's *Civilization and Its Discontents*. I do not see the discontents stemming from repression. There was repression in the Paleolithic too.)

We find this inconceivable because we are trapped within the assumptions of this "historic" period. We label what went before as "prehistory" — a sublime arrogance. To regard at least 2 million (and even upwards of 5

million) years of human history as "pre-" — as simply a run-up to the real
thing — is a pure value judgement for which we have no authority. Before we
knew better — before we knew the human time scale — there was perhaps an
excuse; but there is no longer. We still talk of "early man," and this is man
for 99 percent of his existence! If we changed our terms and called ourselves
"late man," as opposed to "man" proper, we might begin to get a glimmer of
our colossal mistake. The theorists want to "explain history," but their
explanations take history for granted. They do not question the very
phenomenon of "history."

Let us do just that for a moment. Let us take "history" to be a late
development of the human trajectory; so late that it is still in its experimental
stage and has by no means established its inevitability. It is a blip at the end
of the trajectory; a blip that may well disappear as things return to normal. If
we treat history as a possible mistake or disease, then it is a deviation from
some norm; and that norm can only be the culmination of the species' E.E.A.:
the Upper Paleolithic at the latest. Let us then view history as a series of
divergences — swings of the pendulum — from this norm, rather than as a
linear, progressive improvement or a series of cyclical returns. Diagram 5.1
illustrates my own view of the major termini of the major swings of the
historical pendulum. Others might come up with different points of departure,
but the overall picture is the same: ever-increasing, faster swings away from
the norm. Of course, the items listed here as major deviations can only be
rough summaries which require an essay each for justification; but I think the
readers can make their own adjustments. Thus, I do not list "capitalism" and
"socialism," since these are both included under "industrialism" — and so on.

What intrigues me is that the major violent upheavals that have formed the
modern world (which is why the Franco-Prussian War and the American
Civil War are there) all took place on one or other of the great swings of the
pendulum. This makes intuitive sense: the more wildly we swing away from
the norm, the more violently we react. The most violently effective swings
have occurred in the West, which biases our diagram in that direction. But
this is a fact of history that has given rise to a whole industry of
interpretation. Here then is the possibility of a "theory of war," if one wants
one. The penultimate swing was so rapid that no major "deadly quarrel"
occurred: but that may just be an artifact of my choice of conditions for that
arc. I do not know whether World War III will come on the way to the
prophesied postindustrial society, or will be a consequence of our achieving
that state. "Posthistorical society" is, of course, just wishful thinking, but it
puts me in good company. Spelling out this theory in detail is a whole other
task. I offer it here as a first try at looking differently at human "history" and
human violence; a try that seems to me more compatible with what we know
about ourselves in the post-Darwinian world.

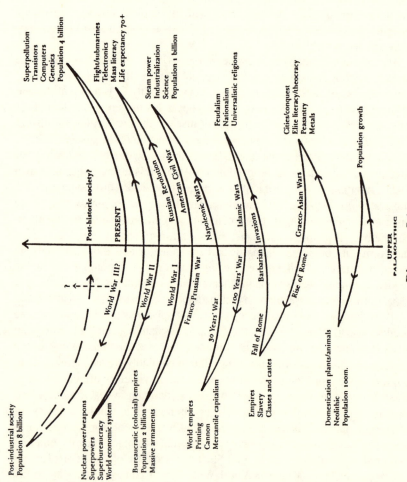

Post-industrial society
Population 8 billion

Nuclear power/weapons
Superpowers
Superbureaucracy
World economic system

Bureaucratic (colonial) empires
Population 2 billion
Massive armaments

World empires
Printing
Cannon
Mercantile capitalism

Empires
Slavery
Classes and castes

Domestication plants/animals
Neolithic
Population 100m.

World War III?
World War II
World War I
Franco-Prussian War
30 Years' War
Fall of Rome
Rise of Rome

Post-historic society?
PRESENT
Russian Revolution
American Civil War
Napoleonic Wars
Islamic Wars
Barbarian Invasions
Graeco-Asian Wars
100 Years' War

Superpollution
Transistors
Computers
Genetics
Population 4 billion

Flight/submarines
Teletronics
Mass literacy
Life expectancy 70+

Steam power
Industrialization
Science
Population 1 billion

Feudalism
Nationalism
Universalistic religions

Cities/conquest
Elite literacy/theocracy
Peasantry
Metals

Population growth

UPPER
PALAEOLITHIC

Diagram 5.1

What hope is there, I am often asked, for a future of peace and nonviolence, in this view? The answer is obviously: not much. But then, I ask in return, what hope is there for a future of chastity and nonsexuality? Not much either. What can we do about violence? Perhaps we can learn to live with it, since we don't seem to have much choice. And this may not be too bad. We know we can lessen the stimuli to violence, and we know that we can inhibit some violence with the threat of greater violence. We can try these things. But unless we can totally dismantle the world as we know it now and return to the E.E.A. equilibrium, we must accept that our huge, industrial world society is bound to provoke high levels of violent response: not because we are killer apes seeking blood and mayhem, but because we are apes that easily resort to violence as a solution. And if we are constantly presented with situations in which violence seems to be the only solution, then we will resort to it with a measure of courage, sadness, dignity, grim determination, cool efficiency, religious devotion, and sheer insane glee. For we can imbue violence with all the shades of meaning our imagination is capable of. And in the end it is our violent imagination rather than our innate violence that will determine the issue one way or the other. But there is no sense berating violence.

It is history that is the disease, not violence.
If you wish to cure the sickness, abolish history.

But, for the sake of an upbeat ending to this apparently pessimistic essay, let me offer the following: In looking at the perturbations of history with a view to fleshing out the details of my diagram, I am struck by one singular fact:

The actual amount of killing per capita in human sanguinary contests is relatively small.

However large the number of those killed, it is small as a proportion of the populations involved. What is more, the amount of energy expended in actual fighting is equally small as a proportion of the total energy expended in any war. Further, the amount of time expended in "diplomacy" — widely interpreted — is greater than that expended on the wars themselves. In going a little beyond Clausewitz, it sometimes appears to me thus:

War is diplomacy's way of creating more diplomacy.
Men love the treaties at least as much as the battles.

And is this so strange in an animal that had to evolve inhibition as well as facilitation of aggression in its long evolutionary history? The cultural expression of inhibition is rules. We are as geared to rules and their keeping as to mayhem and zero-sum outcomes. This is one of our versions of the universal ritualization function. Perhaps we can capitalize on this. We can take some heart from the observation that given the awesome possibilities of violence today, we may just be living in the best of all possible worlds.

6

The Human Nature of Violence

I have been asked to put violence into some sort of scientific perspective, so that we might have a background against which to ask more specific questions. I shall try to do that, but with the usual caveat, so annoying to nonacademic audiences, that this is only one scientific perspective and that others would look quite different. However, that's how we do it with science. We push our modes of explanation (or paradigms, as it has become fashionable to call them) to the point where they won't go any further, and then a bit more. When they start not to work, we know to change the paradigm; or at least our successors know to do it for us. So please bear with me while I push this one as far as I can take it. You will yourselves be on the alert for the places it cannot take us, and that is how it should be. That's how we know we're doing science, not metaphysics.

One of the most common ways for scientists to look at human violence is to ask, What causes violence? I am going to suggest that this is perhaps the wrong way to go about things and one of the reasons we don't seem to get to any very definite conclusions on the subject.

By and large, in the social and behavioral sciences as in life, we tend only to look for the "causes" of things we dislike. Thus, we look for the causes of divorce, but never for the causes of marriage; for the causes of war, but rarely for the causes of peace; for the causes of crime, but rarely for the causes of virtue; and for the causes of violence, but never for the causes of its opposite, however we phrase it — gentleness, perhaps. This is because we see things we dislike on analogy with diseases: they are by definition abnormal states. The normal state is marriage/peace/law/gentleness (or whatever), and this gets derailed in abnormal circumstances. Thus, one of the commonest and most popular versions of the causes of violence is the so-called "frustration-aggression hypothesis," which again assumes the "not-aggressive" state to be normal, but derailed by frustration.

We might call this the "disease" approach to violence: the normal or healthy state is assumed to be nonviolent, and we must therefore explain why violence occurs. (I am using violence and aggression synonymously here as a shorthand.) If we might use an analogy: no one looks for the "causes" of digestion. Digestion is simply there. Any organisms that ingest material and metabolize it have digestion; it is simply what they do: they digest. But when digestion goes wrong, as with, for example diarrhea, then we look for a cause of this in order to cure it. Diagram 6.1 shows a simple model (which was made for a different purpose but will serve ours) of a digestive system, showing how at various points things can go wrong with the normal processes.

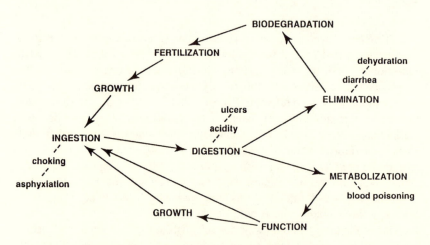

Diagram 6.1: Digestive Feedback System

The assumption that violence is a disease is to make it the analog of diarrhea. But, what if it is in fact an analog of digestion, or of some subprocess like metabolization, ingestion, or excretion? There is no future, in this case, in looking for its "causes" since it doesn't have any. It is just what the organism does as part of its routine of living. One can examine sequences within the routine and see where it fits (what its "functions" are); or, one can ask "ethological" questions about how it came to be there in the first place — evolutionary and adaptational questions. What is it for? What are its adaptational advantages? What survival value does it give the organism? — and so on. But "causal" questions are simply inapplicable.

If we make this analytical mistake when looking at sequences of behavior involving violence at some point, then we will ask, What caused this violence to occur? and expend a lot of mental energy trying to find an answer on the analogy of, Why did diarrhea occur? But if we look at the same sequence in the ethological framework — as we do in "agonistic encounters" between animals of the same species, for example — we can predict fairly accurately when, in the escalation process, violence will occur. It is a natural, expectable, predictable, inevitable part of the process. It is not diarrhea. It is metabolization, if you like.

Whether we like violence or not is not the question here. We are not concerned with evaluating it but with explaining or understanding it. And the causal explanation may simply not be the appropriate one, driven as we are by dislike to look for the cause to remedy the supposed disease.

Diagram 6.2 shows a typical escalation sequence of behaviors during an agonistic encounter (this was derived from observations on macaque monkeys, but is fairly generalizable across species).

The lowest level (1) is arousal: a rival is sighted. This puts the animal into a state of readiness. It will then move on to a display of some kind: baring teeth, pilo-erection, etc. It will then move menacingly toward its rival. This

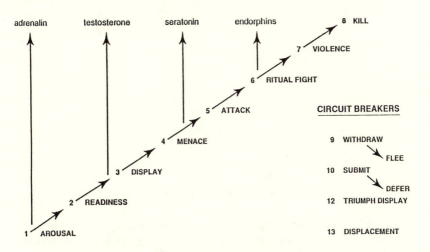

Diagram 6.2: Escalation Sequence

may be followed by an attack, which then will develop into a ritualized fight of some kind. This in turn may spill over into real violence and could end in wounding or killing. There are various "circuit breakers," as I have called them: ways out of the sequence if it gets too hot. An animal can withdraw and flee; it can submit and show deference to the rival; it can indulge in seemingly inappropriate "displacement" behavior (grooming, for example); or it can indulge in a triumph display. This latter is only usual when it has won, but it can be used as a bluff: declare victory and go home, as it were.

Also included on this diagram are some of the hormones involved in propelling the sequence, starting with adrenaline, getting a boost from testosterone and serotonin, and ending with a flood of endorphins if successful. (The trick with serotonin is that very *low* levels seem to be precursors of aggression, but that very *high* levels are associated with success. High levels of serotonin seem to promote calmness and confidence, which is why many antidepressant drugs deliberately seek to increase seratonin levels in humans.)

Of course, there are two animals involved and diagram 6.3 shows the synchronized escalation sequence for such a two-animal encounter.

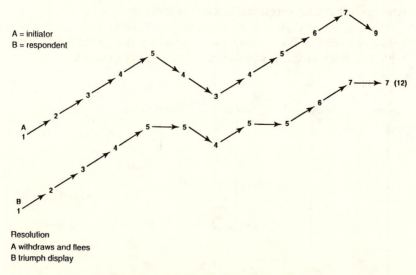

Diagram 6.3: Escalation of Conflict

A initiates the interaction here, and B responds step by step until phase 5: Attack. At this point, B holds his ground, and A falls back one step to mere Menace and then to Display. He proceeds up again to Menace and Attack, but we already see that he has been the one to back down first, and when the

Ritual Fighting spills over into real Violence at 7, it is B again who holds his ground and A who short circuits by withdrawal and fleeing while B goes into a Triumph Display. This is a fairly short sequence and could be over in a couple of minutes. In some species, such escalations and de-escalations can go on for hours.

It is important to note that we are talking here of a fight sequence between conspecifics of the same group — these animals know each other and know the rules, as it were. Between conspecifics of different groups this might be a much shorter and more bloody sequence. As Schaller said of a male lion who strayed into the territory of another lion pride, the only ritualization open to him is to run like hell. Also, this kind of "violence" has to be clearly distinguished from predatory violence between predator and prey species, where the sequence is as in diagram 6.4: the "stalk-attack-kill" sequence. Here the purpose of the encounter is the killing for food, and it is not drawn out. The predator gets on with the job. But that is why the elaborate sequences of escalation and de-escalation among familiar conspecifics are so interesting: there is ample opportunity to break off or de-escalate before getting to the killing or wounding point. And as the ethologists have demonstrated in species after species, the vast majority of fighting stops at the ritual level.

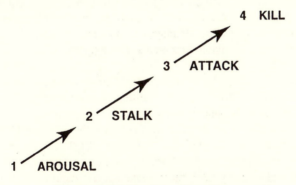

Diagram 6.4: Predator-Prey Sequence

It has been my contention for many years that the vast majority of human violence is of this kind also. It goes on all the time but usually rumbles away at the lower levels of escalation. We waste our time asking what "causes" it: it is as much a part of the human life process as digesting or reproducing. Flirting goes on all the time also, and sometimes escalates to a higher level of sexual activity, and no one asks what causes that. We are a sexually reproducing, sexually competitive, slow-growing, large land mammal. At puberty, our males, for example, increase their testosterone levels as much as ten to thirty times. Given sexual competition, the dominance of older males, and the rise in testosterone, it is entirely predictable that violence will occur. Thus, we find in all cultures young, postpubescent males acting aggressively, and older males acting to restrain and divert them. The females, in their wisdom, pick off the winners. This is what Darwin called sexual selection.

The real "causal" question here then is not why so many young males act so violently. This is digestion; it just happens as long as the appropriate stimuli (the analogs of food) are fed in (females, other males, resources). The real causal question is how so many cultures manage through initiation, intimidation, sublimation, bribery, education, work, and superstition to stop them and divert their energy elsewhere. Sending them off to war is a popular solution, as are dangerous sports and genital mutilations. This is the diarrhea. Lager louts and football hooligans are not a theoretical problem, however much of a social problem they may be. They are expectable and not in need of explanation. Quiescent conformists and career-oriented yuppies are the anomaly. They need explaining. What causes them?

But we could approach them through the escalation model too. Yuppies are known for their competitiveness, but they manage to keep this to the level of display and menace, never taking it to physical attack (verbal attack I count as menace). The question here becomes then, how are they kept to this level? The answer lies in the expanded human capacity for inhibition of aggression — one of the main functions of the evolution of the amygdala and the huge neocortex. This allows humans to indulge in fantastically elaborated sequences that are unavailable to animals. But the structure of escalation is similar.

As I have tried to show in analyses of Irish ritual fighting — a subspecies of pub fighting generally — virtually the same sequence is gone through as with the animal example, and again, serious physical injury is the exception rather than the rule. Major escalation points are the "Taking Off Of The Coat" and what I have called the "Hold Me Back Or I'll Kill Him" phenomenon, in which the spectators are invited to intervene to prevent further escalation. Firmly held, the antagonists can continue the ritualized fight without much fear of damage. Circuit breakers include parading the weeping mother who begs the boy to come home — so he can withdraw with honor. Both sides usually then indulge in a triumph display. (See *The Search for Society*, chap. 7.)

This works, as we have seen, among familiars — among those who, however subconsciously, know the rules and tacitly agree to them. Among strangers there are no rules, and as the ethologists have pointed out, a great deal of human violence looks more predatory than ritualized. The young attackers of the jogger in Central Park — out on their self-described "wilding" — were into the stalk-attack-(rape)-kill mode. The jogger was more like a prey animal, not a conspecific in a more or less evenly matched fight. But here again the question is not what "causes" such violence — predators are violent by definition — but what causes the context to be rendered "predator/prey" rather than "conspecific/familiar." Whether we like it or not, phenotypical racial differences make it very easy to define another human being as a prey animal rather than a conspecific. That this is very deep rooted can be seen from the fighting behavior of chimpanzees. Within the group, fighting is ritualized, but "foreign" groups are attacked like prey, and individuals are often killed and eaten. But given this perception — of the other as prey — the violence follows. Predators attack prey. It is what they are supposed to do. Territory holders attack trespassers. The only ritualization, as George Schaller said of lions, is to run like hell.

(It might be objected that these are not, with humans, predator/prey relationships because humans do not kill other humans for food. But [a] they often do and have done throughout history, and [b] one might use the analogy with rape [which indeed is often involved], where the behavior is gone through with no intention of investing in any relationship or offspring. It is the proximal mechanisms that are operating. Once the "pseudospeciation" of the other is achieved, it is predator motives that operate, not those of — essentially — sexual competition.)

If we are to apply this approach to, for example, pub violence, there is some hope. First, we can assume it to be inevitable; it is going to happen. Pubs are arenas where inhibitions are lowered and conflicts easily provoked. But we do not need to be appalled or disgusted. This is not diarrhea; this is digestion. What we need to figure out, therefore, is not how to "cure" (i.e., eradicate) this, but how to de-escalate in the proper sequence once it occurs. If people are too drunk, this is difficult because alcohol does seem to interfere with the capacity for inhibition so necessary to ritualization, and people can act unpredictably in consequence. They become like the experimental monkeys whose amygdalas have been removed, and who therefore can't get the sequence right.

But usually people are not that drunk, and a good publican, for example, knows when to use humorous diversion, when to appeal to the crowd for support, and when to become suitably intimidating. He knows this because he is going through a process deeply wired into the human animal: he is in a conflict situation in a crowded arena with familiar conspecifics (even if they are not regulars, they are regular pub goers and the setting and rules are known to them). When the whole thing goes wrong it is usually because the sequence has not been respected and gets out of hand — a publican becomes aggressive much too early and triggers a wild response, for example. Or drunken spectators interfere at the wrong moments. Of course, if a motorcycle gang comes in, bent on violent mischief, then we are in a predator/prey situation and we either fight or run like hell. Ethology is not a lot of help; a gun would be more useful.

My only final words of advice — not probably very helpful to this audience — are to treat violent episodes as natural events: not to seek their elimination, but to observe carefully the escalation sequences that seem natural to them, and learn to control these by effective de-escalation through the sequence, or the circuit breakers. Whether we are talking about pub fights, so-called soccer hooligans, or international conflict, much the same rules seem to apply. (The actual players — politicians, military, and diplomats — in international conflicts are in fact usually well known to each other, and they know the rules. The Cuban missile crisis — and a great deal else of the "cold war" — for example, could very easily be mapped out according to the escalation sequence described here. One of the problems with Saddam Hussein is that he is not a "familiar" in the international club, but a local predator running loose.) Thus treating violence as normal, and not as a disease, might in fact help us, paradoxically, to control it better in the end. The temptation is to think in terms of eradication of the pestilence. But if I am right, then this could be the totally wrong analogy, and pursuing it will probably only make things worse.

7

Violence, Ideology and Inquisition:
Encounter with Seville

The 1986 conference of the American Anthropological Association, at its Annual Business Meeting, proposed that the "Seville Declaration on Violence" (also known as the "Seville Statement on Violence") be adopted as the "official policy" of the Association. It was evidently so adopted *nem. com.* This didn't altogether surprise those of us not at the meeting since these agents of righteousness have passed such "resolutions," including condemnations of various heresies and heretics, in the past. (Thus, Derek Freeman and his publishers — Harvard University Press, of all people — had been given the treatment for daring to criticize Margaret Mead and the official party line of cultural determinism, and "sociobiology" had been given an attempted going over. Many members, disgusted at such exercises, had stopped going to the "business" meetings.) At this point, most members of the Association had not seen the text and knew nothing of the provenance of the Declaration. As is the Association's rule, the matter would have to be put to a mail ballot for confirmation.

Before this happened, news not only of the Declaration itself, but of a "Seville Declaration Network" began to percolate. *Vogue* ran a column on the Network, explaining that it was run by one David Adams of Wesleyan University and that it was "promoting the adoption" of the Declaration. If adopted by enough concerned bodies, *Vogue* concluded, the Declaration would not necessarily stop wars, but would "give us one less excuse for having them." The offending "excuse," it seemed, was that we were innately aggressive, and that this innate aggression made war inevitable.

In a further development, the *Human Ethology Newsletter* (5[2] [June 1987]) carried a copy of the text. It also carried a critical commentary by Joseph Manson and Richard Wrangham (University of Michigan) and a reply by Robert Hinde (University of Cambridge), one of the signatories — of which more later.

To be fair here, let us print the document in question exactly as given in the *Newsletter* (a few obvious typos and misspellings of names have been corrected). It evidently derived from a meeting of luminaries in Seville (Spain) on 16 May 1986. The meeting was "supported by Spanish UNESCO." The Declaration was destined to appear in a volume of papers from the conference (which I have not seen) called *Essays on Violence* (Ramirez, Hinde and Groebel, eds.). The Seville Declaration Network is a group of activists whose goal is to get publicity for the Declaration, but especially to engineer its "adoption" as "official policy" by learned and scientific societies. The document is evidently "proposed for adoption by UNESCO" itself, and indeed this may well have happened by now. Here it is:

Statement on Violence

Believing that it is our responsibility to address from particular disciplines the most dangerous and destructive activities of our species, violence and war; recognizing that science is a human cultural product which cannot be definitive or all-encompassing; and gratefully acknowledging the support of the authorities of Seville and representatives of the Spanish UNESCO; we, the undersigned scholars from around the world and from relevant sciences, have met and arrived at the following Statement on Violence. In it, we challenge a number of alleged biological findings that have been used even by some in our disciplines, to justify violence and war. Because the alleged findings have contributed to an atmosphere of pessimism in our time, we submit that the open, considered rejection of these misstatements can contribute significantly to the International Year of Peace.

Misuse of scientific theories and data to justify violence and war is not new but has been made since the advent of modern science. For example, the theory of evolution has been used not only to justify war, but also genocide, colonialism, and suppression of the weak.

We state our position in the form of five propositions. We are aware that there are many other issues about violence and war that could be fruitfully addressed from the standpoint of our disciplines, but we restrict ourselves here to what we consider a most important step.

IT IS SCIENTIFICALLY INCORRECT to say that we have inherited a tendency to make war from our animal ancestors. Although fighting occurs widely throughout animal species, only a few cases of destructive intraspecies fighting between organized groups have ever been reported among naturally living species, and none of these involve the use of tools designed to be weapons. Normal predatory feeding upon other species cannot be equated with intra-species violence. Warfare is a peculiarly human phenomenon and does not occur in other animals.

The fact that warfare has changed so radically over time indicates that it is a product of culture. Its biological connection is primarily through language which makes possible the coordination of groups, the transmission of technology, and the use of tools. War is biologically possible, but it is not inevitable, as evidenced by its variation in occurrence and nature over time and space. There are cultures which have not engaged in war for centuries, and there are cultures which have engaged in war frequently at some times and not at others.

IT IS SCIENTIFICALLY INCORRECT to say that war or any other violent behavior is genetically programmed into our human nature. While genes are involved at all levels of nervous system function, they provide a developmental potential that can be actualized only in conjunction with the ecological and social environment. While individuals vary in their predispositions to be affected by their experience, it is the interaction between their genetic endowment and conditions of nurturance that determines their personalities. Except for rare pathologies the genes do not produce individuals necessarily predisposed to violence. Neither do they determine the opposite. While genes are coinvolved in establishing our behavioral capacities, they do not by themselves specify the outcome.

IT IS SCIENTIFICALLY INCORRECT to say that in the course of human evolution there has been a selection for aggressive behavior more than for other kinds of behavior. In all well-studied species, status within the group is achieved by the ability to cooperate and to fulfill social functions relevant to the structure of that group. "Dominance" involves social bondings and affiliations; it is not simply a matter of the possession and use of superior physical power, although it does involve aggressive behaviors. Where the genetic selection for aggressive behavior has been artificially instituted in animals, it has rapidly succeeded in producing hyperaggressive individuals; this indicates that aggression was not maximally selected under natural conditions. When such experimentally created hyperaggressive animals are present in a social group, they either disrupt its social structure or are driven out. Violence is neither in our evolutionary legacy nor in our genes.

IT IS SCIENTIFICALLY INCORRECT to say that humans have a "violent brain." While we do have the neural apparatus to act violently, it is not automatically activated by internal or external stimuli. Like higher primates and unlike other animals, our higher neural processes filter such stimuli before they can be acted upon. How we act is shaped by how we have been conditioned and socialized. There is nothing in our neurophysiology that compels us to react violently.

IT IS SCIENTIFICALLY INCORRECT to say that war is caused by "instinct" or any other single motivation. The emergence of modern warfare has been a journey from the primacy of emotional and motivational factors, sometimes called "instincts," to the primacy of cognitive factors. Modern war involves institutional use of personal characteristics such as obedience, suggestibility, and idealism, social skills such as language, and rational considerations such as cost-calculation, planning and information processing. The technology of modern war has exaggerated traits associated with violence both in the training of actual combatants and in the preparation of support for war in the general population. As a result of this exaggeration, such traits are often mistaken to be the causes rather than the consequences of the products.

We conclude that biology does not condemn humanity to war, and that humanity can be freed from the bondage of biological pessimism and empowered with confidence to undertake the transformative tasks needed in this International Year of Peace and in the years to come. Although these tasks are mainly institutional and collective, they also rest upon the consciousness of individual participants for whom pessimism and optimism are crucial factors. Just as "wars begin in the minds of men," peace also begins in our minds. The same species who [sic] invented war is capable of inventing peace. The responsibility lies with each of us.

Seville, Spain, May 16, 1986

David Adams, Psychology, Wesleyan University Middletown (CT), USA; S.A. Barnett, Ethology, the Australian National University, Canberra, Australia; N.P. Beehtereva, Neurophysiology, Institute for Experimental

Medicine of Academy of Medical Sciences of USSR, Leningrad, USSR; Bonnie Frank Carter, Psychology, Albert Einstein Medical Center, Philadelphia (PA), USA; José M. Rodriguez Delgado, Neurophysiology, Centro de Estudios Neurobiologicos, Madrid, Spain; José Luiz Daz, Ethology, Instituto Mexicano de Psiquiatria, Mexico D.F., Mexico; Andrzej Eliasz, Individual Differences Psychology, Polish Academy of Sciences, Warsaw, Poland; Santiago Genovés, Biological Anthropology, Instituto de Antropologicos, Mexico D.F., Mexico; Benson E. Ginsburg, Behavior Genetics, University of Connecticut, Storrs (CT), USA; Jo Groebel, Social Psychology, Erzichungswissenschaftliche Hochschule, Landau, Federal Republic of Germany; Samir-Kumar Ghosh, Sociology, Indian Institute of Human Sciences, Calcutta, India; Robert Hinde, Animal Behavior, Cambridge University, UK; Richard E. Leakey, Physical Anthropology, National Museum of Kenya, Nairobi, Kenya; Tana M. Malasi, Psychiatry, Kuwait University, Kuwait; J. Martin Ramirez, Psychobiology, Universidad de Sevilla, Spain; Federico Mayor Zaragoza, Biochemistry, Universidad Autonoma, Madrid, Spain; Diana L. Mendoza, Ethology, Universidad de Sevilla, Spain; Ashis Nandy, Political Psychology, Center for the Study of Developing Societies, Delhi, India; John Paul Scott, Animal Behavior, Bowling Green State University (OH), USA; Riitta Wahlstrm, Psychology, University of Jyvskyl, Finland.

The document was signed by some Western savants whose scientific eminence is not in question. It was also signed by people from behind the Iron Curtain. One knows that it is usually hard to get ideological agreement here (or at least it still was in 1986), so this was a curiosity at least. It also seemed that many who would have had something to contribute — for example, me and many who think like me and work in similar areas related to the study of violence — were never invited in the first place. It began to look awfully like a stacked deck — and the equal unease felt by such eminent researchers as Wrangham and Manson showed that there were others who had a strange feeling of being railroaded.

However, the "Network" was squirreling away, and by now the American Anthropological Association was putting the issue to a mail ballot. The only "text" sent out with the ballot was the five "It is scientifically incorrect..." pronouncements, without the accompanying arguments. Around eighty-five hundred ballots were sent out; only about twenty-two hundred were returned. Predictably, 1,669 voted in favor, 230 against; the rest must have been abstentions. Before the results came out, I decided to make some protest. I felt that the *nem. com.* vote at the business meeting should not go unchallenged lest people out there in the world think that it represented the view of all anthropologists. So I wrote the following letter to the

Anthropology Newsletter (28[8] [1987]), the monthly house organ of the Association. They added the title.

Murmur of Dissent

It disturbs me that the "Seville Declaration on Violence" might become official AAA policy without anyone offering a murmur of dissent. It is not that one cannot readily agree with the rather obvious propositions. Indeed, it is a little like being asked to vote in favor of mom and apple pie. But this exercise in self-righteous piety, while leaving its sponsors with a warm glow of moral superiority, does nothing to advance our understanding of the dilemma of human violence. What is more, it raises false hope in suggesting that a condemnation of such simplistic notions as "innate aggression causes war" will remove "pessimism" and therefore lead to peace on earth. It isn't pessimism that threatens peace but fanaticism — even the sober considered kind exemplified by this document. To me, at least, the prospect of being at the mercy of human intelligence and culture, given its record, is far more frightening than being at the mercy of "aggressive instincts," which I think I understand and can handle.

I certainly do not believe that such instincts "cause" war. (See "The Violent Imagination," in P. Marsh and A. Campbell, eds., *Aggression and Violence*, Basil Blackwell, 1982.) But I believe they exist, and that complementary to them are the equally powerful instincts to ritualize aggression. I also believe that in the "normal circumstances" of our species — that proverbial 99% of our existence in the Paleolithic — these would be in some kind of healthy balance, as they were and are for other aggressive animals. But I also know that this is no longer the case and that what we now have to fear is something far more terrible than simple aggression.

Except for a few pathological cases, aggression is not a basic motive for action; it is a tool of other more frightening motives. What the supporters of this resolution do not seem to understand is that their own action in drawing up a list of heresies and pushing for their general condemnation tells us more about our dismal prospects for survival than anything they can say about human aggression. Our worst enemy is *fanaticism* (xenophobic or ideological or both) and our capacity for an intelligent *routinization of fanaticism*. Aggression is merely a handmaiden that can be called into play once the heretics are identified and condemned, ostracized and silenced and eventually tortured and burned. It is ironically appropriate that this document should have originated in that sordid center of the Inquisition, Seville. No, I'm afraid that the absolute "scientific" proof that innate aggression is not the cause of our troubles does nothing to alleviate my pessimism, and this declaration and the thoughtless acceptance of it do a lot to deepen my gloom over the prospects for human survival. The nuclear war they anticipate will certainly not be "caused" by innate aggression, but by mechanisms closer to those that produced this pointless document. It is this that the students of human survival should be considering, not shopworn denunciations of ideas that no one ever really held in the first place. (Reprinted with the permission of the *Anthropology Newsletter*).

The response was quite remarkable. Clearly, a large number of those who did not vote or speak up at the business meeting were nevertheless as disturbed as I was, but — and now we come to the sinister aspect — *they confessed that they were afraid to voice objections*. A whole distinguished department, in fact, voted in support of my letter and condemned the Declaration; but this was never made public. Partly this was because, as stated in my reply, it is hard to disagree with the propositions baldly stated, however much one may dislike such bald assertion or the antiscientific manner of it. But most of the fear expressed was of offending their "morally committed colleagues" (an actual statement from a letter). No one wished to appear to be "antipeace" or "prosociobiology" or "antirelativist" or whatever. The "good people" had claimed the moral high ground here, and managed to make any opposition look like advocacy of nuclear war.[1]

But a surprising number of people (certainly more than the 230 who voted) were obviously disturbed by the dogmatic, assertive tone of the Declaration and its sinister claim to know who the heretics were without naming them (shades of MCarthy). They were equally unsettled by its arrogant insistence that scientific disputes could be settled by majority votes of institutional memberships, and even columns in *Vogue*. In a subsequent issue of the *Anthropology Newsletter* (February 1988), Walter P. Zenner of SUNY Buffalo wrote (again their title):

Making Scholarly Decisions

I am sure that the over 80% of AAA members who voted to endorse the Seville Statement on Violence did so out of a sincere belief that they were taking a step toward the elimination of war and other forms of aggressive behavior and toward disabusing the public of erroneous and unscientific explanations of such phenomena. Unfortunately, this accusation was taken without a thorough public debate, and thus it constitutes a ritual of good intentions.

What offended me in the Seville statement was its dogmatic tone and its assumptions that we have sufficient knowledge to state a correct scientific position. It also distresses me that 80% of my colleagues act as if scholarly decisions can be made by legislation and resolutions rather than through research, open debate, and a free, not majoritarian, consensus.

We also are biased in favor of environmentalist positions and tend to reject any hint that human beings may have tendencies toward risk taking, aggression, violence or sadomasochism, despite the fact that we are, as Doris Lessing suggested, "children of violence." We must explain these phenomena, not shove plausible explanations, however unpalatable to our utopian tastes, under the rug. While we clearly remember the evils of racism, whether Nazi, North American or South African, we forget the atrocities committed under the banner of radical environmentalism by Stalin, Lysenko and others. We must remember that in this century, the road to hell has literally been paved with good intentions. [Reprinted with the permission of the *Anthropology Newsletter.*]

(We should note that it was not in fact "80% of the membership" who voted in favor, but 80 percent of those who returned ballots, itself only about a quarter of the membership.) The motive for all this declamation and heresy hunting did not become clear until the *Harry Frank Guggenheim Foundation Newsletter* asked to reprint my letter and to solicit a reply from Adams. (I had been for twelve years a Director of Research for the Foundation, which is devoted to the study of violence and aggression, so their request seemed appropriate.) They printed the letter, but Adams grandly refused to reply, referring them instead to his original paper at the Seville conference.[2] They printed a précis of it as follows:

126 college students answered questions (and 114 completed follow-up questionnaires a month later) regarding attitudes to peace activity, beliefs concerning human nature and war, feelings of anger about the arms race, and normative attitudes about peace activity of family, friends, and school. 40% of the students answered "very much" to "somewhat" to the question "Do you believe that war is intrinsic to human nature?" 40% agreed that "there is a war instinct" and 33% that "wars are inevitable because human beings are naturally aggressive." The researchers then examined the history of "peace activity" by students holding these views.

As predicted, beliefs about human nature and war proved to be significant correlates of peace activity....

These results support the need for a worldwide educational campaign to dispel the myth that war is instinctive, intrinsic to human nature, or unavoidable because of an alleged biological basis. As shown by the results obtained here, such a myth is widespread and constitutes an important obstacle that interferes with the development of activity for peace....

The data obtained in this study are consistent with similar results obtained in Finland and in a pilot study ... in the U.S. In all three studies it was found that a student is more likely to believe that he or she can do something about nuclear war if he or she believes that war is not intrinsic to human nature.

Since this was evidently the inspiration for the Declaration, let us start with it and return to the Declaration later. The problem with this enquiry into the "attitudes" of 126 students is the problem with all such studies: garbage in, garbage out. Just looking at the nature of the questions shows how loaded the deck was before it was dealt. Adams got the answers he did because these were the questions he asked in the context of a barrage of questions about "peace activities." And we really have no idea why students answered "yes" to these questions — it could have been, for example, on the basis of their deeply held religious beliefs about original sin and the fall of man. It is highly doubtful that their replies were the result of reading abstruse papers on the nature of aggression by neuroscientists. Even if the Declaration succeeds in its inquisitorial aim of silencing such research (however much people like Hinde may deny this is the aim), this does not mean that the "myth" will be silenced or that the majority of people will then take up "peace activities" on a large scale. Millions of people have, after all, held such beliefs for thousands of years in the absence of any research on aggression. Adams fails to make any connection between aggression research, which claims to show that we have an innate aggressive instinct (and that aggression is therefore inevitable), and the beliefs of these 126 students. As I have said, it is far more likely to be religious conservatism that prompts such answers, and religious conservatives are not noted for their fondness for "peace activities" if this means the left-liberal or, even worse, radical, marches, protests, and demonstrations.

And what would Adams do if these people told him that they prayed daily for peace because only God's intervention can save us from the consequences of our innate depravity? One can perhaps be forgiven for assuming that he wouldn't count this as a "peace activity." Perhaps if he *had* made the religion-pessimism connection, then he would have called for a Declaration denouncing religion? Again, we can be forgiven for supposing he wouldn't have done it, and that UNESCO wouldn't have sponsored it.

Again, if he had gone to countries with Marxist-Leninist educational systems (as opposed to Christian-derived ones), and asked, in the context of questions about the causes of war and peace, "Is war between the imperialist, monopolist, capitalist countries and the revolutionary proletarian countries inevitable?" he would have got "yes" answers to that impeccable environmentalist-historicist position. And precious few of his respondents would have been engaged in "peace activities" — at least as he defines these. What then would he have concluded? That we should have a Declaration denouncing the myth of environmentalist causes of war, and that this would lead to massive "peace activities" by all the Marxist-Leninist pessimists? One knows that this would never happen. If anything like it did, then all those signatories from behind the Iron Curtain would never have been in Seville to start with.

Fortunately, Adams found just the thing to bring them all together under the banner of UNESCO: a heresy hunt on which environmental determinists on both sides of the curtain could agree. Let's not, at all costs, look for the real causes of war; let's condemn a few writers and scientists who are easy targets, although let's not name them, for if we did their small numbers and pitiful influence would belie the need for our elaborate condemnation.

If the foregoing implies a certain cynicism about the role of UNESCO itself, this is not accidental. It has become an article of faith among "peace activists" to believe in UNESCO right or wrong. Those who find in UNESCO a spent idea which, because of its internal contradictions, cannot do what it overtly claims to be doing, are automatically condemned as reactionaries or whatever the current term of disapprobation happens to be. But anyone who has read, for example, Peter Lengyel's excellent, honest and disturbing account[3] will be left in no doubt that by its very nature this institution cannot fulfill its functions.

The original UNESCO ideal, embodied in its charter, of a secular humanitarianism, is described by Lengyel as "the last great manifesto of the eighteenth-century Enlightenment, a utopian document reflecting fervid belief in the bases of the liberal democracies that had just triumphed over fascism and pinning hopes on reform through education, science and reason" (p. 5). It was in trouble from the start since the Catholic countries opposed it and Julian Huxley, its first director general, was forced out. Once the Marxist, Eastern, and third-world countries became active members (if not always steady contributors), the ideological quagmire deepened and the "search for a universalist ideology" was doomed. Hence, there was a tendency to find a way of "agreeing on denominators which offended nobody and generalizations so broad that everybody can subscribe to them" (pp. 100-101). This beautifully describes the Declaration, and that it should be achieved by scapegoating a few unnamed offenders is well in line with UNESCO traditions, despite what the optimists would like to think.

But back to the Declaration itself. I said in my protest that the issue was not really any disagreement with the propositions to which "everybody can subscribe," but let's look at these a little more closely. The first two propositions are more or less the same: we have not inherited a tendency to make war from our animal ancestors, and violence and war are not programmed into human nature. In the first proposition, this is "proved" by stating the obvious truth: "that warfare has changed so radically over time indicates that it is a product of culture." Thus, war is possible, but it is not inevitable, "as evidenced by its variation in occurrence and nature over time and space."

Now, while one can subscribe in a general way to the propositions as stated, there is a problem with this spelling out of them. And this is the issue all along: one can more or less subscribe to the bald statements, but not necessarily to the implications read into them. Thus, for example, the fact that warfare is not a *constant* among all societies at all times does not *prove* that it is "culturally rather than biologically" caused. It merely shows that it varies in its incidence, which is as true for biological as for cultural phenomena. Even if war is indeed culturally rather than biologically "caused," variation in incidence does not prove this. And insisting that it does only deters us from looking at the biological components of war and warlike behavior. "Warfare" among those species that exhibit it (as Manson and Wrangham point out) — species which certainly lack language and culture in the human sense — is not constant either. Part of what those of us interested in aggression study is why, for example, chimpanzees under some conditions live peacefully and at other times practice murderous genocidal and cannibalistic "warfare." We can't attribute this to "culture." These wars do not begin, as the preamble to the UNECSO charter would have it, "in the minds of men." But neither are they the direct expression of any genetic tendency as far as we can see. Chimpanzees do engage in predation of other species, and it therefore becomes an open question how far this kind of "violence" is related to their intraspecific violence; one cannot just close this question off, particularly since chimpanzees often eat the other chimps they kill. At the moment we do not know what the exact interplay of innate violent predispositions, ecology, resource competition, mate competition, predation, and territoriality is. But the issue can only be decided by careful investigation, not by majority vote.[4]

I have myself put forward a quite elaborate theory of the variation in the incidence of warfare in human history,[5] so I am able to subscribe to the view that it varies over time. One cannot object to this way of putting it. But to conclude that this "proves" that it is a "product of culture," with the implication that there are no biological components, is not warranted. The statement itself says that its "biological connection is primarily through language" — which at least admits a biological connection. But why stop there? The complex relationship between selection for successful speaking, successful mating, and successful aggression has to be explored. It was to this that Manson and Wrangham addressed themselves, and Hinde's reply that no one wanted to stop such research was nothing if not naive in view of the route the Declaration Network has taken.[6]

While we are on this item, let us note another grand tautology built into the argument: If warfare is declared in advance to be "uniquely human," then, since culture is the species-specific behavior of *Homo sapiens*, war can only be "culturally caused" by definition. But the species-specific behavior of any species is part of its "evolutionary heritage," again by definition. So the fact that war is culturally caused does not cut us off from an evolutionary (i.e., biological) understanding of it. It is all part of the understanding of the biological basis of culture (i.e., specifically human behavior).

The third of the "scientifically incorrect" heresies is that there has been selection for aggressive behavior *more than* for other kinds of behavior. Well, of course. What could "more than" mean here? Has there, for example, been a greater selection for the human "power grip" than for the human "striding walk?" I don't know what "greater" or "more than" could mean in these contexts. In a certain sense the statement is tautological (and therefore impossible to disagree with!). All human attributes have evolved to the same stage — how can some have evolved "more than" others? The rather incoherent justification for this statement, however, seems only to be saying that hyperaggressive animals are not likely to succeed well in social groups. I know no one who would deny this. But a careful mix of aggression with the other factors mentioned — status, dominance, social bonding, affiliation, cooperation, and physical power — is certainly a central part of success, in, for example, competitive mating situations. It may well be the essential part, in the sense that without it all the other items don't ensure reproductive success. On the other hand, hyperaggressivity without the leavening of the rest of the repertoire will rarely, except in some species, have happy results. But to conclude that "violence is neither in our evolutionary legacy nor in our genes" (another tautology), is violently to oversimplify the very complex interaction of aggression with other factors that is, after all, implicit in what they are themselves saying.

In some very real sense it *is* in our genes/evolutionary legacy. If it isn't, how on earth do we and other species come to manifest it so regularly? The complex outcomes of the interactions of our genetic predispositions and our socio-ecological-cultural environments are not "in our genes," and it is this problem of the expression of genetic material and its incidence that is our prime concern, as the authors of the statement seem half to recognize. But they then back off from it with dogmatic and meaningless absolutist statements about what is and is not the case. The fifth proposition about the "violent brain" is again so totally banal it is not worth comment. But again, while being nothing but the truth, it is not the whole truth, and hides the fact that a number of individuals in any population have severe impairment of their capacity to "filter" stimuli, and their neurophysiology *does* "compel them to act violently." It only takes a few of these to wreak havoc way out of proportion to their numbers.[7]

As for the final statement, that war is not caused by instinct or any single motivation, again one asks, who ever said it was? Where people genuinely disagree is on the balance of forces involved. Some, certainly, would put more stress on the innate components than others. But these are hypotheses open to test and refutation. And that brings me to my main point.

The point is not whether one or the other of the positions here supposed to exist is *true* or not; the point is that IT IS SCIENTIFICALLY INCORRECT to say that position X or Y is true or false — especially on the grounds offered in the Declaration. Either position should be stated in a way that leaves it open to refutation: then it is "scientific" and open to argument. Thus, I have quarreled here with the arguments of the Declaration, not to prove an alternative view "true" (even if I believe it is), but simply to show that there are valid objections and alternatives that the document arrogantly dismisses as "impossible." This is profoundly antiscientific. The ideal scientific situation — which Karl Popper called the "demarcation criterion" — would be one in which all could agree on a crucial test that would conclusively refute a hypothesis. If, for example, we could agree that chimpanzees do not have "culture" but do have "war," then we could agree that war does not "begin in the minds of men" and is not "culturally rather than biologically caused." Perhaps one can be forgiven, again, for doubting that we can get such agreement. The Declaration, while reluctantly admitting that a few examples of "destructive intra-species fighting between organized groups" are found in nature (omitting to say that one of these instances involves our closest genetic relatives), throws in the caveat that none of these "involves the use of weapons." If the defining characteristic of "war" then becomes "the use of weapons," that lets the chimps out nicely — sighs of relief all round.

But the basic objection to the arrogance of the Declaration is the same: No position can be declared "correct" or "incorrect" by fiat. The best we can say is that the preponderance of tested hypotheses so far renders it more or less likely that such a position is correct. But we cannot predict future findings. One dreads to think what would have happened to the sciences if a list of "incorrect" positions had been drawn up in, say, 1910, and future research guided by that list. (Since writing this I came across the following quote from Jacob Bronowski: "There is almost no scientific theory which was held to be fundamental in 1867 which is thought to be true in that form today" [*The Origins of Knowledge and Imagination* (New Haven: Yale University Press, 1978)].)

In fact, many of the worst episodes in the history of science have resulted from just such domination of ideology over research. It is ironic, given the dogmatic cultural determinism of the Declaration, that the best example of this should come not from the "theory of evolution," which they single out (significantly) in their preamble, but, as Zenner pointed out in his letter, from the lunatic environmentalism of Lysenko and its implementation by Stalin.[8] Do we need to spell that example out? Or the extension of it to whole programs of "reform" on the environmentalist model which resulted in the genocide of millions of Kulaks and Ukranians, and the death, imprisonment, and ruination of many honest scientists?

Let us remember a few names that were sent into oblivion because they were "scientifically incorrect." Let us remember Vavilov, Levit, Ivanov, Karpchenko, Muller, Dobzhansky, Ephrussi, Sacharov, Zhebrak, Sergeer, Gause, and Stern ... the list, while finite, is very long. Let us hope, comrades, that you will never be forgotten, and that your names will haunt the purveyors of absolute scientific "truth" forever. Perhaps if Adams had given his questionnaires to those few opponents of Lysenko's who survived, he would have got some sobering answers. But he surely would not have got UNESCO sponsorship and all those brave signatures from behind the Iron Curtain appended to tautological declarations that "everyone can subscribe to."

In the end, this is the nastiest and most sinister aspect of the whole tawdry affair. They challenge "a number of alleged biological findings that have been used, even by some in our disciplines, to justify violence and war." It is against the evil influence of these unnamed disciplines and the unnamed colleagues in them that they boldly take their stand. I know of no one in any discipline who has ever used biological findings to *justify* violence and war. This is an outrageous libel. I know many who have tried to understand the terrible persistence of wars and violence with the help of biological insights. But I know of none who would not willingly put these insights to the service of peace, and who are not convinced that the greater the real insight — as opposed to pie in the sky — the greater the chance of controlling whatever biological factors are involved. I know of many, like myself, who think that simply to deny there are any such factors is a potentially dangerous route to take, and is in effect nothing more than a defense of an untenable environmentalist ideology.

But the Declaration actually goes on to accuse us of encouraging war by spreading "pessimism" about the ability to stop international conflict. That this is ludicrous is obvious on two scores: (1) scientific findings on the innate components of aggression are very recent, but wars have existed throughout human history; and (2) there is no evidence that current "pessimism" about the inevitability of war stems from the influence of the biological studies in question. Some of us are certainly pessimistic, but our pessimism stems from the inevitability of human actions like the Seville Declaration on Violence, not from any theories about innate aggression. If wars are indeed "culturally and not biologically caused," then, given the record of culture, we are in deep trouble.

My statement to the signatories remains the same as in my letter: If you truly wish to prevent World War Three, then do not indulge in those activities which, by your own admission, are the cause of wars and of cruel, specifically human, violence. If one starts a punch-up in a bar, one does not risk starting a war. Aggression as such has little to do with the starting of wars; we are all agreed. But, if you try to organize the World Intellectual Community to declare, by the vote of an intimidated majority, that certain testable scientific hypotheses are "incorrect" and, what is more, evil and dangerous, then you are well on the way to harnessing aggressive instincts in the service of the inquisition, the pogrom, the witch hunt, the book burning, the stamping out of heresy, and finally the jihad, the crusade, and the "war to end all wars."

Wars, as you remind us, begin in the minds of men. And today, at least, they begin like this: with a commitment to the true faith and a campaign against unbelievers. It was once the hope, yea even of UNESCO, that the values of science would help transcend this very human and very violent tendency. You seem to have forgotten this. UNESCO seems to have forgotten this. The professional organizations that pass their resolution with such fervor (to which we can now add the American Psychological Association) seem to have forgotten this. Perhaps there *is* an innate tendency in "the minds of men" (which, despite the implications of your use of the term, are most certainly biological phenomena); a tendency more terrible than aggression; a tendency that we are doomed to express and live by and that explains all this passion to lay blame and punish. My letter was impudent enough to suggest that "fanaticism" is such a tendency, and that aggression is merely one of its handmaidens. But one had better not suggest it too loudly without risking the righteous wrath of you who know with absolute certainty what is or is not "scientifically correct"; who, unlike the rest of us struggling with the hard business of finding things out, have a corner on God's truth. From those who know all the answers, good Lord deliver us.

* * *

All has not been smooth sailing for the Network since this was written. Both the Royal Anthropological Institute in Great Britain and the American Association for the Advancement of Science in the United States resisted the blandishments of Adams and Co. But the American Psychological Association succumbed. And *Vogue* declined — very, very politely — to print my (very, very polite) rebuttal. Adams was given a grant by the Harry Frank Guggenheim Foundation to promote his schemes. They told me this was to "stimulate debate" and because he didn't have any other grant (they also declined my not-too-serious request for an equal grant for equal-time rebuttal). In truth, as they very well knew, Adams had a fat grant from UNESCO. A disgruntled signee even wrote me that he and several others were tired of the way Adams was running the Network in great comfort from Paris as a "one-man show" (I quote) while they labored away in their third-world poverty, ignored by the champions of good in the West. Definite cracks in the ideological front here.

A psychologist from Temple University was also given a nice two-year grant by the same Guggenheim Foundation to write a "history" of the Declaration. He interviewed me, among others, spent a fair time traveling the world to garner material, actually wrote a manuscript, and then mysteriously ditched the whole thing. He didn't want to write about it, he said, because he was "disturbed by the ad hominem tone of a lot of the debate." I've never heard such precious crybaby nonsense as an excuse not to do a job one has contracted for. But it's par for the course with this whole thing. And a great pity in some ways since, despite its wholly partisan tone, the manuscript did reveal much interesting dissent from prominent scientists and organizations right from the beginning, when the infamous conference was being organized.

The journal *Encounter* (whose demise is deeply to be regretted by all who value independent and courageous journalism) reprinted my piece and invited two people to write comments and me to reply. This was valuable because one was Robert Hinde, who has been the best spokesman for the Declaration/Statement. In fact, he has been its only really coherent defender. I don't think even he knows of the dissension in the ranks. My reply, if perhaps too ad hominem for the delicate sensitivities of Temple University psychologists, told some more of the story. But in all this soap opera we should not lose sight of the issues as I have tried to lay them out here, because the academies are going to face more and more of this kind of thing as the inquisitors build up a head of self-righteous indignant steam. Those who laugh at the antics of UNESCO in Seville right now might be the next ones on the list. Surely we can learn that lesson from history: once the inquisition becomes self-sustaining, *no one* is safe.

(Since I wrote this, we have seen a wave of political correctness, speech control, and brainwashing surge over U.S. universities. There is a growing literature of alarm on this, and a general feeling that the Temples of Reason are beginning to look more like lunatic asylums where the inmates have taken over. But I suppose, contrary to what we might like to think, this has always been the case. Universities have been a constant pain in the neck since their invention by dissident monks. This is why they have so often suffered attack from outside forces. The difference now is that the attack on their treasured "academic freedom" is coming from within. They find this hard to believe; but it's real, and doubly frightening because those who are longing to send us to the stake — however metaphorical — are our colleagues. Welcome to Seville.

8

Has War a Future?
or,
Goodnight, Eirene

We seem, at the moment, to be going through one of those "war is dead" periods that occasionally try to brighten up the otherwise uninterrupted march of continual human bellicosity. It is a sociological generalization rarely made but easily tested that somewhere a war is always going on and always has been. Very few people today seem to read Lewis F. Richardson's magnificent *Statistics of Deadly Quarrels* (London: Stevens, 1960 — there are later updated editions), but anyone who doubts the generalization should spend a few minutes browsing through these dense pages. The ubiquity and persistence of war, however, is still seen by the "war is dead" movements as some kind of annoying aberration: if it were not for arms races, imperialism or colonialism, class oppression and capitalism, monarchical rivalries, communist expansionism, or the sick minds of evil dictators (the list is endless), we could lay down our swords and shields by the riverside and study war no more.

History is not kind to the hopeful. And it may have the last laugh over the equally perky "history is dead" movement now so popular with the partly informed. Even God is making a comeback, it seems. So it behooves us to tread carefully in the business of proclaiming the end of these obvious human enjoyments. You know the arguments: force is losing its efficacy as a means of extending policy (pace Clausewitz); democracy is now in worldwide demand and democracies are of their nature pacific (Michael Doyle); the growth of transnational corporations aided by better transport and instant worldwide communications is creating a level of international interdependence that will not tolerate war; all this raises the cost of war to an unbearable level (following on Norman Angell) ... and so on.

Very few of these are actually new arguments. During the seventeenth and eighteenth centuries, and even the first half of the nineteenth, no one bothered much to get into the war-is-dead business. It was pretty much taken for granted that war was a normal and natural mode of national policy-making, to be resorted to under fairly specific conditions and ended under equally specific conditions. With perhaps the exception of the Thirty Years' War — a nasty foretaste of things to come — international wars were pretty contained, fought by professional armies, and not troublesome to the mass of the population. Civil wars could get nasty, but the per capita losses were never great and countries recovered rapidly. It was not until the second half of the nineteenth century that the war-is-dead movement gathered force. The unprecedented rises in population, the huge shifts in population, the massive growth of trade and colonies, and the general industrializing of at least the first world, while obviously leading to more potentials for conflict for some observers, were cause for sunny optimism from, for example, the Spencerian laissez-faire liberals, who echoed their master in prophesying that, paralleling the growth from "simple" to "complex" social structures, there would be a replacement of "military" forms of social structure with "industrial" forms, which would be, for reasons pretty much like those advanced at present, inherently inimical to war. Thus, universal free trade would lead countries to specialize, and hence be dependent on each other, and hence not be able to go to war with each other.

I remember when I first read Spencer's arguments as a teenager (along with those of Buckle and Emerson and other nineteenth-century war-is-dead prophets) I found them very convincing, but wondered at the same time how the Franco-Prussian, American Civil, Anglo-Boer, Spanish-American, Japanese-Chinese, Russian Civil, First and Second World, Indo-Pakistan, Korean, and Israeli-Arab wars (to say nothing of numerous minor skirmishes in Spain, Ethiopia, Ireland, and the like, and of course the almost overlooked acts of colonial genocide such as in the Belgian Congo) had managed to happen in the meantime. Diehard Spencerians (there weren't many around) might have argued that these things took time, there could be relapses, etc. Spencer himself had denounced Disraeli's Suez Canal purchase on the grounds that it was a backsliding into the "military" mode, which, of course, would be obsolete if we just left well alone.

But we don't seem inclined to leave well alone and let the inevitability of pacific history take its course. This continues to be annoying to the "inevitability of pacifism" school, which included, in my youth anyway, the two schools of socialism and internationalism. For the socialists, once the proletariat had taken over in enough nations, they would obviously cease to want to fight each other. Or even before, once they developed class consciousness, the proletariats of the world would refuse to fight each other at the behest of their capitalist masters. At the London School of Economics in the 1950s, this was still being seriously preached by the hard core. Even then I felt one could learn more about the inevitability of human folly — including war — from the almost lunatic stubbornness of such foolishness than from the content of the doctrines themselves.

The internationalists, some of whom were moderate socialists but many of whom were not, plied their own version, which included the familiar arguments: reduce the arms races, strengthen the League of Nations, make the cost of conquest insupportable, expand tourism and exchange programs, and teach everyone Esperanto — the language, literally, of hope. (I had an older cousin who actually did part of his language degree — at Liverpool University — in Esperanto. I even bought the basic text and joined the local Esperanto club, only to find it was engaged in a furious feud with the rival Golapuk society. We forget so easily the failed idealisms of the past as we enthusiastically reinvent them for the benefit of the future.) I suppose one must add here the various kinds of isolationists, especially in the United States, who, while not having a truly coherent theory of the end of war, could be said to hold the view that if we all tended our own gardens and didn't go foreign adventuring, then this would at least cut down on wars. We can derive little comfort from the isolationist leadership of such military geniuses as "colonel" Lindbergh, who assured Roosevelt that the Polish airforce would make short work of the Luftwaffe.

War and Social Circumstances

The urge to announce the end of war is thoroughly understandable, and there can be few who would not like to believe it to be true. But war has been a constant of human history, and before we start the celebrations we have to ask ourselves the uncomfortable question whether any changes in social circumstances will affect its constancy. In other words, whether social circumstances alone can account for the constancy of war, such that a profound alteration in them could profoundly affect war's prospects. Or whether war, like sex, is something that can be affected by social circumstances, certainly, but is not necessarily "caused" by them and cannot necessarily be ended by changing them, however radically.

An intuitive appeal can be made immediately on the following lines: those who believe war is "caused" by particular social circumstances have proposed a list of such causes that is almost as long as the list of wars themselves. T. E. Lawrence, lying sick in his tent in Wadi Ais, ruminated over this same problem while trying to figure out just what the Arab revolt was about. "Clausewitz enumerated all sorts of war ... personal wars, joint proxy duels, for dynastic reasons ... expulsive wars, in party politics ... commercial wars, for trade objects ... two wars seldom seemed alike. Often the parties did not know their aim, and blundered til the march of events took control" (*The Seven Pillars of Wisdom* [London: Jonathan Cape, 1935], chap. 23, verbatim). While in each case these particular circumstances might have triggered the conflict, it would appear odd that each war had its own cause and that there were potentially an infinite number of "causes" of war.

No general formula for the "cause of war" has ever held up. (Neither Richardson nor Quincy Wright [*A Study of War* (Chicago: Chicago University Press, 1942)] could come up with a convincing one.) In most cases of "primitive war," for example, none of the proposed "causes" is present, and wars often seem to be fought for their own sake — or for the sake of intrinsic rewards stemming from the very business of warfare itself. It is this that is hardest to swallow: that war may very well have intrinsic, self-rewarding qualities, and that these are easily appealed to, and the emotions associated with them easily aroused. Of course, there have to be "occasions" for war, but these should not be confused with "causes." In basically bellic societies, for example, the occasions were often highly conventional: more like "signals" for warfare than causes. Often they were simply seasonal.

Critics might immediately object that we still have to "explain" why some societies are bellic and others not. Actually, the truth is better stated as "some societies are more bellic than others," in the sense of perpetually geared for war. But very few societies are totally ungeared for potential war, and those that are are usually very small and at the fringes — Pygmies, Eskimos, and the "Gentle Tasaday." Many who have been touted as nonbellic, such as the Pueblo Indians (whom I know first hand) and the Bushmen, in fact turn out to be, or to have been, formidable warriors when the occasion demanded it. The so-called "neutrals" — Sweden, Switzerland, Belgium, etc. (much touted by the war-is-dead crowd) — all maintain efficient and ever-ready armies. There is no question that there is variation in this, but there is constancy across the variation also. And while no one would question that by varying social circumstances — by cutting down on the occasions for war — one could perhaps affect the incidence of warfare, there is no evidence so far, from history or ethnography, that one can effectively eradicate it.

I would like to argue that such a view of warfare actually offers us more hope than the "war is dead because the causes have been eradicated" approach, which may well turn out to be dangerous in itself: just as dangerous as internationalism and isolationism were in their time. If the leaders of the antifascist world in the 1930s had had a more pessimistic view of human nature and its fatal attraction to the appeals of war, then perhaps they might have moved earlier and more decisively to squash the obvious signs of it because, unfortunately, it remains another simple but true generalization that one of the most effective ways to stop the use of force is by the threat of even greater force. Thus, the antibellic school has real problems with the obvious fact that the reason the major powers have not fought directly with each other over the last forty-five years is probably the existence of a nuclear deterrent. It is in fact the threat of the end of this very effective "antiwar" device that seems to have spurred the booming industry of hope in the "universal democracy" solution.

One of the most extensive war-is-dead statements recently came from John Mueller in his *Retreat from Doomsday: The Obsolescence of Major War* (New York: Basic Books, 1989). This trotted out all the usual arguments about war becoming a "peculiar institution," like dueling and slavery.

But what if war is not basically like dueling and slavery, any more than it is like feudalism or bear baiting or any other now obsolete institution? What if it is more like sex or religion? The question is not asked. But the end of religion was also much prophesied and has not happened, while no one trumpets the end of sex as yet — but wait. Not only is the question (i.e., Are dueling and slavery good analogies for war?) not asked, but the Buckle arguments from the mid-nineteenth century are revived with enthusiasm. Buckle noted the long period of relative peace from 1815 to 1862 and decided it heralded a new age (he refused to count the Crimean War). This, said Buckle, was because war was becoming repulsive to civilized people.

Buckle's conclusion came at about the same time as Spencer's, and the subsequent sanguinary march of history has not dampened enthusiasm for this kind of reasoning. Thus, the long period of relative peace (not counting wars by proxy) between the "major powers" — and especially the major democracies — over the past forty years is heralded as a sign as significant as it was to Buckle that war is dead between these enlightened national entities. But this is only if you discount war by proxy, as Buckle discounted colonial wars (they were not between "enlightened and civilized" nations). If you count war by proxy, then "hot" war has been going on more or less constantly over this period. The major powers have simply, in this view, found another, more Orwellian, way to fight each other, and what is more to draw, in the case of Korea, Afghanistan, and Vietnam, one of the players into direct warfare with the third-world country concerned, to the loss and embarrassment of the major power involved.

This will not matter now, the argument is pressed, because with the triumph of democracy and the end of history, even the Russians and Chinese will become democratic and behave nicely like their models in the West (who in the meantime have invaded Grenada and Panama, and fought Argentina over the Falkland Islands, and Libya over Chad). Would the fact that a few months after Mueller's book was published, a major world conflict involving more than thirty nations erupted into large-scale classical war in the Middle East, daunt the prophets of bellic obsolescence? One wonders. Are they going to "exempt" the Gulf War much as Buckle exempted the Crimean — because two of the parties (Russia and Turkey) were "barbaric" — so this doesn't spoil the theory that democracies don't fight each other? Presumably the Argentineans were equally barbaric? Who knows? The definitions are not all in. Germany was, after all, technically a democracy in 1914 — it had an elected parliament; but this too doesn't count, it seems, because it was not democratic "in foreign affairs," which were controlled by the army and the Kaiser. This gets hard to pin down after a while, and wishing so easily becomes wishful thinking, which in turn becomes a refusal to admit the possibility that the basic premise may be just plain wrong.

War and the Older Professions

We have already hinted that the "disease" model of war — in which it is something aberrant that can be eradicated with the proper therapeutic measures — is what is at fault. This is the "epidemiological" attitude optimists and progressives love to take toward all persistent social conditions they dislike and want rid of: divorce, teenage pregnancy, terrorism, illiteracy, rape, juvenile gangs, drugs, domestic violence, poverty, driving deaths, sexual and social inequalities, prejudice, etc., etc. We have already seen that Mueller uses as his prime analogies dueling and slavery, and we have already questioned that analogy. What if war is more like religion or sex? Sex is too general, since war is organized and institutionalized, so let us say like religion or prostitution. These vie for the claim of the oldest profession, and both have been pronounced obsolescent by enthusiastic rationalists and reformers. (We might add in parentheses — as we seem to add so many things in parentheses [because we don't like footnotes] — that the constant in prostitution is not money, which is a recent invention, but the need of many males to have sex without complications or consequences. The two favored methods, where "free sex" is not practiced, are the giving of gifts [payment] and rape. The latter may even be having its own kind of revival if the current publicity is to be believed.)

Let us take the "end of religion" analogy. Religion, the rationalists claimed, boosted by Sir James Frazer's "inevitable" evolutionary sequence from magic through religion to science, would wither away once scientific explanations were available to substitute for superstition. Similarly, with the advent of "free love" (as we used so optimistically to call it), the need for prostitution would disappear, and so would the institution. But as we have seen, both institutions, despite the advent of advanced science and casual sex, remain and flourish and even seem to be staging worldwide comebacks. We are forced to ask ourselves whether the "disease" premise was not false to start with: whether religion is not just "wrong explanation" and prostitution not just an outlet for frustrated puritan males. Hard as it is for rationalists to face, they have to consider whether or not both institutions answer needs that have nothing to do with explanation and frustration; needs which are just as real as the need for rational explanation or easy sex, but basically different from both.

One approach to this problem of the constant elements in war has been to link war to human aggression, and to suggest that wars are in some way a direct outcome of the more basic aggressive "instincts." There is no question that aggression is related to war, just as sex is related to prostitution or mysticism to religion, but neither *institutional* form follows directly from the basic instinctive drive. Much ink has been spilled by the forces of good (see chap. 7) to refute the thesis that "aggression causes war" and the like. And indeed, such a straw man is not hard to huff and puff down. Even the most primitive of wars is a complicated, orchestrated, highly organized act of human imagination and intelligence, of which aggression is a necessary component but often not even the most important one. By the time we get to the large-scale wars of history, the aggressive component is even more reduced, and the logistical factors by far dominate the violent.

Let us put it this way: To run a war successfully, the leaders must tap the aggression of the populace for support of the war and of the fighters for battle purposes. But battles are often spasmodic and episodic parts of the total war, and modern technological war with its distancing of attackers and attacked can often bypass the need even to tap aggression for many of its operations. We might even paradoxically claim that war is "safer" the closer it stays to basic aggression, since aggression seems to have its own inbuilt inhibitions and ritualizations (which readily translate into formalized fighting of one kind or another, from single combat to counting coup), while the cold imaginations of the technowarriors have none. They must depend, as Clausewitz insisted, on "reason," — and this is a far more terrifying prospect than depending on instinct, which takes care of itself pretty well (see chaps. 5 and 6).

But if the constant of war is not aggression (and if it might even be better if it were), then where does its "religious" appeal lie? What is it that makes it so easy to start wars, so easy to make whole populations support them with enthusiasm, and sustain them with courage and sacrifice unknown in peacetime? We all know that William James found this paradox to be at the heart of the issue in his appeal for the "moral equivalent of war." It is a paradox (if it is a paradox) that we have never solved: that while war brings out the worst in us it also brings out the best. (The same might be said of religion, and the more we look at it the more alike they do in fact appear to be.)

I recently bought a second-hand copy of a sad little book, with no specific date but probably brought out in 1944, called *Prefaces to Peace* and containing the collected peace-wisdom of Wendell Wilkie ("One World"), Herbert Hoover and Hugh Gibson ("Lasting Peace"), Henry Wallace ("Free World Victory"), and Sumner Welles ("Blue-print for Peace"). Every peroration — following on the usual list of one standard eirenicon after another — stressed the same thing: that, in the words of Welles, peace could only be obtained and sustained "by sacrifice, by courage, by resolution, and by vision": all the qualities called up with ease in war and almost impossible to maintain in peacetime — especially "the vision thing." Even solemn declarations of "wars" on poverty, or "wars" on drugs, or "wars" on illiteracy, have little effect. People are not fooled: they know a war when they see one, and these are not wars within the meaning of the act. Within a few months again of the publication of this particular call for the end of war, the atom bombs were dropped and the cold war started up to grow hot in Korea, Vietnam, Afghanistan, etc. Six million were to die in wars of partition between India and Pakistan; a million in Nigeria; 2 million in Cambodia — and so it was to go. And the paradox continues that the slaughter in India was the direct outcome of Ghandi's attempt to put "sacrifice, courage, resolution, and vision" into the service of "nonviolent resistance" and avowed pacifism.

Imagination, Symbols, and Intelligence

If the religious analogy is the better one, it may give us some clues. After all, wars and religion have been inextricably intertwined since the beginning. Religion (using a broad definition that would include such apocalyptic or "visionary" doctrines as Marxism and Imperialism) seems to tap some basic need for a wholistic and satisfying view of life in which the individual, otherwise alone and doubtful, becomes integrated into a "church" and filled with certainty. Humans, unlike animals who, with the interesting exception of our closest relatives the chimpanzees, do not seem to fight wars as we understand them, are endowed (blessed/cursed) with imagination and symbolic intelligence.

The roots of war, like those of religion and prostitution, lie in these essentially human attributes, not in aggression per se. Of course, if we were not aggressive by nature then the issue would not arise, but there are many outlets for aggression at a level lower than organized warfare, and these suffice in some very small-scale societies. What war does is to tap the aggressive tendencies, and, using them in conjunction with some others equally basic, orchestrate, with the use of symbols, imagination, and intelligence, a sustained effort of "sacrifice, courage, resolution, and vision." The depth psychologists have their own elaborate versions of what these "other" attributes are, but we need only take a common-sense view here. The main one is obviously the need for an "enemy." This is so obvious it is often overlooked. Our lives do not always go very well and someone has to take the blame, from the primitive scapegoat up to the international conspirators or the yellow peril or whatever. One of the easiest motives to tap is the motive of blame, and one of the easiest solutions to propose is the removal of its object. The number of "causes" of blame is limitless, like the "causes" of war; but what is constant is the need for a blamee.

What does the enemy threaten? Not necessarily even persons and property. The enemy threatens the ideas that we live by. These ideas (our "religions" in the broadest sense) encompass persons and property in that they define our notions of such. Even primitive warfare, which seems perhaps least ideological, is still so at base. The enemy tribe threatens the things that we deem "sacred" — which, in the primitive world no less than our own, includes our "way of life," which is demonstrably different from theirs. Our gods are different. The occasions for each particular war will differ perhaps. But ultimately "we" fight "them" because they are different, and their difference is threatening in its challenge to the validity of the ideas we live by. Thus, all wars are ideological wars. This is why they bring out the necessary element of fanaticism (and why religion plays so large a part in them). It is fanaticism that sustains "sacrifice, courage, resolution, and vision." Since we are an animal that lives primarily by ideas and only secondarily by instincts (or put another way, since it is instinctive in us to live by ideas), we react fanatically when our basic ideas — those that decide our identities individual and collective — are threatened. And a combination of basic paranoia and xenophobia ensures that we will constantly feel such a threat. Extreme fear of the very different stranger is rooted indeed in our animal heritage as much as aggression is, and the combination of these with ideological fanaticism — our human contribution — ensures a constant basis for the appeal of war.

But the sceptical will ask, why war? There are other ways to attack the ideological enemy. Indeed there are, and we will pray for his destruction and invoke sorcery against him and try to best him in commerce. But we have to call the latter a "trade war" to get any steam into it. And the sad fact is that none of these suffice for us. However "civilized" our string of responses, at some point the only satisfaction is the physical defeat of the enemy. We can get by on analogies just so far, but there seems to be no diminution of the need to obliterate the threat physically when it gets too serious. We all know in our own lives how often we have wiped some infuriating obstacle off the face of the earth in our imaginations. Governments get to do this in reality with the infuriating other, while taking a dim view of the citizenry adopting the same tack on a personal level. We mere citizens (now that dueling is obsolete) have to be content with vicarious satisfactions derived from violent entertainment, and the occasional chance to join in a collective expedition with government and usually official religious sanction.

The apostles of peace will protest that I am generalizing from my own nasty motives, and that they and their friends are free from such base thoughts and feelings. People do oppose wars, they will say. I don't need to be told this; I opposed the Vietnam War myself (though not from the same high moral principles as the majority of opponents: I simply thought it was a pointless war, and unwinnable as conducted). But I saw the vociferous opponents in their serried ranks spitting hatred and screaming defiance at the perpetrators of hatred and defiance. The "antiwar" religion becomes itself a set of ideas to be prosecuted and protected with often more fanatical vehemence than that shown by the warmongers themselves. The moral equivalent of war is the antiwar movement because, in effect, it is the same thing. (I was always impressed by the exact equivalence in intonation and stress, with the accompaniment of the same raised-arm threat gesture, between "Nixon OUT! Nixon OUT!" and "Sieg HEIL! Sieg HEIL!") And to those who oppose war from the comfort of their studies, let me say that fanaticism can be a quiet and composed type; it does not have to foam at the mouth. The civilized opposition had as much in common psychologically with the calm, calculated decision making of the war leaders, as the screaming opposition did with the most vociferous hawks. Fanaticism can have an icy heart.

Of course, the mob is fickle, and if wars do not go their way (as with the Boer War — or for that matter the American Revolutionary War — in England) then there will be growing opposition. But there is rarely very effective opposition to a successful war. The Gulf War did indeed, at least initially, kick the Vietnam syndrome. Eighty percent or more of the tax-paying populace were solidly behind it at the beginning, and since, unlike Vietnam, it was (relatively) short and (relatively) successful, the support did not waver. It does not need all of the people all of the time; just most of them some of the time will do.

Again the objection will come: Even if you are right, what if we reduce all the possible "occasions" for war. Won't this reduce war itself? I would like to think so, but I fear that as long as the basics are there — that is, as long as we are human — the occasions will be sought out or even invented (Orwell's insight again). There will always be, for example, the problem of what to do with millions of testosterone-infected, young, rambunctious unemployed males. The solution in the past for the older males threatened by them (an inevitable result of our long evolution as a species with competitive sexual reproduction) was to ship them off to fight their counterparts threatening older males in other countries. They are not growing any less numerous or any less dangerous, the yuppie phenomenon notwithstanding.

The Democracy Argument and the End of History

But let us take up again, in this context, the "end of history" argument (not because it is particularly good but because it is currently chic). Since "liberal democracy" has triumphed, and all that the world can now look forward to is more of the same, and since democracies don't fight each other the way lesser social systems do, then war is probably over (although it may take a bit of time to sort this out — either a few generations or a few centuries, depending on the version). Note how this regards war as a contingency "caused" by conflicting types of social systems, the eradication of which will eradicate war itself (precisely the thesis we have been at pains to refute).

Truly, if people everywhere were indeed exactly the same then there could be no perceived differences for the paranoia and xenophobia to work on. But the "sameness" is not something that universal "liberal democracy" — should that even happen — could produce. Races and religions and customs and laws ("nationalism" is a phase in the history of these) will still differ. In short, ideological differences will remain, however alike the market economies/democracies may become. And the "end of history" thesis wildly exaggerates how alike such economies/polities are. There are, in fact, only superficial likenesses between, say, Japan and Sweden, or Britain and the United States. (Americans, so anxious to export their own version of democracy, do not always appreciate how alien and peculiar, not to say corrupt and unrepresentative, it seems to those from other democratic societies.)

The existence of universal suffrage and stock exchanges only scratches the surface, as recent run-ins with Japan have shown us, to our distress. True, we have not gone to war with Japan again, yet, but don't forget all those prophecies about how free trade, through "interdependency" would make war impossible "in the long run." It was precisely free trade and specialization that led us to abandon our own oil fields and depend on the cheap stuff from the Middle East. And we see where that got us in the "death of war" game. Economic and political similarities do not wipe out perceived threatening differences: they may even exaggerate them as we come to hate those who have stolen our clothes while we were bathing and now look better dressed than ourselves.

The Hegelian "end of history" thesis, with its view of man as a "product of his concrete historical and social environment," is deliberately opposed by

Francis Fukuyama to "earlier natural-right theorists" who would have man "a collection of more or less fixed 'natural' attributes" ("The End of History?" *The National Interest* 16 [Summer 1989]). Clearly, my thesis has more in common with these "earlier" — and, by implication, cruder, less "modern" — theories than it has with either Hegelian historical determinism, or, as Fukuyama rightly sees, the subsequent radical relativism that emerges when the historical process is stripped of its driving force of "progress." Indeed, I have spent a lot of time and effort defending just such a position (as in, for example, *The Search for Society*). And this is because any thesis such as Hegel's or any derivative version (or any of the so-called philosophies of history) are based on a fatal error: They take the historical process itself entirely for granted and treat it as totally self-contained.

Fukuyama wonders if periods of history might simply be "blips" on the total scale, but he never stops to consider that what we choose to call "history" is only a blip on the total scale of man's "concrete historical and social environment." For that environment stretches back at least three and half and possibly up to five million years. To ignore this huge stretch of human history and to privilege a mere few thousand years of good weather in a particularly mild interglacial (now coming to its close, by the way) is to make an arbitrary cut-off as to where "history" begins — as well as where it ends.

Looked at in the context of the whole (and even this whole is part of 72 million years of primate history and 128 million years of mammalian history), the "historical" period can be viewed not as the progressive manifestation of increasing rationality (or whatever) but rather as a series of wilder and wilder swings away from an Upper Paleolithic norm (see chap. 5). The Upper Paleolithic was when we, as a species, had reached the top of the food chain and were in a sound balance with our environment. We hunted successfully, perfected beautiful weapons (we're still doing that), practiced elaborate religions, and created spectacular magical artworks; there were probably about a million and a half of us. We now face a world with a projected population of 10 billion in the year 2000, with a good deal of our environment irretrievably destroyed, and with a state of complexity running beyond our capacity to handle. And we face it, as one of my psychology colleagues put it, with the emotional equipment of a jungle rat (see chap. 14). Actually, it is worse. We face it with the added imaginative and intellectual equipment of a terrestrial primate, evolved, among other things, to be especially sensitive to differences, and warlike about dealing with them. The jungle rat has a better chance of survival, if we leave it any jungle to survive in.

"History" may well end. Indeed, I prophesied this myself about the same time as Fukuyama (*The Search for Society*, p. 216). But I doubt it will end as Fukuyama envisages; that is, because we shall invent happy liberal democracies where we shall live boring but peaceful lives in an increasingly homogeneous world. It will end because it has been an evolutionary aberration that has grown out of hand: too much for its inventors to handle. He allows that the huge problems of the third world (population gets short shrift) and "nationalism" might get in the way for a while until the benefits of liberal democracy wipe away all tears from their eyes. But what he does not realize is that behind the population explosion, and behind tribalism, neofundamentalism, and nationalism (see what was Yugoslavia, the USSR, etc.), lie those "more-or-less fixed natural attributes" that Hegelian historicism and neorelativism would ignore and that liberal democracy will not wish away. Hegel lived before Darwin, and for him there was some excuse (and his basic insight about the role of ideas is obviously right: that men will fight to defend ideas more than material interests is something we can agree on). But more than a hundred years after Darwin there is no excuse for ignoring 99.9 percent of human history and its living fossil record that is human nature.

Two Men at Jena

It has always seemed to me supremely ironic that the battle of Jena, where Napoleon defeated the Prussian monarchy in 1806, was a traumatic event for two great philosophers: Hegel and Clausewitz. Both were students of Kant, and both were at the battle. Hegel prudently watched at a safe distance and rejoiced as the forces of universalization and liberty triumphed and history came to an end. Clausewitz, in stark contrast, fought in the battle, and was wounded and captured. He came, perhaps not surprisingly, to an entirely different conclusion: that as long as we were human, war and history would continue in lockstep. He summed up his findings in the three volumes of *Vom Kriege* (On War) in 1832. We can only appeal to the subsequent two centuries to decide who was the greater prophet, and to watch in wonder as the neoeireneans start the latest wake.

Hear the incomparable Clausewitz:

War is ... a wonderful trinity, composed of the original violence of its elements, hatred and animosity, which may be looked upon as blind instinct; of the play of probabilities and chance, which make it a free activity of the soul; and of the subordinate nature of a political instrument, by which it belongs to the purity of reason.

The first of these three phases concerns more the people; the second, more the general and his army; and the third, more the government.

These three tendencies, which appear like so many different law-givers, are deeply rooted in the nature of the subject, and at the same time variable in degree. A theory which would leave any one of them out of account, or set up any arbitrary relations between them, would immediately become involved in such a contradiction with the reality, that it might be regarded as destroyed at once by that alone. (*On War*, I.i.28)

Thus, the United States fought the Gulf War, in the purity of governmental reason, to protect Western oil interests (other of the allies had other rational interests of their own — the liberation of Kuwait per se not being high on anyone's list despite the lip service paid to this noble goal). It was executed as a free activity of the soul by the generals and the armies. But the people were sustained in it by the blind instincts of hatred and animosity toward a rapidly dehumanized enemy whose uncompromising alienness threatened not only their pocketbooks but their image of the good. The same went in double measure for the other side: reason, chance, and instinct in inseparable interaction. Clausewitz had them pegged in the 1830s, and they remain as stubbornly evident today.

The interaction of these "basic attributes of human nature," not the dialectical evolution of Spirit toward Absolute Freedom, was reality for Clausewitz: reason, chance, and instinct would always interact to produce both "policy" in the first place, and its "continuation by other means" in the second. So to those who ask (as in Washington they inevitably do) if there are policy implications in this analysis, I can only answer in the most general terms: The meek may someday inherit the earth, but in the meantime be vigilant and keep up your guard.

If the general position outlined here be valid — and obviously there is not the space here to argue all the details — then wars are not a disease to be cured but part of the normal human condition. They stem from what we are, not from some contingencies of what we do from time to time ("history"). They are, like religion and prostitution, basic responses to basic human fears and hopes: in the case of war, fanaticism, xenophobia, paranoia, scapegoatism, and the vulnerability of ideology, as well as the positive appeals of battle so marvelously described by Glenn Gray in *The Warriors* (New York: Harcourt Brace, 1959). But the paradox remains: so important is the defense of our ideas — our definitions of ourselves and our societies — that we will willingly strive to destroy their perceived enemies and exhibit the highest forms of human courage, compassion, comradeship, self-sacrifice, and even love in so doing. And who is to say that we are wrong? What is most worth dying for: material interests or diacritical ideas? It is ideas that make us human after all.

Part Three

Ethnology

Introduction to Part Three

"Ethnology" is used here in its wide sense of "general anthropology" — usually as opposed to "ethnography," meaning the detailed descriptions of particular peoples. As used in the subtitle to *The Keresan Bridge* — "A Problem in Pueblo Ethnology" — it meant more specifically "historical or developmental anthropology": the old British usage. The first essay serves two purposes: to make a general point about social rules (that they are often more like rules of a game than rules of law, and that the rules for breaking the rules are as important as the rules themselves), and secondly to add to the information on Tory Island contained in *Encounter with Anthropology* for those who don't want to plough through the detailed analysis in *The Tory Islanders*. (I really shouldn't make it easy for them since I still think this is the best thing I ever did and that they are missing a lot by not tackling it. Anyway, there is some fun stuff in there among the details.)

The second essay was written for a symposium to celebrate the centenary of Sir James Frazer's *The Golden Bough*. This has not yet materialized for the usual reason that chapters were promised but not produced, forcing the editor (H. Philsooph) to delay — and perhaps even abandon. This is a pity since, as readers of *Encounter with Anthropology* will remember, I feel deeply about Frazer, and this includes celebrating the book that so profoundly influenced intellectual life beyond the boundaries of anthropology well into the twentieth century. Readers can pick up some of my "lost" intellectual autobiography here too, particularly the love-hate affair with the classics described in part 2 of *Reproduction and Succession,* where Greek got its turn in the essay on Antigone and tragedy. I was never a very good student of the classics since I wouldn't put in the effort. But I do have a lingering fondness, and as we hit our late fifties, for reasons I think I understand, we suddenly find these adolescent doings of curious importance, and we make films like *American Graffiti* or *Diner* or *Amarcord* or *Hope and Glory* or *Au Revoir les Enfants,* or we look to the roots of our later obsessions which have, until now, forced the fertile memories underground. We did indeed "put away childish things" — but at some point we have to go back and find them again, or we may not make it comfortably through old age.

The third essay delves into an issue that has continued to fascinate me: the Paleolithic-Neolithic transition; the great breakthrough that started the pendulum swinging with the disastrous results we looked at in chapter 5. How and why did this happen? The verdict is still out, but at least we can ask: what had to happen? And one answer is a growth in social complexity. It was this question that a Leakey Foundation symposium at Rutgers in 1991 sought to answer. Their invitation to me to give the opening address gave me a chance to ruminate on this issue through two of my favorite archaeological peoples: the Anasazi Indians of Chaco Canyon in New Mexico, and the Calusa Kingdom of Southwest Florida on which I have been working for the past few years.

I had looked at the Anasazi for purposes of my Ph.D. dissertation (see *The Keresan Bridge*), but although I had maintained an interest, I had not published anything since, and this was an area neglected in *Encounter with Anthropology.* During my Ph.D. defense (1964), Daryll Forde asked me how we might relate, in general, social anthropology and archaeology. I fear I gave him a very bumbling reply, which he and the other examiners (Raymond Firth and Edmund Leach) generously overlooked. This is a small attempt to make amends, with a promise of more to come. I happen to think that if anthropology is to have any kind of unity and discipline in the future, this will probably have to come from archaeology. Daryll Forde would have been startled by such a reply in 1964 (and indeed I would never have dreamed of giving it), but a lot of spaghetti has twirled round the forks since then, and we cannot be as complacent about a future for social anthropology as we were in those golden days when we were the aristocrats of the social sciences, and when we could only condescendingly think in terms of helping out the other theoretically poverty-stricken disciplines — a little.

9

Principles and Pragmatics on Tory Island

I wish to set forward here in a somewhat schematic way some of the major conclusions concerning the relation between rules and behavior, principle and practice, ideal and actual, that were buried in the ethnographic detail of *The Tory Islanders*. It is perhaps the true mark of human uniqueness that we make rules with avidity and then proceed to break them with no less enthusiasm. What is more, being rational animals, we even more enthusiastically rationalize the whole process with everything from lies and hypocrisy to diplomacy and social science. The Irish, for some reason, have acquired a reputation for being masters at the art of reconciling inconsistencies between principle and practice. It may be, however, that their interpreters, being English and therefore more practiced in the art of genteel hypocrisy than their subjects, do not recognize that the Irish simply have a greater sense of reality, and therefore resignation, about the inevitability of the discrepancy. "They all had beautiful eyes and I'm sure lied freely," said Sir Roger Casement about Irish prisoners of war in Germany — in a phrase strangely echoing the best of Wilde. For all his Irish sympathies, Casement was thoroughly English, and therefore preferred to live a lie rather than tell one. But let me offer one charming anecdote to illustrate what I mean.

We are in nineteenth-century Dublin under the benevolent tutelage of one of those well-meaning Secretaries for Ireland. Grants were being offered for industrial development to districts in the west; all they had to do was present

statistics to show that they had the labor, raw materials, agricultural base, etc.
A deputation appeared before the Secretary with a batch of statistics that were
truly impressive. Their area was the richest in all required resources, their
people were the most healthy and hard working, etc. The Secretary was
initially pleased but then a little puzzled. "Tell me, gentlemen," he said,
"were you not before me, in this office, at this time last year?"

"Indeed we were, your honor," replied the leader.

"And was that not the time we were giving grants to help the poorest and
most backward districts?"

"Ah well, your honor, if I recollect rightly, that was the case, to be sure."

"And did you not then present to me statistics to show that your land was
the poorest, your people the sickest, your resources the most wretched in the
whole of Ireland?"

"Well ... now your honor comes to mention it, we did indeed."

The Secretary looked askance. "How then," he asked indignantly, "do you
reconcile last year's statistics with those you have just presented?"

The leader of the delegation hesitated not one moment. "'Tis like this, your
honor," he replied. "Last year's statistics were gathered for a different
purpose entirely."

What must at first strike the non-Irish listener as typical fey Irishry is
really nothing of the kind. Think. An English — or, even more, a French —
deputation would have replied by weaving some long and more or less
plausible tale to justify the discrepancy. The Irish simply went straight to the
reality of the matter, and with blinding clarity. Indeed, among other things,
the story should be compulsory reading for all statisticians, those masters of
the mathematics of evasion. This should also be worth pondering: so
dependent are our lives on the manipulation of the truth that simple honesty
appears uproariously funny.

I don't mean to dwell on this. Deception, and above all self-deception, are
probably complexly evolved traits in a creature like ourselves selected for
high degrees of reciprocal altruism. Some profound questions are raised about
human nature by our tendency to be so firm in our announcements of general
principles and then so devious in our avoidance of them, and even more by
our verbose attempts to make sense of all this. Whether we are telling a white
lie to explain why we have not fulfilled an obligation, or analyzing the
difference between "overt" and "covert" culture, or "social structure" and
"social organization," we are engaged in that obsession with delusion that is
at the heart of humanity. Indeed, in this view, most of "culture" consists not
in "values of and for behavior," or any of those pompous anthropological
formulae, but in the fantasies we weave to explain away our inability to keep
even the simplest of our self-made rules, to say nothing of those handed down
from heaven.

It has for some time now been recognized that the legalistic framework in which social anthropology developed led to an overemphasis on the rule *per se* and a failure to look therefore at "behavior." This has been corrected to some extent, but has perhaps inevitably led to an overemphasis in the other direction: that rules are meaningless, and that there are "really" only statistical regularities. The truth is there are both, and there is a relation. Just because we break rules does not make it less important to have them. Comparing "what the natives think" with "what the natives do," or what they say should be done with what is actually done, is another honorable tradition in anthropology, and is on the right lines for the reasons only hinted at above: that it probes the essence of humanness. General rules serve a purpose for us that they do not serve for animals, which cannot make them. Paradoxically, one thing rules do is try to render potentially anarchic individual behavior, in creatures endowed with intelligence and the ability to calculate outcomes, more like the instinct-governed behavior of animals. "Social facts" must, as we all remember, be general in the population and exercise constraint on the individuals — like instincts. There is no instinct for uxorilocal residence, so we have to make a rule — which we then proceed to break if at all possible when it does not suit us. But even this is presumably better than saying "Live where you please and the devil take the hindmost." Of course, all rules or principles of behavior are not so stark, and sometimes the problem is finding out what the natives do indeed think. The best social constitutions — even the highly rational written ones — are riddled with ambiguities; this leaves most room for maneuver. Enough of generalities, which at this level cannot rise much above the cliché, and down to cases.

Cognition and Categories: The Genealogical Universe

The original principles on Tory Island are cognitive and categorical; that is, they deal with what people ought to know and how they ought to know it, particularly in the area of genealogy, kinship, and naming. The islanders who are expert in these things have quite articulate standards and principles about them. What I want to show throughout is how these structures of principle articulate the one with the other, and how, when divergences occur, they often occur because of well-understood subprinciples. These we can call "modifiers" of the main principles. My ultimate aim is to show the essential pragmatism of the modifiers, which is achieved by the exercise of what for want of a better term we can call "strategies." Of course, I am not implying that there are never outright contradictions between theory and practice or that no one is ever plain dishonest; only that the relationship is more complex and delicate in many cases.

The Tory Islanders comprise about three hundred Gaelic-speaking Roman

Catholics who live by a mixture of crofting, fishing, and subsidies nine miles from the mainland of Donegal. The island is relatively endogamous, and one of the first principles one encounters is that "everyone is related to everyone else." Since adopted children and those married in are counted as related, this turns out to be true in the sense that *some* connection by kinship or marriage can be traced between any two people on the island. However, *ad hoc* tracing of any kinds of kinship links, while it goes on among the "lay" people — and as we shall see is very important when it comes to the recruitment of boat crews — is not the aim of the island's sophisticated genealogists. In an island where everyone is kin to everyone else — and this is not peculiar to Tory — it is degrees of kinship that count in deciding who is "close" or "far out"; and different kinds of degrees count for different purposes. (I am avoiding the use of Gaelic for its own sake here and using approximate English translations.) One of the primary concerns of the genealogists is with descent. If they have to express a concern at all it is something like: "Everyone should be traceable to an ancestor at least four generations back from the oldest living relative," which in all practicality means, "Every child on the island should be traceable to an ancestor seven generations back." These are pretty close to the statements actually made. Usually they are formed as proverbs or proverb-like statements; thus, "for the souls of the seven generations before you" is a blessing that takes account of what Father Dineen in his dictionary describes as a "measurable ancestral period."

Ideally, that is. In fact, the way the Tory genealogists remember ancestry is to some extent the inverse of this. In a particular case they will link an islander with a remote ancestor by running through the personal names of his forebears in a stereotyped fashion. I will deal with this when I come to names, but even it operates according to the principles of genealogy I am going to elucidate.

In theory, then, one should know all one's ancestors for four to seven generations back. No one, not even the genealogists, in fact, knows this for anyone. What they know are the exact links for varying generations of every islander to a select group of focal ancestors who lived in the latter half of the eighteenth century. Further back than that they know the degree of relationship between some of these ancestors without always knowing the exact link. The "lay" islanders will also usually be able to say within what degree they are related to someone else, and we shall examine this also, but if you first ask an islander who his "people" are, he will usually tell you that he is, literally, "of the progenies of X, Y and Z," or something such. (I translate the word as "progenies" for reasons that will be explained.) Even lay islanders who have little or no knowledge of actual genealogy will be able to state something of this kind and also tell you how progeny X is related to Y and others. This they will do in degrees of "grandchildship." Their "people" (*muintir*) are those who are *Clann agus Ua*. Now it is *clann* that I have translated as "progeny." The whole phrase can be rendered as "children and grandchildren." (*Ua* is the familiar Irish surname prefix O — thus spelled when used alone as a noun.) It really "means," however, something more like "all those who are members of the same progenies as myself."

These progenies, or stocks — rendered in Gaelic by the word *clann* — are the descendants through links of either sex of an identifiable ancestor. But not just any ancestor. Certain ancestors are recognized as the starting point of a *clann*, and all the descendants of the ancestor will be (for example, if the ancestor was called Eoin [Iain]) *clann Eoin*: the progeny of Eoin. (The name will always be in the genitive, which in the case cited does not change. Had the ancestor been Séamus [Shamus or James], then the name would have been rendered *clann Shéamuis* — "clan Hamish.") Sometimes "branches" of these groups will be separated out for recognition. If, for example, Eoin had two children, Anton and Caitlín, then people might identify themselves as either *clann Anton-Eoin* or *clann Caitlín-Eoin*. The deeper the genealogy — that is, the more remote the ancestor — the more likely that these subidentifications will be used.

In principle then, each islander should be able to trace all his ancestors on the ideal (virtually genetic) pattern as in diagram 9.1.

Great-grandparents	H I		J K		L M		N O
Grandparents	D		E		F		G
Parents		B				C	
Ego				A			

Diagram 9.1

This should go on upwards for as many as seven generations. In effect, the whole tracing of ancestry is done in reverse. A remote ancestor is named, and *all* his or her descendants are then recited. I stress recited, for this is almost a formal recitation; the better genealogists aim to get it "right" the first time by naming all the descendants of the ancestor chosen. In the example I gave earlier (chosen from a real case), Eoin would be picked as the starting point, then his two children Anton and Caitlín would be given, then the children of Anton recited until they were exhausted, then those of Caitlín. This is an oversimplification, and the larger and deeper the genealogy — and the largest did span seven generations — the more it would be split up for recitation purposes, and there were various methods of doing this. But the end result would be that all the descendants would be given.

Now, one thing is immediately obvious: these groups of descendants, these "clann" (or, to give the proper Gaelic plural, *clanna*), would be bound to overlap, and indeed they did. Here the genealogists introduced a remarkable piece of economy. They established four major genealogies which were always given in full, overlaps and all. These were the *clann Neilí*, the *clann Eoin*, the *clann Shéamuis,* and the *clann Fheilimí* (Phelim or Philip). Fourteen other ancestors were recognized, but as their genealogies were recited they were endlessly "referred" to the four major ones where they overlapped with them. Thus we might start with the ancestor Paddy (*Paidí*) and recite so far down his line to the point at which one of his descendants marries a member of *clann Eoin*. The genealogist would then refer the listener to that genealogy for the rest of the group. Within the four major genealogies, which accounted for 70 percent of the islanders, five other ancestors were regarded as important enough to count as "independent" ancestors, and a total of twenty-three ultimate ancestors was usually agreed on. The aim of the best genealogists was to complete a tally of the island in which everyone was linked to one of these. This was generally realized. The basic principle of the genealogists, then, could be stated as, "Everyone should be traceable to one of the twenty-three ancestors."

In giving the genealogies (and it should be stressed that despite some literacy in Gaelic this was a purely oral exercise), spouses of descendants would be given on request, but this was, at first glance, a haphazard affair since some spouses of more remote ancestors were remembered and some not; others were disputed. In case of dispute the formula was often that "she came from outside," which neatly disposed of the matter, since there was no cause to remember her. The ones most firmly remembered were those that "linked" various genealogies. Thus, when reciting the offspring of Paddy as above, a descendant would be reached who married a member of, say, *clann Eoin*, and the spouse would be stated with the information, "you have the rest under *clann Eoin*." As we shall see later, this selective remembering has a lot to do with whether or not the spouse in question came from a group with land, for reasons we shall also explore.

We should pause on an anthropological note here to state the obvious fact that what we are dealing with are bilateral or cognatic descent groups: groups of kin tracing descent through both sexes from a fixed ancestor. We have become familiar with these over the last few decades and have stopped regarding them as inferior forms of unilineal descent. But this was not before the profession had appropriated the word "clan" to mean exclusively unilineal descent groups (apart from those who erroneously use "sib"). This is embarrassing for the anthropologists of Gaelic culture, who can claim to be the only ones using the term correctly — but for *non*unilineal descent groups! There is no help for it. I have adopted the compromise of always spelling it with two final consonants even in English to establish the difference. Thus, "clan" = unilineal descent group; "clann" = nonunilineal descent group in

Celtic cultures. Even this is not clear, since it has acquired a different meaning in Scots Gaelic for some purposes. The Highland "clan" was in fact more of a *fine* or tribe, but the principle of cognatic descent was maintained in the claim to membership of the mother's clan and the use of the matronymic. Again this stresses that the cognatic principle results in overlapping and that people can therefore be members of several such descent groups automatically. Theoretically this is as many groups as they have ancestors, but in fact it works out to be, even theoretically, as many groups as they had ancestors who were members of such groups. If only certain ancestors are recognized as having started such groups, then one can only trace back to those, and other ancestors are irrelevant.

In fact Tory islanders never even try to trace "upwards." They might if asked (the genealogists, that is), and if so would use the personal name system we are going to look at. But it was to them a meaningless exercise; that is, the attempt to list a complete set of ancestors for each generation as in figure 9.1. Ideally one should know them, but in fact all genealogical thinking was "downwards" from the ancestor, and all the layman needed to know was to which *clanna* he belonged, and how they were related by degrees to the others.

Degrees of Relationship: The Naming of Names

Let us pass on to this notion of degrees of relationship, since on Tory it too is framed in descent terms. This method was once perhaps more widespread, at least in Donegal and other parts of the northwest, but Arensberg and Kimball did not find it in County Clare, for example. There the reckoning was the traditional one of degrees of kinship distance from ego in terms of *col*: literally degrees of "forbiddenness." These correspond to the church's degrees of consanguinity. On Tory, reckoning of kinship is done by reference to an ancestor — exactly as with genealogy.

The children of two siblings, for example, who would be first cousins on our reckoning, on Tory are literally "grandchildren only," and their children will be to each other *da ua* — second grandchildren. It would be easy to say "and so on," except that on Tory "third grandchildren" are *fionn ua* — fair grandchildren — and "fourth grandchildren" are *dubh ua* — dark grandchildren. The numbering system picks up again with fifth grandchildren. Exact degrees of relationship are stated descriptively. Thus, two people may be *fionn ua*, but the relationship will be explained as "my father's father and his mother's mother were the children of brother and sister." More interestingly, whole "branches" of the cognatic lineages — the *clanna* — would refer to each other this way according to the degree of relationship of the founding ancestors.

While the reckoning is in terms of the degree of distance both parties have to the ancestor, the description of the relationship is always given as above: in terms of the ultimate sibling pair. "My mother and her father were the children of two brothers" is the correct — and as far as I could tell the only — way to state exact degrees. Beyond fifth cousinship, except in rare cases of detailed genealogical knowledge, the exact links were not given, simply the degree of "grandchildship" and the information that it was "far out." Often, however, islanders felt it enough to state a clann affiliation and leave it at that: they were *fionn ua* and *clann Eoin*, for example.

Thus the reckoning of descent and the reckoning of kinship completely parallel each other. In each case what is theoretically possible cannot be realized, but if we accept as first principles the actual practices of the genealogists, then the two articulate perfectly: both genealogical reckoning and the reckoning of degrees of kinship are done with reference to commonality of descent from an ancestor. Let us look at the naming system to see where it fits in.

Kinship terms are not much used on Tory, which is initially baffling to an anthropologist, who likes reality to imitate his art as much as anyone else. Personal names are used, but in a very special way. Every person will have an everyday name used for talking to or about him which consists of his given name plus the name of either his mother or his father and including perhaps an epithet (big, fair, wee, etc.). Sometimes he takes only the given name of one parent, but, since the parent is also sometimes known by *his* parent's name, a person very often ends up with three names strung together. This can be extended, but five is the longest I came across; three is quite common.

Since in Gaelic these names can be quite unpronounceable to the outsider, I will use English names in the examples here. English names are in fact used freely and mixed with the Gaelic, although they are often Gaelicised. We might take, as a simple example of the kind of name anyone would encounter, "Willie-Hannah-Tom." Thus, Willie's mother was usually known as "Hannah-Tom," and he picked up both names, making up his own. He might have been "Willie-Paddy Mór" after his father, "Big Paddy" — and indeed there might be the odd reference to him as such from time to time.

My attention was drawn to the extensions of this system when I questioned the genealogists about the ultimate relationship of certain people, and they would run through "strings" of names until they found one in common. Thus, to take our example (fictional but close to a real case), we might want to know the relationship between Willie-Hannah-Tom and Kitty-Mary-William. They assert they have one: what is it? Well, they are both, say, clann Rory. The genealogist would recite "Willie-Hannah-Tom-Jimmy-Shamus-Rory" and "Kitty-Mary-William-Annie-Willie-Rory." Thus, the common ancestor was Rory; our pair are descendants of his two sons Shamus and Willie, and are therefore *dubh ua* — fourth grandchildren. To spell it all out I would be told, "His mother's father's father and her mother's father's mother were the children of two brothers."

Now, the interesting thing here is that neither Willie nor Kitty need have any idea of the way their names can be extended back like this. These are not the names that are ever used, except in some very rare cases. At most, the ordinary islander is aware, sometimes, that it is important to know one's "name" on both father's and mother's side, but even this will be usually limited to two or three names in the string. And, of course, it will almost never include all the possibilities, even for the genealogists. If we go back to diagram 9.1 we can see that it can stand for names. Ideally, everyone has as many strings of names as he has ancestors in any generation: two in the parental, four in the grandparental, eight in the great-grandparental, etc.

The genealogists will admit that in an ideal universe this should be so, but "the names get lost." What they mean by this is that, from all the theoretical strings of names a person might have, he will only in fact have a few of these "activated" on his behalf for the simple reason that at some point an ancestral link is missing; the names "freeze" at that point. At what point? If, again, we turn the system on its head and stop thinking about working "up" from ego but look at it "down" from the ancestor, what we find fits exactly the scheme of genealogical reckoning. What the strings of names converge on are of course the focal ancestors, the founders of the *clanna*. Thus, no one — not even the genealogist — remembers all the possibilities, but only those which might link a person to one of the focal ancestors. Thus, in tracing "upwards," certain lines will fade rapidly because they do not lead to one of the eighteen. Some people will have only one significant string because they have only one significant clann connection — their father could have married in, for example, from the mainland, or he could have been the last member of a dying group.

Even in cases where the potential was there, it was often realized only with difficulty because there was "no use" in remembering names to no purpose. In the cases where a focal ancestor was involved, the names came trippingly off the tongue, and thus constituted a mode of checking genealogical accuracy. If a link was disputed, then the names could be recited to double-check genealogical memory. It makes more sense, then, if we see the names as "descending" along "clann" lines. It is curiously like the naming of goats. Thus we get Redfern's Tommy's Billy — and since each name following the original in Gaelic would be in the genitive, the Tory names mean much the same thing, except that the order is reversed: "Willie of Hannah of Tom," etc. Naming after ancestors is not uncommon, of course, but usually it is — in most patriarchal traditions, anyway — only the males who are so named over many generations to establish their lineages. On Tory the cognatic principle reigns supreme and is beautifully brought out in the naming system: the names freely cross sex boundaries as they converge toward the ultimate ancestor.

What is a name? I am referring to two kinds of name: the everyday name and the "genealogical" name. Of the former, the islander has one that is enough to distinguish him from all others. It may be a simple William Rua — red William — or, after his father, William-Rory. But to a genealogist he may have three or four "names" which fix his place in the kinship system, or more particularly in the system of descent from recognized ancestors. Let us phrase the genealogist's subprinciple like this, then: "Everyone should be able to trace his name to one of the ancestors" (old ones, meaning the eighteen mentioned). A corollary: "Any people who claim an ancestor in common should find their names converge on that ancestor." If, in the jargon, we take an "ancestor focus" and not an "ego focus," then the whole thing articulates beautifully. Names, pragmatically, converge only on the focal ancestors. It is now time to ask why this should be so and who these fabulous ancestors are (in fact they are very real). But let us first offer a substitute diagram for the "ego focus" table we have been using, to bring these points home and see how they articulate with inheritance.

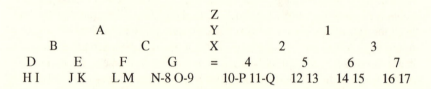

Diagram 9.2

Here, purely schematically, we have two groups I have represented by letters and numbers: a group descended from A, and a group descended from 1. I have had G from group A marry 4 from group 1. The children, with both numbers and letters, being the offspring of this union, belong to both groups. If they in turn have children, these will continue to belong to both groups. Putting names to this, the two descent groups are *clanna*; A and 1 are ultimate ancestors of each clann; and the numbers and letters represent persons of either sex. As for names, the children of the marriage could be, for everyday purposes, named after one or the other parent: N-G, O-4, P-4, Q-G. But, for genealogical purposes, 8(N) could be 8-4-2-1, but also remembered as 8-G-C-A if the need arose. If his grandparent 2 had married into an important clann — say person X with ancestors Y and Z, then 8(N) could also be known as 8-4-2-Y-Z. This would happen if Z were an important focal ancestor, and therefore it was worth 8's while to make the connection — or ask the genealogist to make it.

But why make it? Love of genealogy for its own sake is the preserve of the experts, of those whose skills lie in the old bardic tradition of tales, genealogies, cures, prayers, and the traditions and usages of the island. Getting it right is for them an end in itself. For the people at large this is not the issue. They know who their "people" are without all this paraphernalia: to acknowledge relationship, they only have to know that they are of the same clann. And indeed, for most of the time the knowledge is not put to much more use than gossiping. It becomes crucial, however, on certain occasions such as marriages, when degrees of relationship must be known, and even more importantly when the inheritance of real property is at stake. It is to this we must now turn, to see how it articulates with the principles just outlined.

Inheritance and the Land: Owning, Holding, and Claiming

The Tory principle for the inheritance of land, houses, etc. is very simple. In the first instance the immediate heirs of the present holder each have an equal entitlement. This is absolutely firmly stated and commonly agreed. No Land Acts, no reforming landlords, no bailiffs, no Congested Districts Boards or Land Commissions can shake this island tradition. In this as in all things they pay scant attention to the writ that runs on the mainland. The right of every child to "a place on the land" is sacred. It seems simple, but even a moment's thought would show that if carried to its logical conclusion it would be self-defeating if only because of infinite fragmentation. And indeed, in many parts of prefamine Ireland where "rundale" persisted, and many other parts of Europe where partible inheritance was the rule, subdivision resulted in "ruinous fragmentation," as the chroniclers lament. The peasant was trapped: with nothing to give his children but land he could not refuse them, but in dividing it up he rendered each piece eventually too small to support those on it.

But note that I have stated the principle of inheritance somewhat cautiously here, and indeed this is how the islanders state it. "In the first instance" they have an "equal entitlement." But in fact, when one looks at Tory land holdings over the last hundred years or more, although there has been subdivision, the size of the average holding remains fairly constant. Ideally, then, everyone is entitled to a share but not everyone gets a share. How, given the firmness of the principle, does Tory escape "ruinous fragmentation"?

We should first note that in being crofters, in living by a mixture of very small-scale farming and fishing, they escape the worst pressures of the land-locked peasant. There is always the sea and its harvest to be balanced against the land. If we add to this the lure (or necessity) of emigration, then we see that there are alternative sources of income to the land, and this obviously relieves pressure. But that is not the answer.

However else he might try to make a living, every islander values a stake in the land above anything else. There is a sureness to the land that other forms of income lack: if the worst comes to the worst, one can always grow some potatoes and tether a cow. So, while the alternative forms of earning relieve pressure on the actual *use* of land, they do nothing to relieve *claims* on the land. Thus, a subprinciple has to be stated here: "All the heirs of a landholder retain a claim to the land in perpetuity no matter who is actually using it." This is a basic clue to understanding much of the Tory obsession with genealogy. In principle one has a claim to any piece of land that belonged to any ancestor. But of course not all the ancestors owned land. So in fact one has a claim to the land of any landholding ancestor, and it is to these that the links are remembered. These, in fact, and in particular the major four, are the focal or ultimate ancestors that we have already discussed.

I have spoken here of land "holders" and only hesitantly of "owners." An islander (man or woman) is certainly seen as in a sense "owning" the one or two acres he holds in his lifetime. He can do as he pleases with it — except for one thing: he cannot alienate the land if someone else can lay a legitimate claim to it and if that person objects. Land that the "owners" would like to sell, for example, lies idle for years because some "cousin" in Australia or England has objected to the sale. In this sense, then, the current "owner" of any piece of land (as recorded, for example, for rating valuation purposes) can be seen as holding it in usufruct. He is one of the heirs of the original holder, and the land "came down to him" direct; but he does not have rights of ultimate disposal. Should he himself have immediate heirs, he has the right to pass the land to them. This has the effect of making the system look like one of individual ownership if it lasts over several generations: land passes direct from owner to heirs. But the test comes if the "owner" dies intestate (no pun intended), or if the immediate heirs do not want the land, or if he has no children. I say "intestate," but with one known exception the islanders do not make written wills. I mean here simply that the owner has not made any disposition of his land before dying — a publicly declared disposition, that is. In such a case his immediate heirs would have first claim, but it might be an occasion for others to press theirs.

Let us take the case of a man who held (I am now using "held" and "owned" synonymously) a piece of land and died without heirs, or without heirs who wished to press a claim (they had left the island, perhaps). Under these circumstances, in the old days, the king (an elected arbiter of land and shore disputes) would have been called upon to adjudicate. This office has now lapsed (although there are pretenders), but in any case the king would have called upon the genealogists. The question they would have had to settle was, "Who are the nearest legitimate claimants?" This would be settled by deciding on the provenance of the land in question: from whom had it "come down"? It would then "revert" to the descendants of that owner through the nearest link to the deceased. It can thus easily be seen that land stays with its *clann*, and within the branch of the clann to which it most nearly belongs.

If we go back to our diagram of the two descent groups, we can follow this easily. Say that of our married couple, G and 4, the land belonged to 4. Let us assume further that, rather than having the four children noted, they had died childless, or that the children had emigrated and were not interested. For purposes of assigning ownership, the question would then be, "Where did the land come from?" Had it come from 1, then it would have reverted in the first instance to the descendants of 5. But remember that we had assumed that 2 might have married X, with ancestor Y. It is possible that the land in question might have come from Y. In that case it would revert to clann Y — the descendants of Y, and firstly the children of X. Again this would give 5 and his children a claim, but one only equal to that of the other children of Y. If 5 had died childless or the children had left, then the land would revert wholly to the clann Y: the descendants of 3, for example, would have no claims at all. They would only have a claim on land coming from 1 himself.

Of course, people try to manipulate the situation to their own advantage, and one of the commonest ways is to claim that all the land of the present owners "came down" from one ancestor; that is, the ancestor of the claimant. Indeed, in an early version of this analysis that I presented, I gave a description of the devolution of the land of Eoin as it was given me by an informant of that clann. This showed all the land coming neatly from Eoin himself. Checking with other informants, and particularly with the land records at the Valuation Office, I discovered that only about one-third of the land now owned by clann Eoin came from the eponymous ancestor himself. This was corrected in the book (with one confusing graphical error in figure 9), but the interesting thing was that I am sure the informant in question knew full well what the "truth" was. It was, however, in his interest, in view of a pending reversion, to have the land all come from Eoin, and that is how he presented it. Since most of the old genealogists are dying off, this kind of thing can happen more frequently now, although it was not unknown in the past. Today, also, the islanders are more likely to resort to written wills, and in some cases to a blatant flouting of custom. They can do this because the custom, of course, runs counter to the law, which can always be invoked, although never without bad feeling. In any case, the land is falling into disuse, and disputes are not what they used to be.

What comes out from this, then, is the perfect articulation between the system of genealogical reckoning, the reckoning of relatedness, and the rules for the inheritance of land. It also all articulates with the naming system. In our example above, it was important to know that the children of 4 and 5 had names that ran back to X and Y; it was an important cross-check on the genealogy. It also shows why certain strings of names (those that converge on the apical ancestors) are remembered and not others. It all ties together.

As to "ownership," this has to be seen as "holding" a piece of land. The land itself is the center of a web of claims according to its original ownership, hence it is only "in the first instance" that the immediate heirs get preference, and it is not enough to say that in their absence "next of kin" get it. Nextness of kin is defined, as we have seen, according to the principles of cognatic descent from a fixed ancestor. You might well ask why these ancestors are fixed on, stemming as they do from the late eighteenth and early nineteenth centuries. It may be that oral memory can only go back so far, and this fixes the limit. Some of the older ancestors are already being forgotten, and it is their children — from about the 1830s and 1840s — who are being cited as "as far back as we go," with only dim memories that one clann is "*fionn ua*" to another, and so on. The Dineen principle of "seven generations — a measurable ancestral period" does indeed seem to set the outer limit, with five being more likely.

Now, what we have stated above suggests a quite close fit in the matter of land inheritance (including houses) between principle and practice. If we interpret in island terms the island assertion that "all children get the land," by understanding "get" as "are able to exercise first claim on a share of...," then it is accurate enough. If we ask further, "What if there are no children?" and are told, "Then it goes to those it came down to," and for this read, "To those who are descendants of the original holder in degree of closeness to the deceased," it is pretty accurate. But none of this solves our original question: If everyone gets a share, why is there not perpetual fragmentation? How is it that rather than a fairly random distribution of land — some long accumulation in some descent groups and dispersing in others — there is a fairly constant amount of land *per household* over time?

The Land of the Marriage

Here we must move to subprinciples, pragmatics, and strategies. The principles of inheritance are maintained through the doctrine that no one ever loses a *claim* to land that has "come down to" him. The pragmatics are that not everyone exercises the claim.

As a first step we should note that, if land is divided, it is usually on the marriage of one of the children. It is not otherwise usual to divide land during the owner's lifetime. He, or she, is expected to care for all unmarried children from the land, and they can expect a share on the parent's death. Marriage is relatively late on Tory, as in Ireland as a whole, although the range of "age at marriage" is wide: from twenty-two to forty-two; the average is around thirty-two. Usually, by this time, the complement of siblings is known, since the mother is past child-bearing years. Hence, some rational decisions can be taken about the dispensation of the patrimony. The principle which the islanders invoke to explain which of the marrying siblings should get the land, is stated as that of "the land of the marriage." If it has to be stated as a norm, it comes out something like "the land should go to the one most in need of it," the latter being defined usually as "the one who married somebody without land."

To put this in an example: If a man has, say, only one sister and he gets married to a woman who has three brothers, then he should "put land into the marriage" by asking his father for a share. It would be unfair to ask the girl's father to divide up his land when there are three brothers to take care of. On the other hand, if the situation were reversed, and the man came from a large family and the girl from a small one, then it would be proper for *her* parents to provide the land of the marriage. It is not just family size, but the relation of this to the amount of land each family owned, the marriageability of the other children, the availability of other sources of income, and various such factors that would determine the outcome.

There was no possibility of a mechanical application of a rule here. The principle (or at least subprinciple) was clear enough, but few cases were as clear-cut as the ones I have chosen for ease of exposition. There are no dowries on Tory (as was the case in many parts of "rundale" Ireland before the famine and the Land Acts) and the children were all provided "from the land." But all the debate, negotiation, bad feeling, double dealing, use of intermediaries, and intense fun that went into dowry negotiation elsewhere (and is enshrined in story, song, and ethnography) went on over the land of the marriage on Tory. Here strategy was at its height. But the matter had to be settled; the weight of island custom and the pressure of public opinion demanded it; a settlement was always reached.

Obviously there was no overall planning, and some families and households came out better than others in the short term. But by the very nature of the thing, in the long run, a balance was indeed achieved, and the uncannily constant ratio of households to landholding size was maintained (about one and a half to two acres). No household had less than one acre, and only a handful more than three. What happened to the children who did not get land? Some did not marry, others left, others worked as migrant laborers, others earned a living as fishermen. They never, of course, relinquished their claim on the land, and several "bachelor uncles" have come into land left by childless siblings or nephews, only to leave it in turn to perhaps more distantly related members of its clann of origin. I have not mentioned houses and bogland separately from arable land, since the same principles applied. But often compromises were made such that a daughter (or niece) got the house and a son or sons the land. The daughter had perhaps married a man with land and so they had both land and house, while the sons either married women with houses, or built houses on their land. Women ended up "owning" more of the houses than did the men as a result (which accounts for the high level of uxorilocal residence at marriage that we shall encounter later), while men tended to be recorded as owners of about 70 percent of the arable land and bog. (In the records, men are overwhelmingly recorded as "owners" of all real property, but this reflects the evaluators' notions, not the island customs. Land was often recorded as a man's, but on examination it turned out to have "come down to" his wife. If they were to die without children, for example, it would revert to her clann, not his.)

There is a lot more that could be said about land, but the aim has been to present a schematic outline of the principles and pragmatics, and this will suffice. A whole other essay is due on the relations of this system to all the other systems of partible inheritance in Europe, and in particular to the whole concept of "common ownership" in the village cluster as opposed to either the joint-family holding or the single-family estate based on unigeniture. But this is perhaps better left to the historians.

Boats and Crews: Strategic Networking

Let us now proceed to two other areas: boats and households. For the recruitment of crews to the large herring fishing boats — they were each in need of at least ten men — the islanders faced a dilemma. A principle of recruitment had to be devised that could not be the same as that of the clann. The latter unfolds slowly over time as generation succeeds unto generation, and therefore is perfectly adapted to tasks like the redistribution of land through inheritance. But the large boats which came into use at the end of the last century needed a crew each season (not out of season) and specific skills within the crew. The "ideal" thing would have been for the owner of the boat to recruit those islanders best suited for the tasks. For whatever reason, this was not exactly how it was done, and it was just as well. More successful owners would have monopolized skills to the disadvantage of the less entrepreneurial. As it was, the method of recruitment, odd as it might appear on the surface, probably achieved a fair distribution of various skills and strengths among the boats — but not by randomizing recruitment.

One thing was certain: the clann was not the appropriate unit of recruitment. There was no guarantee, for a start, that within the males of a small clann, for example, all the necessary skills could be found. Also, since the clanns overlapped endlessly, a man might find himself with multiple allegiances. This did not matter — indeed, was an advantage — when it came to land, for it meant that he had many claims. But with boats you could only be in one at a time, and this necessitated an absolute choice — at least for one season. Also, the recruitment of crews would depend on just how the "ownership" of the boats came about in the first place. If one man built the boat and was the outright owner, then he would build up his own crew; if a couple of men were partners in building a boat, then they would share the responsibility. Sometimes a "club" was formed to build a boat, and then there might be half a dozen men charged with bringing in others. But the main point is that the crew had to be recruited at the beginning of the season from scratch and in competition with other owners (although membership did persist over the years in some cases), and this was something new.

It was foreign to island ideology to allow this to be a free-for-all. If asked how crews were assembled, the principle stated was that the owners put together a crew from their own people (*muintir*): that is, their relatives. Again, therefore, we are in the area of "all people are related but some are more related than others." In this case, however, it was not so much relationship by descent that counted — although a crew might be started by paternal cousins, for example — as relationship by marriage. Or at least we can say that relationship by marriage loomed as large as the principle of descent. It was, as I have said, unconceivable that one should not turn to relatives. The island was not seen as a pool of "free labor" from which the entrepreneurs could draw. Nonrelatives were sometimes included in crews, but usually only as a last resort. Given, however, that everyone on the island — including in-marrying males — was related to everyone else either by kinship or marriage, why could the owners not simply pick whomever they chose and then claim these people were kin? For a start, this would never have occurred to them, and secondly it could never have worked that way.

The way a crew was assembled always followed the same line: The "core" of owner or owners called first on immediate kin, who in turn called on their kin or affines, who called on their kin or affines, and so on. The crew was then linked by chains of kinship and affinity, moving "out" from the core. The old men who crewed the boats in their heyday (1890-1920) remembered the process well, and some boats were still in use in the 1960s. They were able to reproduce well enough the process of recruitment — from the core out. Rather than give an ideal example, I will list here the process of recruitment of one boat, using the standard anthropological abbreviations for kin. This boat was known as "The Lads' Boat" because two young men started it. They were paternal cousins, and I shall take the senior of them as the starting point (the "owner"). The recruitment went — they told me — like this:

Owner's FaBroSo then his FaBroSoSisHuMoBro
Owner's SisHuSisHu then his SisHuBro
Owner's BroWiMoBro then his BroWiBroWiFaBro
Owner's BroWiBroWiFaSisHu then his BroWiBroWiFaSisSo

There were other connections between them, but these were the ones cited. There were of course almost an infinity of possible routes along which the recruitment could proceed — in theory. But the owners wanted effective crew members and so proceeded along those routes that would produce them. In this way the ferocity of competition for members that might have resulted in a "free labor" situation was considerably mitigated, and each crew had to take some kin whom no one would have otherwise chosen, since the ten or eleven boats between them demanded most of the able-bodied young men and adult males.

The genealogists were never consulted for boat recruitment. The islanders exploited the links of kinship and affinity that they knew themselves. Indeed, the diagrams of kinship links between crew members look much more like the accounts of their "people" that the lay islanders would give if asked, than the neat pyramidical *clanna* of the genealogists. To use the overworked jargon, then, they exploited the network (ego-centered) rather than the descent group (ancestor-focused); a network which included affinal nodes as well as consanguineal. In fact, it was the ingenious exploitation of affinal links — links by marriage of often a remote kind — that was necessary to the production of the better crews. But one always, if possible, went "through" the intervening relatives. Again, strategies loom large here, and certain smart boat owners, I'm sure, picked the crewmen first and rationalized the link later. I know this because in retrospect several of them gave me affinal links as crucial in attaching a member that only occurred *after* the crew in question had been recruited. This was not rank dishonesty, since people did change boats, and crews persisted over time. It was, rather, interesting in showing how the old men *conceptualized* the recruitment process. There *had* to have been a direct traceable link; therefore one was provided. But everyone agreed that the members had to be "brought in" by the process described.

Marriage and Household: Holy Family and Visiting Husband

We now come to the interesting problem of the relationship between family, marriage, and household that has given Tory its unwelcome notoriety. Again I only want to deal with the "principles and practices" issue here, so I will not go into all the statistical details which the interested reader can find in the book. It is here, however, that the clash of principle and practice — or rather the modification of principle and the resultant strategies — can best be seen at work.

People on the mainland will tell you that on Tory husbands and wives don't live together. Like most things the mainlanders say about the island, this is an exaggeration. Yet, in 1963, of roughly fifty married couples, ten (20 percent) were indeed not living together. On further enquiry, and on checking through the genealogies, I found that earlier this century the figure would have been as high as 50 percent, and during the last century even higher. The population was much larger then, and the pressure on housing greater, but this was indeed a striking feature. Such a strong statistical trend, one might suppose, must be the result of following a "rule of residence."

However, if you ask the islanders what the ideal family situation is, they have no hesitation in telling you that it is that of the "Holy Family": parents and dependent children together under one roof. Even further, they would prefer that this ideal unit never break up. There is great resistance to the children marrying, and it should ideally be put off as long as possible, even until after the parents are dead. That the two attitudes are contradictory does not strike anyone at all. They will agree that all couples should get married and live in a house of their own, but insist that young people should not leave their parents to get married. There is no question that for the islanders marriage presents real problems of social upheaval (including, as we have seen, very often the division of the land) and that it is seen as disruptive. While officially, for example, illegitimate children are disapproved of, in fact no stigma attaches to illegitimacy and the rate is quite high. Better an illegitimate child than a bad marriage, I was told. Children do not disrupt households.

Underlying the contradiction is a subprinciple that says: "Duties to parents (particularly widowed) and siblings take precedence over those to spouses." This enables a solution to the contradiction to be realized: people marry but continue to live in the natal home rather than setting up a common household. On a small island this is possible, since no one is more than a brief walk away from anyone else. In the days of higher population (up to 600) and small houses this must have seemed a sensible solution for reasons other than the solving of a contradiction. But even so it depends on another subprinciple or modifier. After all, no matter what the inconvenience, people could have moved into the spouse's house (husband's or wife's). But this is abominated on Tory. After all, it goes against the ideal — the single family in its own house. Therefore, if this ideal cannot be realized, it is better to marry and not move than to create an extended household with "two women in the kitchen." With the "not moving" solution, at least you satisfy the church's need for a legitimate union while not disrupting the existing household arrangements. This way you get half the Holy Family ideal realized while avoiding the even worse alternative.

The important subprinciple would be stated in various ways. If someone had an old mother to care for, I was told, it was wrong to leave her while she still needed care in order to move in with a spouse. Some of the "living separate" couples were, however, well over forty and had no parent alive. What is more they had married quite late. Well then, I was told, they wouldn't want to go upsetting a situation they had known for more than thirty years and go leaving their brothers and sisters for some stranger, would they? Mostly they would not, although today with the declining population and greater availability of houses — many owned by women — men are more often moving in with their wives. But never in with a wife and her siblings, for example (or vice versa — a woman would not move in with a man and his siblings). Women often bargain with brothers to get the patrimonial house, giving the land over to the brother entirely, so that they can move a husband in. The brother in turn may either build a house or look for a wife who has one.

Thus, while we have some principles and subprinciples working here, we do not have any "rules of residence at marriage." The rules are more like the rules of a game. They say: "Here are certain ideals to be striven for, but here are certain situations to avoid at all costs. Now you put the two together and come up with a solution that is most to your advantage." Thus the "separate living" arrangement is a compromise, but an almost inevitable one for certain people at certain stages of the domestic cycle. And this is important, because household composition changes over time with the death or movement of members, and so different strategies can be called into play. If all a woman's brothers move out, for example, she can move her husband in. Or if a brother and sister, both married, have been living with a widowed mother and she dies, then there is a possibility of a move. But it is striking how often the arrangement, once made, sticks. There is a great conservatism to household arrangements, and since people do not marry until their thirties as a rule, they often stay with whatever arrangement they are used to, despite chances to change.

The statistics show, for example, that many of the "separate living" (called "natolocal" in the jargon) households now composed of relatively old siblings started as households with widowed mothers. The children married but did not move. This is the strongest tie of all — to a widowed mother. It would be considered sacrilege to leave her against her wishes. But often, even once she had died, the siblings would stay together and refuse to move. One old man had renovated a house and spent twenty years trying to get his wife to join him in it, but she wouldn't. She had two brothers and a granddaughter with an illegitimate child to take care of. One of the brothers was married and living apart from his wife, who was living with her sister, who was also married and living apart from her husband! The other brother was a widower. Island opinion had it that it was hard for the old man, but he had a sister to look after him, and the wife in question should not leave her kinsfolk for him. He died without his little Holy Family ever being more than half realized.

I don't want here, and cannot for reasons of space, go into the details of the statistical evidence for the nature of the place of "natolocal" residence in the domestic cycle of the Tory household. All I want to do is again show how certain principles can be firmly enunciated in a way that is unrealizable; how modifiers or subprinciples are stated that allow for compromises; and how strategies evolve — in this case, the shifts in the domestic cycle — which allow the compromises to operate. This comes out beautifully in the case of residence and household composition, but was equally well demonstrated for boat crews and land inheritance and even in the cognitive realm of genealogy and naming. The general principles are usually too general and often self-contradictory, but they do their job in stating an ideal to be striven after. In not achieving that ideal, people are not liars, hypocrites, or fools; they are following out the logic of the modifying subprinciples by means of strategies, often of startling rationality, that allow for pragmatic solutions. The "rules" here are best seen, then, on analogy with the rules of a game — albeit the very serious game of reproduction and survival. The rules do not mandate a simple one-to-one solution, but tell the players the parameters within which they can develop whatever strategies they choose. Of course, as in so many games, the strategies themselves are often time honored and not independent inventions. They are of the collective wisdom, not of individual genius. But it is always open to some enterprising person to find a new loophole and start a new strategy — which may become not only time honored in its turn but eventually a part of the rule structure itself, like handling the ball in rugby, or the forward pass in its American counterpart.

A striking example of this is the way the islanders moved immediately into the exploitation of the kinship and alliance network for the recruitment of boat crews. And who knows how many people, for how many years, failed to get married at all (as happens in the rest of Ireland) until some genius hit on the solution of marrying but not moving? The theoretical importance of all these issues for the social sciences and particularly anthropology will be obvious, and I am not going to belabor them here. All I want to do is use the Tory material to suggest a closer look at the relation between principles and pragmatics that goes beyond the mechanical notion of "norm" and "deviance" and sees the two in a dialectical relationship. We should then go on to ask the questions about "human nature" that I hinted at in the beginning: Why should we have this extraordinary charade at all? Why don't we just do what we say we should be doing? But that would not be human. We did not develop the brain to reason, but to act, and this is the only way it can operate at all, for it is the supreme organ of self-deception. But that is to go into heady realms too far from Tory Island and its specific processes, except that the Tory Islanders, like the rest of us, cannot avoid the burden of being human. In the very specificity of their own charade they illustrate the universality of the human dilemma.

10

The Golden Bough
and the Descent into Anthropology

Every anthropologist knows (or used to know) how Malinowski, studying chemistry and mathematics at the Jagellonian University in Krakow, was preparing for his compulsory exam in English language. *The Golden Bough* had been recommended to him as the best example of English prose style, and in reading it he was so enchanted by its ideas that he abandoned natural sciences and took up anthropology. (See his "Dedication to Sir James Frazer" in his *Myth in Primitive Psychology*.) His version of anthropology became very different from Frazer's, but the two had a respectful and even affectionate relationship, as Frazer's warm and generous preface to *Argonauts of the Western Pacific*, and Malinowski's "Biographical Appreciation" in *A Scientific Theory of Culture*, testify.

Frazer saw no incongruity between Malinowski's self-appointed "functionalism" and his own "comparative method." The better the quality of material coming in from the field the more secure comparative analysis would be. The incompatibility was rather the other way round, with Malinowski's insistence that "context" was all-important, rendering comparison more difficult. His main praise of Frazer's *Totemism and Exogamy*, for example, was that it was the best collection of "rounded descriptions" of primitive tribes before Murdock's *Our Primitive Contemporaries*. But comparativists continued to look at context, and functionalists continued to compare, and the whole thing, from a distance of years, looks almost trivial, however momentous it seemed to the participants at the time. Whatever the final attitudes to Frazerian theory, Malinowski was one of many who came into the dark realms of anthropology, like Aeneas into the underworld, bearing before them the glittering magical object that was the Golden Bough (whatever that was, which remains to be seen).

I came into anthropology later in the game — the early 1950s — and via the same route as Malinowski: *The Golden Bough*. But by a serendipitous series of steps, I ended up being taught fully fledged "Malinowskian functionalism" (with a leavening of Radcliffe-Brown) at his own LSE, in his own department. He, of course, was gone, but his ghost brooded over the department, unwilling to depart thence until properly exorcised. (This happened later with the institution of the fraternal cannibal feast called The Malinowski Memorial Lectures. I gave one — 1967 — and followed the Freudian formula already established of invoking the Father and then demolishing him with the connivance of my confreres, after which spiritual parricide the celebrants retired to the director's dining room for a ritual totem meal. I even suggested that the main dish should be "Boeuf Bronislaw" — some Polish concoction, of course, with potatoes, cabbage, and dumplings — but this was dismissed as too frivolous.) But it was here, after transferring from economics to sociology with the social anthropology concentration, that I discovered to my surprise that Frazer was old hat, the comparative method "totally discredited," and some form or other of "functionalism" (confusion here) the only alternative to vapid generalizations, diffusionist fantasies, and evolutionary speculation ("conjectural history" — remember?).

I have told the story partially in *Encounter with Anthropology*, and to save time I'll quote that account here to get us started.

I approached Maurice Freedman of the anthropology department (now professor at Oxford), who did his best to deter me. "What have you read that is relevant?" he asked. "*The Golden Bough*," I replied, "abridged edition." He was skeptical and told me that if I thought *that* sort of thing was what I would be doing I was mistaken. Nevertheless, I transferred to the social anthropology option of the sociology degree. We did not do much of *The Golden Bough*, it was true. We did a lot about lineage systems and some of the other things that follow in this book, and I was not enchanted.

This had followed an account of how I came to the book via a crisis of religious belief, in which I and my fellow backsliders

searched for allies, for comfort in literature, for a feeling that we were not alone. We discovered the Rationalist Press Association and Bertrand

Russell; Voltaire and anticlericalism; Spencer and agnosticism; Huxley and evolutionism; Bernard Shaw and Shavianism — and above all, for me, Sir James Frazer and *The Golden Bough* (via, in my case, T. S. Eliot and *The Waste Land*).

That was enough detail at the time, but this is my chance to dig a little deeper into memory, aided by faded school exercise books my mother had, unknown to me, kept in one of those chests of family memorabilia: trivia of our personal pasts that only mothers would find virtue in preserving.

My hunger for rationalist allies in the antireligion campaign had led me to Frazer, but only over the tussle of conscience I was having with T. S. Eliot. Eliot was my hero, *The Waste Land* my manifesto, and yet, confound it, the man was an Anglican and a sincere believer! (The two don't always coincide.) His high Toryism and his pessimism I could appreciate, but I was obviously uneasy with the religious preoccupations. The famous footnote in *The Waste Land* was not initially encouraging since I assumed that the Frazer in question must be a fellow traveler: another of the running dogs of Anglicanism. But it was enigmatic. After praising Jesse L. Weston's *From Ritual to Romance,* he continues:

To another work of anthropology I am indebted in general, one which has influenced our generation profoundly; I mean *The Golden Bough*; I have used especially the two volumes *Adonis, Attis, Osiris.* Anyone who is acquainted with these works will immediately recognize in the poem certain references to vegetation ceremonies.

Well, maybe. It didn't seem immediately obvious to me, but then I didn't know anything about "vegetation ceremonies" — whatever they might be. I could think of "Harvest Festival" — a ceremony, certainly, and to do with vegetation, surely — but that didn't get me far. Yet how could I resist "which has influenced our generation profoundly"? Obviously one had to look into this.

The school library, well equipped in other ways, did not have *The Golden Bough*, but the admirable Bradford Reference Library, faithful friend of desperate students, had one of the multivolume editions (the third I suppose), and to these I repaired, expecting the philosopher's stone. What I got — and I was only about seventeen and relatively untutored, don't forget — was massive puzzlement. I read the *Adonis, Attis, Osiris* volumes as indicated, and grasped the "dying god" and "vegetation ceremonies" themes. In a way it was exciting. Jesus was just another of these: a latter-day vegetation deity, dying and rising on cue. Fine. My rationalism was bolstered. But how did this jibe with Eliot's solemn Christianity? Hadn't he got the point? Or was I missing it? It seemed he had taken an argument intended to discredit at least the objective claims to truth of Christianity, and somehow turned it into an argument deploring the modern "lack of faith." That modern civilization was a "waste land" made sense; but that the answer lay in the mummeries of High Anglicanism rather than in rationalistic science seemed to me an outrageous conclusion and a positive sell-out. It was certainly not what Frazer had intended — or so it seemed to me. Of course, I knew nothing else of Frazer at the time, but when I began to find out more, I was confirmed in my opinion. (Thank providence it was the third edition I read and not the second, otherwise I would have found in the text, not hidden away in an appendix, the Frazer theory of Jesus as Haman, and Barrabas as Mordechai, playing out their roles in a ritual sacrificial drama, courtesy of the book of Esther. I would unquestionably have embraced this as, dare we say it, gospel truth, and annoyed my miserable elders and betters even more with my persistent and earnestly insistent explanations.) Of course, at the time, I did not realize that Eliot had only officially been confirmed in the Church of England as late as 1927 — *The Waste Land* dating from 1922. But he had been "taking instruction" since 1925, so he was obviously a fellow traveler before that.

At that time (around 1951-52) a remarkable preacher graced the pulpit of the Bradford Unitarian Church in Town Hall Square. I attended regularly, not because I was a Unitarian but because I loved the sermons. Frank Bullock's "sermons" were really lectures on literature, history, theology, philosophy — whatever took his capacious fancy, and they were wonderful things to hear. His fame was never more than local, although his son, Allan, went on to become a famous historian, master of an Oxford College, and Peer of the Realm. But from Frank Bullock, who, of course, knew Frazer as all intellectuals of his generation knew Frazer (Eliot was right about this), I pieced together a more coherent picture. I remember him telling me: "Don't start in the middle, whatever he [Eliot] says. Read it from the beginning. But use the abridged version. It will make more sense and save a lot of time." When I asked about the riddle of Eliot's devotion to the two opposed doctrines, he told me: "Why do you think I celebrate a form of Holy Communion? Not because I believe in the real presence or even because of the explicit Christian symbolism. Or why do we [Unitarians] celebrate Easter and even Harvest Festival? All these key ceremonies go back to something older and more profound. They have been borrowed and adapted by our religious tradition, but their origins, and therefore their meanings, are derived from the things Frazer displays for us. Eliot understands this."

I remember this so vividly because for me it was an incredible intellectual breakthrough — I mean that one could even *think* like this. It was a different kind of thinking to "school thinking." It was heady and exciting. I wanted more. It was this as much as anything (and the other thing was Mr.

Whatmuff, my wonderful history master) that kept me from leaving school to become a journalist and rugby player, and set me on course for university. Thank you Messrs. Bullock and Eliot. Thank you Sir James.

This conversation took place just before I heard that I had been awarded the school prize for English: a "suitable book." The headmaster wasn't sure that *The Golden Bough* came under the heading of "suitable," but in previous years for the art prize I had chosen Byron, and for the history prize the essays of Sir Lewis Namier, so I figured I had paid my dues to suitability. I persisted as usual and got my way in the end. (My quoting the authority of Eliot was no help. Eliot was "modern" and therefore suspect!) I still have that *Golden Bough* — the 1950 reprinting of the 1922 edition: the green binding with the gold lettering; the mistletoe motif embossed on the front, with, in my case, the school crest stamped in gold underneath it with the three thorn trees and the stern motto Stulti Doctrinam Spernunt. Inside, the bookplate reads:

Thornton Grammar School
1673-1953
Theo Peel for English Prize
J. R. Fox

T. R. Frame M. A.
Head Master

In the days when I did that kind of thing, I pencil underlined and annotated a good deal of it, then tried, messily, to rub out the offending scribblings. But it is still legible and I still use it for teaching. And the estimable Mr. Bullock was quite right. The abridged edition did enable me to grasp the whole of the argument, including the logical playing out of the questions as posed concerning the strange goings-on in the grove of Diana at Nemi, and the theoretical framework concerning the Laws of Magic on the one hand and the evolutionary progression from magic through religion to science on the other. It put Eliot in some better perspective for me. The progression was inexorable, I was glad to note, but that didn't mean we automatically abandoned old ways of thinking and reacting to the mysterious universe (yes, I had read Sir James Jeans on same). The seasons continued their changes into which we were locked by our dependence on nature — science or no science — and we did seem to feel a need to "celebrate" these. So Christmas trees and Easter eggs fell into place with (divine) birth, dying, and renewal. Eliot, of course, feared we were trapped in the dying phase and that there would be no renewal. But he lacked faith in science. At the time I had no such qualms. Most of this is my memory of Mr. Bullock's magical sermons, of course. But I must have worked through some of it in my own confused head. .

This, however, was not an easy time for the leisurely perusal of Frazer, Harrison, and the like, since the newly instituted "A levels" had to be dealt with (three of them) and I was more or less trying to teach myself "A level" economics since we had no economics master at the school and I was applying for the LSE, which was where I really wanted to go even though applications to several places were thought prudent as insurance, and teachers were still nagging me to do English at Oxbridge. I also had to "keep up" Latin since it was still required in some scholarship exams and by most arts faculties. So while I had to abandon Frazer as full-time study, I did find an interesting overlap: we were doing book 6 of Virgil's *Aeneid*, either as a "set book" or as a source of examples for the compulsory Latin verse translation, I forget. (At roughly the same time, that lovely poet of upwardly mobile guilt, Tony Harrison, was writing "My mind moves upon silence and Aeneid VI" at nearby Leeds Grammar School.) Given my Frazer obsessions, the reader will appreciate my delight in finding that this was the book in which the fabled Golden Bough makes its appearance. Frazer, in his penultimate chapter, suitably titled "The Golden Bough," makes extensive reference to the passages in Virgil, translating some of them, to justify his contention that Virgil's "Golden Bough" and the oak-growing (and specifically holm-oak-growing) mistletoe which was the instrument of Balder's death, are one and the same.

It is not a new opinion that the Golden Bough was the mistletoe. True, Virgil does not identify but only compares it with mistletoe. But this may only be a poetical device to cast a mystic glamour over the humble plant. Or, more probably, his description was based on a popular superstition that at certain times the mistletoe blazed out into a supernatural glory. The poet tells how two doves, guiding Aeneas to the gloomy vale in whose depths grew the Golden Bough, alighted upon a tree "whence shone a glittering gleam of gold. As in the woods in winter cold the mistletoe — a plant not native to its tree — is green with fresh leaves and twines its yellow berries about the boles; such seemed upon the shady holm-oak the leafy gold, so rustled in the gentle breeze the golden leaf." Here Virgil definitely describes the Golden Bough as growing on a holm-oak, and compares it with the mistletoe. The inference is almost inevitable that the Golden Bough was nothing but the mistletoe seen through the haze of poetry or of popular superstition.

Later he takes up the theme again:

It only remains to ask, Why was the mistletoe called the Golden Bough? The whitish-yellow of the mistletoe berries is hardly enough to account for the name, for Virgil says that the bough was altogether golden, stem as well as leaves. Perhaps the name may be derived from the rich golden yellow which a bough of mistletoe assumes when it has been cut and kept for some months; the bright tint is not confined to the leaves, but spreads to the stalks as well, so that the whole branch appears to be indeed a Golden Bough.

Then he summarizes:

These considerations may partially explain why Virgil makes Aeneas carry a glorified bough of mistletoe with him on his descent into the gloomy subterranean world. The poet describes how at the very gates of hell there stretched a vast and gloomy wood, and how the hero, following the flight of two doves that lured him on, wandered into the depths of the immemorial forest till he saw afar off through the shadows of the trees the flickering light of the Golden Bough illuminating the matted boughs overhead. If the mistletoe, as a yellow withered bough in the sad autumn woods, was conceived to contain the seed of fire, what better companion could a forlorn wanderer in the nether shades take with him than a bough that would be a lamp to his feet as well as a rod and staff to his hands? Armed with it he might boldly confront the dreadful spectres that would cross his path on his adventurous journey. Hence when Aeneas, emerging from the forest, comes to the banks of the Styx, winding slow with sluggish stream through the infernal marsh, and the surly ferryman refuses him passage in his boat, he has but to draw the Golden Bough from his bosom and hold it up, and straightway the blusterer quails at the sight and meekly receives the hero into his crazy bark, which sinks deep in the water under the unusual weight of the living man.

There we have it: the "goldenness" and the magical power of the Golden Bough eloquently explained.

So I turned to book 6 and the passages in question. I know I did this because in the faded notebooks (or what tattered remains there are of them) I had copied out the passages quoted above, along with the relevant passages from Virgil. First I had noted: "Frazer misses Sybil's instructions to Aeneas," and wrote out lines 136 to 145:

> Latet arbore opaca
> aureus et foliis et lento vimine ramus,
> Iunoni infernae dictus sacer; hunc tegit omnis
> lucus et obscuris claudunt convallibus umbrae.
> Sed non ante datur telluris operta subire
> auricomus quam quis decerpserit arbore fetus.

Hoc sibi pulchra suum ferri Proserpina munus
instituit. Primo avulso non defecit alter
aureus, et simili frondescit virga metallo.

I noted, cryptically, the following:

Sacred to *Juno*, not Diana

Leaves gold, not *like* gold

Leaves *metal*

Proserpine demands it as tribute — to get into the underworld

It was pure carelessness (for which, lord knows, I was chastised often enough by Mr. Evans, the classics master) that led me to miss that it was not Juno, i.e., the wife of Jove, who was meant, but Juno Inferna — the infernal Juno, i.e., the queen of the underworld, i.e., Proserpine, as the later line confirms. But at least it wasn't Diana; I got that right.

Next to Frazer's translation of the passage about the doves sent by Aphrodite, Aeneas' mother, I wrote out the relevant lines — 201-211:

Inde ubi venere ad fauces grave olentis Averni,
tollunt se celeres liquidumque per aera lapsae
sedibus optatis gemina super arbore sidunt,
discolor unde auri per ramos aura refulsit.
Quale solet silvis brumali frigore viscum
fronde virere nova, quod non sua seminat arbos,
et croceo fetu teretis circumdare truncos,
talis erat species auri frondentis opaca
ilice, sic leni crepitabat brattea vento.
Corripit Aeneas extemplo avidusque refringit
cunctantem, et vatis portat sub tecta Sibyllae.

Again the cryptic notes:

Like mistletoe — yellow in winter

Tree with Bough holm-oak? not quercus, not ilex.

Discolor = many colored

The tree of the Golden Bough itself is simply described as "many colored" — *discolor*. Only after the simile (introduced by *quale*) does Virgil mention the holm oak — *ilex*. Frazer has it *"upon* the shady holm-oak," but this is doubtful since *ilice* is the ablative and hence open to interpretation. Translations differ, with Rhoades, for example, agreeing with Frazer:

> Such was seeming of that leafy gold
> On the dark ilex...

While Fitzgerald has:

> So bright amid the dark green ilex shone
> The golden leafage....

Then again, Cecil Day Lewis, has "upon that ilex dark." But the main point is, as I seemed to see at the time, that Virgil does not describe the actual tree of the Bough as anything but "multicolored." There is even a wrinkle in this, however, that only Day Lewis of all the translators seems to see. The Latin dictionary we used at the time — piles of dog-eared copies were distributed at the beginning of the year — was affectionately known as "Smith's Smaller." This has metamorphosed into the Chambers-Murray of today, and on looking up the infamous *discolor* in it, I find I had plumped — as had most of the translators — for one of the meanings: "variegated" or "parti-colored." But there is another sense to the word that conveys the meaning of "different from surrounding objects" — or of a different color from surrounding objects. Now note that Day Lewis opts for this usage, which therefore makes *discolor* refer to the bough itself, not to the tree it is on — quite plausible if one looks at the sentence structure, since the adjective is separated from *arbor* by a comma, thus giving:

> a tree
> Amid whose branches there gleamed a bright haze, a different colour,
> Gold.

I suspect this is the most secure translation of this difficult passage. (Virgil was not here above a sly pun: Dis-color = the color of Dis, i.e., Hades, the destined venue of the bough. If it wasn't a pun, it should have been!)

Finally, I noted the passage where Aeneas comes to the Styx and confronts Charon, paraphrased by Frazer in the third passage (lines 403-410). The Sybil is speaking:

> Troius Aeneas, pietate insignis et armis
> ad genitorem imas Erebi descendit ad umbras.
> Si te nulla mouet tantae pietatis imago,

at ramum hunc" (aperit ramum qui veste latebat)
"agnoscas." Tunida ex ira tum corda residunt;
nec plura his. Ille admirans venerabile donum
fatalis virgae longo post tempore visum
caeruliam advertit puppim ripaeque propinquat.

The notes:

Blusterer quails, etc. Charon — admirans venerabile donum — rage
subsides — he is *reverent*. This is Proserpine's (his queen's) tribute.

Sybil shows bough, *not* Aeneas

So, my first (and last) run-in with Frazer's legendary classical scholarship
was not an altogether happy one. I obviously figured he had, to say the least,
overstated the case for the Golden Bough as mere mistletoe seen through a
"poetic haze." It was a magical *metal* bough, of real gold, in a grove perhaps
of holm-oak, but growing in fact on an unspecified species of tree or one
simply described as "many colored"; it was shown to Charon by the Sybil,
not by Aeneas; it was sacred to Infernal Juno (not Diana), and was destined
(*fatalis*) for this same Infernal Queen — Proserpine — as tribute, which is
why the surly boatman accepted Aeneas and his metal leaves aboard — not
because of its powers as "magical mistletoe." After all, golden objects
growing on trees, like apples in the Hesperides, or fleeces in Colchis for that
matter, were a fairly common mythical theme.

By this point in *The Golden Bough* Frazer was ready to tie the whole thing
together: he was bringing the argument full circle to the Turner painting of
the Virgilian scene with which he began. He had laboriously proved that the
"external soul" could indeed be contained in the mistletoe suspended between
earth and heaven and hence the source of Balder's downfall. It would
somehow have been unthinkable that the Golden Bough of his title would
have been something other than magic mistletoe "seen through a poetic haze"
— and so he went with the interpretation of an admittedly murky piece of
Virgil that suited this conclusion. He opted for "pattern consistency," as the
linguists would say. And indeed his interpretation is as viable as any of the
others, apart from the slip about Aeneas showing the bough to Charon when
in fact it was the Sybil — a minor point. Some people have asked if this does
not, even so, call into question his "legendary classical scholarship." I don't
think so. From the few examples I know, his rendering of classical sources
was accurate enough, and better scholars than I have vouched for his
accuracy in this respect. But I do think we should differentiate between his
legendary *knowledge* and his skills as a *translator*. His knowledge of classical

sources was indeed unrivaled, but I have never thought much of his actual translations. His own tendency to write English "golden prose" was, as in the case of so many nineteenth-century translators, his own worst enemy. Accuracy of translation was often sacrificed to goldenness of prose.

But I didn't pursue this at the time. How could I? I didn't know there were any issues to pursue. The rest of the notebook is largely bits of verse translation and lists of vocabulary queries. The only thing that emerges from them is the entry:

discolor — Dryden = double tree??

The line — an alexandrine — from Dryden's *Aeneid* (6:296) is:

Perched on the double tree that bears the golden bough,

a translation about as misleading as Rhoades' "wished for tree"! (Fitzgerald has "two-hued tree.") I would have been relatively familiar with the Dryden since our English teacher, Mr. Birrell, was a redoubtable Scots classicist only made over into an English master in an emergency. He taught Milton by making us translate him into Latin so that we understood the structure of his sentences. He was fond of renderings of Catullus in the manner of Robert Burns:

Weep, weep, ye loves and cupids all,
And ilka man o' decent feelin' —
My lassie's lost her wee, wee bird,
And that's a loss, ye ken, past healin'.

(How *do* we remember these things? Actually, as a rendering of "Passer mortuus est meae puellae" this isn't half bad.)

He was most comfortable teaching the Augustans because of the classical background, so we were heavy into Pope and Gray; but he insisted we know the seventeenth-century forerunners, which had us equally devoted to Dryden and Swift. Anyway, I was obviously on the trail still of the elusive tree (Frazer just slipped past the problem of *discolor* to hurry on to the holm-oak); but it went no further. It was many years later (quite recently, in fact) that I found that scholars had shared my doubts, and that it might not even have been mistletoe that killed Balder in the first place! See Theodore H. Gaster's (1961) learned footnote on page 382 of *The New Golden Bough* for more details. (This is so learned that I haven't been able to track down most of the references — *Mel. Smets.*?!)

By the time I arrived at the LSE and the fateful interview with Maurice

Freedman, I had obviously forgotten, in the rush of events, this bit of my encounter with Frazer (it was a memory only recently revived) since the issue I had to contend with was not anything so simple as shaky scholarship and deceptive golden prose, but his status even as an "anthropologist." Freedman's curt dismissal (he handed me Radcliffe-Brown's *Structure and Function in Primitive Society* and told me to "learn it by heart") was a shock. To me Frazer *was* anthropology, and his concerns were my concerns: the origins of religious ideas and therefore their status as "truths." Freedman was a sound rationalist and approved my membership in the Rationalist Press Association, but he had little time for Frazer. My attempts to turn the first-year anthropology seminar into debates on Frazer were soundly sat upon. "We haven't time for that," he would say. "In the old days we had to read all that old stuff before getting on with the real thing; you're lucky, you can get started right away on the real thing, so don't worry about all that."

The "real thing" was of course British social anthropology from Malinowski onwards. And even Malinowski, while treated with some piety (as was L. T. Hobhouse in sociology, because, as Donald Macrae used to say, "he's all we've got"), was pretty suspect. He had little to contribute to "lineage theory" which seemed to take up all our time. There was some "History of Anthropology" taught (I remember Barnes and Schapera), but here again references to "the evolutionists" were largely dismissive, and used to show how backward the subject was before the shining light of "structural-functionalism" lit up the murky scene. In "Anthropology of Religion" lectures, we learned thoroughly and well — largely from Raymond Firth — about Trobriand magic, Tikopia rituals, Azande witchcraft, and the newly minted *Nuer Religion*. Frazer again was only mentioned in passing during the first lecture on the "old stuff."

I got a little revenge — this time against Maurice Freedman. He had set me to reading Lévi-Strauss's *Les structures élémentaires de la parenté*. There was no translation, and in any case it was considered somehow sissy to read translations if you were capable — insofar as "school certificate" French rendered you capable — of reading the original. I ordered a copy from the estimable house of Hachette in Regent Street, and was ploughing away through this acknowledged modern masterpiece when lo and behold, there at the beginning of chapter 10 (a chapter, I note in my battered copy, where I had stopped writing translations of "difficult" words in the margin) the following tribute to my hero:

On doit reconnaître à Frazer le mérite d'avoir, le premier, appelé l'attention sur la similitude de structure entre le mariage par échange et le mariage entre cousins croisés, et établi la connexion réelle qui existe entre les deux institutions. Le point de départ de sa démonstration est l'observation que, dans certains systèmes de parenté comportant le mariage préférentiel avec l'une seulement des cousines croisées (habituellement la fille du frère de la mère), on rencontre cependant la double identification du frère de la mère avec le beau-père et de la soeur du père avec la belle-mère. Cette seconde identification ne se comprendrait, pourtant, que dans l'hypothèse du mariage avec la fille de la soeur du père. Cette difficulté s'éclaire, remarque Frazer, si l'on suppose que les deux cousines croisées se confondent, c'est-à-dire si la fille du frère de la mère est en même temps la fille de la soeur du père, situation qui se trouve automatiquement réalisée dans le cas où les cousins croisés sont issus de frères qui ont échangé leurs soeurs. (For a literal translation, see the notes to this chapter.)

The reference is to *Folklore in the Old Testament*, volume 2, page 104. I drew a diagram of the details of this "double cross-cousin marriage" which stayed with me ever after and turned up eventually in *Kinship and Marriage*. (It was not at all original but I didn't know that then. See chap. 12, diagram 12.1.) I was even moved to write a song about it which, in elaborated form and with one verse in French and a banjo-ukulele accompaniment, has helped me to social success at anthropology conferences ever since. It was like a blaze of clarity in a murky world of "kinship theory" — and I was delighted to point out to Freedman and anyone who would listen, that this brilliant insight came from J. G. himself who was therefore no intellectual slouch and had indeed something to contribute to "lineage theory." So be it, Freedman told me. Plough through *Totemism and Exogamy* and see what you can extract from that. Let me get through Lévi-Strauss first, I whined, and the matter was dropped.

But despite the odd flourish like this, Frazer had obviously, from being God, become the fall guy, the scapegoat even: useful to point out known error. The "comparative method" came in for particular scorn. My weak attempts at defense were quickly brushed aside. They went something like this: You say that Frazer simply "lists examples" and does not "test hypotheses," for instance by looking at negative instances. But he isn't trying to test hypotheses; he's trying to establish that some belief or practice is widespread, that's all. True, not all pastoralists taboo the cooking of a kid in its mother's milk. One wouldn't expect them to. But enough do to make us consider seriously the relationship of such a taboo to pastoralist ways of thinking about the world. (Yes, I'd read *Folklore in the Old Testament* by now — abridged edition. And not only because of the endorsement of Lévi-Strauss but, to be fair to him, at the instigation of Isaac Schapera, who loved it as a source of examples to shock pious undergraduates in his introductory anthropology lectures.)

I remember that John Barnes, in his response, pointed me toward Popper and the "principle of refutation" and toward G. P. Murdock and the burgeoning "cross-cultural method." Now, this was good teaching. Trying to follow Popper — in person and in print — forced me back to Ayer (in person at University College then) and the "principle of verification" before I could master the then-considered superior version of the "principle of falsification." Was Frazer indeed setting up "nonfalsifiable propositions" which would then be, Oh Horrors! — unscientific? I got the point, I think; but it seemed a bit like breaking a butterfly upon a wheel. Frazer was not, I countered, trying to be "scientific" in the "proposition and refutation" sense. Contagious and sympathetic magic were indeed "there" in the world. All Frazer was doing was pointing to the ubiquity of examples, not trying to falsify hypotheses. It seemed somehow that while Popper was right with his notions of what constituted the criteria for "science," these criteria were not sensibly applied to whatever it was Frazer was doing. This didn't help me much in the arguments, since in those days it was "science or nothing," and we spent endless hours with elegantly sceptical Popperians debating and defending the status of social anthropology as science.

The happy result for me was the baptism of fire in modern philosophy. I read *Language, Truth and Logic* and my mental life was as profoundly changed as it had been by Frazer; only Sartre had a comparable effect. And all this left me uneasy about Frazer, but still touchily defensive. He did not, I was told, "look for the negative instances"; he simply "instantiated" rather than "tested" his hypotheses. Well, I again countered, so did Darwin and so did Marx. I didn't see any "testing of hypotheses" there either; just massive "instantiation." Their propositions weren't something you could probably "test" in a scientific sense, although testable hypotheses could be derived from them, as they could from Frazer. (Popper of course agreed that they were not open to falsification and thus read them out of the scientific canon.)

This massive instatiation made the *Origin* and *Capital* (which seemed to be a deliberate imitation of the former — compare with earlier Hegelian stuff) pretty unreadable, as Frazer himself can become when he piles on example after example. The fact that Darwin simply instantiates and doesn't test, I argued, doesn't mean that he isn't *right* about natural selection. In fact, he most certainly is. And whatever we might think of Marx's theories and prophecies, his diagnosis of the ills of capitalism — with those endless Darwin-like or Frazer-like examples drawn from the Blue Books — seemed to be sound.

Even with the "cross-cultural analysts," I persisted, they certainly acknowledged "negative instances," but, providing these were few enough, they were ignored. This might seem an odd way to phrase the principle of "significant correlation," but that is what it amounts to. Thus we could set up

Frazer's "hypothesis" about pastoralism and milk-meat taboos in the standard
manner as a two-by-two table:

	Taboo	No Taboo
Pastoralists	(A) High	(C) Low
Nonpastoralists	(B) Low	(D) High

To confirm a "statistically significant correlation," the numbers in cells A
and D would have to be "significantly" higher than those in B and C by the
appropriate test, in this case probably Chi-square. Indeed, Tylor as early as
1889 had done this with the "adhesions" between customs of in-law
avoidance and patterns of residence at marriage in his famous essay "On a
Method of Investigating the Development of Institutions: Applied to Laws of
Marriage and Descent." Frazer refers to this a couple of times, but he never
appears to have explored the possibility of its application to his own data. In
this he was certainly not alone. Thus the sheer *existence* of negative instances
was not the issue in establishing that two elements were significantly
associated, i.e., greater than one would expect by random distribution. One
expected negative instances. Indeed, if there were no negative instances we
might suspect we were dealing with a tautology. It was the greater-than-
chance preponderance of positive instances which established the correlation.
And a "significant correlation" could be established in fact with a fairly
minimal preponderance of positive cases: that is, the correlation (r) could be
low, but significant at the .05 level. Cross-cultural analysts seemed happy to
accept quite low correlations (many negative instances) as long as they were
thus "significant." (Unfortunately for my unfortunate anthropology mentors,
the sociology syllabus required us to know some statistics: not a subject very
dear to their hearts. As I remember, they dropped statistics as soon as social
anthropology got its independent degree.)

My own problems with Frazer were somewhat different. I had started my
Rationalist crusade on the common assumption that religion and magic were
about "explaining" the world, and that as such they were false explanations
and so would soon be displaced by science. This was of course Frazer's root
assumption also. But in reading voraciously, as I did in "primitive" religion
and magic, I soon changed my opinion. The explanatory function was there,
to be sure, but it paled into insignificance beside the expressive and social
functions. Freud started me on the former, and Durkheim (via Radcliffe-
Brown) on the latter. Donald Macrae was instrumental in guiding me away
from my overrationalized view of religion. When I entered the Rationalist
Press Association national student essay competition — whose subject was
"Can Society Survive Without Religion?" — I argued the negative: No, it

can't. At least within a broad sort of Comtean or Durkheimian definition of religion it couldn't. The Press kindly gave me the prize: a free trip to their conference at Oxford. But I felt I was there under false pretenses. My guilt about deserting religion was now replaced by my guilt at deserting strict Rationalism. Well, we have to have something to be guilty about.

I suppose after this my pressing of Frazer and his case became less fervid. The only other thing of that exciting undergraduate career that survived, relevant to Frazer, is a short paper I did for a class presentation, or it might have been a tutorial essay. I think it must have been for Schapera and on the history of anthropology, but it might have been for Macrae, who always reveled in detailed examination of "the old stuff" for its own sake. (Who else would have acceded to my demands to read and write essays on the whole of Herbert Spencer's *Principles of Sociology*, a great set of which I found for a shilling a volume in a second-hand law bookshop in Grays Inn Road.) The paper is in my "Miscellaneous Religion and Magic" file along with old lecture and book notes, and is undated but must have been from about 1955-56. It shows both my continuing interest in Frazer and the details of *The Golden Bough*, and my distancing from the partisanship of the earlier days.

Divine Kings: The Cycle of the Seasons

Why did the king have to die? What was his relation to the wood? To the Goddess of the grove? To the mistletoe?

Frazer continues to probe in the same manner as he did in the foregoing sections, by looking for analogies: examples of the death of kings ritually carried out; of vegetation and seasonal ceremonies carrying the themes of death and of succession or rebirth.

On the principle of imitative magic, the health of the magician-king, the semi-divine ruler — is held to be intimately connected with the health of the crops, animals and people. He will, in later sections, look at the translation of this into pure myth with the death and resurrection of the Gods themselves. Here he is concerned with the living representatives of the God.

What he finds is a twofold pattern. In the first type, the king-god is put to death if he shows signs of aging, sickness or impotence. He cites examples from east, south and central Africa, especially the well-documented (Seligman) Shilluk and Dinka cases. He includes an amazing anecdote of the great Zulu king Shaka who pleaded with the Europeans to bring him hair oil to darken his hair. Further examples from Old Prussia and the west coast of India (Malabar).

In the second type, rather than leave this ritual killing until the king shows signs of wear, he is killed at regular intervals; eight, nine and twelve years being popular — all based on calendrical/astronomical considerations (8 years = periodic conjunction of solar and lunar calendars, e.g.).

He notes that one development of this was that kings found substitutes to die in their places, and that these substitutes enjoyed brief periods of kingly glory in return for their sacrifice.

Greek kings reigned for eight years then were either killed, found a substitute (sometimes the eldest son) or had to withdraw and regenerate themselves (as the King of Israel had, every eight years, to read all the laws aloud to the people to renew his reign). Minos of Crete observed this temporary abdication every eight years during which the seven youths and seven maidens were sent as tribute from Athens, viz., Theseus, Ariadne, Minotaur, etc. The Babylonian king had thus to reclaim his throne annually — leading to some empty thrones.

He picks up again on the notion of substitutes, who can be eldest sons (Abraham and Isaac), other royal family members, special families of peasants, strangers or criminals. This is played out seriously, says Frazer, and the "mock king" is allowed to have the king's wives and concubines before dying. Greek legends (e.g., origins of the Golden Fleece) testify to this custom also.

If the king dies, then what status has his successor, especially if not related? In a weakly argued and supported passage, he maintains that it is believed that the soul of the king passes into his successor (metempsychosis). Sometimes this resides in relics or regalia — hence the tremendous importance of crowns, crown jewels, etc. — and eventually he will get to the mistletoe.

Having established that the king must and did die to preserve the health of the kingdom, he turns to his favourite subject of "survivals" of this custom in folk practices. Most of these take place at Easter and Whitsuntide — the Christian overlay of the traditional festivals of spring and the vernal equinox — the retreat of winter and the onset of summer. Many representations of this transition involve the "killing" of some effigy or other and its rebirth or replacement. This is often quite obviously a "tree spirit" —

like Jack-in-the-Green (Oxford) or a "King of the May." Often there is a mock pursuit or contest and if the "wild man" wins he is not killed.

Around the Med. (his examples come from Provence and Italy, Greece and Malta) the killing of the figure of Carnival at this period is noted. Often quite elaborate ceremonies. In other parts of Europe similar figures of straw are burned or hanged or drowned. Sometimes they are brought back to life, sometimes another "summerlike" figure is put in their places. This is also the case in similar ceremonies in which the killed figure is explicitly Death or The Old Woman — both, he supposes, representing winter and the death of vegetation. He then details the opposite and balancing custom of "bringing in summer" (which he ties in with the May Brides, Queen of the May, etc.). Typically trees, branches and decorated trees are used, sometimes wearing the clothes of the executed death figure. He concludes with mock battles in which "teams" representing summer defeat those representing winter as far apart as Sweden, Germany and the Eskimo and Canadian Indians. To this he adds Russian "mock funerals" in which the "spirit of vegetation" is solemnly buried and resurrected.

Frazer, of course, sees all of these as "survivals" — dim memories of the real thing (human sacrifice) sometimes given a semi-Christian gloss. By now he is seeing vegetation deities under the bed. But he never seems to ask why they persist and seem so alive and meaningful to the participants if all they amount to are these dim memories. At least Freud tries to account for the *persistence* with which we kill fathers and then desperately try to resurrect them, and feel alternately gleeful and guilty about the whole thing. Also, we might rather see all these activities as getting their motivation from our need for symbolic statements of the same theme — less bloody but as poetically apt. The expulsion of Death/Winter/ Famine/Disease and his resurrection as (or replacement by) Life/Summer/Health/Plenty. But Frazer is unquestionably right that it all has to do with deep concerns about fertility and its continuance and effectiveness, and the belief that these rites could somehow influence it all. Next we must tackle the Gods themselves who died and lived again.

Obviously this essay/paper was one of a series, as the last sentence testifies, but this is the only one remaining. And after this I was swept up into other things and the rest is history.

In *Encounter with Anthropology*, in the section on religion, I invoke Frazer, defend him from critics, and suggest that anyone interested start with The Master. I really meant this, and obviously had in mind my own pilgrimage. I still mean it, and I still find that a good freshman class (such as the Scholars' Seminar I teach at Douglass College) responds wonderfully to Frazer, golden prose and all. "It's like a fantastic trip!" one student told me in the early 1970s, bombed out as he was on grass and dying gods. And indeed it is!

Occasionally I show the film *The Wicker Man* — perhaps the best filmic tribute to Frazer yet, thanks to Anthony Schaffer's brilliant script. Christopher Lee was the star, but it was also the film in which Edward Woodward first made his mark as the prudish, virginal policeman-sacrifice, marvelously tempted by Britt Ekland. I also, having had them first read *The Heart of Darkness*, point out the scene in *Apocalypse Now* where the camera pans in to doomed jungle-king Marlon Brando's bedside table, showing copies of *The Golden Bough* and *From Ritual to Romance* just before the ritual killing and ascension to (temporary) kingship by Martin Sheen. (A sacrificial ox dies in flashbacks during the fight — just to make sure you get the point. Coppola doesn't like leaving these things to chance.) And so it goes. Coppola crosses Conrad with Frazer and you have the ultimate modern myth. John Boorman marries Malory with Frazer (with appropriate leitmotifs from Wagner) in *Excalibur* to produce an Arthurian version of the Waste-Land/Sick-King/ Dying-God theme. In *Eye of the Devil* — originally a novel — David Niven plays one of a line of feudal French landowners sacrificed by their tenantry when the vines are blighted. And on and on. Frazer might have been drummed out of anthropology, but he is drummed into the public imagination. Mary Renault — especially in the appropriately named *The King Must Die* — if no one else, has seen to that. Even Anne Rice, the elegant reigning queen of the epic of the undead, laces *The Vampire Lestat* with Frazerian motifs.

He crops up in the most unlikely places too. In one of the funnier satires on American government, P. J. O'Rourke's (1991) *Parliament of Whores*, the author speaks of the president as follows:

We treat the president of the United States with awe. We impute to him remarkable powers. We divine things by his smallest gestures. We believe he has the capacity to destroy the very earth, and — by vigorous perusal of sound economic policy — to make the land fruitful and all our endeavors prosperous. We beseech him for aid and comfort in our every distress and believe him capable of granting any boon or favor.

The type is recognizable to even a casual student of mythology. The president is not an ordinary politician trying to conduct the affairs of state as best he can. He is a divine priest-king. And we Americans worship our state avatar devoutly. That is, until he shows any sign of weakness and disability, as it were. Sir James Frazer, in *The Golden Bough*, said:

"Primitive people ... believe that their safety and even that of the world is bound up with the life of one of these god-men.... Naturally, therefore, they take the utmost care of his life.... But no amount of care and precaution will prevent the man-god from growing old and feeble.... There is only one way of averting these dangers. The man-god must be killed."

Thus in our brief national history we have shot four of our presidents, worried five of them to death, impeached one and hounded another out of office. And when all else fails, we hold an election and assassinate their character.

Much was made of the elderly Ronald Reagan's use of "grecian formula" to darken his greying hair and thus give the impression of youthful vigor. Few perhaps remember what I noted in the undergraduate essay: Frazer's remarkable story of the great and terrible, but aging, Shaka Zulu's desperate and persistent request to his European visitors to bring him hair darkener so that his subjects would not see his greying patches and put him to death (*The Golden Bough*, abridged edition, p. 272).

The reasons Frazer persists, as I dimly foresaw in the undergraduate essay and later argued at length (*The Red Lamp of Incest*), may rest in a Freudian-evolutionary scenario of some complexity. "We consistently reproduce that which produced us" was my formula. And what produced us were traumatic evolutionary events in which younger males battled older for the fertile females, the outcome being a somewhat tamed but still feisty growing male always ready to challenge, but also able to defer gratification (unless under a spell, of course). The stuff of the epics: Diarmud vs. Finn for Grainne; Tristan vs. Mark for Isolde; Paris vs. Menelaus for Helen; Telemachus (and Odysseus) vs. the Suitors for Penelope; Shiva vs. Daksha for Sati; Lancelot vs. Arthur for Guinevere; Siegmund vs. Hunding for Sieglinde; Oedipus vs. Laius for Jocasta; Aeneas (and Turnus) vs. Latinus for Lavinia; and above all, Achilles vs. Agamemnon for Briseis, and Siegfried vs. Wotan for Brunhilde.

At the root of the great quarrels that are the driving force of the epics is the basic struggle between young men and old over the disposition of fertile women, and this is what is at the base of all kinship systems too. These are systems of rules that make sure that the marriage choices of the younger generations are determined by the choices already made by the older: either that, or custom allows direct intervention in such choices by the older generations (usually the males), if the system lacks a positive rule. Most of the rules and customs surrounding marriage are to do with this ongoing struggle. What makes both *The Divine Comedy* and *Paradise Lost*, while grand and profound poems, so exceedingly dull, is that no one is fighting over Beatrice or Eve. Thus, the young agree that the king (read — older male with power over access to females) must die (i.e., lose his power). But they know that there must be kings and that they in turn must become kings themselves and hence vulnerable to the fatal divinity that doth hedge them, the divinity that decrees their defeat and death in turn. The cycle unfolds not only in the sacred grove at Nemi, but in the life of every boy growing into a man and facing the stony phalanx of older male rivals. Meanwhile, the women look on in pragmatic amazement at the male antics and pick off the winners for their breeding experiments. Darwin called this "sexual selection" and pretty well got it right. Freud called it "the Oedipus complex" and confused future generations thoroughly. Yet, put the one with the other and the confusion becomes intensely creative, and the clue to the making of man.

But where would Freud have been without Frazer in the first place? Darwin was not enough: a bridge was needed between the sexual selection process in animals and its peculiar turn in specifically human evolution. Frazer (inextricably intertwined with his lifelong friend and mentor Robertson Smith) provided the bridge. Our symbolic capacity helps us turn dominant males into divine kings, and makes the process of their dispossession, while fundamentally the same as in the primate horde, a richer psychological experience derived from an enriched brain which can reproduce through archetype and myth the memory of its own formation. Yes, Jung gets in here too.

Even without his role in this line of evolutionary and mythological thinking, which for anthropologists is still something of an acquired taste, perhaps Frazer's intellectual obituary is premature. Looking to the future "mainstream" in anthropology, Adam Kuper (1988), in *The Invention of Primitive Society*, concludes that the anthropology of the future "is embracing the second tradition of anthropology, the anthropology of Tylor and Frazer rather than Morgan and Rivers, the anthropology of culture." And indeed some of the pursuits of "meaning" are less on the "contextual" and more on the "universal" pattern. The Structuralist paradigm has to do with universal laws of thought, which is pure Frazer, even if the laws are different. And need they be so different? After all, in currently fashionable jargon the Law of Contagion could be rewritten as the Law of Metonymy, and the Law of Similarity as the Law of Metaphor. So perhaps the wheel has come full circle, as it must. The Fathers were killed and descended into the hell of oblivion; the Sons briefly reigned, but the Fathers are inexorably resurrected and live again — for a while. As it was in the beginning, is now and ever shall be, world without end. Amen.

11

The Origins of Social Complexity

Cousins and Caciques: How Complex is Complex?

We must start by recognizing that *complexity* is a relative term. It is not the case that there was once a period of no social complexity and that suddenly (or gradually) social complexity appeared. Social complexity occurs in insect societies — but that is another, if parallel, story. There is social complexity in monkey and ape societies of varying kinds. We now know a great deal of the complex social organization of chimpanzees, and I have written that macaque kinship systems are only "a naming system away" from human counterparts, and that even the basic human kinship systems are not original in their elements, but only in the combination of their elements (Fox 1975). These "basic" or "elementary" human kinship systems, as we find them among the traditional, and still technically Paleolithic, Australian Aborigines, for example, appear as of a baffling complexity to observers who have not assimilated their fairly simple rules. Readers may briefly look ahead to part 4 at the diagrams there to appreciate the complexity of "primitive" systems of kinship and marriage or consult my book of the same name (Fox 1967a). A great deal of this kind of complexity in fact turns out to be the application of simple rules producing complex situations, viz., chess (see Fox 1989, chap. 9). Not only in kinship, but in ritual, pre-Neolithic societies showed considerable complexity — echoed in the ritual complexity of their modern counterparts. Ritual centers, like those at Niaux, Altamira, and Lascauax, were as elaborate as modern cathedrals. John Pfeiffer (1982) has even appropriated cathedral terminology to describe their apses, naves, rotundas, aisles, transepts, side chapels, etc. Also, as far as cultural complexity is concerned, Marshack (1972) makes a good case that even in the Lower Paleolithic there was an accurate system of recording phases of the moon by incisions on bone, etc., and Ucko and Rosenfeld (1967) have shown that geometric abstraction, not just "primitive realism," characterizes all cave art, which was therefore a system of "signs," not just "pictures."

The *Oxford English Dictionary* is not much help:

complex. a. Consisting of parts, composite; complicated; [complex] *sentence*, one containing subordinate clause(s).

The etymology is from the Latin *plex,* meaning to plait. But it is interesting that one of the earliest sociologists to take this issue seriously, Herbert Spencer (1879), adopted the grammatical criterion for a complex society — although he called it a "compound" society — namely, "a society containing at least one subordinate society." Thereby hangs a tale to which we shall return. (For an interesting critique of the whole idea of "complexity" as a Western capitalist loaded concept, see Rowlands 1989.)

But if the kinship/social systems of the pre-urban humans were "complex," it was a particular type of complexity. The best phrase to describe it I have heard is that of Germaine Tillion (1983), who called it "la république des cousins" in her book *Harem et les cousins.* Those Aranda and Murgin systems may look complex, but each member of these societies knew whom to marry, and that person was a particular type of cousin. Paradoxically, the situation in later societies was in fact much more complex even if the kinship systems were simpler. (This is why Lévi-Strauss distinguishes between "elementary" and "complex" systems. See chap. 13.) With the decline of kinship to the level of the extended family, and in the towns even the nuclear family, the choice of mate became highly probabilistic. No specific cousin was marked down; the choice was technically all the unmarried eligibles in the town or village. The choice would in fact be determined by complex considerations of class, caste, status, dowry, and the like.

If we want to invent terms, let us call the type of complexity that existed in pre-urban, tribal society "horizontal complexity." In the post-Neolithic cities of the Near East this was replaced by "vertical complexity." The complexity of marriage rules might have been reduced, but the social hierarchy produced a new kind of complexity to replace it. Divine kings with their courts and nobles came to dominate. Often the kings made sacred marriages with their sisters, and a tendency to caste divisions in marriage increased. Women of upper castes were not available to those of lower, although the upper-caste males could usually appropriate lower-caste females (and often a lot of them). This, along with the expropriation of the agricultural surplus of the peasantry, was the new element. It was completely unknown to the republic of the cousins, where even chiefs — or the gerontocrats of the Australians — had to marry their specified cousins, and where there was no surplus of anything to expropriate.

It is a commonplace that this new kind of "vertical complexity" needed a surplus to work on: the upper classes or castes did not produce for themselves. Again it is inconceivable that this could have occurred in hunting societies, or probably even with the very early planters and herders. It took the revolution in Neolithic agricultural technologies — planting, breeding and irrigation, and eventually the plough — to achieve this. But these, while the commonest causes, were not strictly necessary. Vertical complexity was possible simply as long as there was a surplus, however this was come by.

Calusa: The Seashell Kingdom

One possible source was fish. Fish had to be hunted (shark) or gathered (shellfish), as it were, but they were not cultivated or domesticated. Societies of great vertical complexity have been built on fish in at least two known instances: the Northwest Coast of America, and the Gulf Coast of Florida. Take the latter (because it is the less well known). The Calusa empire, which was flourishing at the first Spanish contact in the early 1500s (they were the Indians who killed Ponce de León in 1521), was eventually finished off in the second half of the eighteenth century, perhaps by the Creeks/Seminoles armed with British guns (or perhaps not — their end is murky), having successfully fended off the Spanish for two hundred fifty years. This long period of contact, however, had the serendipitous result of much documentation about a society that otherwise would have been hard to reconstruct (see Hann 1991).

The original Calusa were Muskogean Indians, probably from Georgia, who were in place with their pottery and mounds by 200 A.D. and flourishing by 800 A.D. Theirs was a society built, literally, on shellfish. At one period, during the sixteenth century, the empire and its vassal tribes covered the whole of south Florida, linked by a system of well-constructed canals up to twenty feet wide and lined with shell, and stretching from the present Fort Myers to Miami via the Caloosahatchee River and Lake Okeechobee, and south via the barrier islands to the Florida Keys (see map 1 and Luer 1989). Their population has been estimated at about ten thousand souls. Substantial towns were built on the barrier islands from Charlotte Harbor down to Key Marco, centering on Mound Key, the capital in Estero Bay. These towns were built up on the used shells from the numerous varieties of shellfish caught, and included temple mounds as high as sixty feet (according to Cushing 1897), huge plazas, internal canals, fish tanks, and gardens.

On Pine Island, one such city, substantial remains of which are still being excavated, covered three miles of seashore and went inland for three-quarters of a mile. (This is what is now "inland" — water levels have fluctuated over the centuries.) The "water courts" (Cushing's term) often covered at least an acre, and had pile dwellings on the sides and burial mounds in the centers.

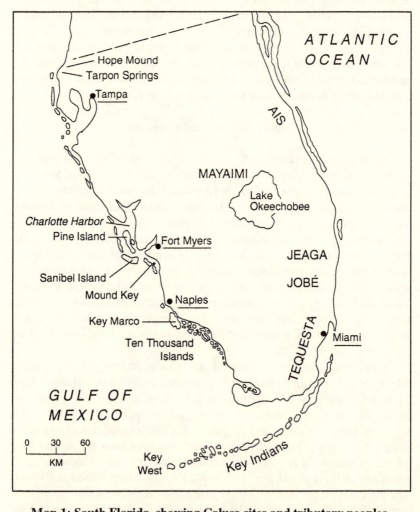

Map 1: South Florida, showing Calusa sites and tributary peoples (modern towns underlined)

The high "temple mounds" were faced with elaborate mosaics of shells in overlapping patterns; similar mosaics were used to make pathways. Canoes made from cypress were the mode of travel; some of them were huge, holding forty to sixty warriors. The Calusa independently invented the catamaran by lashing two canoes together with planks for carrying especially big loads. There was a limited lithic industry, but an extensive technology in shells: Cutting instruments, sinkers and floats, hooks and awls, etc., were all made from seashells (Gilliland 1975). Most of their fine art is lost, since it was in wood (carved with sharks' teeth), but what remains, largely rescued by Cushing's famous expedition of 1895-96, rivals the finest in the Americas (Gilliland 1989).

The canals helped to connect all parts of the Calusa kingdom to huge ceremonial centers inland near Lake Okeechobee. Some of these earth-mound structures are massive: 12,000 cubic yards of sand went into one mound at the Ortona site, and it was one of dozens. (We know the exact size since it was torn down and sold for landfill.) Tony's mound, the most elaborate, is 1,665 yards long and 580 feet wide. Big Mound City covers half a mile across in two directions. These mounds, often semicircular with "fingers" leading off them, must have required a tremendous amount of labor, yet there is no evidence of nearby habitation. They seem to have been purely ceremonial centers where the Calusa gathered with their vassal tribes for periodic rituals before returning to the shore cities (Allen 1948; Willey 1949).

The ruler (called "Carlos" by the Spanish — obviously a version of "Calus") was a "sacred king" who married his sister, Inca style, the only case in North America of incestuous royal marriage. Marquardt thinks these were at best half-siblings or first cousins. But the Spanish report an insistence on "sister," and it became a big bone of contention with the missionaries. Succession to the chieftainship and the higher offices was from father to son, but we do not know what the order of succession and inheritance was in the lower castes. The greater Southeast is almost exclusively matrilineal, and it could be that the common people retained this form of kinship while the nobles and priests moved to a patrilineal form. The polygamy they practiced would have encouraged this. The king's caste of nobles, and his priests and chief warriors, were exempt from work. He was reported to have a "war chief" (called "captain general" by the Spanish) and a chief priest, both relatives. This sounds like the old American "war chief and peace chief" pattern, but now subordinated to a ruler — one step up the social evolutionary ladder.

There was an elaborate ritual system including human sacrifice (with heads on poles), the fate of most early Spanish captives, and a belief system that included a trinity of "great" gods controlling the weather, the sea, and war, together with "totem" animals and elaborately carved idols. Children and captives were sacrificed on the death of a queen or nobleman. The Spanish describe elaborate ceremonies including masks, processions, songs, dances, and retreats. The "sorcerers" they describe sound like healing shamans with paraphernalia common to such practitioners in North America. This religion had the devotion of the people and was highly resistant to missionary activity. The Franciscans were stripped naked and shipped off, and the Jesuits defeated.

The various kings in fact successfully manipulated the Spanish. "Carlos II" even forced Pedro Menéndez de Avilés, in 1566, to marry his adopted sister (after divorcing her himself and sending her to Cuba with the Spanish as a spy). The Spaniards killed two Calusa kings in an effort to suppress the kingdom, but they were forced to accept their successors or lose the labor of the natives. Finally, three years after they arrived, to try to "colonize" the Calusa in earnest, the Spanish gave up and left in 1573. In 1697 the Franciscans made another well-documented attempt, which ended in failure (see Hann 1991, part 1).

Exactly how the Calusa came to their end we do not know, but some might have been assimilated. The Seminole of the area still maintain that some of their "old songs" are Calusa (Densmore 1956). One story is that Key West — in Spanish, Cayo Hueso (Bone Island), so named from the huge piles of human bones found there — was the place of the last stand of the Calusa survivors. Others are said to have gone north or to Cuba (see Hann 1991, part 3). One way or another, this amazing civilization finally met its end, but not from internal collapse. And this remarkable kingdom was sustained by fishing — mullet being the favorite — and built on old oyster beds at the edges of shallow islands whose interiors were almost impenetrable mangrove swamp. The only high places existing in this totally flat part of Florida are in fact Calusa shell mounds, except where a later and more advanced civilization has bulldozed them to make way for luxury retirement complexes and golf courses. (For a description of the Calusa, see Goggin and Sturtevant 1964; Marquardt 1988, 1991; Widmer 1988.)

There is still dispute on the origins of Calusa vertical complexity. Widmer favors the view that it was a slow process brought about by the need to organize and feed an ever-growing population, while Marquardt favors the view that it was in fact a product of the acquisition of Spanish trade goods and their control by certain leaders (these trade goods, or captured goods, seem to have been a major component in tribute). It could of course be both, the Spanish intrusions accelerating an already existing development. More research on what little is left of the Calusa might help to resolve this and many other enigmas of this fascinating civilization, including the problem of how exactly a surplus such as fish could be expropriated and redistributed.

The Southwestern Desert: The Living Neolithic

Thus the initial conditions for vertical complexity seem to be a surplus of whatever kind, even fish and shellfish, and intimidation, religious or military, or both. Yet a system like the Calusa grew out of typical North American Paleolithic, tribal, nomadic material as did all the high civilizations of the Americas (even allowing for some diffusion from the Pacific). There was a transition point in all their developments to the "Neolithic village," just as there had been in the Near East and the other centers of eventual "civilization." This is why, for example, the Pueblo (town dwelling) Indians of the American Southwest are so fascinating. In studying them we are looking at living examples of what happens when this transition is made. Our archaeology is precise: we know exactly when and where they did it and what they did. But we also have their living descendants operating modified versions of those transitional social systems to this day, as is unhappily not the case with the Calusa. In looking at the Pueblos, we can, by stripping away the Spanish and Anglo accretions, take a kind of peek into the Neolithic transition in action.

Joseph Campbell (1959), when discussing the transition from the tribal power of the shaman to the urban power of the priest, says, "The situation in Arizona and New Mexico at the period of the discovery of America was, culturally, much like that which must have prevailed in the Near and Middle East and in Europe from the fourth to second millenniums B.C., when the rigid patterns proper to orderly settlement were being imposed on peoples used to the freedom and vicissitudes of the hunt" (vol. 1, pp. 238-39). Indeed, reconstructions of the earliest Neolithic "pottery" villages like Çatal Hüyük in Anatolia (6500 B.C.) even look like Pueblo villages with their multistory adobe dwellings clustered around courts and plazas (Mellart 1966, 1967). They too were practicing either dry farming or minor irrigation, and they too had domesticated grain, which was their basic crop. They also clearly had a well-established mother-goddess cult.

What of the Pueblo Indian stage of social complexity? Well, it shows a very definitely transitional character. Shamans have indeed become priests, and there is a "chief priest" (Spanish *Cacique*) who is exempt from field work, but he is the only one. What is more, while there is a rigorous theocratic hierarchy, it is open to anyone. Any male can join one of the "societies" that are the route to ritual power. And there is no caste system, only grades of ritual authority which any novice, after the appropriate ritual tests and initiations, can achieve: a little like a modern university, in fact. There is no expropriation of surplus by anyone. Except among the Rio Grande Pueblos with their extensive irrigation farming, there is very little surplus anyway, if any. Dry farming rarely gets to that point.

In the Rio Grande Pueblos, the Cacique is exempt from planting and harvesting, and here we may have the beginnings of the social differentiation we are looking for. The Pueblos stayed relatively small, with only at most a few hundred people per village. Zuni is unusually large (2,500 plus) but is probably an amalgamation of as many as seven villages. Among the other language groups the tendency is to small villages, with the Keres having seven, the Tewa five, the Tanoans five (one now extinct), and the Hopi, traditionally, seven. The average population was probably about three hundred per village. The ancient Anasazi sites show towns/villages of similar size and distribution.

This is not a basis for expansion of production and a surplus. But elements were there, taken over from the nomadic tribal stage: There were "medicine societies" of differing degrees of power and status; there were "clown societies," better understood as "managing societies," for complex ritual performances; there were "warrior societies" which speak for themselves, as well as a "war captain" and his assistant named after the hero twins of myth, who were a kind of ceremonial police force but had the right, for example, to execute witches; there were "hunt societies," often associated with the warriors; there were women's societies; and so on. All these were part of the tribal system simply moved into the villages. But the greater emphasis on the collectivity and on collective enterprises (like ditch digging and cleaning), the greater discipline, the greater dependence on trained priests and priestly societies rather than individual ecstatic shamans, all pointed to a possible development: Once a surplus could develop, these "egalitarian" or "meritocratic" fraternities could easily become differentiated classes or castes.

There was in every Pueblo a distinction between the "made" and the "unmade" people, or the "cooked" and the "raw" people — it was variously phrased. But essentially it differentiated the ritual specialists from the "common" folk (see Fox 1967b; Ortiz 1969). It would not take much to turn this into a class/caste distinction. The rest would easily follow. The clan system as it existed in the Pueblos was something of a brake on vertical differentiation since clans cut across the societies and fraternities. But, as eventually in China, for example, the clan itself could become internally differentiated, or "aristocratic" clans could emerge. The republic of the cousins is fragile once "le snobisme" has something — like the surplus — on which to work, as Tillion shows so brilliantly. It is a short step (although it may take a long time) from "les cousins" to "le harem."

As to their kinship systems, while they show great variety, they are essentially the "elementary" systems of the republic of cousins, again moved into a settlement. There is considerable evidence of preferential marriage practices, but various Pueblo groups show different stages in a shift from "elementary" to "complex" systems. Only with the Northern Tanoans, however, do we seem to have shifted from dominance of clan and cousinship altogether (Eggan 1949; Fox 1967a). Thus the Pueblos show a truly fascinating transitional picture, but have rarely been looked at as such. The next transition comes with greater population density, and hence the fabled surplus and a shift to vertical complexity when, for instance, the whole clan of the Cacique is exempted from labor, and his "sisters" (i.e., clanswomen) become his only suitable brides; when the various "societies" become specialized castes equally exempt: the warriors becoming the army; the sacred clown/managers becoming the priests; and so on. But this requires an ever-expanding agricultural base to support these specialists full-time.

Chaco: The First Apartment Dwellers

Again in the Southwest we get the possibilities of this in the great Anasazi cultural complex of Chaco Canyon and its environs in what is now northwestern New Mexico (roughly from the tenth century through the twelfth century A.D.). In the canyon itself there were seven to nine great "towns" — unitary apartment dwellings either semicircular (D-shaped) or rectangular (E-shaped) and rising to as many as six stories on the outer walls. They usually had two "great kivas" — semiunderground circular temples — and numerous smaller kivas. (Plate 11.1 shows the largest town, Pueblo Bonito, from an artist's reconstruction; plate 11.2 shows its current condition, diagram 11.2 its excavated floor plan. Rectangular rooms are dwellings; round rooms are kivas.) The main town complex in the canyon itself was surrounded by numerous outliers and related towns, with an extensive irrigation system and roads covering a hundred miles north and south (map 2). For an excellent general description see Frazier 1986.) These roads were a regular thirty feet wide — no one seems to know why — with signal towers at strategic intervals. Like the Calusa canals, their purpose might have been as much ceremonial as utilitarian.

Such a complex must have had a pretty extensive agricultural base, achieved by ingenious irrigation in a semiarid climate, and yet we do not have any evidence that it achieved a *social and cultural* complexity greater than that of the present-day Pueblos, despite claims to this effect. (See Lynne Sebastian's chap. 6 in Crown and Judge 1990 for an excellent discussion of Chaco complexity.) The towns were magnificent pieces of architecture, but they did not house more than a few hundred souls, and each was more or less a D-shaped or E-shaped replica of the others. They could have been built over periods of years with not too large a labor force (Lekson 1984).

Estimates of the Canyon population differ, depending on the method of calculation (there was a paucity of burials for some reason), but most realistic ones fall between two thousand at the beginning and decline, and about six

Plate 11.1
Pueblo Bonito ("Beautiful Village") at the time of the Chacoans
(in an artist's reconstruction)

Plate 11.2
Pueblo Bonito today, as seen from cliffs above and looking west.
(National Parks Service)

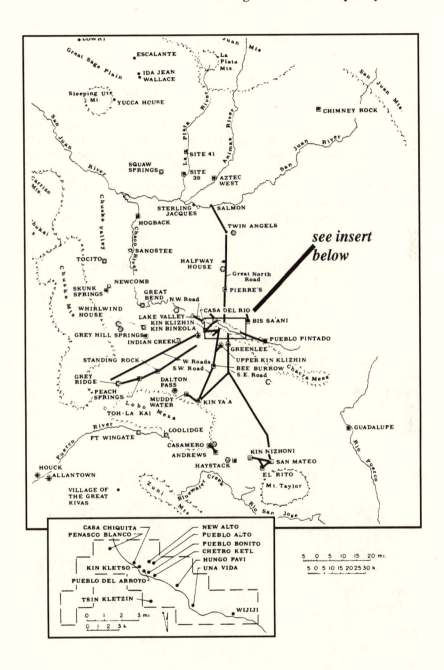

**Map 2: Chacoan roadway system and outliers
(National Parks Service)**

thousand five hundred at the peak (see R. Gwinn Vivian's chap. 4 in Crown and Judge 1990). One method not yet tried is to assume that each "small kiva" belonged to a clan (they are sometimes referred to in the literature as "clan kivas," but this is not followed up), as in present-day Hopi for example, and do the calculation based on median clan size for the present-day Pueblos comparable in size. The figures I have to hand are for Cochiti (Lange 1959), where the median size in 1897 was twenty-four (population = 271, clans 11), and in 1948 again twenty-four (population = 378, clans 10). (The mean had shifted from 24.6 in 1897 to 37.8 in 1948, but the median is the better measure because of extremely lopsided clan sizes, varying from 2 to 114, a common feature of Pueblo demography.) From Sia (White 1962) we get a median of nineteen (population = 329, clans 9) in 1957. For the Hopi, Titiev (1944) gives us a median of twenty (population = 622, clans 22) for Old Oraibi in 1906.

These numbers seem representative, and give a rough median clan size of twenty to work with. If we then go back to Chaco Canyon at its peak and take, for example, the very large Pueblo Bonito, there are thirty-two small kivas. Assuming them all to be in use, this makes for a population of approximately six hundred forty. This is the biggest, and gives us a population and clan number uncannily close to traditional Old Oraibi — itself the biggest of the Hopi Pueblos. Continuing with small kivas, Chetro Ketl has eight, Pueblo Aroyo eight, Pueblo Alto eight, Penasco Blanco eight, Una Vida four, and these seem nearer the kinds of numbers we get today in the

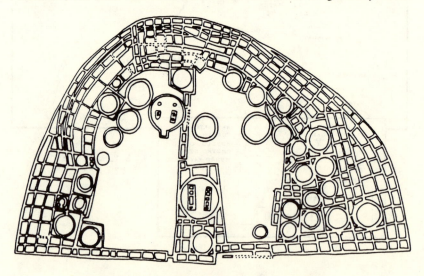

Diagram 11.1: Floor plan of Pueblo Bonito
(National Parks Service)

Pueblos. If we total up the "clan populations" of these Pueblos, we come up with a rough estimate of one thousand three hundred sixty. Assuming half as many again lived south of the Chaco wash and between the "great" towns, we would have a population of roughly two thousand forty (plus) in the main canyon at the peak of Chaco development. This is certainly on the low side since there are some small towns where the great-kiva/clan-kiva distinction is hard to fathom, and I have left these out, e.g., Wijiji, Tsinkletzin, Hungo Pavi, etc. But if we assume that at least four clans would be a minimum, this gives us a sum of eighty people for each of these. Then we can add approximately another four hundred, giving us an estimated total of two thousand four hundred forty.

There has been much controversy over the size estimates for Chaco Canyon itself, varying from a few thousand to twenty-five thousand and more. It is now generally agreed that figures much over six thousand are exaggerations, and the estimate here agrees with the "low" side of the reasonable figures: compare Windes' (1984) figure of "no more than 2,000" based on firepits (hearths), with Hayes' (1981) maximum of 5,652, based on room occupancy. Vivian, in Crown and Judge (1990, chap. 4), cites estimates based on space usage in modern Pueblos (5,836), construction labor (2,762), land cultivation (2,667), and ratio of fallow to cultivated land (2,885-4,576). Thus we can say with confidence that the population probably never exceeded five thousand.

However one looks at it, this is not exactly a large population. And it makes sense. There is no way primitive irrigation and dry farming techniques could have supported a much larger one. As the Chacoans expanded outward they tended to produce smaller versions of the Chaco pattern at Aztec, Salmon Ruin, Kin Bineola, and the like. Even if they doubled their population with the "outliers" it would not come to much more than ten thousand given the most generous high estimates — about the same as the Calusa. And despite the roadworks there is no sense of any real vertical complexity being arrived at. Chaco Canyon itself is central and might well have been a "ritual center" in the manner of Stonehenge. Yet even this is not incompatible with modern Pueblo ideals. Each group of Pueblos seems to have a "central" member preeminent in ritual affairs: for the Keresans it is Santo Domingo, for the Tewa, San Juan, and for the Hopi, Oraibi. Similarly, all Pueblo Indians turn to certain centers for very special rituals peculiar to them, the best example being the spectacular Zuni Shalako.

But despite the canyon's "centrality" there are no palaces, no barracks, no great royal burials (although some people have detected a different "pattern" of burials — based on very few cases — between the Great Houses and the others), and no evidence of any occupational specialization. The possible exception is the making of turquoise jewelry. Large amounts of turquoise are found at Chaco, although the deposits are sixty miles east at Cerillos, New Mexico (and toward which, interestingly, there is no great road). But this kind of rudimentary specialization is found today in the Pueblos: the Cochiti make drums, the Hopi make dance kilts, the Tewa make glazed pots, and these are traded between villages. But until the coming of Anglo markets, no one was a full-time specialist in these items.

Thus, for all its sophistication and obvious long-distance trade contacts, there is no evidence of central organization or advanced specialization in the Chaco complex. It is almost like a cell continually dividing and producing more and more clones, loosely linked but never combining into a more complex organism. Yet, with their extensive trading contacts and obvious ability to engage relatively large labor forces, it seems the Chacoans were on the brink. But Chaco was abandoned before the tipover into vertical complexity could be achieved. (McGuire's insistence that people called "lineage heads" controlled the trade and distribution of "prestige goods" seems to be based more on the requirements of theory than the evidence of archaeology, history, or ethnography [McGuire 1989].)

Organic Solidarity and Moral Density

That is where it leaves us: with the essential clue as to the tipover. If you like: What did *not* happen at Chaco Canyon? I would sum it up under three heads:

1. Elaborate differentiation of tasks leading to a true division of labor.

2. War and conquest combined with widespread trade leading to tributary kingdoms.

3. Some system of record keeping leading eventually to the emergence of elite literacy.

These are what seem to be needed to produce what Durkheim (1893) called "organic solidarity": the necessary cooperation of unlike, hence mutually dependent, parts. This gave the impetus to "history" as we understand it.

Chaco was operating at the level Durkheim called that of "mechanical solidarity." This means that society consists of units — clans, families, villages, etc. — that are basically replicas of each other. Each one does everything the others do. One might protest that among the Pueblos the clans are ritually differentiated, in that they perform different ritual functions. But each clan has its ritual functions, and in this sense they are all alike. There is not, for example, a clan of smiths, a clan of potters, a clan of merchants, etc. Until something like the latter occurs you do not get any real "change of gear" in social complexity to a system based on "organic solidarity," which, as we have seen, is based on the mutual interdependence of *unlike* parts: Adam Smith's "division of tasks" that was the basis of the wealth of nations. We may simply not find it in the early Neolithic towns any more than we do in the traditional Pueblos — although my archaeological colleagues can correct me here. If there is any way we can decide that a division of labor existed from the material record it would be interesting to know.

Durkheim's catalyst for this change was population growth. In his quaint, nineteenth-century French way of putting it, greater social density led to greater moral density. But he might well have been right. The less than ten thousand populations of the Chacoans and the Calusa did not give enough critical mass to get beyond their interesting but relatively uncomplex cultural forms. The Calusa had moved to vertical complexity and warfare with tributary states. But again there is no evidence, beyond the castes of the vertical system, of any extensive division of labor in the population at large. Without the coming of the Europeans, would the Calusa have moved on to a complexity like that of Central and South American urban civilizations? I doubt it because of the dependence on small-scale fishing and the inability to develop agriculture in the mangrove swamps. But who knows? We never shall.

The development of extensive metal technology is not a prerequisite of this organic kind of complexity. We get it in the New World cities where the only metal working was in precious metals and some copper (which found its way as far north as Chaco). And even when tribes develop smelting, etc., they often stay at the tribal level. But the extensive use of bronze, tin, copper, and iron certainly speeds things along. It is a cliché that the calling of blacksmith is the "oldest profession" (despite claims made for more exotic vocations). While every Pueblo family makes its own pots, and, in the old days, would have made its own arrow heads, jewelry, etc., with the advent of metals there was need for a full-time specialist. Making things in metal is arduous and time consuming. People cannot do it in their spare time, as it were. And when metal weapons become important on a large scale, armies of smiths are needed, as well as full-time miners to provide the raw material.

In all the post-Neolithic mythologies a smith god eventually appears — perhaps the first specialized god, the others being general vegetation or hunt deities. But whatever kicks it off, once the division of labor becomes established, once potters only make pots and do nothing else, then true social complexity of a dynamic kind enters the picture. Specialization in the towns means that masons, artists, glassworkers, potters, tile makers, jewellers, metal workers, weavers, dyers, chandlers, bakers, vintners, etc. have to work full time. They are therefore dependent on the peasantry for food, expropriated by the gentry and paid out to the workers. Even the peasantry now become specialized food producers, obtaining their pots, clothes, and other necessities from the specialized manufacturers, at first by barter.

As we have learned by now, this can make for rapid expansion and the development of cities and empires, but it has inbuilt limits. Peasant farming does not produce much of a surplus, and as empires expand they must rapidly add more land to feed their armies and urban populations. This means adding more peasants who can barely feed themselves and who are usually hit with heavy taxation. Slavery is added to the complexity of the system, but it too has productive limits. These systems can last a long time if they can expand indefinitely, like Rome, or have a rich and constantly renewable agricultural base, like Egypt with its Nile floods. But otherwise they hit an upper limit and collapse. The collapse is both external — threats from the nomadic barbarians — and internal — the limits to the productive system and the burden of taxation (Grant 1990; Tainter 1988). There then has to be a further change of gear to move to the next stage of social complexity (usually some form of feudalism), but that is beyond my brief.

I mentioned trade. Chaco had a wide trade network and might even have had specialized traders. But judging from what we know of Pueblo trading in historical times, it is more likely that the traders were simply agricultural clansmen who dropped farming for a period (winter) to go off trading, and then returned. But if one adds widespread trading to the division of labor, then the existence of a class of trading specialists — "merchants" — enters the picture and the world changes. The mercantile mentality and mercantile values begin to have their effect on what was once a simple subsistence farming community. Media of exchange (money), and wealth acquired other than by expropriation (profits), move to center stage, along with numeracy and record keeping.

Note I have not put literacy as such first in this third condition. Societies of great vertical complexity, such as the Inca of Peru, existed without literacy as we know it. But they had elaborate systems of notation, mnemonics, and computation in the "quipus" — knotted and color-coded strings — which were capable of storing huge amounts of information. Similarly, the early cuneiform "writing" of the Near East was not the transcription of language that we usually mean by the term, but rather again a series of lists, mnemonics, and quantities. At first these were enough for the purposes of administering tributary and conquered states (see the excellent account by Larsen 1988). The development of true literacy came later. Again, this is a vital and far-reaching transition but beyond my limited brief, which deals only with origins. (See Goody 1968 and Havelock 1963 on literacy, and Gellner 1990 for the cognitive consequences of the changes.)

Large-scale trade also means the mingling of populations, with all the consequences of breaking out from the tribal mode of thinking and the growth of, for example, universalistic cults and religions, even scepticism and philosophy. For my money, the real founders of Western civilization are not the Greeks but the Phoenecians, who taught the barbarian Greeks to read and write in order to trade with them!

With the development of warfare and conquest, as opposed to the skirmishing that passes for war at the tribal stage, Spencer's "complex" (or "compound") societies are formed. With rare exceptions such a development is impossible for the Neolithic hunting society, or even the early Neolithic town. Conquest is of little use without some central and minimally literate (in our earlier sense of numerate and record-keeping) government to administer conquered territories, and slaves are simply more mouths to feed, as are standing armies. With the development of a centralized theocratic government, aided by a literate clergy, conquest and slavery became possible and led to the incorporation of whole societies and ethnic groups within other societies.

There is no need to elaborate on this — we all know it from the stories of Israel in Egypt, and the Babylonian captivity, and it is indeed the whole story of the so-called "development of civilization." But whether it leads to cultural mongrelization, as in the Near East, or, as in India, to a hardening of ethnic differences into castes, it moves at one stroke to multiply social complexity by many powers. Chacoan civilization never made it to this point, but in Middle and South America, the tipover into complexity of this kind occurred, along with the predictable crashes. (The Maya were once thought to be an exception to the "warfare and conquest" condition, but recent work makes it clear that they are not.) And it happened without bronze and iron, and with the only metalworking being in copper, gold, and silver. This might seem rather charming, but with the advent of the mercantile capitalist adventurers from even more complex postfeudal Europe, it became the undoing.

Part Four

Kinship and Marriage

Introduction to Part Four

Kinship, as I said in part 1, is central to the anthropological enterprise. In *Kinship and Marriage* (1967) I said it was what logic was to philosophy and the nude to art. Philosophers and artists now tell me that this is not a correct "postmodern" view of their subjects, and I have watched with dismay as kinship has slipped from its central position in anthropology over the years. (Sales of *K and M* are still steady, so someone is teaching it somewhere — probably in undergraduate introductory courses where the syllabus tends not to catch up with the trends for about a decade.) Partly this decline is a result of the general run of fads and fashions (and the speeding up of these) that plague expanding disciplines with too many people and too few original ideas. Partly it is the result of the "deconstruction" of the idea of "primitive society," where kinship is the major diacritic to be deconstructed. Partly it is because, like logic, kinship is often hard to understand unless you are willing to put in some real effort, and despite my own and others' attempts to render it intelligible. But the issues are still there; they don't go away simply because they become unfashionable. And the deconstructing of primitive society does not, for me, render kinship any the less important, because I have always maintained that it never really disappeared in "modern" society, even though the sociologists said it did. The "resilience" of kinship, and the "war between kinship and the state" were the themes of *Reproduction and Succession*. And I boldly predicted a revival, a revival that will, as usual,

195

leave the sociologists scrambling from behind with rationalizations and excuses (insofar as sociologists will still be interested in real events by then).

The two essays here — classic exercises in kinship analysis with no apologies — hark back to the point made in part 1: that the rules of classical kinship systems render the marriage choices of the younger generation contingent on decisions made by the older generations. This is built into the rules of the system laid down "in the beginning," thus taking the heat off the older people and putting the blame, as it were, on God. (This has been a major function of religion too, but that is going a bit far afield at this point. However, as a rationalist parent who didn't want to scare his kids with bogey men, I invented a deity called "The House," whose rules had to be enforced, regretfully, in the interests of the house. It worked for a while, until the kids deconstructed "The House" with the kind of manic intelligence only kids can muster.)

The first essay, on the Murngin system, was in fact buried in a chapter on sexual selection in man that sought to lead up to this basic point, through the process of evolution, and then illustrate it with Australian aboriginal material (in Bernard Campbell, ed., *Sexual Selection and the Descent of Man 1871-1971* [Chicago: Aldine, 1972]). As usual, this effort to bring together the evolutionary biologists and the social anthropologists fell between the two stools. (This has been the story of my academic life!) Although I say this somewhere in the text, it is worth repeating here: Biologists just didn't appreciate the kinship material, and social anthropologists don't read chapters on sexual selection in the first place. (Eric Wolf is one of the few I know who grasped it and used it, at least in teaching.) When it came to redoing this whole argument in *The Red Lamp of Incest,* I wanted to spell out these details, but the publisher panicked at the sight of all the diagrams and saw his popular audience deserting in droves. So I could only get in one little diagram and a fairly weak statement and hope to put the rest in somewhere else later. Here it is. Those who have read *Red Lamp* can read it as an extension to the "Alliance and Constraint" chapter (the title in fact borrowed from the sexual selection piece).

The second essay, on Crow-Omaha systems, is another of those that was written for a *festschrift* that never appeared. This one was for Lévi-Strauss (in 1969, I think), and seemed all set, when the editors, having delayed several years, axed the project, leaving the article high and dry. It had already been circulated and even quoted in a few places, but it never appeared in print. I hung onto it and fiddled with it further because I had a projected book, which I even announced in the second edition of *K and M,* to be called *Kinship and the Natural Order,* where I was going to include it. But that project — due to shifting editors and policies — also fell through, so poor Crow-Omaha was still orphaned twenty years after being written. The "fiddling" concerned an attempt to draw the Southeastern tribes (Cherokee, Choctaw, Yuchi, Seminole, etc.) into the same web of explanation I had used for the Southwestern Pueblo tribes. In 1966 Eggan had published his *The American Indian,* in which he had a whole chapter extending his "acculturational" hypothesis to these tribes with their problematical "Crow" systems. I didn't think it worked any better for them, and so tried to reexamine them in my own framework. This is completely new stuff that readers of *Keresan Bridge* will be able to add to the analysis there.

I didn't worry too much about my Crow-Omaha piece not being published since it was essentially another "condensation and retelling" piece based on the argument of *The Keresan Bridge* and a follow-up chapter in a later book (Fox 1972 — see notes to chapter 13). And, with the arrogance of youth (or even the reasonable expectations I had been reared with), I assumed that all my kinship colleagues would have read these and understood the argument. Why, I don't know, but almost everything written on the subject since has simply ignored this crucial issue, which was spelled out by Lévi-Strauss after all in his pivotal chapter 28 of his magnum opus. So here I return the compliment. I have revised and rewritten the article to make the point as clear as I can, but I have not "brought it up to date" by citing all that has been written on Crow-Omaha since. I did think of putting the whole bibliography (some forty-seven items) in an appendix, but then I figured that I had spent enough time embarrassing my colleagues and enough was enough. But sometimes I wonder about them, or about the private little mutual admiration cliques they live in, handing out their little annual prizes to each other.

I would like to think that a major part of the problem here lay in my concern with the speculative reconstruction of kinship systems. This was an odd concern for a British social anthropologist even then, being completely out-of-fashion post-Radcliffe-Brown and having never come back into fashion since. But I am not so sure, because even when I propose solutions to kinship problems that have nothing to do with speculative reconstruction — the relation between the consanguineal household and the domestic cycle and the relevance of this for understanding matrilineal descent, for example — they get ignored too. As I said in "From Science to Survival: Twenty Years On," I sometimes begin to feel like one of Orwell's "unpersons." The attention paid to my kinship efforts has something of a Cheshire Cat quality to it: all polite smile and no real substance.

So be it. Enough whining and complaining. I should know that if you don't constantly push things down their throats in the ongoing journals and the lecture circuit they won't bother themselves with you. Also, if you don't "train" students to do these things and pursue the issues you set up for them, there will be no "school" of Foxism and kinship. In any case, I have always been too impatient to move on to something else and have never tried to create an academic industry out of my ideas. But the issues, as I have said, will not go away. There are clans and moieties, there is exogamy and preferential marriage, and there is a classificatory language in which this is all couched. It is perhaps about time that instead of "deconstructing" it (a petulant adolescent activity at best) we started taking it seriously again. The last living examples of the classic systems are fading before our very eyes. We still have the literature, and now we have computers. All is not lost, and a few brave souls are persevering. God bless them one and all. They get precious few thanks in these postmodern, critical, interpretative days.

Many people, like the humanist publisher, panic when they see kinship diagrams; but really they are ridiculously simple to follow. There is nothing here that a reader of goodwill and serious intentions cannot grasp with a little patience. This stuff cannot, as my friend Ashley Montagu put it so charmingly, "be read standing on one foot." But as with chess, a few simple rules generate a large number of games. The rules really are simple, and once you know them the games become a challenge and even a lot of fun. Even so, it is fun about the most serious sequence in human life: "birth and copulation and death." Kinship is what we do about reproduction and succession, birth and continuity. And we must never lose sight of that in our fun with the diagrams.

And it is why it will continue to be relevant at least for the foreseeable future. The systems described here may seem to belong to an archaic world, but they are dealing with problems we are still dealing with, and they are part of the route by which we got to our own solution — or lack of solution. We can still learn from them about our progress through time on the one hand, and about alternative ways of handling eternal problems on the other. And if the revival I predict in fact occurs, they may come to have an even more immediate relevance, perhaps as models for the crystalline structures that Lévi-Strauss predicts we may end up playing with in the future world of infinite leisure.

I am somewhat sceptical of this, but not in the least sceptical of the continuing importance of kinship, even without a world of leisure in which to enjoy it. Kinship is not only a fun game but an adaptation to the harsh realities of a tough existence that may yet be what will face us, rather than a technologically engineered world of luxurious indolence. My formula, as stated in various places (the latest being *Reproduction and Succession*): When the state fails to protect, people turn to the security of kinship. And the protective powers of the state (itself no friend to kinship) seem to be eroding at an alarming rate.

12

Will the Real Murngin System
Please Stand Up?

In 1967 I published a "solution" to the celebrated "Murngin Problem." To be fair, my solution was a synthesis of previous ideas, original only in its rearrangement of these. But being fair to my predecessors may not be all that complimentary to them — read on. This problem had plagued anthropologists ever since it was first described in the nineteenth century, and various attempts had been made to solve it. In 1967, John Barnes also published a monograph, the main conclusion of which was that the problem was basically unsolvable. This didn't stop the intrepid, including your author, who continued to "solve" it to their own satisfaction. My solution was generally praised and accepted — even deemed elegant by fastidious critics like Rodney Needham. It worked, it fit the facts as we knew them, it explained the basic mechanism: how asymmetric alliance could articulate with moieties and direct exchange. It had all the virtues except for one minor problem: it was wrong.

So this is an anthropological cautionary tale: the model that works does not necessarily explain. What I presented in a sense "happens" among the Murngin, but it is an accident, an artifact of the real situation in which something quite other than asymmetric exchange is going on. The Murngin may appear to be doing what I describe them as doing, but this is not what they set out to do. And when we are proposing models to "explain" native behavior, as opposed to playing hypothetical kinship games (which is not wholly frivolous, as we shall see in the next chapter), then the only model worth anything is the model that explains why the natives do what they do. As Lévi-Strauss has reminded us, while all models are interesting — in telling us, for example, what the possibilities are — the model that fits reality is ultimately the best one. And indeed, the only one if explanation is our goal.

We might compare the situation to that of an analyst watching a chess match. He sees all the moves and then presents an analysis of the winning strategy, showing how the player began with a typical Brodsky opening, progressed to a brilliant Mindelevsky middle game, and ended with a sterling Bognovitch end game (I made these up). This might very well accurately describe what happened in the match. But then we discover that the player knew none of these games and was not using them in his strategy. There is nothing wrong with the analyst's description as a description of what happened in the match, but it is not in any way a description of what went on in the intentions of the player. If we want to know what the player was doing to win the match, we cannot claim that he was using some specific chess strategies if he didn't know them. (The argument that he really was using them even if he didn't know it gets metaphysical and therefore silly.) What is more, he perhaps presents us with three other game plans that equally well "describe" his win, and claims he was in fact following these. What then is the status of our analyst's description? It remains interesting that the match can be described by his analysis, but it still holds that this does not describe how the player played the match.

We want to know how the Murngin of northern Australia play their game, not how cleverly we can describe how they play it. So let us begin as near the beginning as possible and sort this thing out. The Murngin appear to do the impossible in combining two different principles of marital exchange: symmetrical and asymmetrical. The symmetrical version is common in Australia, and has variously complicated forms, but is in essence a matter of direct exchange between two groups: for simplicity, A and B. The men and women of A cannot marry each other but must marry the men and women of B, and vice versa. In its classic form it involves the division of the tribe into two named and intermarrying "moieties." But it can take place between any two units: families, clans, hordes, etc. In Australia these are usually patrilineal units, with descent in the male line, and the basic situation of direct exchange is usually as in diagram 12.1.

Here we have two patrilineal units exchanging spouses (the symbols can be taken to represent either individuals or collectivities of individuals). I have taken the middle generation to represent that of the focal ego and written in some of the relationships that ensue. We shall return to these, but for the moment let us look at how we might describe the mechanics of direct exchange from the outside. It can be seen, generation by generation, as classic "sister exchange" (although it could just as well be described as brother exchange). In each generation sisters are "exchanged" between the men of A and the men of B. It is often the case in such systems that members of the same generation in the same clan or moiety all call each other "brother" and "sister." So even if the symbols are taken to represent collections of individuals, "classificatory" sisters will be exchanged. So this is one model.

But another way of looking at it is that people marry "bilateral cross cousins." The ego in our example is marrying someone who is both his mother's brother's daughter (MBD) and his father's sister's daughter (FZD) because his mother's brother married his father's sister (real or classificatory). This is the native description of "what they are doing" in many cases: looking for the appropriate cross cousin. Yet again, if we view it from the perspective of the parental generation, it could be seen as "daughter exchange" (or son exchange, of course): the elders in each generation exchange sons and daughters (I give my daughter to your son; you give your daughter to my son, etc.). Or, as we have seen, viewing the units as

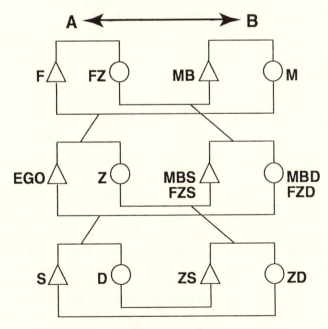

Diagram 12.1

Key: $\triangle$ = male; $\bigcirc$ = female; $\sqcap$ = siblings; $\sqcup$ = marriage; F = father;

M = mother; B = brother; Z = sister; S = son; D = daughter

collectivities, we can simply say that there is a direct or symmetrical exchange of spouses between two groups. The "system" can be described in all these ways, but we can only know what the natives think they are doing by asking them. For the moment let us just fix this notion of direct exchange in our own heads and move on.

We have seen that the cross cousin married here is "bilateral" — the product of the marriage of the mother's brother with the father's sister. This will always produce the symmetry of the A ↔ B kind. But a simple rule forbidding marriage between these two relatives produces an alternative: ego can then marry the daughter of *either* the mother's brother *or* the father's sister. We can put the latter case on one side since it will not affect the Murngin problem, and look at the consequences of opting for the first as a systematic form of cousin marriage. If again we have patrilineal units (it will work for matrilineal too, but the Murngin are patrilineal, so we will stick to this), and they systematically practice marriage with the mother's brother's daughter (MBD), then the relationship between the units will be "asymmetrical" — flowing in one direction — as in diagram 12.2.

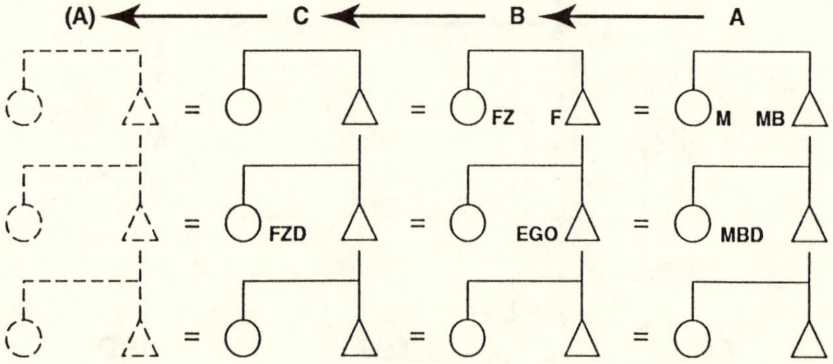

Diagram 12.2

There must be three units at least, and we can see that the system can be "closed" by unit C marrying back into unit A on the classic A → B → C → A pattern. Of course, there can be more than three units; theoretically there can be any number, but practicality will determine it to be small and finite. The main thing to note is the absolute difference between this and direct or symmetrical exchange. With asymmetrical exchange, the exchange, if it can be called that, is entirely indirect. If A gives wives to B, it cannot collect wives back from B. B must give them to C, and A can then collect from C. This is often referred to in anthropology as the "circulation" of wives (or, more correctly, of spouses since the men are circulating too), and with their love of

Latinisms anthropologists have dubbed it "circulating connubium." Again it can be seen from a variety of perspectives, like direct exchange: as the marriage of "matrilateral cross cousins" (MBD/FZS); as a rule that spouses can never be exchanged — that "wife-giving" groups can never be "wife-taking" groups; as a rule that men must take wives from groups which have previously given wives — and so on. But the basic fact is what I continue to stress: the absolute incompatibility of this with a system of direct exchange.

Then we come to the Murngin — or to that group of northern Australian tribes in Arnhem Land loosely designated "Murngin." They present us with the supreme anthropological impossibility. They are divided into two moieties, and spouses are indeed exchanged between the two moieties. But their rule of marriage for men demands marriage with a mother's brother's daughter or with a second-cousin version, a mother's mother's brother's daughter's daughter (or, interestingly, someone who is both MBD and MMBDD). Or, to put it more correctly, the system *ends up with* them marrying the matrilateral cross cousin. This might not seem like an important distinction, but in view of what we have been saying, the reader will be alerted to the interpretative problem.

The "objective" problem for the anthropologists was to figure out how the two seemingly incompatible systems could be made to mesh. This is not the place for a history of these attempts, which Barnes covers very well. Enough for our moral tale to look at my synthesis of solutions. It seemed simple enough once one grasped that moiety exchange could involve more than one subgroup of the moiety. The Australians themselves gave the clue to this by naming "marriage classes" or "sections," which were indeed such subunits and by which they "explained" who could marry whom. Also, in a simple expansion of the "two unit" system, one could produce a form of direct exchange that needed at least four units (e.g., patrilineal clans), as with the famous "Aranda" system named after the central Australian tribe that employed it. The expansion occurs (never mind the reasons) by invoking a "second cousin" rule of marriage. Thus, from the man's perspective, he cannot marry directly back into the clan into which his father married (as in diagram 12.1), but must marry into the clan into which his *grandfather* (paternal) married. The second cross cousin will not then be a MBD/FZD but a MMBDD/FMBSD — the same cross relationship, but through the grandparental and not the parental generation. I diagrammed this possibility in diagram 12.3.

A and B again are the two moieties, but this system will split them into four submoieties: A1, A2, B1, and B2. We can see how the various relationships that in the simple model were confounded are in this one separated out, and how the first cross cousin (MBD/FZD) is separated from the second and placed in the "forbidden" patriunit. We can see how in the top generation there is simple sister exchange between units of the moieties: A1 with B1, A2 with B2 — but how in the next generation this cannot be repeated, as it would be in the simple system: A1 has to go to B2, and B1 has to go to A2. In the next generation we are back to the original exchange, and so on alternating down the generations. It looks formidable, but the rules are really very simple and easy to follow: You do what your paternal grandparents did. The native does not have to know much more than this, and it is made simpler for him by the use of names for the combinations of moiety and generation (the "sections" or "marriage classes") that enable him to place himself accurately vis-à-vis his fellows and to know into which "class" he can and cannot marry.

We had to introduce the "Aranda" complication — the second-cross-cousin rule and the four units — because the Murngin superficially seem to operate on the same principle. They too have the moieties and the four units and the marriage classes and all the paraphernalia of the Aranda system, but with the puzzling rule that we have already observed and which seems to go against the whole Aranda logic. Among the Murngin tribes, one may not

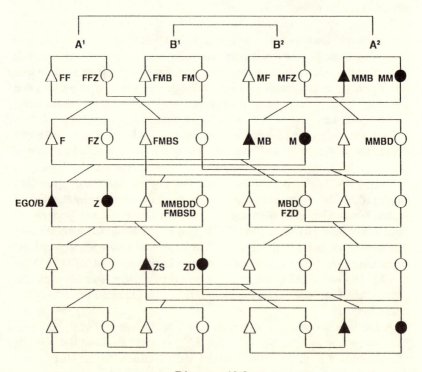

Diagram 12.3
(The shaded figures are for future reference.)

marry a bilateral cousin — one who is both MBD and FZD. Thus, one must marry a MBD who is *not* a FZD; or a MMBDD who is *not* a FMBSD. Now, a quick glance at the Aranda system (diagram 12.3) shows immediately that these two relatives, whom the Murngin treat as absolutely distinct, are absolutely the same for the Aranda and must be by the logic of the system. And as we have seen, systematic practice of the forms of marriage the Murngin require will lead automatically to asymmetric exchange (circulating connubium — diagram 12.2), which is the structural opposite of the direct exchange system of the Aranda!

Here was my solution, and it was ridiculously simple. Let us take the same four units as in the Aranda case (and don't forget the Murngin have these units) and see how they could engage in circulating connubium among themselves without disobeying the rules of moiety exchange, which are after all the same as for the Aranda. Look at diagram 12.4.

Thus, if A1 marries B1, B1 marries A2, A2 marries B2, and B2 marries A1, we have a perfect circulating connubium of:

$$A1 \rightarrow B1 \rightarrow A2 \rightarrow B2 \rightarrow A1$$

So all is for the best in the best of all possible Murngin worlds. Everyone marries a matrilateral cross cousin (MBD), the four subunits marry "in a circle," but moiety exchange is perfectly preserved. (For the sake of accuracy we should note that there can be any number of subunits — e.g., clans — on either "side" of the moiety system. What this is a model of is not some total system, but how the system would work between any four subunits practicing it systematically. Note and pass on.)

We can diagram the outcome with the same structure as the Aranda system, but showing how in each generation the four subunits will marry in a circle (this will be repeated in each subsequent generation), and how each man will marry a MBD who is not a FZD, and thus how the "opposite" systems of symmetrical and asymmetrical exchange, of direct and circulating

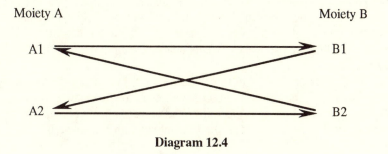

Moiety A   Moiety B

A1   B1

A2   B2

Diagram 12.4

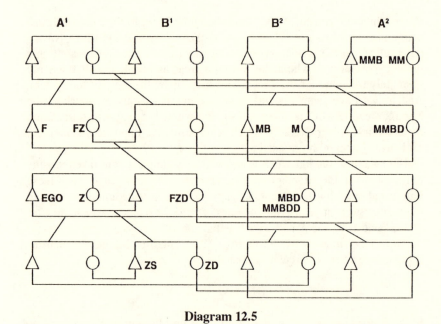

Diagram 12.5

cunnubium, can be neatly accommodated in the one system. See diagram 12.5.

The rule is not hard to follow: A man in A1 knows he must marry a woman in B2; a man in B2 knows he must marry a woman in A2; a man in A2 knows he must marry a woman in B1. No one has to know how the whole system works — although Australians are as adept as anthropologists at diagramming and describing their systems — but only what one's own rule of marriage is, and that is quite simple. And as for the total system, the anthropologists can see it plainly as one where the daughters and sisters pass between the moieties in "direct" exchange, but where the subunits (clans in this case) "circulate" spouses in indirect exchange. Like the observer of the chess match, we have identified the strategies, which are easily recognized, and perfectly represented the match in terms of them. But now comes our come-uppence: the wretched players turn round and say, "Very pretty indeed, but that isn't what we do: We exchange nieces between men of the same moiety but different patriclans." Exeunt unhappy anthropologists. Back to the drawing board.

I have a personal stake in this issue because, just after I proposed my pretty solution I moved from the London School of Economics to Rutgers University. While looking for recruits to the new department of anthropology there, I received a letter out of the blue, along with a manuscript, from a young man in California called Warren Shapiro. He was recently back from Australia, had studied a "Murngin" tribe (the Miwuyt of Arnhem Land), and was looking for a job nearer New York City, his home. He warned me that he would use my book in his classes only to show how wrong it was. I liked this immediately, and saw that his findings contained the basis for a true solution of the problem. I hired him. His paper was called "The Exchange of Sister's Daughter's Daughters in Northeast Arnhem Land" (Shapiro 1968), and it was later worked into a book (Shapiro 1981). I tried to convey the new truth in a chapter I wrote for a book on sexual selection in 1972, but social anthropologists don't, on principle, read books on sexual selection, so my effort was wasted on them, and the biologists who read the chapter didn't understand the kinship analysis (Fox 1972). My effort fell (as have so many) nicely between two stools, so there is no harm in repeating it here.

"The exchange of sister's daughter's daughters." How does this come about? Actually, what really happens is even simpler than this sounds: it is what Shapiro calls "mother-in-law bestowal." A man will "bestow" his sister's daughter as a "mother-in-law" on another man of his moiety (but a different patriclan). Thus, in effect, he promises that any daughters born to his sister's daughter will be brides to that man. These then are the sister's daughter's daughters in question who are thus "exchanged" because the arrangement is reciprocal: If I bestow a mother-in-law on you, you must bestow one on me. This is the simple rule. But the problem comes in following out the mechanics of its consequences. We have already, however, stored up most of the mechanisms needed for the answer in our previous models. Let us here note that even in this primitive stage of analysis we can see that moiety exogamy is maintained. The moieties are patrilineal, so a man's sister will have married into the opposite moiety, and her daughter would belong there by birth. If he controls the marriage destiny of his sister's daughter, he can give her to a man of his own moiety but of another patriclan.

But what about this exchange of nieces? What are men in patrilineal clans doing controlling the destiny of their sisters' children? Here we must hark back to the Aranda system, where I shaded in the "implicit" matrilines that cycled through the generations (diagram 12.3). We can see here that the mother's mother's brother — a senior male in the matrilineal line — is also a senior male of ego's own patrilineal moiety. In the Australian scheme of things this makes him a doubly powerful male since he represents both lines of descent. These two lines are indeed recognized by the natives, and the "matriline" often has a name and official recognition. The natives can, with dazzling accuracy, rearrange their kinship terms, on request, to conform to matrilineal as opposed to patrilineal descent. If we stay with sister's daughters for the moment (ZDDs involve eight units and get difficult to handle diagrammatically, but the principle is the same) then we can see that the MMB's sister's daughter is in fact ego's own mother. If the MMB had then given his sister's daughter to ego's father — a man of the same moiety (A) but a different patriclan (A1) — then that would have produced ego and his sister. By following the shaded members down the line we can see how this would repeat itself when ego (from A1) in turn gave his ZD to a man in A2, and so on. So the Murngin are not doing anything remarkable in using the matrilines to control marriage. Because, in a sense, the matrilines "straddle" the two moieties (or, in the classical language, cycle through them), they are in fact the appropriate units to handle intermoiety marriage.

Again, if we extract out the two matrilines implicit in any dual system of the simple type in diagram 12.1, we can see that matrilines always "exchange nieces." Diagram 12.6 shows the logical opposite of 12.1, with matrilineal units instead of patrilineal.

Looked at within generations, this is "sister exchange" as in the patrilineal model, but from the point of view of the older generation, men of A are exchanging nieces — sister's daughters — with men of B. They are, in effect, giving nieces to sons, that is, to men of their own patriline. I hope the logic of this, and its essential simplicity despite its unfamiliarity, is becoming obvious. But the Murngin proper (as in the Miwuyt) add a wrinkle, which is what makes their system operate on the circulating connubium principle

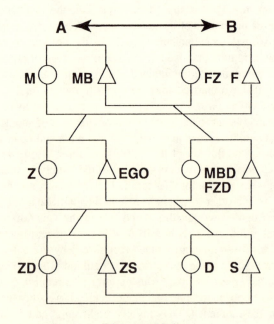

Diagram 12.6

rather than simple direct exchange: the men do not give sister's daughters to their sons, they give them to each other!

One of the charms of kinship analysis is the challenge of rendering left-brain logical sequences into right-brain graphic diagrams. As with geometry, everything could be spelled out as mathematical equations, but I would never have passed school geometry had it not been for the fascination of the diagrams (I barely scraped through algebra). So here we have the challenge of (a) coming up with a diagram showing this form of niece exchange, and (b) transferring this into a diagram showing the total Murngin system incorporating all the features. Here goes. Diagram 12.7 shows our two matrilines, with the men exchanging nieces with each other.

The letters represent the two patrilines, which in this "mirror image" cycle through the two matrilines. We can use the letters here and they will help us when we come to the summary diagram (12.8). What we have here then is two matrilines (A1-B1-A2-B2 and A2-B2-A1-B1) exchanging nieces. I could take the reader by the hand through the diagram, but said reader should now be adept at following out the relationships unaided. The patrilines can be easily verified: sons of A1 are in A1, sons of B1 are in B1, and so on. So this system is easily compatible with the existence of patrilineal units, and indeed, as we shall see, the letters here will become the four patrilineal subunits of

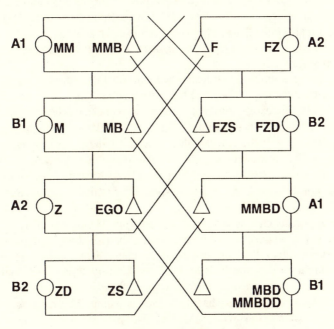

Diagram 12.7

the total-system diagram, identical to those of diagram 12.4. We can see from the example given that by the simple application of this rule a man *must* marry someone who is both MBD and MMBDD (the "Murngin" rule), and that he cannot marry a FZD. In fact, the father's sister's daughter has, by the rule, already been appropriated by the mother's mother's brother! This then sets up the rule of "asymmetrical" marriage: with MBD rather than with FZD. We can also see, by simply following the marriage lines, that women pass in succession A1 → B1 → A2 → B2 → A1: exactly the requirement of my "solution" in 12.4. But not because of the direct pursuit of MBD marriage: because of the symmetrical exchange of nieces between men of the same patrimoiety. Let us try then for the total diagram that will put all these elements together, and set the exchanging matrilines in the context of the two patrimoieties and the patrilineal subunits (clans). This is attempted in diagram 12.8.

Here we have the two moieties A and B, and their subunits A1 and A2, and B1 and B2. We can conceptualize the system either as "sisters" passing asymmetrically, as shown between the four subunits, which encompasses our original solution, or as nieces (sister's daughters) passing symmetrically between subunits of the same moiety (A1 ↔ A2 : B1 ↔ B2), which is not encompassed in our original solution but which is how the natives play the game. The matrilines here can be easily followed: the sister's children of A1 are in B1, those of B1 in A2, those of A2 in B2 (refer back to 12.7). As for the individual relationships, they are given exactly as in 12.7, and we can again see how ego must marry his asymmetrical cousin (MBD/MMBDD) but cannot marry the FZD.

Despite the seeming complexity, we can see that the whole system is produced by two simple rules: (1) the patrimoieties must exchange spouses — that is, they are exogamous; and (2) men must exchange sister's daughters with men of their own patrimoiety but from a different patriclan. This is exactly how some tribes do it; others exchange the sister's daughters as mothers-in-law, thus delaying the acquisition of a bride for one more generation but not altering the principle of "niece exchange." It is in fact the equivalent of the Aranda pushing to a "second cross cousin" level the logic of the basic system.

What is equally clear is that this model does not do violence to my original solution, but is superior in that it incorporates the real strategy employed by the Murngin rather than one imposed on them from the outside. Thus, sisters/daughters do indeed "circulate" in the way I proposed, but this circulation is an *outcome* of another strategy, a strategy that the natives in fact pursue, a strategy of niece exchange. At the same time, the natives recognize that one must marry a MBD/MMBDD, but they do not pursue such a marriage as a strategy; it also is an outcome of the niece-exchange strategy.

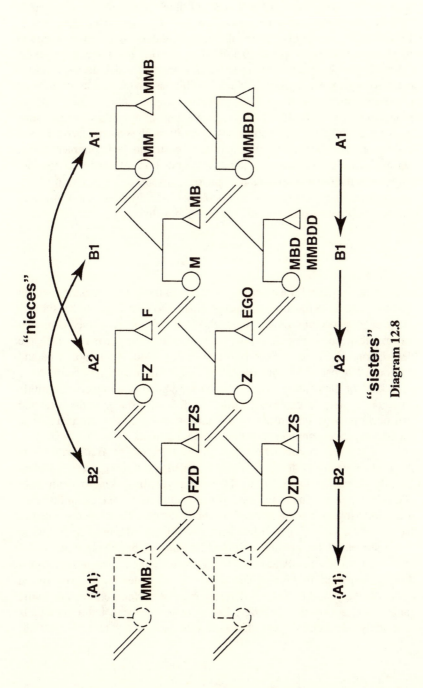

"nieces"

"sisters"
Diagram 12.8

So any model that hopes to describe "how the players play the game" has to include the niece exchange, and that we have done in our final version. Were the earlier models then a waste of time? Not at all. They help us to classify possibilities and to be sensitive to these when analyzing real systems. In fact, there is something to be said for analyzing possibilities as an end in itself, and for using computers to do it. If we can see what systems, given the rules, are possible, then we can see which occur and which do not. And we can learn a great deal by seeing which possibilities are rejected and which accepted by human societies. The possibilities are in fact enormous, but the probabilities rather small. We use a limited range of possible systems, which means that while our imagination may be limitless, the constraints on our social action are rather severe. Whether these constraints lie in our mentalities, our ecologies, our economies, the inherent limitations of our social relationships, or our heritage of evolutionary biology, or some combinations of these, is a question to employ serious anthropologists (that is, those who want to do science) for many years to come — if they choose to try.

* * *

Here again the relevance of this analysis to the crucial remark made in chapter 1 about the function of kinship systems as controls on the behavior of the younger generation should be noted. We are not just concerned here with the exotic peculiarities of a few Australian aboriginal systems (see the descriptions in Goodale 1962; Hart and Pilling 1960; Hiatt 1965; Lee and DeVore 1968, part 4; Meggitt 1962; Rose 1960; Shapiro op. cit.) but with the very kind of elementary system that arose among our Lower Paleolithic ancestors to meet the challenges of the transformed sexual selection situation that occurred with the growth of the human neocortex and the increase in social complexity consequent on the hunting transition.

A system of "gerontocratic polygyny" such as we find among the Australians would perfectly fit the bill, and fit even more perfectly when kinship increased its functions from simply uniting kin to complexly allocating spouses. The beauty of it is that the old men could claim that they were not arrogantly appropriating the nubile females; these were granted to them by "the system" which had been laid down in the dreamtime by the totem ancestors. They simply followed the rule of "bestowing mothers-in-law" — their sister's daughter's — on men of their own moiety but a different patriclan. In this way they were as much under the "control" of the system as the youngsters who had to wait many years for their turns to do the same thing, and in the meantime had to undergo severe initiation rituals (including the genital mutilations of circumcision, superincision, and subincision — the message is pretty clear!) that inculcated these rules and stamped them into their memories.

But the very rules themselves ensure that the marriage choices of the young are constrained by the previous decisions of the old. We shall see in the next chapter that even as systems become more "complex" they still retain this characteristic; that is, putting the burden of marriage control onto the system of exogamic rules but continuing to make the marriage choices of the young contingent on, and restricted by, decisions made generations earlier. The Crow-Omaha systems we are going to examine in the next chapter, on my theory, emerge directly from some of the types of elementary systems we have been discussing here, and therefore are the next installment in the social evolutionary story of "what happened to sexual selection and assortative mating after the transition to humanity?" (This is the basic theme of *The Red Lamp of Incest.*) When even these systems declined with the growth of civilization, the situation became even more "complex" both literally and in the technical sense used by Lévi-Strauss. The reader can ponder the present state of the war between the generations for control of the sexuality of females — and the role of kinship in the process — and estimate where we stand now. If we are not close to chaos, we are far from the pristine order of the systems discussed here and in the next chapter.

13

The Evolution of Kinship Systems and the Crow-Omaha Question

Crow-Omaha: The Child is Father to the Cousin

The general features of Crow-Omaha systems of kinship terms (named after two North American Indian tribes) have been known to anthropology since Lewis Henry Morgan first collected his massive schedules for *Systems of Consanguinity and Affinity of the Human Family* in the 1850s and 1860s (Morgan 1871), although we had to wait for Robert Lowie in the 1920s to sort out and name the types. Morgan's use of these to reconstruct the history of kinship systems was so patently wrong to later anthropologists that the whole effort at such historical reconstructions has more or less been abandoned, with the notable exception of his lineal descendant G. P. Murdock in *Social Structure* (1949). But what was at fault with Morgan was not the idea of historical reconstruction as such, but the manner in which it was conducted. I shall try to illustrate how it is possible to do such reconstructions, not on a scale of worldwide history perhaps, but on a more restricted and local scale which may, however, be the appropriate prelude to a general history of human kinship — or at least to the identification of possible routes that such a history might have taken.

The major features of Crow-Omaha systems lie in what we would now call the "lineal equations" made by their kinship terminologies. The equations tend to be correlated with the type of unilineal descent system practiced: Crow with matrilineal and Omaha with patrilineal. Not all matrilineal systems, however, have Crow terminologies, nor patrilineal, Omaha. It is, as we have said, a correlation: We do not find Crow with patrilineal or Omaha with matrilineal. The lineal equations seem to mark out the "matrilines" and "patrilines" as shown in diagram 13.1, which shows which relatives would be classed together under one term. Exactly which term differs from system to system. Thus, some have a separate term for FZ — some call her "mother." In some Crow systems the MB is called by a special term or is called "elder brother." Likewise, in some Omaha systems he has also a special term or is called (as in Latin) "little grandfather," and so on. What matters, however, for our preliminary purposes, is not the exact term but the "equations" that are made: who is lumped with whom. Thus, in diagram 13.1, which shows an "ideal" version of Crow and Omaha usage, everyone labeled under one kin term, for example "FZ," will be called by the same term as the father's sister, whatever it is, and similarly for the other terms. The same symbols are used as in chapter 12 except where noted.

Here we can see that what appeared to early observers as strange anomalies — calling the FZS "father" in a Crow system (and the MB's children "son" and "daughter," or collectively "child"), or the MBS "mother's brother" in an Omaha, for example — make great sense when we see that in a Crow system all the members of the father's matrilineage or clan are being classified together, as are all the members of the mother's (i.e., mother's brother's) in an Omaha. In many such systems this extends to the "grandparental clans," where again the members are classed together using the grandparental terms. This is shown for the relevant clans (lineages) in each case. This would make second (cross) cousins, for example, terminological grandparents — something that confused several earlier anthropologists who actually thought "the natives" married their parents' parents! The ascending generations in own clan and in father's clan (Crow) or mother's clan (Omaha) vary a lot, but one of the commonest ways of classifying the "affinal" clans is simply to continue to extend the terms upward in a lineal fashion. Thus, in a Crow system the FM and FMB would continue to be "FZ" and "F," with the mirror opposite in the Omaha.

The essence of Crow-Omaha systems then is this "overriding of generations" in favor of classification by unilineal descent. It can be contrasted with those other systems of terminology, especially the Hawaiian, where the generation principle is all important, and our own "Eskimo" version, where generations tend to be treated with greater respect and are clearly distinguished from each other.

This distinction of generations is especially true of the kind of "direct exchange" systems we examined in the previous chapter, where lineage and

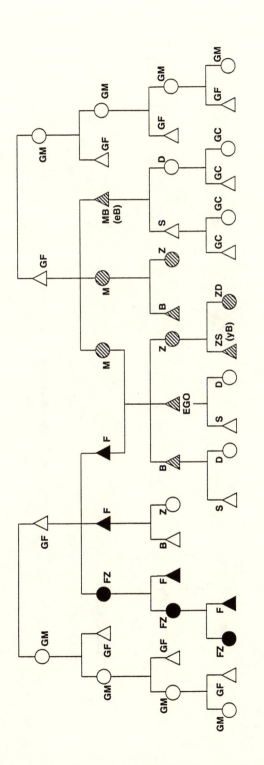

GF = grandfather
GM = grandmother
GC = grandchild

eB = elder brother
yB = younger brother

▲ Father's matriline

◒◯ EGO's (Mother's) matriline

Diagram 13.1a Ideal Crow (Matrilineal)

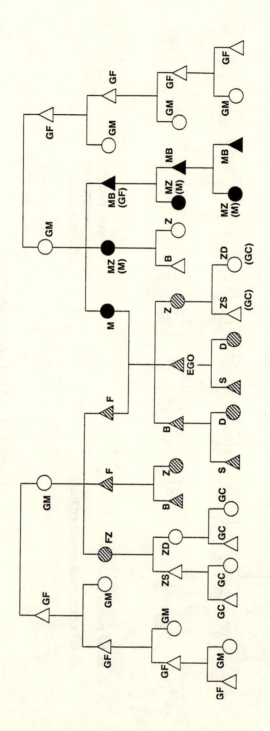

Diagram 13.1b Ideal Omaha (Patrilineal)

Ego's (father's) patriline

Mother's patriline

generation must be clearly distinguished in classification. (For more details see Fox 1967a, chap. 9.) Finally, we should note that the Crow-Omaha systems, given their premises, display great internal logic on most points. Thus, with the cousin classifications in Crow, it is obvious that if I call my FZS "father," he must respond by calling me "son" (or "daughter" if I am female). Hence a MBS must be "son" or "child." Equally in the Omaha system, if a MBS is "uncle," I, his FZS, must be "nephew" (strictly, "sister's child"). This can be easily verified from the diagrams. (The English term "nephew" in fact comes from the Latin *nepos,* which originally meant "grandson." The Omaha-usage Romans called the mother's brother "little grandfather" [*avunculus*], and he responded by calling his sister's child *nepos* [grandchild]. "Niece" comes from the later Latin *nepta. Nepos* traveled through French and Old English to become "nephew," but as late as the seventeenth century, "nephew" was still being used to mean "grandson" as well.)

We perhaps should note one constant of Crow-Omaha systems since we must return to it later and it may prove crucial: parallel cousins (FBD-MZD/FBS-MZS) — the children of father's brother and mother's sister — are always classed with siblings. Cross cousins, on the other hand, are classed in their typical Crow or Omaha fashion — the diagnostics of the system in question. If classification were entirely by lineage, then this would not make sense, since while one's own brothers and sisters are of course of one's own lineage in either system, the father's brother's children are not in a Crow system (matrilineal), and the mother's sister's children are not in an Omaha (patrilineal). On the logic of "lineage identification" we would expect them to be differentiated. Not only do they not become differentiated in the terminology, but exogamic restrictions apply to them as strongly as to "real" siblings, and they are forbidden to marry each other.

This anomaly has led one line of commentators to argue that it is simply the logic of the language that is operating here. If the mother's sister is called "mother" and the father's brother "father" (as they almost always are), then their children will be called "brother and sister" (Lounsbury 1964). But the classification of cross cousins does not follow this logic. Indeed, it defies it, and this defiance is what defines the systems for us. The "logic of language" school has to introduce a "skewing rule" (essentially a convenient exception) to account for this, and is not therefore very convincing. We shall try to turn up a better (historical) reason for the persistence of this interesting constant in Crow-Omaha terminologies, noting only that they share it with the so-called Dakota-Iroquois systems, where it is the crucial distinction between "us" (parallel cousins and siblings) and "those we marry" (cross cousins); that is, systems with bilateral cross-cousin marriage but without Crow-Omaha cousin designations.

Crow-Omaha: The Elementary-Complex Complication

We are talking here of "ideal models" of such systems, of course, and in practice they differ markedly among themselves as we shall see. (In fact, the Crow Indians themselves are not as thoroughly "Crow" as we might wish!) We shall also see that these very differences may give us the clue to the historical evolution of such systems. To understand this we shall pursue Lévi-Strauss's distinction between "elementary" and "complex" systems put forward in his great synthetic work *Les structures élémentaires de la parenté* in 1949, the same year Murdock came out with his own neo-Morganian analysis. We have looked, in fact, in some detail at some "elementary" systems in the previous chapter: systems of direct exchange and circulating connubium; restricted exchange and generalized exchange. However they may differ from each other they have the one specific defining characteristic that the category of spouse is "positively" defined; that is, one must marry a designated category of cousin.

The difference between these and what Lévi-Strauss chooses to call "complex" systems is simple: In a complex system there is only a "negative" definition of the appropriate spouse; that is, we are told whom we may not marry (members of our own clan; all relatives up to third cousins, etc.), but no category of spouse, defined by kinship, is laid down. This makes the determination of the spouse "complex," since that person could in theory be any marriageable person in the society. In fact, such contingent factors as geography, status, wealth, religion, social class, occupation, caste, etc. will make for the "complex" determination of marriage partner.

Lévi-Strauss has described Crow-Omaha systems as being the "hinge" between elementary and complex systems, and hence sees them as crucial to the understanding of such systems (1965, 19). They include, he argues, features of both generalized and restricted exchange (1949, 576; 1958 73-74). And although they are, in a technical sense, "complex," they are the bearers of "elementary" tendencies (1965, 19). No systems better illustrate his point that the "elementary : complex" distinction is difficult to draw precisely and is best considered a heuristic device (1965, 18).

He assigns to elementary systems a "logical" precedence and asks whether or not this indicates a historical precedence. This problem he leaves to "culture historians" (1949, 575). He does, however, sketch the probable development of African and Indo-European kinship systems to illustrate the complexities of these historical problems. I would here like to present a very tentative historical reconstruction of some "Crow" systems in an attempt to sort out the implications of Lévi-Strauss's contention that "la combinaison des principes de l'échange restreint et de l'échange generalisé nous paraît être à la base des systèmes americains dits Crow-Omaha" (1949, 576). We might also note that he confesses to having abandoned writing a book on such systems in despair at handling their complexity (1969, xxxvi). No one, he says, has felt the desire to take the time necessary to clear up the question. I would be foolish to claim to clear it up here, but I would like to suggest a way of approaching such a clear-up, and one, paradoxically, that is contained implicitly in chapter 28 of Lévi-Strauss's *Elementary Structures*.

First, let us try to get clear exactly what Lévi-Strauss is saying about Crow-Omaha systems. Let us first take the point that they are intermediary between elementary and complex systems, being more complex than elementary systems proper and yet more elementary than complex systems proper. An elementary system, as we have seen, is one in which the terminology indicates the category of "potential spouse"; a complex system has no such category. In an elementary system the class of women into which ego *must* marry is laid down, as well as the class of women he may *not* marry; in a complex system only the class of unmarriageable women is designated. Thus, in an elementary system the rules of the system determine the category from which any ego will take a spouse; in a complex system there is no such category, and any pattern of marriage choice that emerges can only be determined statistically. To use the terminology made famous by Lévi-Strauss, in an elementary system there is a mechanical model for both prohibitions and preferences; in a complex system there is a mechanical model for prohibitions but a statistical model for preferences. The elementary systems have both positive and negative rules; the complex have only negative. I think this about exhausts the dichotomies descriptive of this distinction.

Most Crow-Omaha systems appear certainly to be complex by this definition. There is usually no prescribed category of spouse. Ego simply has to avoid marriage into certain clans: in the simplest version, only his own (which is really no different in effect from many unilineal systems lacking Crow or Omaha terminology — a point for further consideration); in more complex versions the clans or phratries of both parents and possibly one grandparent. Thus, in a Crow system (for example, the Hopi of northern Arizona) we may get a prohibition of marriage into one's own (mother's) clan and the clans of father and mother's father.

This undeniably produces a "complex" arrangement of marriage choices. But I think Lévi-Strauss's position is this: In applying the prohibition to whole social groups (clans or phratries), the system is more like an elementary system than one which, for example, simply forbids marriage with some prohibited range of kin; also, because the number of such groups is limited, any ego is in fact faced with a "category" from which to draw a spouse, that is, the category composed of the clans in the system other than those which are prescribed to him. In a system, say, of seven clans, ego cannot take a spouse from perhaps three of them, but "must" take one from the remaining four. This limitation, however, even though it is reminiscent of an elementary system, is determined not mechanically but contingent on the previous marriage choices of members of senior generations.

Thus, insofar as several units are banned from ego, obliging him to choose a spouse from the remainder, and insofar as he has no control over this distribution of "marriageable" and "unmarriageable" units, then the system has "elementary" overtones. But insofar as the rules and terminology of the system do not predetermine marriage choice, it is undoubtedly complex.

What, then, of the "generalized : restricted" distinction? To simplify: all exchange involves "wife-giving" units and "wife-taking" units; in restricted exchange one unit's wife givers are also its wife takers, while in generalized exchange wife givers and wife takers must be distinguished. The two formulae can be expressed as A ↔ B (restricted) and A → B → C → (A) (generalized), whatever units — families, clans, phratries, etc. — A, B, and C may represent. Now, let us take a Crow system as our example, since it is this form that we will consider later. Let us take a simple model of a system with five clans or phratries. If ego is in A, and his father was in B, and his mother's father in C, then the universe of marriage choice *for him* could be represented as follows.

$$[D, E] \to [A \to (B + C)]$$

B and C have taken wives from A. Hence, for ego, A (his own clan), B, and C are banned, and he must take wives from D or E. The world must look to him much as it looks to an individual in a generalized exchange system: There are "us" who are banned in marriage; "wife takers" who are similarly banned; and potential "wife givers." But the italics above are significant: "marriage choice *for him*." These prohibitions apply to the individual concerned and do not follow for the other members of his group. Thus, while ego cannot marry into B or C, there is nothing to prevent the other members of his clan from doing so, provided their fathers and mother's fathers are not from B and C. We can imagine another A whose mother had also married into B but whose mother's mother had married into E:

$$[D, C] \to [A \to (B + E)]$$

and so on for each individual A. With a large number of clans, each with only a few members, the possible number of combinations becomes very large indeed.

The system would become more "elementary" and more like a system of *generalized* exchange if the rules were extended so that ego could not marry into any clan into which women from his own clan had previously married. This would quickly set up "cycles" of clans marrying on an asymmetrical basis. But it would also require a large number of clans or lineages, since with a small number, ego would soon end up with no potential spouses. Thus, the Hopi, with their restrictive rule in this respect, run to fifty or more clans. As it is, the asymmetry of the system is essentially "ego centered." At the level of the total system, clans directly exchange women; every clan marries into every other clan. The "flow," however, has elementary asymmetrical properties.

This then is one way in which Crow systems can be seen as combinations of generalized and restricted tendencies. In this they are not alone, however, for, as I have argued elsewhere, whether or not exchange is restricted or generalized depends on the level of social organization that one takes, and in many systems generalized exchange at one level is converted into restricted exchange on another. (See the previous chapter and Fox 1967a, 206 and 218.) But with the Crow variants we have been considering, generalized and restricted exchange occur *at the same level*. In this they resemble many African unilineal systems where both "cycles" and "direct exchanges" operate at the same level. (Clans, for example, both exchange spouses directly and at the same time circulate them.) They differ in the manner in which prohibitions are applied to the individual, and hence in the more precise and limited nature of the category of his "potential spouses." Somehow, American Crow-Omaha systems are "more elementary" than their "simple unilineal" African counterparts, and it seems to me not insignificant that they are found in an area where the *moiety principle* looms large in social organization — a principle virtually absent from Africa. In a letter to me commenting on the original version of this chapter in 1968, Lévi-Strauss said that African Crow-Omaha systems made use of several parameters not present in America, "where the model appears to be better conceptualized in the native mind." It is legitimate, he concluded, to use the American forms as a paradigm.

Not all Crow systems by any means operate in the way described above. Lévi-Strauss (1969, xxxvii) quotes Deacon (1934) on the Seniang of Melanesia who seem to operate on almost the opposite principle: a man should not marry a clan into which a man from his own clan has married within living memory. Here we get the generalizing of the rule to the whole unit, but it works in the reverse direction to the logical outcome of generalizing the rule we have just considered. It would be too difficult to follow this out here, as it would go into the Omaha variants which, while in many senses the "opposite" of the Crow, nevertheless can be subsumed under much the same general kind of analysis.

There is another sense in which Crow systems at least "lean" toward elementary tendencies. Lévi-Strauss notes, for example, that among the

Cherokee (see Gilbert 1937) "marriage prohibitions are limited to two clans, that of the mother and that of the father, while it is recommended that a man marry a 'grandmother,' in other words a girl belonging to either the mother's father's or father's father's clan." Thus, while the Hopi version of the system strains, in Lévi-Strauss's terms, "to make it either possible or compulsory for kinship and affinity to become mutually exclusive ties," the Cherokee system aims "to make it either possible or compulsory for matrimonial alliance to be kept within the circle of kin" (1965, 19). The latter, of course, is the basic tendency of elementary systems and the former of complex. (The Cherokee system, if followed systematically by any four units — lineages or clans — would produce in fact a system of second-cousin direct exchange on the "Aranda" pattern, only matrilineal instead of patrilineal — see the previous chapter and the notes to this one.)

Thus, it seems Crow systems can move in either direction. They can turn in on themselves and develop elementary tendencies, or they can change gear and move off in a complex direction by not allowing whole social units systematically to reinforce their alliances but instead "immersing" this tendency in a "flow of probabilistic events." The more in fact that we look at Crow systems, the more do they appear very different from each other, and this difference is based upon their place on the elementary-complex continuum. The question then is: What evidence have we that this theoretical gradation is also a historical gradation? The idea that it is is implicit, for example, in the work of Murdock, White, and Service, all of whom see Crow and Omaha systems arising from "simpler" forms. We shall look at this later. But for now I want to concentrate on the question whether or not Crow systems (in particular) are the outcome of specific tendencies in elementary systems, and hence whether those Crow systems that display more "elementary" tendencies than others are simply more in touch with their past, having moved less far in a complex direction than "pure" Crow systems. I stress that this is only a hypothesis and that it was developed not to prove or disprove anything in Lévi-Strauss, but to counter an alternative hypothesis: that variations in Crow systems represented different stages of "acculturation" (Fox 1967b).

To Crow or Not to Crow: American Southwest

I argued, for example, that the system found among the Keresan-speaking Indians of New Mexico is not, as many observers have thought, a result of a breakdown of a Crow system as a result of acculturation. On the contrary, I argued, for the Eastern Keresans at least it seems more probable that Crow tendencies are an incipient rather than a declining phase. I then reinterpreted the terminology of the Keresans to show that it could easily have evolved from an elementary system involving patrimoieties in direct exchange of spouses. I might add here that patrimoieties are not essential to the scheme, but the fact remains that the Eastern Keresans (living along the Rio Grande) do have patrimoieties, although these are not exogamous. I hypothesized that they might once have been.

To go into all the issues would be too complicated, but we can look at a few of the clues that these systems present. In Cochiti, for example (an Eastern Keresan Pueblo in New Mexico that I studied firsthand), a basic stock of terms seems to be distributed differently in different contexts (Fox 1967b). Sometimes it is used in a "Crow" fashion, and sometimes in a "generation" or "Hawaiian" fashion (all members of the same generation and sex called by the same terms; thus, all male members of ego's father's generation would be "father" for example). The "Crow" usage is illustrated in diagram 13.2 and shows classical Crow features, except that, like the Crow Indians themselves when using terms of address, the Cochiti use the term for "mother" also for "father's sister." There is another root, -ku, more generally meaning "woman" but now used mostly for "wife" (with a first-person possessive prefix, i.e., "my woman") but which some informants say was once used for father's sister, with the implicit meaning "woman of father's clan" (and which would have taken a different possessive prefix meaning "our/their woman"). As we shall see, in other Keresan-speaking Pueblo tribes this usage is indeed found, for example *kuya* at Acoma and Laguna. This, combining *ku* — (woman) and *ya* — (mother), might have been the original Cochiti usage also.

"Pure Crow" usage, however, is usually reserved for ceremonial occasions involving the matriclans (of which there were thirteen). On ceremonial occasions involving the patrilineal moieties, and generally when matriclans are not involved, kinship terms are used quite differently. This more general usage incorporates alternating-generation terms: thus, in the great-grandparental generation, for example, the terms for "father" and "mother" (*umu* and *yaya*, i.e., the parental generation terms) are repeated, and the great-grandchild generation are called "son" (*muti*) and "daughter" (*mák*), or more generally "child" (*ushe*).

Self-reciprocity of terms (if I use a term to you, you use the same one back to me) is common, and of particular interest is the MB = ZS reciprocal (*nawa* for males; females call MB and ZS *nyenye*). The "grandrelative" terms *mumu* and *papa* are also self-reciprocal, as is the "cross-sibling" term *meme* used between brothers and sisters. The term *wawa* (used by males) is very intriguing. It is applied to the MB = ZS reciprocal (replacing the "regular" term *nawa*), but is also used as a reciprocal between cross cousins, and particularly between the second cross-cousins FFZS and MBSS. This usage for a male speaker, in the context of the other terms, is shown in diagram 13.3, with the *wawa* terms emphasized.

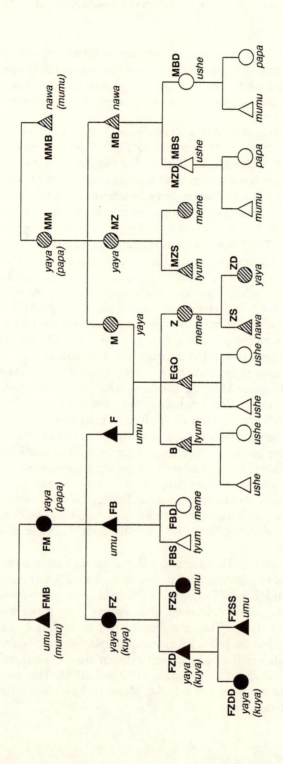

Diagram 13.2 Cochiti "Crow" Usage (Male)

Ego's (mother's) matriline

Father's matriline

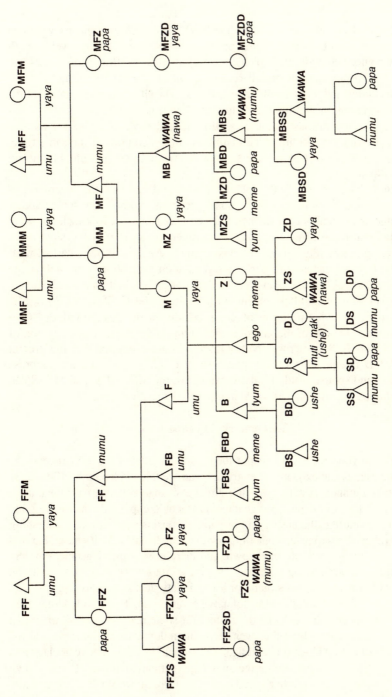

Diagram 13.3 Cochiti "Non-Crow" Usage (Male)

Parallel cousins are always classified with siblings, and, as we have observed, the FB's children are forbidden as marriage partners even though they do not belong to one's own or one's father's clan. But cross cousins can either be designated by the self-reciprocal *wawa* or given the "grandrelative" terms *mumu* and *papa*, again self-reciprocal. The alternating-generation terms are interesting in that they seem to be a way of having lineal equations that "override generations" (their repetition up and down the generations of a lineage) and yet recognize the distinction of generations at the same time. Again, analysts of Crow-Omaha systems have not known quite what to do with them.

In a sense, they defy the "skewing rule" and insist on the separation of generations. Sometimes, as we shall see with another Keresan-speaking Pueblo tribe, males of a lineage may be classified in Crow fashion while females are classified by alternating generations, as if the system were hovering between two modes of classification. Analysts have not asked what kind of system actually *requires* this generation distinction — as well as the self-reciprocal MB-ZS terms, the equation of parents' siblings with parents, the equation of parallel cousins with siblings, the FFZS = MBSS = MB equation, the identification of cross cousins with "grandrelatives" (and sometimes the use of the grandparental term for spouse), or the equation of MBS and FZS by *wawa*. Note also for future reference that the crucial MFZDD is equated with the symmetrical FFZSD as *papa*, same as cross cousin and spouse. And, as alternative terms, the MB, MBS, and MBSS can be classed together also as *wawa* in true Omaha fashion.

Elementary, My Dear Crow

But anyone who cares to put these facts together with the existence of patrimoieties and exogamous matriclans can see that hidden in the "flux" here is an elementary system involving direct exchange between patriunits, as in diagram 12.1 in the previous chapter. This would explain the major anomaly we noted earlier: the classifying of parallel cousins with siblings; something that otherwise defies the logic of Crow-Omaha "lineal" classification. Parallel cousins always fall into one's own, and therefore "unmarriageable," moiety (matri- or patri-) along with one's siblings; cross cousins are always in the opposite (marriageable) moiety (or if not moiety then at least lineage).

The Cochiti moieties are not now exogamous. I concluded that they probably once were, but that the system for some reason "opened up" into a Crow direction, without this ever becoming a dominant trend. If we add the information that Cochiti encourage "sequential" marriage between clans and highly approve and encourage marriage with a member of one's own generation in the mother's father's clan (which would be, for a male, marriage with a real or classificatory MFZDD — see notes to this chapter for further details), then we can see the strong elementary tendencies in the system, which, I am hypothesizing, derive from an elementary past that has never been shaken off. (And note for future reference the likeness of the Cochiti marriage preference to the Cherokee preference for marriage into mother's father's or father's father's clans.) I am not so wedded to the preexistence of exogamous patrimoieties as I once was, but dropping these would not radically alter the analysis. We only need to accept that "patriunits" were real and were involved for the system to work. And indeed, strong patrilineal extended families do exist as essentially ritual units in Cochiti: subunits of the patrilineal moieties.

Diagram 13.4 shows the possible Cochiti "original" system of kin terms embodying an elementary exchange system with two patriunits. This is arrived at purely by following out the logic of the terminological system as it now stands. The male terms are used here, but as I have demonstrated (Fox 1967b), the female terms follow the same logic.

The reader can go back to diagram 13.3 and verify that the equations made there fit this reconstruction accurately, and that the "anomalies" we now see in the supposed "Crow" usage are more likely to be a reflection of this older but still influential system rather than a breakdown of a perfect Crow system. (Ego's matriline has been shaded to make the identifications easier.) It is the "Crow" usage, in other words, that is newer and more intrusive, operating only in strict "clan contexts." My interpretation of the derivation of the present state of terminology was linear. It envisaged a *passage* from a direct-exchange system to a "turbulent" version of a Crow system. Now there is no reason why, theoretically, the system should not at one point have become wholly Crow and later reverted to elementary tendencies, for example. I can only say that this seems less plausible than what I have conjectured. We know of no examples in ethnography or history of such a drastic reversal of social evolution.

As the Crow Flies: The Same in Laguna

To try to illustrate how this process could have occurred — how the present terminology, for example, could have easily derived from an elementary version of itself — I applied the analysis to a Western Keresan Pueblo that I had not myself studied but that was admittedly "more Crow" than Cochiti: Laguna. Eggan (1949, 268-71) had found difficulty in explaining several facts about Laguna terminology: self-reciprocal terms; alternating generation terms; the use of the "grandrelative" term for the spouse and as a reciprocal between MBS and FZD. I will take the terms Eggan gives for a female ego's own (mother's) lineage and her father's lineage and show how these are

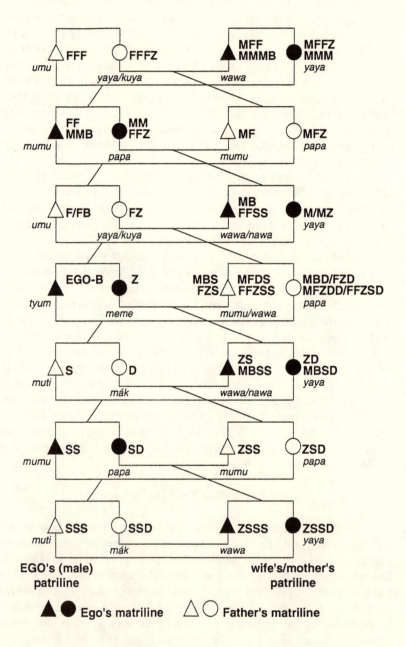

Diagram 13.4 Reconstructed Cochiti Kin Terms (Male)

congruent with the change I have hypothesized. (Men's and women's terms are different, as is common in many such systems, and I choose the women's terms here as they contain several interesting features worthy of comment. The reader could go to Eggan's tables and do the same analysis with the men's terms for confirmation.) Diagram 13.5 is the Eggan data for a woman's own lineage and her father's lineage.

The dialect of Keres spoken in Laguna differs from that of Cochiti, but the terms are recognizably cognate. The Laguna *naicdia* is the Cochiti *nashtyu,*

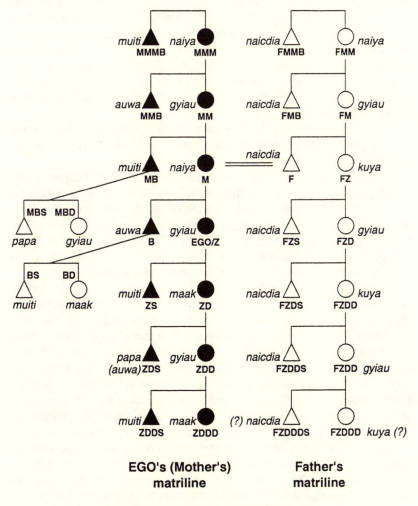

EGO's (Mother's)   Father's
matriline   matriline

Diagram 13.5 Laguna Terms (Female)

used in Cochiti as a term of reference for "father," who is otherwise *umu*; *kuya* we have already discussed; *gyiau* and *gauau* are women's terms corresponding to the Cochiti *ta'o* and *tao* — cognate women's terms for grandrelative and sister respectively; *auwa* is unlike the Cochiti *meme* but remarkably like *wawa*; the terms for "son" and "daughter" are the same: *muiti* and *maak*; *naiya* is the same as the Cochiti *naya*, a term of reference for "mother," who is otherwise *yaya*. Many of the "differences" are differences of transliteration by linguists, not of actual pronunciation.

The interesting features here are the MB = ZS equation, especially as *muiti* is used for own son (the corresponding female term in Cochiti is *nyenye*, which I think could be derived from Spanish *niño*, "son," and substituted for the "old" word *muti*, which is identical with the Laguna counterpart); the alternating-generation terminology in ego's own lineage; the "lineal equation" of all the males in the father's lineage; and the alternating-generation terminology for the females of the father's lineage. The cross-sex reciprocal "grandrelative" term *papa* (same as in Cochiti) is used for both spouse and MBS.

Now, if we rearrange the Laguna terms as a direct exchange system involving two patriunits, as we did for Cochiti, they look remarkably like the Cochiti result (diagram 13.6).

As with any such system, a matrilineal classification is "built in" to the essentially patrilineal alliance terminology. Thus, for our female ego all those kin shaded in the diagram would be members of her matrilineage, "cycling" through the two patrilineages. Her children and her sister's children would be in the opposite unit (husband's), and her son and her sister's son would be "equivalent" to her mother's brother in being "males of adjacent generations in affinal unit" and hence classified together as "unmarriageable."

The unshaded kin would be ego's father's matrilineage, and hence, turning back to diagram 13.5, it is easy to see what happened when (and if) the elementary system gave way to a Crow and complex successor. The most startling thing is that the members of ego's *own* matrilineage continue to be classified *exactly as they would have been under the elementary system*, alternating generations and all. In the father's lineage, the "lineal equation" applies to the men, and a permanent substitution of *naicdia* ("father" — Cochiti *nashtyu*) for *papa* has occurred. But, and this is the fascinating fact, the women of this lineage continue to be classified in alternating generations, *exactly as they would have been under the direct-exchange system*.

Given the Cochiti "clues" — and there are many others that I cannot detail here, including a systematic distinction between relatives designated by the root *mu-* and those by *wa-* (for example *muti*, son, and *wati*, son-in-law or male affine) corresponding to a division between "own" patriunit (*mu* people) and "wife's" patriunit (*wa* people) (see Fox 1972, 79) — it seemed reason-

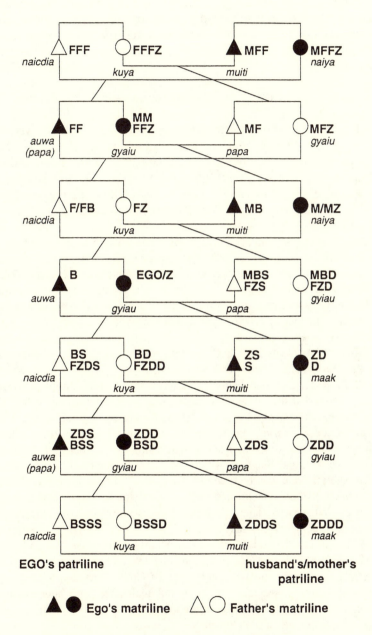

EGO's patriline

husband's/mother's patriline

▲● Ego's matriline   △○ Father's matriline

Diagram 13.6 Reconstructed Laguna Terms (Female)

able to suppose that an evolution had occurred among the Keresans from a system of restricted exchange to a Crow system, and that variants of the Keresan system showed different degrees of adaptation to this change; that is, they lay along a continuum from elementary (restricted) to complex (Crow), with Laguna well along the road, but Cochiti still heavy with elementary tendencies.

The Crow-Omaha Evolution: Wise Words from the Masters

My primary aim in this demonstration was to show that this hypothesis accounted for the data better than the hypothesis that these were Crow systems in states of relative degeneration through acculturation. A prominent exponent of the degeneration theory was L. A. White, and therefore it came as a surprise to me to find him advancing the following argument for the *general* evolution of Crow (and Omaha) systems:

When the clan system is young and weak, the kinship system will be of the Dakota-Iroquois type, regardless of the sex in which descent is reckoned. As the clan system develops, however, and comes to exert its influence more and more upon the social life of the tribe, the Dakota-Iroquois terminology will be transferred into the Crow type in a matrilineal society and into the Omaha type in a patrilineal society. (1939, 569-70)

"Iroquois" systems include those with restricted (direct) exchange (they are the matrilineal version, Dakota the patrilineal), and so this hypothesis would fit the Keresan data better than the one White in fact adopts. However, I don't think that the "weakness" of the clans had much to do with it. The Iroquois and the Navaho have very "strong" clans by any standard, but both have "Iroquoian" terms rather than Crow. Some analysts find this hard to believe, and much time has been wasted trying to "fit" Navaho terms onto Crow-type "lineage" diagrams which make very little sense (Aberle 1961). A much better account can be found in Kaut (1957), where the development of the Southern Athapaskan kinship systems from simple Hawaiian to Iroquoian — in the Western Apache and Navaho — is correlated with the relative degree of settlement of these tribes.

While on the Iroquoian subject, we should notice that G. P. Murdock (1949, 244) classifies Cochiti as "Normal Iroquois," and Acoma (which parallels Laguna in most respects) as "Bi-Crow." Iroquois can become transmuted, in his system, into Crow, and again this "fits" better than the decline and fall theory. Another anthropologist, E. R. Service, also expresses the proposed change in some detail:

In some cases where lineages and clans are strongly corporate, the widespread bifurcate-merging terminology undergoes further specific change. Clan and/or lineage membership may become such an important aspect of social interaction that the status of a person of ego's affinal group — his father's clan in a matrilineal society, the mother's in a patrilineal society — becomes more importantly a matter of group membership than of the more individualized, more specific, egocentric relationship. Thus the bifurcate-merging type of egocentric nomenclature remains characteristic of ego's social relationship to members of his own clan and lineage, with whom he has close and frequent interaction, but in dealings with members of the affinal lineage or clan the terminology normally used is sociocentric, meaning something like "male (female) of the such-and-such clan (or lineage)." Generic terms have been given this overriding of the egocentric terminology by a sociocentric term in situations like the above: "Crow system" where the affinal group is father's (i.e., a matrilineal society) and "Omaha system" where it is mother's (a patrilineal society). (1962, 132-33)

His "bifurcate merging" terminology is essentially one appropriate to a direct-exchange system, or, as he would call it, a system of "reciprocal exogamy." His characterization of the process of change fits closely our proposed sequence for Laguna and Cochiti.

I do not want to discuss the various evolutionary schemes, but simply to point out that they are all concerned in various ways with the *passage aux structures complexes* — although none of them analyze this in quite the same way as Lévi-Strauss does. He prefers the role of culture historian to that of speculative evolutionist. They are all unfortunately based on an inadequate classification of kinship systems which lumps together disparate types on the basis of a few superficial resemblances ("fish and whale," as Lévi-Strauss puts it).

What they describe are general tendencies in social evolution. What I have described is a particular case in which a particular type of elementary, restricted system probably evolved into several types of Crow or near-Crow systems. This could not possibly be the only way in which the *passage* is effected, but it seems the most probable in this instance. It is interesting that a direct development from a *restricted* exchange system should produce a complex system which is itself a combination of restricted exchange and a "complex formula" of generalized exchange. But perhaps it is precisely *because* the development is of this kind that we get this result. I have been misled in the past by thinking that when Lévi-Strauss spoke of Crow-Omaha systems as such a combination, he must be implying the separate existence of each type in successive stages of the development of the system. There is no reason why this should be so, of course.

The Many Routes to Crow: American Southeast

Do Crow systems always "emerge" in this way? I doubt it, because other Crow systems seem wedded to matrimoieties, which are just as likely as patrimoieties to be the units in a restricted or generalized exchange system. Let us approach this by taking the Cherokee. We have already seen that a Cherokee should marry a "grandmother," that is, a member of his father's father's or mother's father's clan (see diagram 13.1 for the ideal Crow pattern that would produce this result). Again the rule applies to *individuals* and not to whole groups, so what we have are elementary tendencies to "second cross-cousin marriage" (FFZDD and MFZDD — note Cochiti preference for the latter) and hence *restricted* exchange, which are immersed in a probabilistic flux, just as with the Hopi, for example, we had elementary tendencies to *generalized* exchange similarly immersed.

The Cherokee did not have matrimoieties, but their neighbors (and linguistic relatives) the Choctaw did, and these moieties were exogamous. Eggan (1966, chap. 2) has difficulties with these systems similar to those he had in explaining the Keresans, and with the Southeastern tribes he similarly resorts to an acculturational explanation. (See my diagram 13.7 taken from Eggan's chapter: his symbols are slightly different from mine — S for him is "sister," for example — but the pattern is clear.) The problem with the Cherokee and the Choctaw is the persistence of non-Crow elements in what appears superficially to be a "Crow" system. For example, in both systems, FZS = F in true Crow fashion, but then FZSS = F, which contradicts Crow usage and is decidedly "patrilineal." The Cherokee system according to Eggan is "complicated in part by patterns of preferential marriage," and the Choctaw, as we have seen, had matrilineal moieties. If we regard "pure Crow" as the baseline for these two systems, then these annoying features become, like the alternating generation terminology of Laguna, inexplicable "interferences" in the working of the system. But could it not perhaps be that these features, rather than "acculturation," explain the deviations from Crow usage? That is, as with Cochiti, the elementary tendencies in each system lead to alternative means of classification.

These systems of classification can either be true alternates within one system, or "crystallized" (Lévi-Strauss's term) in one direction or another. Thus, the Laguna terms crystallized further in a Crow direction than the Cochiti, and Gilbert (1937) found that the Eastern Cherokee were more Crow in their terminology than were the Western. If we take the Cherokee and Choctaw usage seriously, then we could argue that what they are emphasizing

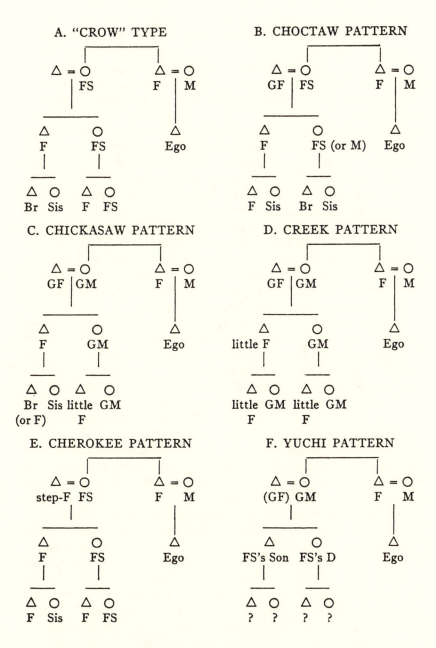

Diagram 13.7 Southeastern Kinship Structures (after Eggan)

in the seemingly un-Crow classification is the patrilineage of the father's sister's husband (FZH); that is, the one she has married into. In a patrilineal direct-exchange system, these men would be identified together as members of ego's affinal lineage. (Alternatively, see the system diagrammed in the notes to this chapter for systematic marriage with the MFZDD, where the FZS and the FZSS would indeed fall into the same clan [father's] and be classified together. Either alternative would easily explain why the equation is made.)

While in the Southeast we might look at Eggan's other problem children, the Yuchi, because he maintains that they have "gone through the whole sequence of changes from a Crow to an Omaha type of kinship system." One possible factor, he notes, "is the greater emphasis on patrilineal institutions among the Yuchi" (1966, 34). In fact, the matrilineal clans of the Yuchi were "cross-cut by a division of the men into two patrilineal societies." (Murdock [1949, 247] classifies the Yuchi as "Duo-crow," which, among other things, lumps them with the Murngin! And it is worth noting that the Murngin are willing to arrange their own kinship terms — which show the "elementary tendencies" of alternating generations, self-reciprocals, etc. — in either "patrisequences" or "matrisequences" as we have been doing here. In other words, the recognition of both "lines" in elementary systems is not some artifact of anthropological analysis, but is seen clearly by the natives themselves: see Hiatt 1965.) These patrilineal societies of the Yuchi "tended" to be endogamous, but even so the situation is remarkably like that in Cochiti, where two nonexogamous patrimoieties cross-cut the exogamous matrilineal clans, and where the system of terms refuses to be wholly Crow but carries "reverse" (i.e., Omaha) tendencies.

I hope to have demonstrated that these "Omaha" tendencies in Cochiti are in fact compatible with a restricted-exchange system based on patriunits. Perhaps a fuller knowledge of the Yuchi would reveal something similar and show that acculturation, rather than "causing" specific changes in the system, serves to "strip away" certain features while leaving others intact. In other words, it does not "cause" the Omaha tendencies; it reveals them. (I find it hard to understand in any case how acculturation to Spanish or Anglo-Saxon kinship systems should produce lineal equations of FZS = FZSS or MB = MBS; or again, "generational" terminology. Any of these alternatives are as foreign to European systems as they are to Crow.) I am not denying the role of acculturation in change — that would be absurd — but suggesting that perhaps in these cases its role may be different from what has been thought.

We have then two types: the Cochiti type with its patriunits and "Omaha" elements immersed in a Crow flux — with perhaps the Yuchi as another possible example; and the "Cherokee type" with matriunits engaged in restricted exchange. Both types have strong Crow components, but in both there is a strain toward restricted exchange. This makes them very different from, say, the Hopi, whose "purer" Crow system strains toward generalized exchange.

Les Passages aux Structures Complexes

All these systems are "complex" in one sense, and yet veer toward the elementary end of the continuum in another.

I have suggested that they might possibly be a development from a system such as we find among the Shoshone of southern Utah (Steward 1938) or the Dravidians in south India (Dumont 1953). Here there are no unilineal institutions, but bilateral cross-cousin marriage (possibly deriving directly from sister exchange) is practiced, and terminology "strains" toward an accommodation of such a system (parallel cousins are distinguished from cross; MB = FZH, etc.). Such a system can then move off in a variety of directions. It can crystallize into a restricted exchange system involving unilineal descent groups; it can, with the advent perhaps of matrilocal residence and the strong matriclan, move off in a purely "Crow" direction — as happened with the Hopi, whose system is derived directly from the aboriginal Shoshonean pattern; it can likewise move in an Omaha direction — a possibility inherent in the patrilineal/patrilocal tendencies of the Ojibwa and the Great Lakes Indians (see Eggan 1966, chap. 4), or even the development of patrilateral cross-cousin marriage (FZD or FFZSD) as in New Guinea (see the summary in Rubel and Rossman 1978); it can develop a system of restricted exchange between patriunits which are later superseded by matriunits — as might have happened with the Cochiti; it can develop a system of direct exchange between matriunits which can crystallize at that stage (see, for example, the Siuai of Melanesia — Oliver 1955), and perhaps develop matrimoieties — as among the Iroquois; or it can fail to crystallize and move directly into a Crow system by ceasing to apply the marriage-exchange rules to whole units and confining them to individuals.

Now, these illustrate some of the many *passages* from a simple system of bilateral cross-cousin marriage, and some of these can produce Crow and Omaha systems. What I am suggesting is that the variation we find in terms and rules, among Crow systems at least, probably represents various "outcomes" of these different "strategies." These outcomes can of course be affected strongly by acculturation, but we may be misled if we see the outcomes simply as various stages in the "decline" of "pure" Crow systems. The term "Crow" (and by implication "Omaha" also) should perhaps be reserved as a term descriptive of certain *tendencies* in systems hovering between restricted exchange and complexity. This state of hover perhaps also produces the strains toward generalized exchange. But there is the possibility that some Crow systems have themselves been derived from systems of generalized exchange between matriunits. The ones I have looked at do not seem so derivable, but the possibility should be explored. On the whole, I see "Crow-Omaha" systems on the one hand, and the "simple formula of generalized exchange" on the other, as alternative strategies, with Crow-Omaha leading more easily to "complex" systems. Thus, the proto-Indo-European kinship system was "Omaha," and this can be clearly seen in various aspects of Latin kinship terminology (Friedrich 1966; Benveniste 1969).

Lévi-Strauss notes the confusion that arises when Crow-Omaha systems are classified with systems having asymmetrical cross-cousin marriage. A similar difficulty arises, for example, in lumping restricted-exchange systems in with those designated "Iroquois." Perhaps the next step in research should be a closer examination of Iroquoian (and Dakotan) systems that do not have restricted exchange, to see where they fit on the continuum (Buchler & Selby 1968, chap. 10). Basically, they have the similar feature we found in most Crow systems with preferential marriage patterns: the rules apply to individuals, not to whole social groups; they are therefore "sectionless" (see Shapiro 1970).

I would hope that an examination such as the above, if carried out generally, would marry the evolutionary interests of Service, Murdock, White, etc. with the cultural historical interests of Eggan and Lévi-Strauss, and that the marriage would be under the auspices of the latter's theory of elementary and complex tendencies in kinship systems. This approach would require a reclassification of systems in terms of the theory, and would concentrate on discovering processes of change in particular areas with a view to understanding the many forms of the *"passage aux structures complexes."* Eggan's summary of the changes in kinship structures among the Algonkian peoples is an excellent example of such a possible analysis (1966, chap. 4). These changes are not inexorably unidirectional, but may fluctuate between the opposite poles of "elementarity" and "complexity."

On closer examination, I have suggested, Crow-Omaha systems will turn out to be examples of a certain type of fluctuation. They are not a "stage" because clearly many societies have not gone and will not go through the Crow-Omaha experience. They are, if I am correct, *one mode of transmutation by which elementary structures pass into complex.* Another step in research, then, is to identify the elementary tendencies in these systems. Once this is done we can attempt to derive the various types of Crow-Omaha system from their elementary foundations, and hence perhaps reach a better understanding of their place on the elementary-complex continuum.

Crow-Omaha: Why They Are Where They Are

We must then ask why they occur where they do. That they seem most prevalent in North America is interesting since American culture (like Australian) is relatively "archaic," having been isolated on the continent and existing at a low population density for upwards of twenty thousand years. The prevalence of moiety systems and cross-cousin marriage in many areas, and the widespread occurrence of Crow-Omaha structures, suggest strongly that the latter are indeed an adaptive response to a slow change from the "elementary" systems of the primitive hunting/gathering base culture, representing one form of the "opening up" of such elementary structures. (We get a similar mixture in South America, with moieties, direct exchange, and Omaha-type systems preponderant.) New Guinea systems could also be an Omaha way of opening up the elementary structures of an Australian type (or both may derive from some Dravidian-type Ur structure with bilateral cross-cousin marriage and correlated terminology, but without unilineal descent groups). The Melanesian examples also need to be looked at carefully since they too may have ultimate historical associations with the Australian (see for example the varying interpretations of Mota in the Banks Islands — Needham 1964).

Lévi-Strauss suggests that in Africa the evolution of bride wealth and its associated practices was another "opening up" in the direction of a complex system of generalized exchange with long cycles, suitable to a continent of agriculturalists and pastoralists living in areas of high population size and density. Central African matrilineal systems show definite "Crow" tendencies. Among the Indo-Europeans, on the other hand, it was the fact of generalized exchange running up against hypergamy and ranking that produced such solutions as caste (India) on the one hand and the truly complex "European" solution of "prohibited degrees" on the other, with China, for much of its history, hovering on the line between generalized exchange and true complexity (Lévi-Strauss 1949, chap. 28).

We can (roughly) contrast these as areas of rapid social change (Europe — including Slavic countries), moderate social change (Africa, China, Southeast Asia, India), and slow social change (North and South America, Australia-Melanesia-New Guinea). In each case the rise in population size and density is relative to the rapidity of change, and of course the evolving social systems were very different in features other than kinship. It may be that eventually we will be able to put all these facts together and understand better the

242 The Challenge of Anthropology

adaptational significance of "elementarity" as opposed to "complexity" on the one hand, and of the different forms of each on the other. At the moment we can only say weakly, for example, that "Crow-Omaha" systems seem to be a complex adaptation of the middle range; that restricted exchange systems are geared to small and stable populations; that generalized exchange has advantages to expanding populations but soon reaches limits; that large and mobile populations in highly differentiated societies seem to require a complex kinship system, but that this does not preclude small populations with simple structures from having "complex" kinship, etc., etc. Complex kinship systems in small and relatively endogamous populations must, however, be very different from the same systems in large and mobile populations, for, as Lévi-Strauss notes, in such a population with only a "negative rule" of "prohibited degrees," after the lapse of the required number of generations (usually two or three), consanquines will begin marrying each other again. (See Fox 1978, chap. 8, for an expansion of this idea with an empirical example from Ireland.) Similarly, generalized exchange among the three hundred egalitarian Purum is something very different from the same among three hundred thousand hierarchical Kachin (Fox 1967a, chap. 9).

But these figures give point to the fact also noted by Lévi-Strauss: that Crow-Omaha systems seem confined to populations of five thousand or less (the outer limits of the Paleolithic linguistic tribe). And indeed it is difficult to imagine such a system working in a population of five hundred thousand, especially one characterized by some degree of social differentiation. Such considerations may help us to fix the "adaptational level" of the systems. Thus, it could have been the modest population growth during the Anasazi period in the American Southwest that rendered a simple system of moiety exogamy unworkable and pushed the system in the direction of clan exogamy and a "Crow" solution, but not beyond that point. Looking at kinship systems in this way enables us to take advantage of the insights of demographers, zoologists, ecologists, and geneticists; for, in essence Lévi-Strauss is asking, "What types of assortative mating systems operate in the various populations of *Homo sapiens*?" To those of us interested in "culture as adaptation" and the ongoing evolution of the species, such considerations are of obvious importance.

We must not leave aside the problems of definition. As it stands, the definition of Crow-Omaha systems, if we go beyond the merely terminological and try to include rules of marriage, etc., is negative and inadequate. They seem to be systems that make lineal equations in terminology but do not have systematic, generalized exchange. This has to be so since the latter type of system ("circulating connubium") also makes "lineal equations," but not on the same basis as Crow-Omaha systems.

Strictly speaking, the term applies only to systems of terminology, but Lévi-Strauss uses it in a much wider context than just terminology, and I have followed him here in that use. It is perhaps because of their transitional nature, because they are tendencies, not fixed types, that Crow-Omaha systems are so difficult to pin down with rigorous definitions; yet they seem easily recognizable when we come across them. They have, in Wittgenstein's words, "family resemblances" that enable us to identify them, even if no two are exactly alike. This may seem an unsatisfactory place to leave the question, but it may, paradoxically, also be the answer to it.

I have been deliberately uncritical of many of Lévi-Strauss's notions here (for example the idea of harmonic and disharmonic regimes, which is a total red herring) in order to push his ideas as far as possible to see what they may bring to light. The exercise has been, as one might expect, well worthwhile. The riches to be mined in his work seem endless, and will keep we lesser spirits suitably busy and out of mischief in the ethnological years to come.

Part Five

Mind and Myth

Introduction to Part Five

Observers often show surprise when they ask me to sum up the basic question asked in "Prejudice and the Unfinished Mind" and I reply: "What happens when we think?" I seem to have a knack for inventing catchy titles that unfortunately give a mildly wrong impression. Thus, people — including reviewers who claimed to have read it — thought that *The Red Lamp of Incest* was about incest! As though, I think I wrote somewhere, *The Golden Bough* were about arboriculture. But it really is my own fault. The trouble is, I really couldn't think of a snappy title for the piece that would somehow sum up all that is in it. It *is* about prejudice, as indeed *Red Lamp* is about incest — sort of. But it is much more to do with what happens when we think — the unfinished mind.

An interest in mentation, the thought process, cognition, or mind (as we used to call it) has run through a lot of previous ruminations. The chapter on "The Matter of Mind" in *Red Lamp* actually started as a talk at the American Anthropological Association meetings sometime in the early 1970s when structuralism was still in fashion and I was interested in totemic categories as a subset (as we said freely) of categories in general. A version of it appeared as "The Evolution of Mind: An Anthropological Approach" in the *Journal of Anthropological Research* 35(2) (1979). This was expanded as a talk to a conference on science and religion, published in an obscure journal devoted to same, and eventually appeared as "The Passionate Mind" (an obvious play

247

on Lévi-Strauss's *The Savage Mind*) in *The Search for Society*. Meanwhile, I had edited, with Jacques Mehler, the book *Neonate Cognition,* which was the outcome of a conference we organized on thinking in babies (or the baby mind, or what you will). Even chapter 9 of the present book could just as well be seen as an essay on cognition as on ethnology.

Indeed, the early "science of man" in Morgan, Tylor, Frazer, Durkheim, Mauss, Lévy-Bruhl, and Boas, for example, was strongly mentalist, and Boas did call his great general work *The Mind of Primitive Man.* Morgan had written interestingly of the mentality of beavers, which he thought compared favorably with our own. Lévi-Strauss maintained the French end of this through his structuralist approach, and the cognitive anthropologists (and some of the linguists) kept the flag flying in the United States. British anthropologists like Evans-Pritchard and Mary Douglas revived the tradition in England in the face of functionalism, and Malinowski, as we shall see, was interested in such things as "Myth in Primitive Psychology." All in all, then, an interest in what happens when we think, and even further in why we think the way we do when we think, is as good an anthropological tradition as a philosophical or psychological one.

I say this obviously a bit defensively, since "the unfinished mind" is not at first glance an obvious anthropological topic. But I think it is at the heart of the anthropological program. "What about kinship?" you will ask. Look at my essay on "Kinship Categories as Natural Categories" — whose latest manifestation is as a chapter in *Search for Society* — and all will be clear. But I must admit that the piece reproduced here in chapter 14 was not published in an anthropological journal but, much to my surprise, in a rather strict psychology journal with peer review and peer commentary and all that. Some friends of mine, psychologists (some of my best friends are psychologists), who had heard it as a public lecture to a general audience, were moved to recommend it to *Psychological Enquiry*. I was sceptical, because it was obviously not written at all in the pristine way usually required even of think pieces in the psychology journals. But to my delight the editor, Lawrence Pervin, and the reviewers, while having some serious criticisms and excellent suggestions for improvement, actually seemed to welcome the change from the run-of-the-mill psychology pieces and approved it. This meant it had to go out to some fifteen psychologists — almost all social psychologists — for "peer commentary." I had never been subjected to this hazard before, especially not with such (for me) a strange audience. But again I was amazed at the playfulness and wit that so many of them wove into their altogether serious and critical critiques. If nothing else, I can claim to have turned an entire issue of a solemn psychology journal into a lively discussion of the real meaning of *Star Trek.* If I manage nothing else, this should count for something. There is simply not space enough to print the commentaries here, or my lengthy reply, so the reader must consult the journal for these. I think perhaps they got me on base rates and probabilities, but I think I won the *Star Trek* debate.

As it turns out, I seem to be on the same lines as those contemporary "evolutionary psychologists" who see the mind, and thinking, not as some general, all-purpose, computer-like operation but as a collection of rather specific mental functions cobbled together in the process of natural selection and adaptation (see Jerome Barkow, Leda Cosmides, & John Tooby, *The Adapted Mind* [New York: Oxford University Press, 1992]). If the mind is, as Lévi-Strauss claimed, a *bricoleur*, it is because it is itself the result of an evolutionary *bricolage*; or, as I have put it several times already, the mind reproduces that which produced it — in this case including its own structure. Who would believe that this was all to do with prejudice? But it does. I seem fatally attracted to unpopular causes, and when something like "aggression" or "prejudice" gets a terrible press, but is nevertheless stubbornly persistent, I am drawn to it like the moth to the proverbial flame (and, in the opinion of my colleagues at least, with a similar result). But I'll risk the burning if you will join me and find out what Charles Lamb, Mr. Spock, and Paul Robeson have to do with it all.

The second essay, on myth and psychology, seems to me to fall into this same tradition. We are back to wondering why, universally, there seems to be this urge to make myths, an urge not in the least diminished by the triumphs of science and technology but if anything aided and abetted and extended by them, viz., *Star Trek, Star Wars,* and the whole cinematographic paraphernalia of modern mythmaking. If our notion of an "adapted mind" is on the right track, then we might perhaps cautiously ease into this matter of myth via a modified version of Jungian archetypes. I flag this in the first essay, and it gets an airing in the second. The essay does not expand on this because again it was written as an encyclopedia exercise, not as a theoretical exploration. But the extended section on the "Fragmentation of Trickster" shows how the thinking might go. Something is "in the wiring" (Primordial Trickster?), but the expression of it in mentation — in this case, in myth — is not wholly pre-determined; it filters through in many colors like light through a prism. I confess I don't quite know where to take this at the moment, but perhaps the reader will be interested enough to want to join in the search.

14

Prejudice and the Unfinished Mind: A New Look at an Old Failing

Dinner in Jerusalem

Just outside the old city of Jerusalem there is an area, Miskenot Sha'ananim, beautifully restored by the generosity of Sir Moses Montefiore. It is largely inhabited by writers and artists, but it is also home to a magnificent, continental-style restaurant serving food in the classic manner. My hosts in the city told me that Henry Kissinger liked to dine there when he was in town (which was frequently in those shuttle-diplomacy days of 1974). I decided this was reference enough, and there retired with two colleagues, both psychologists, to discuss papers we had heard at the fiftieth anniversary proceedings of the Technion in Haifa. One of the papers had particularly intrigued me, and I invited the authors, Daniel Kahneman and Amos Tversky, to share the repast. The evening had two major surprises for me. One was the discovery after lapping up the excellent wild duck with wild berry sauce and a halfway decent Israeli cabernet courtesy of the Rothschild family, that this was a strictly kosher establishment. Perhaps this shouldn't have surprised me, but it did. The other was a remark made by either Kahneman or Tversky (the passage of time tends to merge them in memory) which came at the end of the evening when, after a second bottle, we were beginning to drop our defenses and tell it like it is.

I shall keep you in suspense about the remark which so shook me until I have described the paper in question and why I was so fascinated with it. The authors were interested in the capacity of people to think consistently and logically, which they define simply as being able to reach incscapable conclusions based on premises previously agreed upon as absolute. In some simple cases there is no problem. If we agree that two plus two equals four, we have to accept that three plus one equals four. The logic of the first implies the second. But when we move away from certainties to probabilities, it appears that our capacity for consistency and logic breaks down. The example our authors gave in their paper ran something like this. They set up an experiment with a group of people chosen from the general population. They first got the group to agree on a specific premise, which they called The Law of Large Numbers. It is in effect a basic principle of probability: If one has a large sample in which one item is overwhelmingly represented (say, more than 90 percent), then if an object is picked blindly and randomly from that sample, the probability of its being the overrepresented item is also more than 90 percent. If, for example, we have 100 golf balls in a box (90 white and only 10 black), then if we pick blindly from the box and offer you the choice of color, you will be bound to opt for white. Odds of 9:1 are pretty overwhelming, and people readily agreed that they must choose white under these circumstances.

Our authors then set up a neat test. The conditions were as follows: The sample was a farming community in the Midwest where at least 90 percent of the men were farmers. We pick a name out of the census list at random. What is the occupation of the man so picked? Obviously, we must opt for "farmer" — the agreed-upon principles leave us no choice. The odds are overwhelmingly — stupendously — in this direction. If we had money on it, that is the way we would bet. But our subtle, even cruel, authors decide to put us on a mental rack. They append a description like the following to the person picked (I am doing this from memory, so the details may be a bit different, but the principle is not affected).

The person is male and well educated. He likes reading — especially serious non-fiction. He is fond of classical music and plays the piano reasonably well. His hobbies include chess and crossword puzzles. He likes good wine and good conversation. His favorite television is Masterpiece Theater and his favorite films are foreign.

And so on in the same vein. Now, this information should not, if we have indeed accepted the Law, affect our decision in the slightest. It does not matter what the man's characteristics and preferences are; the chances are so slender of not picking a farmer that we should stick to our decision, however unusual a farmer he may appear to be. Nevertheless, when presented with this description, the subjects of the experiment deserted in droves and decided that their random pick was in fact a schoolteacher or librarian — the two most popular choices (even though these represented only a fraction of 1 percent of the population in question).

Lunch in Evanston

To illustrate how deep seated is this tendency to buck logic, I will take you to another gracious meal, this one in the charming town of Evanston, Illinois. (Thai cuisine this time and just as delicious). The guests included a famous BBC producer and an even more famous zoologist. These were unusual men and certainly not of the common herd. In fact, they were deploring human illogicality — in the context of a discussion of the function of religion. I thoroughly agreed, and as evidence told them the Kahneman and Tversky tale of the illogical subjects. To my surprise, they joined the droves of deserters and protested that what the description did was provide "extra information" on which to base a judgement. They presented arguments to back this up. The BBC producer insisted that it was like telling you that the person in question had "white soft hands" and therefore, one supposes, couldn't be a farmer. The world-famous zoologist gave the analogy of a box with 99 white and 1 black stones. If we picked at random, yes, he said we would have to say that the unseen stone was white. But if we were then told that the stone was carboniferous and ignitable, we would obviously change our minds and say we got the one piece of coal in the box.

These are smart characters, and they made their case forcefully. Let's admit it: You're nodding in agreement with them. But consider: There is nothing in the description that is even close to "having white soft hands," and even if there were, is this cause to deny farmer status to our random pick? He could have a skin condition and wear gloves all the time. I know lots of farmers who always wear heavy work gloves and whose hands are not particularly gnarled. As to the coal analogy, the only thing that would count would be something in the description which definitely ruled out farmers, like, "He has no idea how to use a tractor" or, more analogously, "He works full-time in a library." There is nothing like that in the description. Thus, I countered, unless the description gives unqualified evidence that the man is *not* a farmer, given your acceptance of the Law, you have no cause to conclude he is anything else. He may be a very unusual farmer, although, again, I know a lot of farmers with pretty refined tastes and college educations. (In fact, legally, I am a farmer, and I have letters from the state addressed "Dear Farmer" to prove it.) The point is, absent conclusive evidence to the contrary, whatever description is given, if we are to be consistent and logical we must stick to the decision that our random pick is overwhelmingly likely to be a farmer. But not only do we not do so, we feel decidedly uncomfortable with this decision, much happier with the schoolteacher, and tend to get, like my eminent friends, heated and argumentative if the point is pressed.

Kahneman (or was it Tversky?) gave many such examples over dinner, and, at the close of the evening, shaking his head, he sadly concluded: "In evolutionary terms we are an imperfect creature; we have an unfinished mind." That was my second shock of the evening.

I had not expected a cognitive psychologist to invoke evolution, but to hear one deplore our "unevolved" condition was even more striking. The logic was implacable: If we are capable of accepting logical premises, we should be capable of acting on them. We seem incapable of doing so. We prefer intuitive judgments to logical arguments; we are hopelessly deficient thinking machines. It perhaps is not strange that cognitive psychologists should have a totally logical thinking machine as an ideal — a computer, in fact. The computer would have remorselessly turned up "farmer" every time. It is not burdened with human intuition; it does not get heated and emotional; it does not prefer to base its judgments on qualitative evidence when it has accepted quantitative premises. In this respect it is a superior thinking machine. But, one asks, how long would it survive in the real world of human decision making?

You may perhaps think that, recollecting in anything but tranquillity, I exaggerate the position of the psychologists. Indeed, the original conference paper has long since disappeared from my files. But a portion of Kahneman's conclusions survives in print. "There is an element of incongruity," he says, "in the image of an organism equipped with an affective and hormonal system not much different from that of the jungle rat being given the ability to destroy every living thing by pushing a few buttons." But if that is not bad enough, he adds:

Another source of danger is to be found in man's cognitive limitations, which make it quite likely that the fate of entire societies may be sealed by a series of avoidable mistakes committed by their leaders. The increase in man's power over his environment has not been accompanied by a concomitant improvement of his ability to make rational use of that power. Crucial decisions are made, today as thousands of years ago, in terms of the intuitive guesses and preferences of a few people in positions of authority. Since our ability to predict social events is not equal to the increasing complexity of social systems, decisions that affect the lives of millions are typically made in a state of extreme uncertainty concerning their consequences. Unfortunately, our cognitive limitations are nowhere

more evident that in our ability to make intelligent decisions under
uncertainty. Recent advances in decision analysis and in cognitive
psychology have uncovered systematic inconsistencies in our preferences
for uncertain outcomes, and systematic errors in our intuitive reasoning
about uncertain events. These errors and inconsistencies appear to be
essentially universal. They are not overcome by experience and are not
prevented by merely trying. Their prevalence increases the likelihood of
negative consequences of decisions, well beyond the lower limit that is set
by the existence of uncertainty. (Melvin Kranzberg, ed., *Ethics in an Age
of Pervasive Technology* [Boulder, CO: Westview Press, 1980], pp. 191-
92)

In other words, conditions are always uncertain and we are more or less
bound to make a hash of any decisions about them. As things get more
complex, this gets worse. Not a happy picture of "the human condition." Nor
do I exaggerate the "logical computer" solution. Here is Kahneman again:

Human engineering starts from a dispassionate appraisal of the operator's
limitations and attempts to structure the environment in which he will
function so as to circumvent these limitations, both by assigning some
tasks to the machine [computer] and by designing man's tasks so that his
limited capacity may be used to full effectiveness. (Ibid., p. 192)

I used to ask students: "Suppose we had a really super computer that could
analyze perfectly all the facts we fed into it and come up with the highest
level of probability possible of a Russian first strike. Would you be prepared
to let it press the button, or would you prefer to leave that decision to a duly
elected, but fallibly human, President of these United States?" I think I asked
Dan Kahneman the same question after that memorable dinner; but, as with
so many similar memorable occasions, I've completely forgotten his answer.
Frailty, thy name is memory.[1]

Where No Man Has Gone Before

The ideal evolutionary model, at least of these cognitive psychologists,
from which we fall short in reality, has been realized often enough in fantasy.
Most of the plot of *Star Trek* — I mean the real *Star Trek*, not the over-
talkative, tarted-up modern version — rests on the inability of the totally
logical Vulcan, Spock, to comprehend the intuitive thinking of the humans,
especially the good captain Kirk. Yet the story always leaves us with the
moral that good intuitive thinking is really to be preferred. Spock is fine when
working out strategies in the abstract, but when it comes to dealing with the

fallible human creatures who inhabit the *Star Trek* universe (and who all conveniently speak English), he is at a disadvantage. Kirk's intuition wins the day; Spock is like a superuseful computer. Sometimes he can be annoyingly so. When stuck in a particularly tight corner, Kirk asks rhetorically, "I wonder what our chances of survival are?" Spock without a blink answers "2,427.736 to 1, Captain." Kirk gets understandably irritated. In the new *Star Trek*, they have gone the whole hog and replaced the half-human Spock with the totally android Data, who, of course, yearns to share those endearing human imperfections with which he has not been programmed.

Thus, I wondered at the time and have wondered since if our cognitive psychologists, distressed as they might have been over the refusal of their subjects to follow their own rules, really had in mind a totally logical animal as some kind of ideal end point of evolution. Or had they perhaps missed the point? Were the defectors, including the famous producer and the famous zoologist, perhaps operating on some better principle than "logic" (the quotes obviously indicating "logic at least as Kahneman and Tversky define it")? Could not they have been correct in following intuition and bucking overwhelming odds? And, if so, what principle were they following? Because we have to admit that, flying in the face of logic as they are, they are guilty of, yes, *prejudice*. We have to face up to this because prejudice has been getting a bad press lately, and perhaps it is time for a new look at an old failing.

What is happening to the subjects of the experiment — the principle they are falling back on — is our old friend stereotypical thinking. We should perhaps be aggrieved at their defection. Especially if we are farmers, we should perhaps set up a committee to protest against the slur cast on the farming community which suggests it is incapable of culture and refined tastes. After all, I have known a good may farmers in my time who played the piano, many who enjoyed a good wine, and at least one Southwestern farmer who had recordings of everything Bach ever wrote. Of course, the reaction was a prejudice plain and simple; farmers are conceived of as a type that excludes these things, ergo, this man could not be a farmer. We only have to expand the logic of this thinking a bit further and we have the whole range of social stereotypes, sexual stereotypes, and ethnic and racial stereotypes, with which we are unhappily familiar. And of course we are righteously against all such stereotyping, are we not? — all of us who knew, in our heart of hearts, that *the man was not a farmer.*

Let me ram this home with a more uncomfortable example. Let our sample be the population of a district in a West Coast city that is 90 percent homosexual. Let you pick again a name at random and agree that we must opt for homosexual. Then let me give you the description.

The man is a construction worker who likes bowling, football and car racing. His favorite music is country and western; his favorite drink is straight bourbon and a Bud chaser. He is a union organizer and a member of the National Guard and the NRA.

Need I go on? The whole logical mob of you, despite your firm commitment to observe the laws of probability, has now deserted "homosexual" in droves. Think about it. Actually, since academics tend to be more sensitive to the feelings of homosexuals than farmers, some of you will be a bit more ambivalent about this one. Think about that too.

Well, I don't know what the conditions of evolution were on Vulcan. The canon is not consistent on this. In one version the Vulcans evolved beyond emotion into pure logic; in yet another, they so fear the emotional parts of themselves that they suppress emotion in favor of logic in their training. Either way, they must have had a peculiar environment of evolutionary adaptation. If, for example, they never think in stereotypes but only on the merits of the individual case and according to strict induction, it is hard to see how they might have survived. Perhaps their environment was so benign this could happen. But again the canon implies a warlike and competitive past, so this seems unlikely. And in such a past — so like our own (as they often stress with a smugness unbecoming creatures of pure logic) — any organism acting on pure induction would have lost out in the struggle. While Spock was consciously calculating the odds of being hit by the sabre tooth tiger springing at him — calculating its arc of approach, estimating its weight and velocity, working out its ETA and point of impact, etc. — he would have been cat meat. Kirk, on the other hand, rolling swiftly to one side, yelling "zap that tiger" and aiming with his phaser on kill, would have been saved — or at least have had a better chance of being saved.

Similarly, we are at war with tribe X, and a member of that tribe in full war paint appears suddenly before us with spear at the ready. There are a number of logical possibilities: He is out to get us; he is a defector from them to us and we just startled him; he really wants to surrender; he is one of ours in disguise just back from a spying mission; he is a supernatural entity and will not harm us; he is an hallucination, etc. All these are interesting possibilities; they, and countless others, all could be true. But we suspect that anyone acting on the logic of that assumption and stopping to explore them would have less chance of contributing to the gene pool than someone who acted on the first and disposed of the stranger.

But, the purist might say, in each case we are acting in terms of extreme prejudice. (Isn't it interesting that this term, prefaced by "to terminate with," has become a spy novel euphemism for "to kill"?) To which we can only answer, "And a damn good thing too." For in these instances "prejudice" can be defined as the making of a quick decision in a survival situation. By definition, the information will be inadequate in such circumstances, and we would be obliged to act in terms of superficial indicators. In other words, we would act in terms of stereotypes. We are certainly capable of switching to that other mode of thinking: the exploration of all logical alternatives. But this was perhaps better done at night, round the campfire, when the clear danger was not present. And of course we might often have made mistakes. The tiger might have been jumping into a tree to catch a monkey; the warrior might have been on a peace mission. Perhaps. But in the long run these mistakes would be more than offset by the survival benefits of killing enemies first and thinking about it afterward.

But let us not be led into making a false dichotomy here between thinking and acting — just as we must avoid the implicit one between emotion and thinking. The brain evolved to do both and do them at the same time. Kirk is not *thinking* any the less than Spock when he rolls away and fires the phaser. If anything, he is thinking harder and faster — so fast that we don't want to call it "thinking" at all. We want it to be "reflex" or "automatic." Even if it is, it still involves thought. Kirk was presented with data, he analyzed it, and he acted on it — in a split second. He drew with astounding rapidity on a huge bank of stored information and put it into action. I doubt the computer programmer exists who could ever get close to simulating that speed of retrieval and translation into action. (Something similar prevents even the best computer chess programs from beating human masters, although I am told they are rapidly catching up.)

In effect, Kirk was doing everything Spock was doing only at a trillion times the speed. And he could not have done it without a tremendous upsurge of adrenaline kicking the whole thing into action. The process could have failed, of course, and he could have stood rooted to the spot. But training to act involves thought, which cannot be separated from action. And in the course of evolution our brains developed to achieve just such thought-action in the struggle for survival. Our ability, when recollecting in tranquillity, to dissect such activity in the Spock fashion and reduce it carefully to possible alternatives, mathematical formulae, and the like, is in effect a by-product. Removed from the need to act, we can think in this disembodied way. But that is not how our thinking evolved, and in that sense, it is not what it is *for*.

The essence of stereotypical thinking is that it is fast and gives us a basis for immediate action in uncertain circumstances. But its legacy is that we are happier and more comfortable when thinking in ways that promise to ensure immediate survival than in ways that appear to threaten it. This may no longer make much sense, but unfortunately our brain doesn't know that, or if it can be persuaded of it, it still has a hard time bucking a system which got it to this point in the first place. Presented with the need for a quick decision, it will prefer stereotype to logic.

Backgammon in Edinburgh

Let us digress for a moment to ask a question which is at the base of all modern philosophy and which exercised another dedicated winer and diner, in Edinburgh and France, in the eighteenth century. David Hume is a charming writer and was obviously a charming man, although the description by the Earl of Charlemont is scarcely flattering:

His face was broad and fat, his mouth wide, and without any other expression than that of imbecility. His eyes vacant and spiritless, and the corpulence of his whole person was far better fitted to communicate the idea of a turtle-eating Alderman than of a refined philosopher. His speech, in English, was rendered ridiculous by the broadest Scotch accent, and his French was, if possible, still more laughable. (McNabb 1951, 9)

But this grotesque figure faced a cruel death with great dignity, literary failure with composure, and the world of philosophy with a daring scarcely matched by anyone since. How can you not like a man who says of himself:

My company was not unacceptable to the young and careless, as well as the studious and literary; and, as I took a particular pleasure in the company of modest women, I had not reason to be displeased with the reception met with from them. (McNabb 1951, 11)

I think we would have all liked to dine with David Hume and he would have been at home among us. Mrs. Adams, the mother of the famous architect, said of Hume, "He is the most innocent, agreeable, facetious man I ever met with." What a nice epitaph.[2] Also, my own prejudices lead me to quote with glee his statement that "there cannot be two passions more nearly resembling one another than philosophy and hunting" (*Treatise of Human Nature* 1738, II, 3, x).

Yet, this innocent, by virtue of his very innocence, set the agenda for modern philosophy. He was the complete sceptic and forced us, in the *Treatise*, to examine our most cherished assumptions about human thinking. First among these was the assumption that there is a necessary connection between cause and effect. There are certainly connections — of contiguity in time and space, for example — but on what basis do we impute a necessary connection? All we in fact know, says Hume, is the spatial and temporal contiguity: Flame causes heat. This is a "constant conjunction" and exists in the real world. The idea of necessary connection (or, as he would have written, connexion) exists in the mind of the observer. Hume does not, as superficial readers sometimes imply, deny that there are causes and effects in nature. He does deny that the "necessary connection" is there in nature; it is by way of an inference from natural succession and contiguity. He will have nothing to do with attempts to define forces or powers that are inherent in things. Gravity is an inference from the behavior of bodies in space, not a property of the bodies.

Now all this is very familiar. It is, as I said, the foundation of modern philosophy. It woke Kant from his "dogmatic slumbers" in an attempt to find the *Ding-an-sich* which was a constant reality behind the appearance of things. Hume ruthlessly applied it to the idea of the "self" — to our very personal identities — and showed this too to be an inference, not a property of something called a "person." At its most fundamental, our belief in the constancy of physical objects is a colossal act of faith.

One might suppose that Hume would have been devastated by his own scepticism, and he confesses it should have this effect.

The intense view of these manifold contradictions and imperfections in human reason has so wrought upon me, and heated my brain, that I am ready to reject all belief and reasoning, and can look upon no opinion even as more probable or likely than another. Where am I, or what? From what causes do I derive my existence, and to what condition shall I return? Whose favour shall I court, and whose anger must I dread? What beings surround me? And on whom shall I have any influence, or who have any influence on me? I am confounded with all these questions, and begin to fancy myself in the most deplorable condition imaginable, environed with the deepest darkness, and utterly deprived of the use of every member and faculty. (Ibid., I, 4, vi)

Such vast philosophical despair — he even invokes a metaphor of shipwreck — surely makes Hume a candidate for the first existentialist. And note that as with Kahneman and Tversky it is "the imperfections of human reason" that are the basis of this empiricist angst. But note also how he gets out of his difficulty.

Most fortunately it happens, that since reason is incapable of dispelling these clouds, Nature herself suffices to that purpose, and cures me of this philosophical melancholy and delirium, either by relaxing this bent of mind, or by some avocation, and lively impression of my sense, which obliterate all these chimeras. I dine, I play a game of backgammon, I converse, and am merry with my friends; and when, after three or four hours' amusement, I would return to these speculations, they appear so cold, and strained, and ridiculous, that I cannot find it in my heart to enter into them any further. (Ibid., I, 4, vi)

This is scarcely a solution that would have recommended itself to Kierkegaard or the Left Bank crowd. We can be certain of nothing, says Hume, but it doesn't matter. "A serious, good-humored disposition" will not be overtroubled by the fact that we have no better reason than custom to believe that tomorrow will resemble today in any respect. "If we believe," he says, "that fire warms or water refreshes, it is only because it costs us too much pain to think otherwise." Scepticism, in other words, is for philosophers in their studies; "honest gentlemen ... being always employed in their domestic affairs, or amusing themselves in common recreations" (ibid., I, 4, vi) have no need of such scepticism, and indeed are better off without it.

Most philosophers, of course, accept this as a charming aside from Hume. It certainly didn't satisfy that honest German gentleman Immanuel Kant, whose massive rebuttal of Hume's scepticism was a far remove from the "spleen and indolence" preached by the facetious Scot. But this is where I want to press the matter a little. Kahneman and Tversky's subjects were honest gentlemen (and gentlewomen), and they too preferred to avoid the pain caused by ruthless reasoning. They followed what Hume was never afraid to call Nature with a capital "N," in deserting reason for intuition, or what he would have called "custom" — habitual kinds of thinking resistant to sceptical incursions from clever students of probability theory. Fire *does* cause warmth; a man so described is *not* a farmer. In our philosophical moments, like the scientists or like Hume in his study, we can go into black despair at this imperfection of human reason, this evidence of the unfinished mind. In the real world of domestic affairs and common recreations it doesn't matter a damn.

Now, Hume did not think that in proposing this way of avoiding angst he was proposing anything more than a therapy. It was not a solution to his problem, Why do we imagine a necessary connection between contiguous events? This imagining was simply "custom"; it was "Nature"; it was blind habit; it was just what we did. What Hume does not seem to have seen, and neither have his successors, is that he was implicitly proposing a solution; but it was a solution that would have been better understood a hundred years after his death in 1776, once Darwin's two major works had come off the presses, and even more so a hundred years after that. The solution is simply that natural selection has programmed us to respond to constant contiguity in time

262 The Challenge of Anthropology

and space with a mental image of necessary connection because our survival depends on it. (Forgive the anthropomorphising of natural selection here. This is just for literary effect.)

Imagine the creature that evolved without making this connection. You cannot, anymore than you can imagine a creature evolving with a total scepticism about the existence of external objects. The totally sceptical creature — our completely rational computer — would never survive. We have to make the assumption of necessary causal connection in order to survive. It is that simple. Creatures with brains that did otherwise might have existed, but they are not here to tell the tale. The philosopher in his study may have no good reason to suppose that if fire burns today it will do so tomorrow, but the first *Homo erectus* to utilize fire some million years ago had better have operated on this assumption or the philosopher might not be here to doubt it.

Hume actually teetered on the edge of this answer in a remarkable but short chapter in the *Treatise*, "Of the Reason of Animals" (ibid., I, 3, xvi). He was concerned to make the point that our imputation of cause and effect as well as our imputation of continued existence of bodies, was not a result of "reasoning" or "speculation" but of "custom." He has just (in section xv) given eight pretty straightforward rules by which we judge cause and effect, and, he insists, "our scholastic headpieces and logicians show no such superiority above the mere vulgar" when it comes to making such determinations. If this is so, one simple demonstration will clinch it: Animals are not capable of "subtilty and refinement of thought"; nevertheless, they operate as soundly on the principles of cause and effect as we do "for their own preservation, and the propagation of their species." He gives examples from the behavior of dogs toward their masters, and birds building nests. A dog avoids fire and precipices, shuns strangers, and caresses his master, he says, and does so on the basis of experience that he generalizes, exactly as we do. If this is so, then what does human "reason" add?

> Reason is nothing but a wonderful and unintelligible instinct in our souls, which carries us along a certain train of ideas, and endows them with particular qualities, according to their particular situations and relations. This instinct, it is true, arises from past observation and experience; but can anyone give the ultimate reason why past experience and observation produces such an effect, any more than why nature alone should produce it? Nature may certainly produce whatever can arise from habit; nay, habit is nothing but one of the principles of nature, and derives all its force from that origin. (Ibid., I, 3, xvi)

He goes on to elaborate this in the subsequent sections:

Nature, by an absolute and uncontrollable necessity, has determined us to judge as well as to breathe and feel; nor can we any more forebear viewing certain objects in a stronger and fuller light, upon account of their customary connection with a present impression, than we can hinder ourselves from thinking, as long as we are awake, or seeing the surrounding bodies, when we turn our eyes towards them in broad sunshine. (Ibid., I, 4, i)

...

Nature has not left this to his choice, and has doubtless esteemed it an affair of too great importance, to be trusted to our uncertain reasonings and speculations. (Ibid., I, 4, ii)

In 1738, appeals to Nature were certainly often made, but no one had much idea how it was that Nature came to "endow" creatures with such propensities. Hume offers "their own preservation and the propagation of their species," and it is obviously a very small step to the principles of mutation and selection and the obvious conclusion that, unsubstantiated as they are by subtle reasoning and philosophy, the power of ideas, like necessary connection between cause and effect, derives from their survival value to the creatures so endowed. This "uncontrollable necessity," which is as strong as seeing and breathing, is "of too great importance" to be left to the possibilities of reasoning. It has to have the automatic qualities of instinct; it must operate without the intervention of subtle thinking. Hume could offer no reason why Nature should so endow us, thus leaving himself open to attack from just those he sought to undermine. His enemies could insist that it must be a benevolent act of God intended for our preservation. We can now invoke a different sort of deity and come up with a similar answer; except that our deity is blind and lacks compassion. It is only interested in survival and not particularly interested in us. If logic serves survival, so be it; if it does not, so much the worse for logic.

Thus Hume unwittingly proposed a solution when he thought he was merely giving sensible advice on avoiding a philosophical hangover. His honest gentlemen, and the ranks of the vulgar, as well as his philosophers, did indeed operate on principles of necessity rather than of rationality. And they were absolutely correct to do so. Creatures ignoring the inner prompting to attribute causal efficacy, or assuming that objects drifted in and out of existence, or supposing that they were not the same people today as yesterday, would not have been able, to use his words, to protect themselves and propagate their species. The honest gentleman, therefore, and even the philosopher Hume when he was playing backgammon or enjoying the company of modest women, and blindly acting on assumptions of causal necessity, was acting according to Nature and entirely as he should be acting. Hume's therapy was indeed the source of his necessity, and hence the solution to the problem. Equally, we must conclude that the experimental subjects were right to reject their agreed-upon logical assumptions and go with their intuition: the man was *not* a farmer.

But is this not, to follow the logic of the argument here, to say that we are right to engage in stereotypical thinking? In a sense, yes. But in exactly *what* sense we must explore a little further. And as a little footnote to the philosophers let me say that while we can indeed go straight from Hume to Darwin without passing through Kant and collecting the synthetic a priori, it would be unhistorical to do so. I recognize this, as I recognize that Kant's thoughts on the categories of the understanding, and his very insistence on their a priori character, is an important stepping stone. Konrad Lorenz has forcefully put this case, and I have in fact dealt at some length elsewhere with the means by which they might have become lodged in our mental processes by natural selection. Unfortunately this was in a book that appeared to be about incest (it was confusingly titled *The Red Lamp of Incest*), and few philosophers read it. I mention this for the record. One who did read it was Willard van Orman Quine who commented:

> Chapter seven was gratifying for its philosophical position, so congenial to my own: the naturalistic conception of mind and the recognition of natural selection as the origin of mind and language. (Personal communication, 1983)

He later elaborated a very similar view to the one put forward here regarding causation, but in this case with regard to prediction, or as he charmingly renames it, "veridical expectation": the expectation that similar events will have similar sequels.[3] Of these expectations he says:

> We take their fulfillment hour in and hour out as a humdrum matter of course; the occasional unexpectedness is what we notice. Our standard of similarity, for all its subjectivity, is remarkably attuned to the course of nature. For all its subjectivity, in short, it is remarkably objective.

> In the light of Darwin's theory of natural selection, we can see why this might be. Veridical expectation has survival value in the wild. Innate standards of subjective similarity that promote successful expectation will tend to be handed down through the survival of the fittest. The tendency will have favored us and other species as well. These considerations offer no promise of future success if nature takes what we would regard as a

sudden turn, but they do account plausibly for how well we have been doing up to now.

To Blame or Not to Blame

Another digression, into moral philosophy this time, may help to make the point. I shall here invoke another article, this time by Peter (now Sir Peter) Strawson, which I read in 1962, with the prescient title "Freedom and Resentment."[4] Articles sometimes hit you and stay with you and nag at you, the way the Kahneman and Tversky article did. I had always been puzzled by the issue of free will. In fact, it was to finish a thesis on that topic that I first ventured to the United States in 1957, only to be sidetracked from Cornell to Harvard where I was kidnapped by the anthropologists and brainwashed. But the topic continued to bother me in the irritating way the basic problems of philosophy tend to do: they are very boring but you can't let go of them. Of course, like any sensible philosopher, if not like the ranks of the vulgar, I was a determinist, since I could find no precise meaning to the idea that any act could be "free." The network of causation going into any action was so complex, what sense did it make to say it was a "free" act if by free one meant "uncaused" or "without influences external to itself" or whatever. There was no such act by definition. But then came the philosophical conundrum: if no act is free then how can we attribute responsibility, and, horror of horrors, how can we ever BLAME anyone for an evil deed? For, without the possibility of holding people responsible for their actions so that they might be blamed for wrongdoing and punished (and vice versa), the whole structure of law and morals, to say nothing of the upbringing of children, was meaningless.

Strawson addressed just this point, and interestingly invoked Hume on causation as his model. As far as morals were concerned, Hume had fallen back on the Moral Sense theory of his Scottish colleagues in formulating a moral system of his own, the Moral Sense being as original and natural as our intuition of causation. Darwin took off from exactly this point in *The Descent of Man*, and I have tried to show in some detail where he went from there.[5] Strawson, however, wants to compare our insistence on seeking justification for moral praise and blame to our insistence on justifying causation:

Compare the question of the justification of induction. The human commitment to inductive belief-formation is original, natural, nonrational (not irrational), in no way something we choose or could give up. Yet rational criticism and reflection can refine standards and their application, supply "rules for judging cause and effect." Ever since the facts were made clear by Hume, people have been resisting acceptance of them.

His point is that, while we must accept the nonrational origin of the necessity of causal connection, this doesn't prevent us from rational discourse about it. This, after all, is what science is about. But there is nothing (in his opinion) we can say about the principle itself: it is just there, as Hume insisted. *In like manner*, says Sir Peter, there is a "web" of human attitudes and feelings which are equally just there. In order to have moral arguments, we have to take these for granted and then argue within these given premises:

Inside the general structure of the web of human attitudes and feelings of which I have been speaking there is endless room for modification, redirection, criticism, and justification. But questions of justification are internal to the structure or relate to modifications internal to it. The existence of the general framework of attitudes itself is something we are given with the fact of human society. As a whole it neither calls for nor permits an external "rational" justification.

Thus, we may argue endlessly about the details of, for example, how praise and blame should be apportioned, but the fact that we wish to heap praise and lay blame in itself is just a given fact of what we used to call "human nature" — Strawson's "web of human attitudes and feelings."

He makes a psychological point in pressing his argument. The logical determinist, he says, must always maintain an "attitude of objectivity." He must never lay blame or feel resentment, since he knows that no one is "responsible" for his acts and that therefore these attitudes are illogical. Need we hark back to Mr. Spock, the ultimate determinist, who always refuses praise for doing what was logically necessary even at the risk of his own life, and is rarely — except in his half-human moments — perturbed by the wickedness of others since they are doing what they must. We lesser creatures, says Strawson, simply cannot sustain the "objective attitude" as a matter of psychological fact.

We have the resource [the objective attitude] and can sometimes use it: as a refuge, say, from the strains of involvement; or as an aid to policy; or simply out of intellectual curiosity. Being human, we cannot, in the normal case, do this for very long, or altogether.

We can do it for special classes of people for some of the time, he says: the insane, children, addicts, etc. If people are acting under obvious duress, or under some "irresistible impulse" we may excuse them. But even here there are casuistic concerns. Sometimes we may allow jealousy as a plea, but we never allow ambition, even though the compulsion is arguably as great. (This is my example, not his.) But even making these exceptions is hard. Multiple

killer Ted Bundy was clearly not "responsible" for his slew of insane killings
— he actually bit chunks out of his victims in a startling regression to
paleoviolence — but very few people could maintain the "objective attitude"
about him.[6] For a start, it is too frightening. It is the thin end of the wedge. If
Bundy is not responsible, then what about lesser offenders? Where does it
stop? Those generous liberals who insist that there are no criminals but that
society and poverty and maternal rejection make them so, are the first to howl
for blood when their children turn out to have been sexually molested by
trusted adults. Even the Christian principle of turning the other cheek
assumes that the offender was responsible: It says, "Blame, but do not
retaliate."

Well, we may not always retaliate, although that is hard, but what
Strawson is saying is that we cannot live without blaming. We MUST
attribute responsibility, and we must do so on the same basis as we attribute
cause and effect — as Hume would say, by "custom," by an emotion
implanted by Nature, because it is something too important to be left to our
rational, logical, decision-making processes, which would lead us to
speculate endlessly on the chains of causation leading up to the act in
question. Our hypothetical Spock, early in human evolution, would never
have survived, because in neither accepting moral responsibility nor attaching
moral blame he could not have functioned in a human community. Whether
or not it is rational to lay blame and attribute responsibility, we must do it to
make people conform to rules and expectations; we must act "as if" we are
responsible, just as we must act "as if" effects follow necessarily from causes.
What is more, we are so psychologically constructed that we cannot do
anything else except for short and trying periods of mental effort.

Several biologists and philosophical biologists have gone on to make the
point in their own ways (although without reference to Strawson).[7] But theirs
is all a reworking in terms of "inclusive fitness" or "reciprocal altruism" or
something such of Darwin's observation in 1871 in *The Descent of Man.*

The following proposition seems to me to be in a high degree probable —
namely, that any animal whatever, endowed with well-marked social
instincts, the parental and filial affections being here included, would
inevitably acquire a moral sense or conscience, as soon as its intellectual
powers had become as well, or nearly as well developed, as in man. (pp.
149-50)

This would include a "sense of responsibility" — one's own responsibility
and that of others — and with it the possibility of living according to rules:
the essence of a truly human existence.

But it has no rational basis. It is, as Strawson is at pains to point out, not irrational but nonrational: given, original, a priori, or whatever. When we act on the authority of "ought," we are responding to an imperative that is just as much a product of natural selection as when we act in terms of cause-effect. This or that particular "ought" will be given by our particular culture; but the compulsion of "ought" itself is given with our brains and bodies. This is why the imperative is categorical. This is why the moral sense of the peasant is as definitive as that of the most refined moral philosopher. This is why Jefferson could argue that all men are created equal in a philosophical climate set by John Locke, who did not believe any such thing.[8] But the system of praising and blaming, or responsibility and resentment — the web of human attitudes and feelings itself — is simply given and beyond rational justification.

Alarms and Excursions

Strawson does not throw up his hands in horror at this, like Kahneman, Tversky, and Hume. But one perhaps senses a kind of ennui; a sort of North Oxford resignation. "Yes, it's a mess, but it's what we've got and we'd better learn to live with it. There are, after all, no real alternatives; we can probably muddle through." There is certainly no celebration of the situation. So perhaps we may say that all four of our thinkers adhere to the theory of the unfinished mind. The picture painted is not so much of a fallen creature as of one who has never risen far enough. The end product should be a totally logical, totally rational, totally objective creature: a Mr. Spock (sorry, like Strawson he has been elevated: Commander Spock). Insofar as we fall short of this, insofar as we cannot think logically or maintain moral objectivity for more than brief privileged periods of ratiocination, then we are imperfect creatures.

But as we saw with Hume's therapeutic solution, the imperfections have one outstanding quality: they work. We are here; we function. We have built an ambitious science on our unwarranted induction of cause and effect; we have built many and varied societies on our unjustifiable systems of blame, praise, and retribution. Despite our brain being a wildly imperfect logic machine, despite its activity being, from a logical point of view arbitrary and contingent, in some way or other it has ensured our survival. Logic nearly drove John Stuart Mill mad (as Hume could have told him it would), and his recovery came partly through reading Wordsworth. I like to think he read these lines from *The Excursion* (1814):

How exquisitely the individual mind
(And the progressive powers perhaps no less
Of the whole species) to the external world

Is fitted; and how exquisitely too —
Theme this little heard of among men —
The external world is fitted to the mind.

If the mind seems to be a logical mess, and yet it deals so successfully with the external world, then surely our conclusion must simply be that logic is not the best way of dealing with the external world. In truth, it may even be a disastrous way of dealing with it. In "prejudging" the world in certain illogical but effective ways, we are acting in accordance with certain natural imperatives as surely as in seeing things in colors and in three dimensions. There is certainly no "logical" reason why we should do this. It is just the way natural selection panned out as a result of living an active life in trees for so long.

In the same way, logic served us no real purpose except for some synthetic propositions we can't very well ignore: those of mathematics, and the law of noncontradiction, for example. Again, individuals who didn't operate on the principle that something could not be both true and false at the same time, would have had an intolerably hard time with the world. But these are principles we operate on in the normal conduct of everyday affairs, not the extended exercises in logic that characterize the classrooms and studies of philosophers. We may have abandoned the idea that the syllogism is the ideal type of logical thinking, but all of us still operate on some principle of rationality which is founded on the idea that rational thinking equals logical thinking. And by logical thinking we mean what Hume, Strawson, Kahneman, and Tversky mean by logical, even if we can't keep it up for long and in the end quickly ditch it for prejudice and stereotype.

Perhaps we should ask ourselves: Why must we burden ourselves with a model of rationality that does not work for us? Instead of bemoaning our unfinished and imperfect state, why should we not accept that there is that Wordsworthian "fit" between mind and the world? This does not even have to mean that we have an accurate picture of external reality; it certainly does not have to mean that the world corresponds to canons of logic as we understand them. The "fit" is as arbitrary as the fit between our bodies and the world. It is just the way it is because natural selection made it that way by a process of chance mutation and ruthless selection. As we have said, if attributing cause and effect and personal responsibility is not logical, and if refusing to act on agreed premises without conclusive contrary evidence is not logical, then we do not necessarily have to despair of our illogicality — our unfinished mind — but rejoice in the fact that our prejudices do our reasoning for us in cases where, to use Hume's words again, it is a matter too important to be left to subtle processes of reasoning and speculation.

Reason Is as Action Does

We shall probably have to come up with a new definition of "reason" itself. Reasoning, from this perspective, is not an exercise in applied logic. What reasoning may be is a complex series of intuitive leaps whose "logic," while arbitrary and contingent, is that they correspond to enough of external reality to enable us to survive in it.[9] And they are that way because Konrad Lorenz's "great constructors" — mutation and natural selection — so shaped them, as they shaped the grasping hand and the well-planted foot. From a logical point of view the mind is a mess — a morass of prejudice and resentment. But so is the body a mess from the viewpoint of the designer of an ideal animal. Why should we expect the mind to be any different? I have always liked the title of James Thurber's lovely little book *Leave Your Mind Alone*. Yes, it operates on prejudices; but these prejudices (in the form, among other things, of a priori categories) are what got it here, so they deserve some respect. If we can learn to see as prejudice our attribution of cause and effect and personal responsibility, as well as our refusal to accept overwhelming probabilities — which is the thrust of all the arguments here considered — then we will have to think differently about prejudice (stereotypical thinking) itself.

George Lakoff, who has done more than any other linguistic philosopher to change, through an examination of metaphor, our notions of rational thinking, pleads for a "richer view of reason" based on the idea of "prototype effects" which are "used in reasoning, though not in logic as it is normally understood."[10] Among these forms of "reference point" reasoning are: "Social stereotypes: making quick judgments about people and situations; Typical cases: making inferences from typical to atypical cases, based on knowledge of the typical; Paragons: making comparisons, using them as models of behavior," and so on. Our task then should be not to try to eradicate stereotypical thinking on some mistaken logico-rational model of human thought, but to consider what our "paragons" and "typical cases" and "social stereotypes" are and to see perhaps how we can (and, realistically, how we cannot) rearrange our metaphors to make them suit our benign prejudices better.

It is surely easy for us to see that we are more comfortable with stereotypical thinking than with logically treating each case on its merits. It is something that our puritan, moralizing selves bemoan daily. But if we stop to consider WHY we are so comfortable, and how hard it is to maintain, as Strawson saw, "the objective attitude," then we might want to rethink some of our own attitudes to prejudice. The first reaction is perhaps that such thinking is lazy. There goes that human moralizing again. People are responsible, and if they don't shape up to our logical expectations, then we use blame words. But if we don't moralize, and if we ask ourselves why there is, in Hume's words, "more pleasure and less pain" in so thinking, then we might conclude that this is a case where our "natural reason" is operating for us. It is saying, "Class these objects together on some principle of resemblance and operate on the assumption that the less familiar they are the more they should be treated with suspicion: insofar as the properties of any of them are known, act as if the rest had the same properties: if these are pleasure-producing properties, approach; if they are pain-producing properties go into a defensive posture; if they are aggressively pain-producing properties, then prepare for flight or attack," and so on.

This is very rough-and-ready. The whole routine would be like an elaborate critical-path analysis and would indeed be like a computer program if we could work the whole thing out (there are hundreds of possible subroutines). But it is not a program for dealing with individuals on their merits. It deals with classes of individuals (human or otherwise). What it does is provide us with an immediate response to an uncertain situation. Not for nothing did Kahneman and Tversky call their subsequent book with Slovic *Judgement Under Uncertainty.*[11] When their subjects opted for "not farmer" as a response, they were operating on a program like the one above: they opted for a stereotype. And they were right to do so. In an uncertain situation — e.g., you are told that "farmers" are going to kill you but "nonfarmers" will protect you, and you are given the description offered as opposed to one of a "typical" farmer — which would you choose? (The same would go for our homosexual example.) I am not saying that prejudice is infallible; it doesn't have to be. To win out over Spockian or other strategies, it only has to stand a better chance than any alternative of getting its practitioners into the gene pool. On average it has to come out a winner, and that will do to establish it.

This of course becomes a real problem in modern society, where we want to be right all the time and "on average" won't do. Bernhard Goetz (a white New Yorker who opened fire on black youths who surrounded him in a subway car and demanded money) operated on a xenophobic racial stereotype, and who knows whether he wounded innocent young men or saved his life from potential killers? The jury gave him the benefit of the doubt (the youths did have sharpened screwdrivers on them) because we have to establish responsibility and lay blame. But he certainly gave us all pause, black and white, because he drove home how much we depend on such stereotypes in uncertain situations, and how deep rooted are our responses, our fears and suspicions and hates, despite what we might wish to claim to the contrary. It struck a nerve because we all realized that we were potential Bernhard Goetzs and in a similar situation might do the same thing. Does it help to know that he was really only taking to a, dare I say it, "logical conclusion" what we all were doing when we opted for "nonfarmer" or "heterosexual"? He was the warrior of our first illustration, faced with alien warriors in a provocative situation. He chose attack. He was prejudiced. He is alive. His antagonists are in various states of disarray.

You might say that my position "justifies" Goetz, but I am a determinist as you know, and as long as I can maintain the "objective attitude," I will insist that justification has nothing to do with it. I want to *understand* the situation, and moralizing doesn't help there. To say that Goetz was responding with intuitive reactions, which have had such a highly successful survival potential that they are now deeply programmed into the human response system, is not to "justify" the action but to try to understand it. If we are interested in somehow or other changing or controlling such reactions, then surely we are better off understanding them than indulging in self-satisfying moralizing. Except, of course, that if I am right then this moralizing is as inevitable as the reaction of Goetz himself, or as inevitable as our thinking of the whole thing in terms of necessary cause and effect.

I do not intend to use this as an opportunity to pontificate on what might be done about discrimination, defamation, racism, sexism, affirmative action, and the like. Indeed, I have very few suggestions of any use. The persistence of xenophobia and its resultant stereotyping obviously has very deep roots. It is there in all group-living and territorial animals.[12] As humans, we add our own cultural trappings. The animal rule is basically the same: Trust the familiar; suspect the unfamiliar. In the animal and early human case this would have been literally true: the familiar would have been "of the family": relatives of a similar phenotype. Recognition would have been easy. In the human case, when other-than-family groups came into contact, some means of identifying "us" and "them" (however defined) would have been necessary. The differentiation of languages would have first served this purpose, but one doesn't always get a chance to hear a stranger speak. So distinctive markings, scarifications, paint, hairdos, etc. would come into play to make the distinctions obvious (and deceit a constant possibility; hence the hatred of the spy and the passions aroused in moralistic aggression against traitors).[13] Of course, when one crosses significant phenotypical boundaries — to other skin colors, for example — nature again does the job for us.

Many of the marks of distinction — the tribal totems, the mythological knowledge, songs, cries and chants, etc. — would be laid down early and traumatically in initiation procedures designed to make fixed and lasting these diacritics of group membership. Certain even deeper and more unshakable discriminations would have been, and continue to be, laid down in early childhood during the "fear of strangers" period between six and eighteen months. The "typical" faces laid down then as "familiar" will continue to be the basis of stereotyping for ever after. A specialized area of the visual cortex will repeatedly sort through and compare future faces.[14] Thus, all the cultural signals add amplification to the basic "fear the strange, trust the familiar" response.

Stereotypes, Prototypes, Archetypes

You might object to such a view of human action as too much based on animal models. Surely human thinking is of a different order than animal instinct. After all, it might be argued, we can revise and reject stereotypes; animals cannot reject — even if they may in some cases substantially modify — their instincts. At some level this is surely true: at the level of specific stereotypes. But whether it is true at the general level of thinking I'm not sure. Thus, Hume could reject the necessary connection of cause and effect in his study, but not in his life. Thus, we can sustain the objective attitude in a clinical enquiry, but not in running a society. And we can act on the Law of Large Numbers in principle, but not when faced with a specific instance. We perhaps make too much of the leap from instinct to "thought." The core of Niko Tinbergen's definition of instinct was "stereotyped behavior" — his very words.[15] This had to be independent of learning and complete at first attempt. But it was stereotypy (if there is such a word) that was of the essence.

In animals that develop large prefrontal cortexes, foresight, planning, and the elaboration of memory storage become more important. But as Bergson so brilliantly showed, these features of "intelligence" have to get the same job done as instinct used to do.[16] They cannot therefore depart too much from the same principles. So, for "stereotypical behavior" we substitute "stereotypical thinking." In the same way that the stereotypical behavior of the animals "fit" the world of their environment of evolutionary adaptedness, so the stereotypical thinking of *Homo sapiens* equally "fits" its world. Some things didn't even change. The deep-level "thinking" in terms of cause-effect and veridical expectation was there in the animals anyway, as Hume and Quine were at pains to point out. It is very hard to make an "instinct" versus "thinking" distinction here — Hume's point again.

This is a crucial point because it is what renders most of the work on "stereotypes and prejudices" of the past sixty years, in social psychology in particular, largely redundant. Ever since Walter Lippmann in 1922 appropriated the term from the vocabulary of printing has it been used with an almost totally negative connotation.[17] "Stereotypical thinking" has come to be synonymous with "unfavorable prejudices directed against another ethnic, sexual, or religious group." Lippmann himself, and other influential thinkers in this area, like Gordon Allport (with whom I studied for a while when being brainwashed at Harvard), did see the absolute *necessity* of stereotypical thinking. "A normality of prejudgment," Allport called it, while for Lippmann: "For the most part we do not see first and then define, we define first and then see." An eloquent expression of the basic truth. But in each case they, and everyone after them, rapidly back away from this insight and concentrate on the wholly negative picture. All "prejudgments" become bad judgments, and the problem then is how to get rid of them. Lippmann's own proposal for a specialized class of guardians to handle decisions has strange overtones of Plato and of John Stuart Mill's "those best qualified to judge" — his own rather desperate solution to the problem of Utilitarian head counting. For Lippmann, democracy was not to be trusted because of the stereotyping tendencies of the masses; but he never addressed the question of how the specialized elite were supposed to rid themselves of the tendency to form "pictures inside our heads" — his famous and vivid phrase for the stereotyping process. He lived in the days before computers, but he would have rejoiced in the Kahneman solution of fallible, stereotyping humans hooked up to logically thinking machines; he could only think in terms of vast, Orwellian "intelligence bureaus." (Haven't we tried that?) He (and most of the subsequent prejudice industry) never followed up their insight that we must think stereotypically to think at all. And this is the real issue. They have some of them seen, following Lippmann's lead (although with typical academic arrogance rarely acknowledging his originality), that stereotyping, in "reducing complexity" and the like, can perform "useful" functions. But they have gone no further than this into understanding that the useful functions are not some kind of serendipitous by-product of otherwise objectionable thought processes, but are the "useful functions" that natural selection has programmed into the fundamental processes of thought and action to ensure survival and reproduction. Let us try to push this insight a little further.[18]

The work of the psychophilosophers of mind at the moment seems to turn on what they call "categorical perception."[19] The essence of this is that perception consists not of the raw reception of sense data, but rather of the moment-to-moment placing of things perceived into categories. The most obvious example is that of the phonemes of a language. These minimal units of meaning (in English, consonants and vowels, and a few things like stress, juncture, and intonation) are often in fact "clusters" of actual sounds (allophones) which can be, phonetically, quite different from each other. But we "hear" the phoneme rather than the differences. Thus, the aspirated, alveolar, unvoiced stop /t/ — as in "tin" — is a phoneme in English, contrasting with its voiced counterpart /d/, as in "din," in making for a "minimal unit of meaning." As English speakers we can take in all kinds of deviations from the sound "t" — glottalized, retroflex, unaspirated, labio-dental, alveopalatal, and so on — but, so long as it is unvoiced, we still "hear" /t/ because that is the phoneme. In languages that do not have the voiced-unvoiced contrast, and where, for example, it is the aspirated-unaspirated contrast that is phonemic, the speakers will hear sounds fall into these two categories as opposed to our /t/ and /d/. Our /d/, for example, they tend to hear as an unaspirated /t/. Thus, when moving between languages, we tend to organize pronunciation according to our native phonemic system. This accounts for the strange phenomenon of "foreign accents." But the point is that we do not deal with raw sounds, rather with sounds arranged into categories around a central, prototypical sound.[20]

What is true of phonemic "perception" of language sounds is thought by some researchers to be true of all categorical thinking about the world. Another paper that stuck in my head long before I appreciated the true significance of it was Eleanor Rosch's "Natural Categories" in 1973. Taking off from the work on color categories, she showed how each category had a "central" or "prototypical" member, and how the categories got fuzzy at the edges. Later she went on to show how this applied to all of our categories. Membership in them was not all-or-none but more-or-less. Thus, experiments showed that the category of "bird," for example, has a sparrow-like central member, with owls and eagles further removed, and oddities like penguins, emus, and ostriches at the fringes.[21] Lakoff, as we have seen, expanded these observations into a new view of reason and the nature of thinking based on taking metaphorical thought seriously, and with it the basic nature of categorization in the operation of mind.

The question is, how are these categories formed and what relationship do they have to the "real" world? Often this relationship is problematical, not one-to-one, as with color categories. But there does seem to be an order to color classification that is "given" and not dependent on the terms of a specific language.[22] It is not an order that makes any logical or scientific sense, but to an animal with color vision it is again an order that has obviously had survival value. The range of such perceptions is itself dependent on the range of visible light, and, as we know, this is only a tiny part of the full light spectrum. But it is enough. It could become a disadvantage in changed evolutionary circumstances where the ability to see, say, ultraviolet light, might mean survival. But nature is concerned with ongoing adaptation, as Quine so clearly saw, not with future contingencies, and this small slice of the full spectrum has been enough for our needs so far. This logical arbitrariness, then, is generally true of our system of stereotyping and categorical perception, which in turn interacts with our system of praising and blaming to produce what we call "human behavior." It is pragmatic, not logical. It exists because it works, not because it is rational.[23]

It must immediately have occurred to some of you that there must be a connection between what I am saying and the Jungian concept of archetypes.

For are not archetypes a kind of prototype or stereotype? Indeed they are. For us to "fear the stranger" or "love the hero" or "hate the villain," it seems it is not enough to have general emotions of fear, love, and hate; we must have general notions of stranger, hero, and villain as well. I don't want here to get into the issue of whether these archetypes are "innate" or "learned"; they are probably a bit of both, but if learned they are learned easily and quickly and early, and therefore may well be subject to some basic program in the genome.[24] They are part of our essential moralistic sorting of the world that allows the praise-blame system, the system of allotting responsibility, to work smoothly. Otherwise, we would again have to take every case on its merits, and as we have seen, life is too short for that. We do not have the "survival time" for such a luxury.

When we put together our archetypal stereotyping and our urge to assign responsibility and blame, we get the basis of mythology and its successor, literature. For all the ink spilled in the analysis of the codes and functions of mythology, something is so obvious that it tends to get overlooked: The story is always about identifiable archetypes, and the story always has a moral. We may need the aid of psychoanalysis or structuralism or whatever to get at the *specific* moral; but that there is a moralizing, responsibility-assigning, praising-and-blaming function is ubiquitous; and the moralizing is always about villains and heroes, however disguised. If this were not so, then it would be impossible to explain its persistence, from the Paleolithic to the present, in mass entertainment, where the customers call the tune and get the entertainment they deserve, whether it be epic poetry, religious ritual, fairy tales, morality plays, knightly romances, gothic horror stories, Punch and Judy shows, comic book violence, the Western, the cop show, the A team, the soap opera, *The Bonfire of the Vanities,* or professional wrestling.[25] We mess endlessly with the archetypes to render them recognizable to our times, and the content of the moralizing changes constantly. But archetypes and moralizing there will be, and that is what it is all about: stereotypical thinking and the attribution of blame.

Again I repeat my basic point: that in our more lofty moments we tend to treat our stereotypical moralizing, either at the level of logic or at the level of social action, as some kind of pathology, as evidence of the unfinished mind, as a serious defect in human nature. But if it is persistent and seemingly ineradicable, if it is lodged in the very process of thinking itself — if we MUST attribute necessary connection, if we MUST assign responsibility, if we MUST think stereotypically — and if we must do these things because we did them throughout evolution to survive and propagate, then how can they be defects? What we mean, when we say they are defects, is that we would really like ourselves to be otherwise than we are, and we believe we can reshape ourselves not to be this way. I gravely doubt it.

As Strawson said about moral discourse, there is room for a lot of discussion within the web of human attitudes and feelings. This is true. One thing we can do, as conscious cultural humans, is conjure with definitions of the familiar. We can try to have more people fall into the familiar category. Of course, we will continue to stereotype — the familiar is automatically good — but this is a stereotyping we reckon we can live with. The problem is that it tends to reduce variety and plurality. What is to be, for example, the human prototype of the familiar? At the moment it seems to be individualistic, entrepreneurial, law abiding, tax paying, urban, white, monogamous, middle-class and male. Well, dem's mah peeple, as they say, but they're not everyone's notion of the good life. And will the two sexes ever be able to overcome a perception of difference, a difference that is great enough to cause difficulties? And should they? "Vive la difference" is not an idle cry. It is what makes life interesting.

You will perhaps counter, "We don't want people to be the same. We just want them to tolerate differences." But that isn't true. "We" don't want to tolerate differences of which "we" don't approve — if you like, differences "we" are prejudiced against, such as cannibalism, devil worship, lynchings, abortion, smoking, infibulation, censorship, gun clubs, polygamy, blood sports, flag burning, bigotry, child molestation, pornography, integration, or wearing animal furs. The list is endless. And those campus pundits who thunder that they will not tolerate intolerance are in danger of emulating the Cretan liar, with the same contradictory results. What we are really saying is that our set of prejudices, which are good prejudices, must replace your set of prejudices, which are not.

Is there then nothing to be done? Of course not. There is much we can do to make people live in more civilized concert with each other, if that is what we want. We can punish them for not doing so and reward them for cooperating. The praise-blame system can be quite effective. We can make it clear that certain intolerant behavior will not itself be tolerated, without fear of being self-contradictory. We simply define what is acceptable and insist on conformity to it. But what we cannot do is change *the established, physiological, stereotypical basis of thinking itself.* We are locked in stereotypical-prototypical thinking and cannot live outside it. We are not, through tolerance education, sensitization seminars, attitude-change programs, consciousness-raising sessions or anything else, going to get rid of that fact.

What we will do is substitute one set of overt prejudices — of which we approve — for another. I say overt because we really do not know (even after sixty years of diligent effort by social psychologists) to what extent we change basic attitudes as opposed to verbal expressions of them. And perhaps we have to settle for the latter. Don't say the wrong things and don't do the wrong things or you'll have to join another club. And why isn't that enough? Probably because that old blame-laying Adam (and Eve) won't let us alone. That particular prejudice urges us to treat those with other prejudices as responsibly evil people rather than just people going through their own stereotypical paces. And our puritanical, moralistic tradition insists that we "convert" them: that we make them over into good people, like ourselves.

Imperfect Sympathies Revisited

But most of the time we are not dealing with "offensive prejudice" — with taking the battle to the enemy without waiting for provocation. Most prejudice, like the very a prioris of our basic thinking processes, is defensive. It says, "Fear the strange initially, and only revise your opinion if the facts warrant it." It does not usually say, "Go out and get the stranger first." This latter usually depends on a lot of social orchestration, and we can certainly do a lot to control that. But we should not confuse prejudice in this offensive sense with mere dislike of other groups, or even just a lack of interest in them. Nor should we confuse it with a mild discomfort in dealing with other groups. All these defensive prejudices are normal, and it is hard to imagine how we could ever produce human beings free of them. The whole point of this argument has been to show that we have no choice but to think in stereotypes. That is what thinking is. What is more, we are "comfortable" with such stereotyping, and our better selves only deplore the fact when some particular stereotype lacks social approval or conflicts with our current moralistic stereotyping. As long as it does not, we are happy to sink into it. Thus, in certain circles, "All big corporations are polluters" would not be challenged, while "All gay men are untrustworthy" would evoke horror. In other circles, of course, this would be reversed. You know who I mean.

Let me take a literary "case history" of mild, defensive, even fairly benign, "prejudice" from a writer who actually sets out to lay his "imperfect sympathies" bare. We can do this without too much discomfort since the essay was written in early nineteenth-century England, and this is far enough removed in time and place for us not to take it too seriously. What is more, we have to go out of our own time to find such an example. It is something to ponder that such a charmingly honest portrayal of genuine feeling would not be publishable today, even though it is, as I am trying to show, essentially nonaggressive and concerned not with invidious judgments but with mere discomfort at cultural differences such as we all feel. This gentlest of essays on prejudice, "Imperfect Sympathies," appeared in Charles Lamb's *Essays of Elia* in 1823.

Lamb was a gentle soul who cared for his intermittently mad and matricidal sister (with whom he wrote the *Tales from Shakespeare*), worked hard as a clerk at the East India House, and was the best friend of Coleridge for all his difficult life. He never harmed another soul, although he had a sharp wit, and could deliver a good verbal riposte when required, despite his stutter. Coleridge, when speaking of sermons, asked him in all innocence, "Charles, did you ever hear me preach?" Lamb unhesitatingly replied, "I n-n-never heard you do anything else." When a fussy lady pestered him with questions about how he liked the "little ones," he replied with annoyance, "B-b-b-boiled, madam." He could be a bit disconcerting — after all, he spent some time, like his sister, in the madhouse, and when he met the great Wordsworth, whom he revered, he was so moved he shook him not by the hand but by the nose, and cried out "How d'ye do, old Lakey poet?!" When as a small child his sister took him round a graveyard to read the lapidary inscriptions, he asked her, "Mary, where are all the naughty people buried?" But I ask you, how could one not like such a harmless, quirky, agreeable fellow?[26]

He begins by quoting Sir Thomas Browne, in the *Religio Medici*, who claims to have no national or other prejudices. Well, says Lamb, we are not all such perfect beings:

I confess that I do feel the differences of mankind, national or individual, to an unhealthy excess. I can look with no indifferent eye upon things or persons. Whatever is, is to me a matter of taste or distaste; or when once it becomes indifferent, it begins to be disrelishing. I am, in plainer words, a bundle of prejudices — made up of likings and dislikings — the veriest thrall to sympathies, apathies, antipathies. In a certain sense, I hope it may be said of me that I am a lover of my species. I can feel for all indifferently, but I cannot feel toward all equally.

This applies in particular to one national group:

I have been trying all my life to like Scotchmen, and am obliged to desist from the experiment in despair. They cannot like me — and in truth, I never knew one of that nation who attempted to do it. There is something more plain and ingenuous in their mode of proceeding. We know one another at first sight.

He then describes with exquisite accuracy the constitution of the "anti-Caledonian" — i.e., English — mind, which is "suggestive merely," and its total failure to mesh with the literal Scots mentality which "stops a metaphor like a suspected person in an enemy's country." He ends with his despairing story of attending a party where a son of the recently deceased Robert Burns was expected. In his daffy English fashion, he dropped the remark that he wished the guest could have been, not the son, but the father. Four Scotsmen started up at once to inform him "that was impossible, because he was dead."

We can laugh a little at that still, I hope, because it is far from us in place and time; it is gentle and playful in its characterizations; no one is hurt or insulted. But even so, Lamb is creating a national stereotype here, and he acted on it. He steered clear of Scotsmen, fearing the worst from such encounters. We might be a little more uncomfortable when Lamb comes to Jews. And we must remember that in the eighteenth century, Jews in general were as distinct in their dress, speech, manners, religion, customs, and the like as are, for example, the Hassidim from the rest of the population today. It was about this visibly distinct subculture that Lamb was talking:

> I have, in the abstract, no disrespect for Jews. They are a piece of stubborn antiquity, compared to which Stonehenge is in its nonage. They date beyond the pyramids. But I should not care to be in habits of familiar intercourse with any of that nation.

He certainly recognizes the "centuries of injury, contempt, and hate" which have been visited upon the Jews, and fully understands why they must hate the Christians. What he dislikes is what he sees as the hypocrisy of pretending it could be otherwise; of "affected civility" between those who know they are irretrievably different from each other. "The spirit of the Synagogue is essentially *separative*," he says. Jews are concerned to emphasize their *differences*. It is what being a Jew is about. And that is how it should be. Either we should all convert one way or the other or stay separate, is his conclusion. He does not mind dealing with Jews at the 'Change, for "the mercantile spirit levels all distinctions, as are all beauties in the dark." He admires this mercantile spirit and insists that he has "never heard of an idiot being born among them." "Some admire the Jewish female-physiognomy. I admire it — but with trembling. Jael had those full dark inscrutable eyes."

We should note that there is nothing here, as there is nothing in his discussion of Scotsmen, that can be remotely described as "racist." He is talking all the time of cultural differences. He never slanders the "blood" of other groups or says they are racially inferior. Far from it. His description of the Scots mentality does not rank it with respect to the English, for example. It is as with the Jew and the Christian: they are different; they are incompatible. He does not want to mix with them or pretend to have to like them. It is the same with Quakers. And again we should remember that sharp differences of speech, dress, custom, etc. marked off the Quakers of his day. He is full of reverence for Quaker ways, he is in awe of Quaker rectitude, but, he has to admit, he cannot *like* Quakers. "I must have books, pictures, theatres, chit-chat, scandal, jokes, ambiguities and a thousand whim-whams, which their simpler taste can do without." We might compare a modern romantic idealization of Amish life, which goes along with a horror of having to live it. This whole tenor of Lamb's honest confession comes out with respect to Negroes:

> In the Negro countenance you will often meet with strong traces of benignity. I have felt yearnings of tenderness toward some of these faces — or rather masks — that have looked out kindly upon one in casual encounters in the streets and highways. I love what Fuller beautifully calls — these "images of God cut in ebony." But I should not like to associate with them, to share my meals and my goodnights with them — because they are black.

We must again remember that Africans would have been many times stranger to Lamb in those days than Scotsmen, Jews, or Quakers. But here again, despite his "yearnings of tenderness," again his almost awe, he does not want to associate with them — because they are black. Throughout the essay he is simply trying to illustrate the impossibility of the lofty tolerance of Browne. He does not hate any of these other groups — on the contrary, he admires, is in awe of, and respects many things about them. But they are too different, and he cannot like them "as to live with them." Browne, in his smug metaphysical moments, may feel totally free from prejudice, he says, but mere mortals think otherwise. Lamb's disarming honesty, and the very benignity of his attitude even to wildly different cultural groups, ram home the point that being uncomfortable with the different is not the same as ethnic or religious hatred. It can be quiet and inoffensive, even humorous and kindly.

But even if it is not, we must accept that people have a God-given right to dislike other individuals or other classes of people on whatever basis they choose. They even have, in this country, a constitutional right to say so. Other people will think they are wrong. Fine. Let's argue. I have written at length to try to set right some erroneous thinking about race differences. I doubt I have changed many attitudes, but I have helped take away some of the armory of argument used by the other side. Thus, if a white student tells me that he does not like blacks because they are genetically inferior, then I can point out to him that such a belief makes no sense, and why. But if he says he does not like black people because they are black, and persists in this attitude even if told it is inappropriate, etc., then I have really no useful argument against him. Like and dislike are not open to proof and disproof. I can disagree, but that is all.

But if people have a right to cling to their dislikes despite the evidence, what they do not have a right to do is, to repeat a well-worn but still brilliant example, shout Fire! in a crowded theater. It is sometimes difficult to sort this out, but we have to try. We cannot prevent or cure dislike. (What on earth are we to say to Charles Lamb to change his mind? And what right do we have to do so? Our very act of prevention is an expression, often fanatical, of dislike in itself.) But as long as we get to make the rules, we can prevent *provocative expressions of dislike* such as might lead to physical or mental injury. We are prejudiced in favor of a certain kind of world, so let's go for it. But not because we are trying to compensate for a deficiency in human nature. (Lamb certainly had his problems, but morally, compared to any of us, in what way was he a deficient human being?) Rather, we are building on human nature to bring about a self-correcting mechanism whereby we try, not to replace stereotypical thinking — we can't do that — but to edge out unwanted stereotypes and replace them with those we approve.

At the same time we are constantly trying to make the unfamiliar more familiar — our only real strategy to beat stereotypical thinking at its own game. Most Jews that I know are really not very different from me in most significant respects. In this sense my situation is very different from Lamb's, and those ethnic or religious groups he found strange I find relatively familiar. However, while middle-class, intellectual, nonreligious Jews are so familiar to me as to be perceived as essentially "the same," I do still have, like Lamb, difficulties with the Scots. There may be a moral here. Perhaps if I had gone to Edinburgh and not to Harvard I would be singing a different tune. Perhaps if we could have got Lamb together with Hume over a good dinner and a game of backgammon, he might have felt differently about the Scots.

Lamb's difficulties with Africans, for example, stemmed from a total lack of familiarity with any one of them. I was brought up in a part of that same country equally devoid of Africans. I never knew any intimately until I was an undergraduate, and then they were exclusively black intellectuals. But I am leaping ahead. In my youth I was not without a stereotype of black people. And this category had a central member — a prototype, or paragon — who is well enough known to this audience: Paul Robeson. In our household he was a hero, and rightly so. My image of him is always as Othello in his robes. He *is* Othello, much as Sean Connery is Bond. Any others are strained imitations or conscious attempts to be different (yea, even Lord Olivier). My father had a nice bass voice and knew all the Robeson songs, which he taught to me. My mother had seen and heard him in person at Harrogate, and never stopped talking about it. We watched his films, however bad they were as films (I didn't know that then) as many times as we could get to see them. The moment my voice broke I began practicing "Old Man River." In my fantasies I was the young district officer in *Sanders of the River*, and Robeson/Bosambo was my friend. My sadness was that I could never be Bosambo.[27]

Around this beautiful prototype of the black man swirled a Kiplingesque cast of noble savages. There were the great Fuzzy-Wuzzies of the Nile, whom Kipling celebrated, for they did the unthinkable:

So 'ere's *to* you, Fuzzy-Wuzzy, at your 'ome in the Sudan;
You're a pore benighted 'eathen but a first-class fightin' man;
An 'ere's *to* you Fuzzy-Wuzzy, with your 'ayrick 'ead of 'air —
You big black boundin' beggar — for you broke a British square!

which was more than Napoleon's cavalry, even led by the redoubtable Ney (the bravest of the brave), ever managed!

Then there were the frightening and victorious Zulus, whose *impis* did the same at Isandhlwana, with assegai and shield against rifle and cannon. And my favorites, the Ashanti, whose king did not sit, but rested his elbow on a golden stool, and whose warriors, again with reckless bravery, defied the British guns. My father was an old soldier, and an old Tory, but he would never hear any disrespect for these people. (The same was not true for the Ghandian agitators whom he had, to his great distaste, to put down in India. "Nonviolent resistance" was simply an obvious oxymoron to an old soldier who had fought hand-to-hand against the Pathans on the Northwest Frontier.) And always at the center was Robeson, and the constant sound of spirituals from scratchy 78's on a wind-up gramophone.

The first black men I ever met were MP's near a U.S. airforce base in Norfolk during World War II. I was perhaps eight or nine and had strayed near the base into a forbidden zone. These two kind soldiers took me home to tell my mother that I shouldn't go there — for my own safety. They were so tall — I had never seen such tall men — and they had beautiful uniforms and large guns in white holsters, and they were soft spoken and impeccably polite. (I had never heard my mother called "ma'am" before.) I asked them in awe if they knew Paul Robeson. "Sure son," they said laughing. "We know him." I was in ecstasy for weeks. I tell this personal anecdote because I think it was for me a matter of tremendous good fortune that my stereotype of black people was thus formed. When I see a black face on campus, I see a potential Robeson, not a potential mugger. And I find that my experience has been the opposite of what it has been for most of my white American, liberal, Northern friends. The central item of the stereotype is the crucial one.

But we can't be everywhere with everyone, and as long as perceivable differences exist we can only hope constantly to revise our stereotypes in a more favorable direction, not try to outlaw what is evidently not a disease of the mind but part of its basic constitution. We have to come to terms with the idea that prejudice is not a form of thinking, but that thinking is a form of prejudice. Then we can deal with it more or less rationally. This may not seem as grand an objective as "abolishing racism and sexism" or something such, but I suspect it is a more achievable one, and in a real sense a more human one. And being human is the only job opening we're offered.

15

Myth and Mind

(With a Note on the Fragmentation of Trickster)

Myth can be treated as "contemporary" wherever and whenever gathered in space and time, and used as evidence of universal psychological (or sociopsychological, or biopsychological) processes. Alternatively, a historical or evolutionary view can be taken in which myth shows definite changes over time, reflecting different stages in the development of consciousness, or at least reflecting a different psychic reality at different times, a reality corresponding to a different sociocultural situation at each time. A good example of the latter would be Joseph Campbell's *Transformations of Myth through Time*, which starts with the myths of the hunter-gatherers, moves up through the Neolithic agricultural myths to the myths of the great civilizations, then to the period of "creative mythology" — the Middle Ages. We shall take primarily the first view here — myth as evidence of universal processes, with a few side glances at the developmental approach. For convenience we shall list these processes under nine headings, while understanding that the categories overlap and are heuristic rather than objective. One may either view these headings as psychological processes or as social and psychological functions. It is simply a matter of emphasis. Each of the processes mentioned serves some social or psychological function, or both. The headings do not exhaust the possibilities but are what I can handle in the space allotted.

The material for the study of myth comes from three basic sources: the collections of mythical tales by folklorists, anthropologists and philologists, spurred in many cases, such as the brothers Grimm in Germany and Lonnrot in Finland, by nineteenth-century nationalism; the classical texts of literate societies that give us the myths of Rome, Greece, Egypt, Persia, India, and China, for example; the medieval and later transcriptions of oral traditions that give us the myths of Iceland, Finland, Ireland, and Central America; and finally, such archaeological evidence that these societies leave behind, such as monuments and inscriptions. The material is vastly uneven, of course, but even more impressive is the evidence of the universality of themes. The greatest attempt to make order of these is in the work of Aarne and Thompson (1961). The greatest previous attempt at synthesis was that of Frazer (1891), but this represented a particular theory now much disputed, and the same can be said of the massive synthesis by Lévi-Strauss in his four volumes (1964a) of *Mythologiques*. Perhaps the most interesting recent synthesis is Dudley Young's brilliant *Origins of the Sacred* (1991), and perhaps the best recent general introduction is Leeming's *The World of Myth* (1990). It should not be forgotten, however, that myth is continually being produced, and some brief reference will be made to this continuity of mythical production up to our own times in both high and popular culture.

Myth as Explanation

This is perhaps the commonest suggested sociopsychological function of myth and the one most readily invoked by common sense. Myths are seen as stories that explain natural phenomena in the first place, and social institutions, or psychological dispositions, in the second. Typical examples of such theories are the rationalistic evolutionary theories of Sir James Frazer in *The Golden Bough* (first published in 1891). For Frazer, myths represented primitive man's attempt to explain the universe — its origins and nature. He gathered myths from primitive and peasant people the world over and used them to illustrate the passage in mentality from magic, through religion, to science. The magical element in myths involved a primitive theory of causation in which either like produced like (thus, the planting of prematurely forced seeds in "gardens of Adonis" in honor of the consort of Venus was expected to produce the same effect on the real crops) or separated parts of a thing were supposed still to be connected to it (thus the use of nail parings, hair, etc. in sorcery to inflict injury on the owner). For the most part, Frazer used myths connected with vegetation ceremonies to show that these two basic ways of thinking lay behind most magical and ritual practices. Most famous among these were the various myths of dying and rejuvenated gods and their mother-lover consorts: Venus (Aphrodite) and Adonis, Attis and

Tammuz, Isis and Osiris, etc. The "high" versions of these were concentrated in the areas of original cultivation: the Fertile Crescent, the Near East, and Egypt. But similar stories are found, connected with the idea of the death and rebirth of nature, in all agricultural societies. Thus the annual cycle of nature is, in this view, explained as the cosmic working out of the death and rebirth of the gods, as with Perspehone's six months in Hades and six months with her mother Ceres (the corn goddess) on earth. Frazer also pointed to the profound identification of the ruler (who developed from a rain magician) with the health of his people and particularly their land. This magical connection between the king and the land was a basic theme among agriculturalists to the extent that if a king's health were to fail or if he showed weakness or impotence, he would often be put to death. The theme of *The Waste Land* — devastated by the king's illness or insufficiency — was the basic inspiration for the great poem of that name by T. S. Eliot, a poem redolent with mythological themes and which in turn became a kind of defining myth of modernism.

Another theory of explanation, which gained wide currency, was that of Evans-Pritchard (1937), who studied magical explanations among the Azande of the southern Sudan. The Azande understood that bad luck could happen, but they needed an explanation of why it happened to some people at certain times. The answer to this they found in the practice of sorcery. Termites may have eaten through the supports of a granary, but why did it fall on this man at this time? Answer: sorcery practiced by an enemy. Evans-Pritchard pointed out that the system, like any conspiracy theory, was self-reinforcing. If one could not find the sorcerer, for example, this only served to show how cunning he was and hence how dangerous. Myths explained the origin and nature of the powers of sorcery. Again, the stress here is on the explanatory function.

In general, myths have been seen as having a whole range of explanatory functions, in particular in explaining the origins of things. Thus, Malinowski (1926; 1948) shows how myths in the Trobriand Islands explain, for example, the origins not only of natural phenomena but of such things as love magic, born of a mythical sexual union between brother and sister. Since any sexual connection between brother and sister is most stringently tabooed, this very danger became the source of power in love magic. Myths of the origin of the world itself and of mankind, whether from the actions of an earth diver, the fiat of a high god, the union of a sky father and an earth mother, or an act of masturbation by the divine Atum (Egypt), have again been taken as essentially explanatory.

The problem with attributing a primarily explanatory function to myths lies in their failure to disappear once more rational and scientific explanations are available. These should, in theory, as Frazer expected, supplant the inadequate "explanations" provided by myths. But myths continue to flourish and new ones are constantly invented. This suggests that something other than simple explanation lies behind the persistence of mythology.

Myth as Charter

The view of myth as a social or cultural charter was popularized by Malinowski, who was impressed by the Trobriand myths of clan origins. In each case, the totemic ancestors of the clans were seen to have originated in certain specific places, and their origin there validated the clan's claim to the territory. This was the "mythological charter" of the clan. Many myths provided this kind of validation. Thus, among the Hopi (Waters 1963) there is a ritual hierarchy of clans, and this hierarchy is validated with reference to the original wanderings of the clans after they left the original underworld and came up into this one, and the order of their eventual arrival on the Hopi mesas. These, of course, are the "origin myths" that we have seen under the heading of "explanation." But here they are seen as fulfilling the function not so much of explanation as of validation; of staking a legitimate claim to territory, in particular. Thus, the Jewish claim to Israel (Palestine) is based on a validating myth in which it was given to them in perpetuity by Yahweh as part of their covenant with him. This does not so much explain why the Jews are there as validate their claim to be there legitimately. The "charter" does not only validate territorial claims, of course, but the succession in royal houses, for example (myths of ancestral descent from Adam, complete with detailed genealogies, were common in European nobility — e.g., the O'Neills of Ulster) and the proper performance and power of ritual. Every Navaho ritual, embodied in a sand painting, has its validating myth, which the sand painting symbolically represents.

Myth as Rationalization

This is close to the former category, but its proponents do not stress so much the validating function of myth as its attempt, again, to "make sense" of certain puzzling phenomena. But this time it is not natural phenomena but rather the phenomena created by ritual and religion itself. Let us take the famous "myth versus ritual" quarrel, which occupied a great deal of effort from anthropologists and classicists (see Versnel 1990). One side saw myth as primary, and ritual simply as a playing out of mythical themes in dramatic fashion. The other side saw ritual as growing up out of magical practices in an ad hoc fashion, and myth as coming along later to rationalize the practices.

Since the origins of both the myths and the rituals are lost in the proverbial mists of history, it is often impossible to prove one way or the other; and indeed there must be constant feedback. But some investigators have taken a particularly firm stand in favor of myth as rationalization of ritual. One of the most extreme of these was Lord Raglan (1936), for whom all myth was a rationalization of ritual drama. The ritual drama itself did not have a "story" but was simply a set of magical formulae: for example, the installation ceremonies of a god-king, or the ritual sacrifice of a victim at the spring equinox. What later "tradition" did was to render these formulae more meaningful as tales of actual adventures of hero figures. Thus, according to Raglan, arose most of the famous "hero" myths: Robin Hood, King Arthur, Cuchulainn, Oedipus, Theseus, Perseus, Jason; in the Bible, Joseph, Moses, Elijah; and, among primitive tribes, Watu Gunung (Java) and Nyikang (Shilluk). He shows that a fairly tight pattern of events characterizes the lives of all the heroes — he scores them on a 22-point scale from birth from a royal virgin, through victory over giant, dragon, or wild beast, to eventual mysterious death or assumption to heaven. All these correspond, he claims, to stages in ritual drama. He is mostly concerned with proving that such heroes are completely unhistorical and thus refuting the "myth as distorted history" school, but his method (first promulgated in 1936) interestingly anticipates the "structural" approach, which we shall examine later, and is suggestive of a psychological need to render ritual into narrative.

An even more unusual version of the rationalization theme is Robert Graves' (1946) theory of "iconotropy," in which many myths are the attempts by a conquering people to rationalize the icons of the conquered and bring them into line with their own beliefs. Many biblical myths are Hebrew attempts thus to rationalize icons of the earlier Canaanites (see chap. 19), and similarly, many classical Greek myths were the confirming of Olympian myths at the expense of displaced Minoan ones. Thus, "For example, the story of the unnatural union of Pasiphae ('She who shines for all') and the bull, the issue of which was the monstrous Minotaur, seems to be based on an icon of the sacred marriage between Minos, the king of Cnossos (pictured with a bull's head), and the representative of the Moon-goddess, in the course of which a live bull was sacrificed." Similarly with Europa, Oedipus and Lot, and Lot's daughters — all rationalizations of indigenous icons. Again, the psychological process involved seems to be the need to rationalize, not so much to "explain" as to "make sense of," in one's own cultural or folk psychological terms, alien symbolic expressions that one wishes to assimilate. The alien cannot simply be left alien; it has to be reinterpreted and then integrated into one's own idiom.

290 The Challenge of Anthropology

Myth as Code

Known as the "structuralist" approach to myth and associated primarily with Claude Lévi-Strauss (1958), the main feature of myth as code is the abandonment of the idea of narrative as essential to myth. A myth, in this view, is a "story," but its meaning lies not in the plot but in the underlying relationships of the basic elements of the plot (or "mythemes"), which are revealed by looking for "structural contrasts" between the elements. Thus, in the story of Oedipus, several "mythemes" are in play throughout the plot. Lévi-Strauss sees them as pairs of opposites (he calls them "contradictions," but it is hard to see in what sense they contradict each other), such as:

overvaluation of kinship vs. undervaluation of kinship

bisexual origins of man vs. autochthonous origins of man

Thus, in the Oedipus legend, when Cadmus refuses to search further for his sister Europa (who has been raped by Zeus), he undervalues kinship, while when Oedipus marries his mother Jocasta, he overvalues kinship. But in each case the result is bisexual human reproduction. When Cadmus kills the Dragon — whose teeth sown in the ground produce the Spartoi, the first men of Thebes — and Oedipus kills the Sphinx, they are "denying the autochthonous origins of man." This is further reflected in the fact that all the male members of Oedipus' lineage have names referring to difficulty in walking, a feature of autochthonous origins in most myth, and that male relatives kill each other throughout the cycle.

The "meaning" of the myth then lies not in some moral tale about patricide and incest, but in a "resolution" of the contradictions between the theories of autochthonous human origins (held by most agricultural peoples on the model of plant emergence) and the knowledge that they are in fact the product of bisexual union between humans, and the fact that humans must value kinship, but not to the extent of investing genes in kin who are too close (this is my formulation, not his). Ultimately, all myth is reduceable to the resolution of the contradiction between Nature and Culture, the constant in the web of human puzzlement. We are part of nature and yet defiantly different from nature. Thus, he often uses the formula for ratios to illustrate this:

Nature : Culture :: Raw : Cooked

Nature is to culture as raw is to cooked. This formula lies behind many South American myths of the origins of humanity characterized by the cooking of food (and hence the invention of fire) as opposed to the eating of it raw (Lévi-

Strauss 1964b). Myths of the origin of fire characterize all cultures, and, in the structuralist version, have to do with the resolution of this basic contradiction.

The essence of this theory is that no inherent meaning resides in the items, symbols, and plots of myth in and of themselves. Myths are a code, and the various elements can be arranged and rearranged in different ways to produce "messages" about basic human dilemmas (contradictions) and their resolution. The mind is compared to a "bricoleur" who cobbles together useful objects out of whatever material is to hand. The psychological process here is essentially "intellectualistic" rather than emotional. It is as though these constant problems produce a strain for resolution, and the myth provides the resolution, although with a covert rather than an overt answer. The resolution is "understood" by the audience not at the overt level of plot and story, but at the subconscious level of the resolution of contradictions.

Also important is the issue of "transformations" of myths. Thus, neighboring peoples often take the theme of a myth and transform it into its opposite, as with the myth of the star-husband in North America and the myth of the bird fallen from its nest in South America. Thus, the essential similarity between two myth "series" may lie in their opposite statements of the same theme. It could be argued, for example, that Little Red Riding Hood is a structural transformation of the myth of Santa Claus. The reader can work this out as an exercise.

Perhaps the clearest example of the structural approach lies in Lévi-Strauss's (1962) treatment of totemic myths. The gods of ancient Egypt are almost always presented as having animal or bird heads, and this probably derives from their origins as clan totems in the previous tribal stage of Egyptian existence. The gods of the ancient Semitic tribes, before the advent of the monotheistic Yahweh (Jehovah) cult, were similarly "totemistic" according to Robertson Smith (1956). The totem represented the original animal ancestor of the tribe or clan, the bridge between Nature and Culture, and so could be seen as an explanatory myth, or an origin or charter myth. Such totemic myths are extremely widespread, cropping up on most continents. They are often accompanied by rituals involving the reenactment of the myths, and food taboos that prevent the "descendants" of the totem creature from eating the animal (or plant or whatever) in question, except perhaps on ritually prescribed occasions. Freud traced this back to the original "primal crime" of killing the horde father, who is now represented by the totem. Several other commentators, however, including Radcliffe-Brown, had seen the interest in the natural world shown in totemic myths as essentially utilitarian, especially as members of the totem clans, among the Australian Aboriginals, for example, held regular "increase ceremonies" to promote the fertility of the totem. But Lévi-Strauss sees it differently. From his intellectualist point of view, such explanations do not take into account the universal features of totemism which, he says, boil down essentially to the *classificatory* functions of the totems. Often they are inedible things, or supernatural things, or certainly things of no utilitarian concern. But by using such categories as separate but opposed species (e.g., Raven versus Wolf, Eaglehawk versus Crow, Emu versus Crocodile, etc.) to classify moieties, for example, people are setting up metonymical systems of classification of their social worlds. This leads to his famous formula that totems are not so much "good to eat" as "good to think." The totemic myths serve to emphasize the separate but totally interdependent nature of the social units involved.

Myth as Projection

Once we move to the subconscious, it is inevitable that we invoke psychoanalytic theories. These differ from the structuralist in that they are primarily concerned with emotions rather than the intellectualist solution of contradictions. Thus, Freud (1938; 1957) saw in the Oedipus myth not some code about human intellectual dilemmas, but a "projection" of real human anxieties onto the mythical figures (Oedipus, Laius, Jocasta, etc.). These anxieties, stemming from our own "unresolved Oedipal conflicts" in the sexual dilemmas of the human family, could not be dealt with directly, but they could be displaced, as it were, onto the figures of myth, where their awful consequences could be played out. Thus, the ubiquity of incest myths, and particularly of the awful consequences of incest, illustrates the constant human state of anxiety over incest temptations projected onto mythical personages. (Still one of the best summaries of the psychoanalytical approaches to the Oedipus myth is Mullahy 1952.)

In a bold but much misunderstood work, Freud (1952) attempted to show how this anxiety might stem from deep-rooted biological memories of events in human evolution — the primal horde and primal crime that we have already mentioned — but his followers have been happier with the original idea that there is a recurrent human family drama in each generation, with the unresolved conflicts handled by myth and religion. Thus, children have their first libidinous attachments to their parents, and this causes intense same-sex rivalry, especially between fathers and sons. This rivalry has to be suppressed by the sons, who must strive both to identify with their fathers and to achieve sexual and social independence. The "hero cycle" then for the Freudians is in effect a retelling, with larger-than-life mythical figures, of the family drama wherein the boy struggles to reach maturity. The Oedipal version, for example, shows both the awful consequences of not suppressing the killing urge toward the father and the libidinous urge toward the mother, and at the same time, how Oedipus, in finally recognizing and atoning, does reach maturity, independence, and heroic stature. It is fair to say that no culture so far studied has not produced a myth, or series of related myths, of this kind, and this the psychoanalysts would take as evidence of the projective realization of a universal human anxiety.

Various offshoots of psychoanalysis, such as the culture and personality school of anthropology, have taken the idea of projection even further. This school attempted to blend the "hypotheses" of psychoanalysis with the rigors of experimental behaviorism. The basic theory is perhaps best exemplified in Whiting and Child (1953), who, using the method of cross-cultural statistical comparison, test a series of hypotheses derived from psychoanalytic ideas and show how these are reflected in belief systems about the causes of illness. Thus, they claim, certain child-rearing practices lead to the intensification of various anxieties, which will then be projected onto mythical figures: Early indulgence by the mother followed by later rejection will result in paranoid personalities who will project their paranoia onto myths of aggressive witches who cause illness. Other investigators found that severe fathering will lead to strong castration anxiety in men, producing myths that are either quite literal — as that of Cronos castrating Uranos (and giving birth — obliquely — to Aphrodite) — or more disguised, as in the common myth of the vagina dentata with its castrating potential. Severe toilet training will produce myths concerned with anal functions either directly or in disguised forms, such as myths of miserliness — Midas, Scrooge, etc. In the projective scheme of things, as with structuralism, the processes are subconscious and disguised. But the Freudian projectionists do not see the symbols and persons of myth as arbitrary elements in codes; They take them to have substantive meaning. Incest is incest, not one sign in a code to be read as "overvaluation of blood relationships."

We cannot leave the Freudian projectionist scheme without mentioning the importance of dreams. Anthropologists had always recognized the importance of dreams as sources of myth material, and "primitive" people had always recognized the connection. But Freud made them absolutely central: they were the "royal road to the unconscious." Dream symbolism was the source of myth symbolism. Part of the "dream work" was to translate primary material into symbols so that repressed material could be experienced in a disguised form in the dream. Thus, a parental problem that could not be directly faced in consciousness could be realized in a dream of giants and monsters or kings and queens; sexual problems could be translated into dreams of flying, or of phallic snakes, and the like. Now that we know the crucial importance of dreaming for long-term memory storage (see Winson 1985) and the direct involvement of the emotional centers of the brain in the dream (REM sleep) process, Freud's observations take on a new strength. Myths become a kind of prepackaged dream work, readied for long-term memorization. This becomes extremely important when myths are used as methods of education in adolescents, as we shall see (Fox 1980, chap. 7; 1989, chap. 8).

Myth as Archetype

Closely related to the Freudian and successor schools is that deriving from Jung (1971) and his followers. It starts from much the same premises but differs sharply on the meaning of the symbolic content of myths. For the projectionists, meaning is in a sense created in each generation when the basic personality patterns are set down in child training. The universal patterns observed are the result of universal human features, but their translation into myth has to be achieved anew, as it were, in each generation, and can change as child-training practices change. The relative conservatism of such practices usually means that there is a constancy in projective myths over time. The Jungian approach disputes this. For Jungians, myths are not primarily reflections of childhood experiences but constants stemming from the inherited experiences of the human species itself. Calling this the "collective unconscious" has somewhat confused the idea, but Jung was simply stressing that the archetypes were the common property of the species occurring in all individuals. Thus, to use the example we used earlier, the "hero" theme is indeed universal and indeed does have to do with the boy's saga of maturation into manhood. But it is not created anew in each generation; it and its basic symbols and symbolic themes are part of the genetic heritage of the species. Thus, we do not "project" our anxieties in the *creation* of heroes and villains, tricksters and witches, demigods and fatal enchantresses, and the like. They are in a sense there, in dream material, waiting to be realized in story. We may project *onto* them, but we do not bring them into being. A Jungian would ask, with some reason, how it is that, despite the huge variation in human cultures, certain quite definite and recognizable characters and situations crop up universally, if these are supposed to be constant "recreations" in the form of projections of childhood anxieties. The fixed characters, situations, and their accompanying symbols Jung called "archetypes," and, quite contrary to the structuralists, he saw their content as having explicit meaning, which could be recognized quite easily. The witch or wicked stepmother was a "split" of the mother — her evil side feared by the child — while the good queen or fairy godmother was the mirror opposite — the good qualities of the mother. There is a "code" here, but its message is not to be deduced from intellectualist combinatorial properties. Rather, it is to be directly read off from the actual content of the myth: wicked uncle = feared aspects of father. (In the Hamlet myth, which long antedates Shakespeare's version of it, the wicked uncle *becomes* the [step]father.) And these meanings do not change. The archetype is eternal.

Archetypes should not be confused with "innate ideas." They are more like the "innate releasing mechanisms" of the ethologists: instinctive responses that arise in response to certain environmental stimuli. (For an excellent discussion of this idea, and the general relation of archetypes to biopsychological processes generally, see Stevens 1982.) The major ones have to do with the same aspects of the family drama as in the Freudian version. But for Jung, for example, the "mother archetype" existed in the human psyche *ab origino*; what individual — or group — experience achieved was a particular realization of the archetype: a matter of emphasis on the good or punitive sides of the mother, for example. In myth, the mother could be symbolized as Mother Earth in her various manifestations (the Corn Goddess, the Fertility Goddess, the Divine Queen, the Mistress of the Animals, Spider Woman, etc.); or, as the feared version in the Death Goddess (Kali), the Evil Enchantress (Vivien), the Witch (as in Hansel and Gretel), the Gorgon, the Dragon or Sea Monster, etc. The creative Greeks could split the mother-female archetype many ways, from the sexual Aphrodite through the virgin Artemis to the motherly Demeter and the dominating Hera (see Friedrich 1978, who sees this as a way of dealing with a "repressed mother-lover archetype"). Robert Graves (1948) expanded this with the idea of the "triple goddess" who, while the same person, appears as the young girl, the mature woman, and the old crone in different manifestations of the stages of womanhood. The father, in turn, appears as the Sun God (Aztecs), the Sky God (Yahweh, Zeus), the Divine King (Caesar), the Magician or Wizard, and, in his bad forms, as the vengeful deity, god of wrath, or evil magician (sorcerer). The "split" between bad and good fathers is at the base of many successful modern myths, such as that expressed in the conflict between Bram Stoker's Count Dracula and his nemesis, Dr. Van Helsing. (For other good examples of this "splitting" in English literature, see Brewer 1988.) One might even see the rise of the idea of Satan in Judaeo-Christian mythology as an attempt to overcome the impossibility of trying to contain both the good and evil father archetypes in one Father God as demanded by strict theology. The rise of Marianism equally represents, in this view, an insistence on reinstating the Mother archetype (and especially the *mater dolorosa*, the sorrowing mother-goddess with her dead-but-to-be-resurrected son) in a religion in which she had been seriously demoted by celibate misogynist male priests (Carroll 1986).

Jung also postulated various other aspects of the archetypal psyche, all of which emerge in myth (as they do in religion, politics, music, and popular culture). Thus, the psyche is always split into the *animus* and the *anima*: the masculine and feminine aspects. In Greek myth, Athena springs full-born from the head of Zeus — his feminine aspect; and many gods and goddesses have a decidedly androgynous look. It is also open to introversion and extroversion: Sherlock Holmes is perhaps the ideal introvert, and Falstaff perhaps the extrovert. Especially compelling is the archetype of the *shadow*: the evil side of the self that is rejected and feared. The fascination in legend with twins (and the real fear of twins in many societies) reflects this notion of two sides of the self that are at once identical but antithetical to each other. The fascination moves from the Hero Twins of primitive myth, through Cain and Abel and Castor and Pollux, to the constant use of the "good and evil twin" theme in modern soap operas and miniseries, and was evident in much folklore as the Doppelganger, or exact double theme. Its most graphic modern mythological expression is, of course, in the tale of Dr. Jekyll and Mr. Hyde, and even Dr. Frankenstein and his "monster," whom he must destroy and by whom he must be destroyed. (See Twitchell 1985 for an extended discussion of such themes in modern "horror" literature and films.)

We could go on identifying the major archetypal systems — for example, the powerful Mother-Son combination central to many mythological systems and even higher religions, or the *puer aeternus*, the golden youth who remains a youth forever, as in Horus, Peter Pan, Ganymede, or even Dorian Gray and Elvis — but these must suffice. It should be mentioned, however, that it would be wrong to think of archetypes as solely concerned with personages; they can equally be places (magical islands like the Hesperides or Atlantis, gardens like Eden, and forests and underworlds) or events and processes, like the Quest or the Monster Struggle, etc. The major processes represented are, of course, individual maturation and the life-death barrier. The "death and resurrection" theme, which Frazerians would see as a magical-explanatory fertility myth, or the structuralists as overcoming an intellectual contradiction, would be seen by the Jungians as a major archetype dealing not only with the problem of real death and the possibility of an afterlife, but with any kind of major life-transition involving the death of one "self" and the re-creation of the other. (The basic meaning of the "Death" card in the Tarot pack in fact is "change.") One of the most beautiful modern mythical expressions of this is in the final act of Mozart's *Magic Flute*, where the young hero and heroine survive trial by fire and water to be reborn into a new life. This sequence is based on Masonic mythology, itself derived from the great Mystery Religions (Isis, Demeter, Mithras) in which Christianity, as it developed, also has its roots. The Hero or Heroine's triumph over death, and the promise of eternal life to believers who follow the same "path," is a powerful archetypal theme. (See Turner 1991 for a sensitive discussion of *The Magic Flute* as myth, as well as of *The Tempest* and *The Wizard of Oz* as quintessential modern myths.)

The Jungian tradition has been carried on most successfully not by anthropologists, who tend to be suspicious of claims to psychic universals even while they preach the psychic unity of mankind, but by mythographers like Joseph Campbell (1949; 1959), especially on the Hero theme. Indeed, his essentially Jungian analysis of the Hero archetype (as we have seen, the basic story of male maturation) was the source for George Lucas's highly successful movie trilogy *Star Wars* — one of the most spectacular cinematographic tributes to archetypal theory. With its creation of Obe Wan Kenobe and Darth Vader on the one hand, and Luke Skywalker and Hans Solo on the other, it followed to the letter the "good father/bad father" and "older brother/younger brother" (hero twin) themes, and even included the princess-anima and the "animal helper" themes. (Many movies that have become "classics" seem to have done so on the basis of their tapping of archetypal images: the lonely hero in *High Noon,* for example. *Shane,* considered by some to be the greatest "western," is redolent with father archetypes in a seesawing competition-cooperation scenario, with the soul and ultimate adult identification of the hero boy at issue throughout. It is only a short step to the Navaho/Pueblo myth of "How the Two Came to Their Father," or, for that matter to the Arthurian cycle.)

It is probably useful to include under this general heading the influential work of Eliade (1965), such as "Myth as Education." Essentially what Campbell did for the Hero Eliade did for the process of initiation, which he linked closely to the death and rebirth theme. It is during this process that young boys, particularly, are introduced to the basic wisdom of the tribe, and this information is conveyed largely by myth. This is true both in primitive tribes and modern societies, the latter having just as strong a tendency to convey important messages about behavior and conduct through myths of, for example, sports heroes (Knute Rockne and "win one for the Gipper") or rock stars (Elvis the King — the *puer aeternus* who refuses to die). Whatever view of myth we take, it is clear that it exerts a peculiar kind of power over the developing psyche that makes it a suitable vehicle for impressing eternal (or parochial) verities on impressionable minds. This is particularly true when it is conveyed through music and drama, and it is for this reason that Plato wanted both banned from his ideal, rational Republic. He would thoroughly have understood, and deplored, the powerful appeal of MTV. The role of graphic imagery in producing dreams, and dreams as producing long-term selective memory, which we have previously discussed, is clearly important here. Graphic, even terrifying, myths and rituals for adolescents will have the actual physical effect of "stamping in" the messages conveyed by the myths.

As an exercise, students could take something as archetypally loaded as, say, a football game, or more graphic even, a modern bullfight (where the fragile matador wearing the solar "Suit of Lights" either penetrates the huge dark bull of the moon with his slender sword, or slays the evil "wild" father — archetypes have many resonances), and see where such an analysis takes them, as opposed to, say, a structuralist version. Or they could examine, as

Jung himself did, the contents of the enormously popular Tarot card pack, something that was for Jung a positive encyclopedia of archetypal themes: The Emperor and Empress (father and mother), The Magician, The Lovers, The World, The Tower, The Hanged Man, The Fool (the *puer aeternus*, the holy innocent), Death (change), The Sun, The Wheel of Fortune, The High Priestess (Isis/Mary), The Hierophant, and a welter of cups, staves, stars, and coins with their own kings, queens, knights, and pages.

A Note on the Fragmentation of Trickster

While discussing archetypes, we might briefly look at one of the most powerful — one that fascinated Jung — namely, the enigmatic figure of Trickster. Trickster is placed by Campbell as one of the "primordial" myths: one dating from the depths of the Paleolithic; one of the Ur myths of humanity. Trickster can come in many forms in these ancient versions. He is sometimes an old man or old chief, as among the Winnebago, whose version, recorded by Radin (1956), was the source of Jung's fascination; or among the Hopi a coyote (Malotki 1985); or sometimes, as among other Winnebago versions, a hare; or a raven among other North American Indians. But his shape is not "fixed" and, indeed, one of his characteristics is that he is a shape changer and sex changer. He appears as the spider Anansi in West Africa (and in Caribbean derivations) and in Europe as Reynard the Fox. In Polynesia he is Maui, at once Trickster and Creator, who has an island named after him in the Hawaiian chain.

In the primordial version, Trickster is many things: he is at once stupid, gullible, cunning, and devious; he is the embodiment of chaos and yet can be an important deity of creation; he is totally amoral and yet often the founder of society and moral order; he is relentlessly libidinous and yet cannot control his own penis, which wanders off and has its own adventures; he is scatological in the extreme, and his anus, like his penis, seems to have a life of its own; he is basically male but can change sex and live as a female; he is at once asocial and yet, for example, steals fire from the gods for man. Above all he is funny. Trickster stories are told always for amusement, and most of the current stock of "dirty jokes" have their origins in his adventures.

This primordial figure, who seems to us to have such a rash of contradictions built in, springs from homogeneous hunting groups, themselves equally undifferentiated and "compact." One could see him as a symbolic representative of the basic psychological process of "cheating" so important in the process of evolution itself (Trivers 1985), and something which, after the appearance of language, doubled in importance both as a strategy of individual reproductive success and as something society had to contain and control — but ambivalently so since it was also the basis of creativity and other necessary energies. As society grew in complexity, so the bundle of archetypal material that was Trickster began to unravel and separate out into distinct characters. To trace all of them would be a lifetime's task, and, since the process is ongoing, an endless one, so we can only sketch an outline here.

In the great Iron and Bronze Age myths, Trickster keeps some of his identity, but already is beginning to appear as more than one god or hero with different characteristics. The Greeks, for example, have their "official" trickster in Hermes (Brown 1969), who was indeed the god of trickery, and whose name derives from the Herms, or phallic statues used as boundary markers. He was thus the god of boundaries, but also the god of thieves and, interestingly, merchants and craftsmen. He was the messenger of the gods and brought luck to men. Despite his phallic origins, he was not a particularly libidinous god; this aspect of him was taken over by his son Pan — half animal, half human — and by Dyonisus, god primarily of wine, but basically an ancient, pre-Greek (as was Pan) fertility deity who was lord of orgiastic ecstasy and the period of "misrule." Fire was stolen by Prometheus, and the human-heroic aspects of Trickster are summed up best in the person of Odysseus, who, noticeably, had the second great Homeric epic all to himself and his exploits of trickery, deceit, and triumph. The Norse myths kept him more or less intact in the person of Loki, but he is here transformed into a devil-like figure of ambiguous sexuality who is ultimately responsible for the death of Balder and the doom of the gods. But even here many of Trickster's characteristics are parceled out among the gods, including the basic amorality of Wotan (Crossley-Holland 1980). This is also true of the Hebrew religion once the mountain/thunder/sky god Yahweh displaced his rivals ("Thou shalt have none other gods before me..."). Old leftovers of primordial Trickster are there in the serpent, and in such figures as Samson and Jonah, but it is God himself who seems to have inherited much of Trickster's impulsivity and amorality — indeed, almost everything except his libidinousness and his humor.

We could look further, to the Trickster aspects of the great lord Krishna in India (his stealing of the dairymaids' clothes and his sexual teasing of them is pure Trickster stuff), among the various characters of the Finnish *Kalevala* (Lemminkainen, for example, for whom Sibelius wrote a beautiful tone poem), or to the great Irish and Welsh epics where the "Trickster" and "Hero" archetypes have not, as it were, thoroughly separated themselves out (Finn, Cuchulainn) and would not do so until these characters were remolded in the Middle Ages in the Arthurian epics. As they unfold, the stories begin to make the characteristics of Trickster more fragmented and to assign different aspects to different characters, rather than trying to bundle them all up in one contradictory, protean roustabout. Thus, Merlin is the Trickster-Magician and shape changer; Lancelot du Lac is the would-be hero still enslaved to his libido; Parsifal is the gullible fool who nevertheless is the key to the salvation of the Waste Land; Arthur, Galahad, and Gawain are out-and-out heroes; and it is reserved to Mordred/Morgana to embody the evil and deceitful aspects. (The theme of the gullible simpleton who is in fact a kind of hero continually reappears through *Don Quixote, Pilgrim's Progress, Candide, The Good Soldier Schweik*, up to Charlie Chaplin, Bill Murray, Steve Martin, Radar O'Riley in *M*A*S*H*, and Kurt Vonnegut's Billy Pilgrim and Kilgore Trout.)

The violence and deceit of Trickster were never lost to the "folk" audience and show up in the figure of the devil in medieval mystery plays, and in successor figures like Til Eulenspielgel, Punch, and Pierrot. We have perhaps forgotten the enormous popular appeal of these characters — although Punch and Judy shows, often much bowldlerized, pop up here and there at children's parties. Punch is highly stereotyped, but clearly Trickster, while Pierrot was subject to many interpretations and developed an interesting complexity as the "gullible fool" or "foolish innocent" side of the Trickster equation (with sometimes sinister undertones, as in *Pierrot assassin de sa femme*). (On Punch, see Twitchell 1985; on Pierrot, see Storey 1978.) They all arose from the Italian *commedia dell'arte*, where the Trickster role was split into the three figures of Pulcinella, Pedrolino, and Arlecchino. Punch was discarded in the French versions, where Pierrot and Harlequin in consequence had to develop interestingly complex roles incorporating some Punch characteristics.

The scatological side of Trickster, along with his gluttony and lust, was kept alive by Rabelais in *Gargantua* and *Pantagruel* in the otherwise officially prurient Middle Ages, as was his "outlaw" status with Robin Hood and his gluttonous cowardice by Falstaff and Sir Toby Belch. The Renaissance spawned a whole stable of libidinous and deceitful Tricksters, with Machiavelli unfortunately heading the list. Even if he didn't deserve it (as all scholars agree), the Machiavelli-Trickster equation was too strong to resist. But note that this "Machiavellianism" was the consciously devious aspect of Trickster, not the "innocent fool."

Trickster was being more and more fragmented and "specialized" as society itself became more differentiated and complex. The libidinous aspects of Trickster became woven into the legends or semilegends of Don Juan, Cassanova, and Cellini, for example (with perhaps Carmen as the female counterpart), with the sexual violence taken up by de Sade. The amoral "con man" aspects were taken up by such figures as Tom Jones or Barry Lyndon (who had their libidinous and gluttonous sides as well, of course). The rapid social changes after the mid nineteenth century in both Europe and America saw further fragmentation as more varied social types became available to take up the different aspects of Trickster's multifaceted character.

Thus, the "con man" theme was elaborated in various directions, including the gentleman thief, the gallant highwayman, and the unscrupulous social climber. The enormous popularity of such movies as *The Sting* and *The Hustler*, for example, shows that this part of Trickster's character continues to fascinate — as do the portrayals of all such "outlaws" (the Western hero-villains have a lot of this in them) as long as they amuse and the people they "take" are deserving dupes. (Trickster would have had no such scruples: the Puritan revolution often added a moralizing dimension to Trickster figures not present in the original.)

Marginality, indeed, has become almost a mark of modern Trickster characters. Thus, the Mafia exerts a profound fascination from the margins of society, as do such figures as private eyes (gumshoes, shamuses), with Sherlock Holmes showing unmistakable Trickster qualities, and spies. While there is much serious spy literature (John Le Carré, for example), there is also much that is in the Trickster tradition. James Bond 007, at least in the movie versions, has all the amorality, libidinousness, deviousness, and shape-changing qualities of Trickster, while at the same time being "licensed to kill," i.e., having the power of life and death. All these "agents," even in the serious spy tradition, are obsessed with deceit and deviousness, which is their trade after all; they have mastered it, as they have mastered the double triple cross and the like. To cheat the cheater (especially the "mole") is at the heart of their plotting.

Again, these are not the descendants of Gullible Coyote. The "innocent fool" theme, as we have seen, has also been carried on as a separate tradition and finds curious outlets in the literature of the Beatniks; in such amoral, lustful, but essentially harmless and ineffective creatures as Donleavy's *Ginger Man* or even the Rolling Stones; or equally amoral but creative tricksters as Joyce Carey's Gully Jimson in *The Horse's Mouth* — one of Alec Guinness's best film roles. (See also his foil to Dennis Price's amoral, social-climbing Trickster in *Kind Hearts and Coronets.*) Once on this hunt, one can find specialized bits and pieces of Trickster cropping up all over the place, including the incomparable Jeeves in P. G. Wodehouse's Bertie Wooster novels, The Fonz in *Happy Days*, and even Ferris Beuler in his hilarious day off. We have already mentioned Bill Murray, who seems to have made a niche in the line from Parsifal through Pierrot through Chaplin as the modern foolish innocent. Perhaps the "libidinous-coward-liar-cheater" who nevertheless wins through is best represented in the brilliant character of Flashman, the notorious school bully, carved out of the otherwise sanctimonious *Tom Brown's Schooldays* by the genius of novelist George McDonald Frazer.

The "splitting" of Trickster is especially noticeable in private eye versions. Conan Doyle started it: Holmes and Watson followed directly in the

Quixote/Sancho Panza tradition. The "new" character of Lestrade was introduced: the pompous bureaucrat who is only interested in his image with the public, and who often gets the public credit for our Trickster-heroes' efforts (perhaps foreshadowed by such characters as the Doctor and Pantalone in the *commedia*). There are numerous modern examples, but think of the highly successful *Rockford Files* — still in reruns, with Jim Rockford (played by James Garner, who has had a notable Trickster career, including *Maverick*) as the shape-changing charmer (he has a small printing machine in his car for producing instant business cards to suit the needs of the occasion); his father, Rocky, as the gullible innocent; and the marvelously misnamed Angel as the amoral rogue who will sell out his friends with a smile and still remain funny and likable. The bureaucrat role is split between the frustrated but helpful policeman Dennis, the enigmatic lady lawyer, and various pompous captains and lieutenants who again take our heroes' glory. Equally, *Magnum P. I.* has the likable shape changer Magnum, the gullible and innocent (but heroic and loyal) T. C., and the amoral rogue Rick. All do battle with the pompous guardian of morality Higgins, with the help of a lady lawyer. (Women fit only uneasily into this scheme, as they had only played subordinate roles in the *commedia*: Trickster seems quintessentially male, even in the split version.) *Lovejoy* has a similar trio of Lovejoy (the likable rogue), Eric, and Tinker (a true modern Pierrot figure), the last two sharing the gullible innocent role, with the ever-helpful Lady Jane tagging along. This show lacks a true "Angel" character of the ruthless Trickster kind. The British shun this kind of thing; it is left to the villains, which spoils the effect since Trickster is not a villain. (Knowing the difference is essential to understanding the character.) These are all in the long line of fragmentations starting with the *commedia dell'arte*, but with the various twists added to take care particularly of the public's growing ambivalence toward police and bureaucracy generally. I keep waiting for a convincing female Trickster character, and perhaps Kinsey Milhone, the heroine of Sue Grafton's alphabet series, *might* qualify. But somehow she just doesn't come off as Trickster (or at least only as a female imitation of one), and this is either my simple male prejudice or Trickster has something profound to say about male psychology. When men dress and act as women for deceitful purposes, the Trickster aspect is clearly evident — *Some Like It Hot, Tootsie, Bosom Buddies* — all variants of the classic *Charlie's Aunt*. This awaits further analysis; Miss Marples, for example, while a great detective, is absolutely no Trickster.

It is important to note that just being funny does not qualify one for Trickster status. Circus clowns and stage magicians, for example, have a different lineage, although equally steeped in mythology, and stand-up comics and funny characters need have no Trickster characteristics at all. Some cartoon characters, however, seem to be exactly in the Trickster tradition, led, appropriately, by Wile E. Coyote in his hopeless pursuit of Roadrunner. A true Trickster for grownups has emerged in the work of Poet Laureate Ted Hughes. His *Crow* (1972) is all Trickster, and quite consciously so — alternately hilarious and terrifying, as Trickster should be. Equally, Dadaism and the whole Surrealist movement in art, theater, cinema, and literature has definite Trickster overtones, including so-called "magical realism" which, despite its pretensions to being "postmodern," is really a pale imitation of the Surrealist novel and especially of the great Boris Vian (see *L'écume des jours* for an example of gentle, shape-changing Trickster tristesse).

One could go on almost endlessly, but the point is simple and doesn't need more examples. In a sense, one would have to take all these modern "specialized" roles and bundle them all together into one character to come up with primordial Trickster. This we can no longer do (except perhaps for some poets perhaps more in touch with the primordial than the rest of us). Our archetypal mentalities retain the need for the Trickster "stuff," but we are no longer able to think of him as a single character, as our Paleolithic ancestors did, or even as three or four characters, as our Iron Age forebears could. We have fragmented him into dozens of specialized roles to match our own sociopsychological reality, and even if our primordial imaginations can still contain these contradictions, our modern modes of thinking and feeling require Trickster to be revealed to us through a kaleidoscope of roles and fragments that we must somehow imaginatively reassemble, and probably do, however unconsciously, to reach the almost lost unitary figure of Old Man Coyote, somewhere lurking in our still Paleolithic brain.

Myth as Integration

A powerful school of sociological thought has stressed the sociopsychological integrative functions of myth for the society as a whole. This school, founded by Emile Durkheim (1915) and carried on by Radcliffe-Brown (1952), sees myth and ritual as inextricably mixed, and indeed regards the ritual performance of the myth as far more important than the actual content. In the nineteenth century, the comparative ethnographer Adolf Bastian (1868) distinguished between mythological content based on *Elementargedanke* (roughly, "elementary ideas") and that based on *Volkergedanke* ("ethnic ideas"). Jungians are concerned with the former: the universal themes of myth, folklore, and magic. The sociological school is concerned with the latter: the local expressions of mythical ideas in ritual. If there are any general psychological functions for the Durkheimians, they lie in the *functions,* not the content, of myth. Thus, myth and ritual together serve to promote the integration of the individual into society; in Durkheim's expressive terms: to integrate the individual conscience (or consciousness) with the collective conscience. (Note that this is very different from the "collective unconscious" of the Jungians, which embraces the whole of mankind, not just a particular society.) The individual is in a sense always "alone" in his own perceptions, but he has to be in some sense in concert psychologically and socially with his fellows in order for society to function. This is not achieved simply by coercion or contract, in Durkheim's view, but by the sharing of myths in ritual experience. The myths contain the collective wisdom of the tribe or society, and in coming together in ritual to enact the myths, the members not only share information but share a common psychological experience of being together under the almost objective or external authority of the society itself. This is the source, Durkheim claimed, of the power of the moral imperative that had eluded Kant. It comes from society itself — the ritual, as Radcliffe-Brown phrased it — sustaining certain common sentiments in the believers, and so powerful is their experience that they attribute it to an external source or sources: god or gods in some form or another. But these are nothing more than society itself acting through its rituals on the individual.

Durkheim turned for his major demonstration to the myths and rituals of the Australian Aborigines, which are largely to do with many of the things we have been discussing: initiation of youths, for example, and increase and fertility of the animals of the hunt. The myths derive from the "dream time" — the ultimate beginnings of Aboriginal society when the totemic ancestors laid down the territories, rules of marriage and initiation, rites of passage and hunting rituals, etc. Whatever the psychologists might think of these myths, the sociological view sees them as functioning to integrate the individual Aborigine into his larger society and to keep that society integrated by its common commitment to these ancestral myths. This was especially clear with the Aborigines who lived for most of the year in small wandering families or bands, coming together periodically for their great "collective" ceremonies, like the Intichiuma of the Aranda. Radcliffe-Brown was fond of quoting Confucius on ceremonies, to the effect that it didn't matter much what the ceremonies were about, and certainly not whether the myths on which they were based were "true" — what mattered was that they were performed. Their function was to bring people together with reverence for a body of beliefs and thus reinforce their "common sentiments." To use Durkheim's formulation, the "individual representations" would be brought into harmony with the "collective representations."

One of the more popular and easily most expressive of such forms of integrative mythology/ritual is ancestor worship. Societies that stress the worship of ancestors either stress the belief in a general body of ancestors — as with the Kachinas among the Pueblo Indians — or actually worship specific ancestors — as with the Chinese, whose ancestors are recorded in temples on ancestral tablets for as many as twenty or more generations. Reverence for the ancestors, and beliefs and rituals concerned with placating them and ensuring their continued benevolence, are powerful supports for the family hierarchy and the system of values it embodies. Durkheimians, for example, are less concerned with whether or not child-rearing practices lead to beliefs in punitive ancestors as they are that common worship of clan ancestors by members of the clan — the holding of common beliefs and the practice of common rituals — ensure the social solidarity of the clan itself.

Myth as Expression

All the above theories have in common that they see myth having some instrumental or functional purpose for the believers. But there is another aspect to myth which might be called the expressive, which sees myth as more akin to poetry or drama or opera or even science fiction, and which downplays the utilitarian explanations. The thrust of the work of Victor Turner (1969) has been in this direction. Thus, Tedlock (1972) sees Zuni myths not as explanations or projections primarily (although they may be both these things) but as poetic expressions of Zuni concerns. Written out in a raw prose form, many myths make little sense, a fact that led early mythographers to dismiss them as examples of "prelogical mentality," or later structuralists to seek the hidden messages behind the rambling narrative. But, says Tedlock, a good deal of expressionist poetry would make equally little sense if treated as a version of rational narrative. We do not treat it as such, but realize that if it has a "function" it is indeed expressionistic. Its function does not go beyond its aim to express a particular emotion or sentiment or feeling: to say something poetic about the world. It is primarily metaphorical in character rather than logical. That such an expression has "power" is a common belief, of course — the bard's poetic curse was feared even by the High Kings of Ireland, and this is perhaps the explanation for the often exaggerated respect given to the gnomic utterances of contemporary poets — but the aim is essentially expressive. One of the most quoted Navaho ritual "chants" is used certainly in conjunction with a curing ritual, itself the reenactment of a myth, but it is also a powerful piece of expressive poetry:

House made of the dawn
House made of evening light
House made of the dark cloud
House made of male rain
House made of dark mist
House made of female rain
House made of pollen

House made of grasshoppers
Dark cloud is at the door
The outward trail is dark cloud
The zigzag lightening stands high upon it
....
....
May it be beautiful before me
May it be beautiful behind me
May it be beautiful below me
May it be beautiful above me
May it be beautiful around me
In beauty it is finished
In beauty it is finished.

In taking this tack and looking at the purely expressive functions of myth, which would mean "explaining" them as we would "explain" poetry or music, for example, no one denies that they may serve other functions, such as those discussed above. But it is suggested that they have this other quality of "pure" expression, and that as such they should be treated more as we treat poetry or opera, where we do not make such heavy demands on their instrumental roles as on their success as expressions of emotion. Thus, the great Liebestod of Isolde in Wagner's *Tristan* is undoubtedly archetypycal and may well be subject to structural interpretations, etc., but primarily it is to be judged, in this view, as a successful or unsuccessful expression of the theme of love-unto-death-and-beyond that it is trying to express. It would make no sense, for example, to try to interpret the Tristan legend as a whole as "explaining" anything. What does it "explain"? Rather it *expresses* something: either something universal or something to do with a central emotion of the culture in which it occurs. And it may have no function beyond that expression. (For a vivacious but insightful view of opera as a kind of "alternative mythology" to Western Christian orthodoxy, see Conrad 1987.)

Myth as Knowledge

We have suggested both that myth has strong mnemonic properties and that it may contain a hidden "code." These two properties combine in the view that myth is in fact a form a knowledge passed on in code, but that the knowledge is essentially not archetypal or structural but astronomical. It is, as we like to say, "star lore." We rather take for granted that all the visible planets and constellations are assigned to various Graeco-Roman gods, goddesses, nymphs, and heroes, but we lost touch with the idea that this is their essential meaning. That is, they *are* the constellations and the stars and planets. Their various wanderings, risings and falls, triumphs and deaths and resurrections, are in fact encoded versions of their passage through the heavens — or through the zodiac, as the ancient literate world would have had it. Yet this was indeed the common view of literate minorities of the great post-Neolithic civilizations throughout the world. And there is plenty of evidence that the roots of such astronomical knowledge went deeper into the Paleolithic world of the hunters. Marshack (1972) makes a good case for Paleolithic recording of phases of the moon, for example. The astronomical function of the great megalithic monuments has been determined, and from Yucatan to China, and Polynesia to Persia, a vast system of astronomical information and its accompanying astrological lore was universally known and codified in mythic symbols (Santillana & Dechend 1977). A great deal of this lore — and this is found in so-called "primitive" myth as well as in more advanced literate versions — concerns the world axis, world tree, or world mountain, sometimes pictured as a mill, quern, or churn, on which the whole of creation turns (or is turned by various heroes like Horus and Seth in Egypt or Vishnu in India, or even Hamlet in his pre-Shakespearean incarnations as Amlodhi in Icelandic myth) and which eventually falls into disuse, or becomes a whirlpool or maelstrom. This is seen, with accompanying stories of gods dominant, gods twilit, and gods destroyed, as a coded message about the "precession of the equinoxes" (based on the tilt of the earth and the discrepancy between the global and solar equators of 23.5 degrees) and subsequent "world ages," defined according to the zodiac and taking some 2,400 years to "revolve" plus a "great year" of approximately 26,000 years. Thus, the sun "progresses" though the zodiac from, in say 5000 B.C., Gemini, through Taurus into Aries into Pisces, where it stands now (Christ the Fish inaugurated the present age) before moving into the "Age of Aquarius" in about 200 years' time.

To spell out the numerous "codes" in the great myths that carry this astrological lore would be lengthy, so let us take one example from one of the most famous icons of Near Eastern religion: Mithras slaying the bull. We have already seen how the bullfight survives as a popular ritual and what the psychological theorists might say about it. But Mithraism was one of the great mystery cults that challenged Christianity for dominance of the Roman world, and only the intervention of the emperor Constantine probably prevented it from triumphing. The astrological belief that lay at the foundation of Mithraism — that was revealed only to the highest order of initiates — was precisely the precession of the equinoxes rediscovered by Hipparchus about 128 B.C. (Ulansey 1989). Its great central icon shows Mithras kneeling on the back of a bull, looking away, and stabbing the bull in the shoulder. Wheat ears sprout from the wound (or the tail), and various animals are in attendance — a dog, a snake, a raven, and a scorpion — and sometimes a cup and a lion. For a Jungian "decipherment," one may look to Campbell (1959, vol. 3, p. 257). But the astrological interpretation suggests that this represents the passage of the sun from Taurus (the bull) when the constellation Perseus was directly over it. This ended the "Age of Taurus" (killed the bull) and ushered in a new astrological age. Only a very powerful "god" or force could have ordained this, and he was personified as Perseus/Mithras, the latter identification being either part of the mystery cult's secretiveness or a ready identification of the Persian deity (Mitra) with Perseus on the basis of the latter's name and the origin of the cult within the Persian empire of Mithradites. The attendant "animals" are all constellations that were under the celestial equator, thus "under" Perseus/Mithras, when the change occurred; and the cup is Aquarius, the water bearer, while the lion (Leo) represents the summer solstice, and the wheat ears are the spring equinox.

From M. Vermaseren, *Corpus Inscriptorum et Monumentorum Religionis Mithriacae*, vol. 2 (Amsterdam: Martinus Nijhoff, 1956-60). Reproduced by permission of Kluwer Academic Publishers, Netherlands.

The curious reader must look at the sources and follow out the details which, while strange on first reading, become convincing in accumulation. I have dwelt on this aspect of myth at some length because it has been the most neglected by anthropologists, if it has been paid any heed at all. It is in no way incompatible with other interpretations, since the astronomical significance of the myths was probably never widespread knowledge, and the icons and star lore rapidly degenerated into "myths, legends, and folktales" — and indeed were speeded on their way by the very mythical vehicles in which the lore was preserved. But if, for example, we see the Greeks as the crossroads between the ancient mythical world and the modern scientific one, and the Stoics and Pythagoreans as the first "scientists," then we should remember that both were steeped in the ancient "star lore" that was the basis of their science and the origin of mathematics, astronomy, navigation, and geography. As late as Kepler and Newton, "scientists" were still steeped in this lore, kept alive by the alchemists in the Middle Ages.

Conclusion

It has been stressed throughout that there is no necessary conflict between these various theories of the psychological origins and functions of myth. They are, in effect, different "readings" of the same material, and each has its own validity within its own assumptions and for its own purposes. But the very persistence of the mythological mode of thinking, and its resistance to rationalist onslaughts and refusal to go down in the face of "scientific" alternatives, suggest that we must ask the more ultimate question of its possible adaptive functions in a Darwinian sense. Born of self-consciousness and language, themselves the products of the rapid expansion of the human neocortex over the last 2 million years, yet drawing on phyletically old material in the limbic system — dreams, memory, and emotion — myths are clearly in some way "necessary" to the adaptation and survival of creatures dealing not directly with the world through the immediacy of their senses, but indirectly through the world as their language-consciousness redefines it. We live, in a sense, inside our own heads, and living there with us is the myth material that makes it possible for us to survive and interpret the strange world-as-we-see-it that is peculiar to our species. Myths are, after all, fantasy, and nature knows no fantasy, with the startling exception of one genus, *Homo*. Myths are coterminous with language and consciousness in a way that, for example, logic (a late developer) is not. Myths are a more powerful and satisfying way of apprehending the world than is logic, and, for most people, science. This can be either dangerous or benign, but the truth of it should be the focus of any integrated theory of myth and psychology.

Part Six

Primatology

Introduction to Part Six

Science is tough. The demands it makes on its practitioners are, in a historical sense, very unusual. For a start, it must be objective, replicable, totally open to public scrutiny, and available for refutation. What is more, scientists *must tell the truth all the time* — when doing science, that is. They don't always live up to these demands, lord knows, but in no other field of intellectual endeavor are such demands even made. Yes, we are all supposed to tell the truth, for example, but in science the very enterprise is totally undermined if we do not — scarcely something one could say of law, religion, politics, or literary criticism. Again, the demand for refutability means that a scientist must always present data and results in such a way that they might be refuted. This is not something prelates, theologians, or politicians really understand — nor most practitioners of the humanities. The demands are taxing, and the politics of science — especially "big science" — combined with human (all too human) greed and ambition, mean that results are fudged or even fabricated. But (a) this is true of only a tiny fraction of scientists, and (b) the penalties for this when found out (and it is always found out) are severe beyond the worst nightmares of literary critics.

It is no wonder then that many practitioners of the so-called "social sciences" are in fact unhappy with these demands, and either claim to be doing "soft science," which lets them off the harsher demands, or not to be doing science at all, which allows them to breathe sighs of humanistic relief and go back to peddling opinions and trading in rhetoric. Those of us in anthropology who subscribe to the scientific ethos but who cannot meet the high demands of experimental natural science, nevertheless take comfort from the model of the "observational sciences," where the same basic rules apply — from astronomy through geology to zoology. In fact, in the person of "primatology" we have claimed for ourselves a goodly chunk of one of the observational sciences. Strictly speaking, the study of nonhuman primates is the province of zoology, but the closeness of these primates to the human primate, and their obvious importance in understanding human evolution, has meant that a great deal of impetus for the study of monkeys and apes has come from anthropology.

It is here that "behavioral science" of the human kind has to make its most serious accommodations to "natural science" of the observational kind. (In paleoanthropology, much scientific technology is involved, but I am here talking of the behavioral side.) The anthropologist interested in learning more about primates in order to understand humans better has still to follow the same rules of science as his zoological and biological colleagues who are interested in them for their own sakes. This means, unfortunately, having to stick to the rules of scientific presentation and writing. I say unfortunately because it means that the layman and student, unfamiliar with statistical methods and the accepted way of presenting findings, may be totally put off. But this method of analysis and presentation is necessary if the hard rules of science are to be adhered to. To someone like myself, who is most of the time at the "soft" edge of behavioral science, it can be irksome also. I like to write plain English, and baulk at the jargon. But I have come to respect the need for hewing strictly to the objective and dry language of statistical analysis. For one thing, the very uniformity and impersonality of the presentation helps to ensure unambiguous comparison of results, or to point up areas (as in this study) where such comparison could be improved by sharper analysis. In promoting ready comparability, it means that competing hypotheses can be more easily tested. If every scientist were allowed to "tell the tale" in any old way he chose, the enterprise would rapidly stall on the heap of competing anecdotes, and the cumulative increase in knowledge would never occur. What is more, fudging would become temptingly easy.

The austerity — one might almost say the liturgy — of scientific presentation keeps us and the enterprise honest and egalitarian, as it should be. One hypothesis does not, as in nonscientific circles, win out because it is more plausibly and eloquently argued than the others. It wins out because it "accounts for more of the variance" in an objective, measurable (and replicable) way than its competitors. And not because it is proof against refutation but quite the opposite: because it is vulnerable to disproof in the first place. All hypotheses are equal. Some survive, some don't, and all are always vulnerable. I often tell the story (is this repetition the onset of senility?) of Karl Popper confronted with a distraught student who complained that all his hypotheses seemed to turn out wrong. Popper told him to be pleased. This meant he must be doing science. If all his hypotheses were inevitably correct, he was probably doing metaphysics. Great words from a great man; but we do like a few to come out right, let's face it.

When dealing with primates, we are also under a restraint because, unlike their human counterparts, we cannot talk to them. The only clues we have to their behavior are the observations we make and the correlations we find. Thus, we have to follow the zoological/scientific method in all its pristine impersonality. We cannot simply say some elaborate version of "well it looks to me as if what they are doing is...," even if this is our first approximation and the beginning of hypothesis formation. We have to spell out our observations and correlations with exactitude, tell how we gathered the data and what means we used to interpret it, pay scrupulous attention to comparable findings by other observers, and so on.

I say all this by way of introducing the following "encounter with the primates" since I hesitated to include the piece at first. Primatology is for me an essential part of anthropology as I see it — as will be obvious to anyone who has followed my attempts to introduce and promote evolutionary thinking in the behavioral sciences. To keep myself honest, and to overcome my natural inclination to sit in an armchair and read the work of others rather than get my own hands dirty with data, I have from time to time undertaken some primate studies of varying degrees of rigor, from anecdotal observation to carefully controlled data studies such as this one. (Who was the cynic who said that the plural of anecdote was data?) So I was happy to include some tough primatology here. But nevertheless I saw that the manner of presentation — so necessary, as I have argued, to science itself — might get between the reader and the subject. I have decided to risk it, and to present it with a few prefatory notes to walk the reader through. There is actually quite a bit of "discussion" in this piece — more so than is usual in such articles — so the reader who is willing should be able to make sense of it and perhaps gain a sense of satisfaction from so doing.

The problem addressed concerns a group of stumptail macaques (relatives of the better-known rhesus monkeys) kept in "semi-free-ranging" conditions on a little island off Bermuda. I am not personally crazy about monkeys, and stumptails less than most. People affect to find this astonishing in a primatologist. These are the same irascible little beasts who figured in the aggression studies in chapter 6. But they were there, they had an interesting history, and who can resist Bermuda? The little island in question, sitting in a beautiful bay and guarded by a monster electric eel (it really was) had had a distinguished role in primatology even before the arrival of the macaques, for the great C. R. Carpenter had kept his gibbons there. When I first went, in 1980, there were still extensive rope lines strung between the trees, which he had put there to give his agile apes more brachiating room. The macaque group had been used by a team led by my friend and colleague Dieter Steklis — who recently garnered much public attention for defending gorillas against guerrillas in Rwanda — to do a very neat experiment. The dominant male tended to have favorite females with whom he copulated most, if not exclusively. These were put on contraceptive doses, the same for their body sizes as for a human female on the pill, and the male quickly lost interest in them and turned to the others. Once this reversal was complete, the new favorites were "put on the pill" and the rejected females taken off. The male switched back. The finding was clear-cut, and obviously disturbing in its implications. The popular press picked up on it immediately.

But one professional criticism of it was that it involved only one adult male, whereas the "normal" macaque group would have several competing adult males. Steklis and I looked through the literature and found various discrepancies in findings concerning stumptail sexual behavior. So we decided to try to establish a "baseline" by examining the behavior of our colony, which now had two more adult males — one through maturation and one introduced.

We were particularly concerned to see how sexual behavior of both males and females differed over the different phases of the menstrual cycle. The cycle has three phases — two ends and a middle, as it were. The follicular and the luteal are the beginning and end phases, and the periovular (or ovulatory) is the "midcycle" period, when the female is ovulating and able to conceive. The commonest pattern in primates is for females to become most sexually active (often with genital swellings and scent changes) during midcycle, presenting their genital areas to the males. The more dominant males tend to cluster their copulations during this period — for obvious reasons.

Stumptail macaques, however, seemed to present (no pun intended) an exception to this rule: High-ranking males did not cluster their copulations but copulated at a high level throughout the cycle, and at least in some reports females did not change their sexual soliciting during the cycle either. This had led some commentators to conclude that hormones were not important in determining stumptail sexual behavior. It was this anomalous situation that we set out to resolve by careful measures of all these variables in our group where the animals were relatively free-ranging. This we felt was important and was why we stressed it in the official title of the article. Animals in the wild behave more "naturally" but are not amenable to such procedures as blood sampling or vaginal swabbing, so it is hard to detect exactly what stage of the cycle they are in. Animals in captivity may be easily monitored, but their behavior is less natural, mostly because of overcrowding and lack of natural cover. We felt that our island situation was a nice compromise: the animals could be monitored, but their natural behavior was only minimally interfered with. It led us, as the reader will see, to decide that a combination of hormonal, social, and environmental factors held the answer, and that individual variation was perhaps more important than had been supposed — or rather, had been masked by assumptions about "rank." Of course we could be wrong. And for that reason Popper would be proud of us. The data are there, the methods spelled out, and it is up to any scientist to replicate the study or reanalyze our data and prove us so. That is what science is about.

The only technicality that might otherwise bother the nonstatistical reader is the use of statistical "significance." It is not enough, for example, to find a large correlation, or a big difference, between two averages. We have to know the probability that these are not due to chance in the sample concerned. This is what the intrusive "p" numbers are about: roughly speaking, the lower the "p" the less likely that the result is a fluke. Also, "SE," or the standard error, is often included. This concerns the way numbers are clustered or spread out around an average (r): the greater the spread, the less likely is the difference between the averages to be "significant." This spread is what "SE" measures and what the little lines above the columns on the bar graphs illustrate. (Experts will realize that the verbal description is closer to "SD," the "standard deviation." They will also realize that in a description for the layman the difference is negligible, the standard error being the standard deviation corrected for the size of the sample by the formula $SE = SD/\sqrt{n}$. Believe it or not, in a previous incarnation as a working sociologist, I actually taught "social statistics" to earn my bread and butter. I even helped write an introductory textbook! We all have our little secrets.)

I might add that the way things are presented makes it all look easy and straightforward. It is anything but. What is not recorded here is the amount of preliminary sorting and dog work (over and above the data collection) and the numerous statistical "runs" that got nowhere until we established the variables and parameters that "worked." What you see is the tip of the iceberg of effort. But no one is interested in the stops and starts and abortive tries and frustrations and feelings that one has simply a bunch of random numbers here. For example, we spent ages trying to correlate aggression between females with phases of the cycle, only to discover we had too many categories and too few numbers to be able to reach any conclusions. So this line of enquiry had to be abandoned. (And given the marvels of the computer, we were able to do this at ten times the speed it would have taken in the days when I started statistics with a punch card machine and a slide rule. The computer may not actually help you get the hypotheses right, but it does enable you to discard a lot of rubbish quickly.) But for a flavor of this side of scientific effort, go back to Watson's account of his discovery with Crick of the famous double helix. We're not quite in the same league, I admit, but the majority of the book — in fact, what makes for the tension and the interest — is taken up with their getting nowhere! And if Watson hadn't written about it, all we would have known was the brilliant end result. Science is indeed tough. But to extract even a minor nugget like the one here has a kind of satisfaction in finding out something real about the real world that is worth a dozen brilliant broadsides on conceptual distinctions. Try to share the excitement.

Anne Fox

Stumptail Macaque in Bermuda

16

Sex and the Stumptails
(written with Horst D. Steklis)

Abstract

The sexual behavior and female reproductive cycles of a group of island-dwelling stumptail macaques *Macaca arctoides* were monitored over a six-month period, yielding 530 observation hours and 268 copulations. Compared to nondominant males, the dominant male copulated at a relatively high rate throughout the cycle, but largely with one high-ranking female. The nondominant males copulated most frequently at midcycle. Female presenting was highest at midcycle, but only to the dominant male. Cross-study discrepancies may be due to different observation methods and restricted environmental conditions that mask female-initiated sexual behavior. The more naturalistic setting of this study allowed for a fuller expression of proceptivity. Contrary to some previous conclusions, present findings suggest that both hormonal and socioenvironmental factors influence the patterns of sexual behavior found in stumptail macaque colonies.

Introduction

Previous studies of sexual behavior among captive *Macaca arctoides* have revealed a sharp difference between colonies where the dominant male(s) shows no peak of sexual activity during the periovular phase (Nieuwenhuijsen et al. 1986) and those where a significant between-phase difference in activity is found, with the periovular showing the highest levels (Harvey 1983; Murray et al. 1985). These studies also show a difference between the behavior of high- and low-ranking males. In the study by Nieuwenhuijsen et al. (1986), the alpha male showed no significant variation in sexual activity between phases of the cycle, while the nonalpha males showed a marked increase in the periovular phase. In contrast, Murray et al. (1985) showed no such phase difference for the low-ranking males. Harvey (1983) did not take male dominance rank into account. However, Harvey did find that sexual presenting to males had a significant periovular peak, whereas Nieuwenhuijsen et al. (1986) again found phase to have no effect on presentation rates. Murray et al. (1985) found no significant phase-related variability in total female sexual behavior, but they did not report separately on presenting.

Thus, the studies of Nieuwenhuijsen et al. (1986, table 1, p. 166) not only claim a marked difference between stumptail macaque sexual behavior and that of most other ground-dwelling monkeys and apes, but also are at variance with other studies of the same species. Some of these differences may stem from different study methods, from different captive conditions, and/or from different assumptions about which variables are important in the mediation of sexual behavior of stumptails. However, the finding by Murray et al. (1985), that cycling females engaged in more sexual behavior than noncycling females, suggests that ovarian hormones play a major role in the mediation of sexual behavior in this species.

In our previous studies of a semi-free-ranging island group of stumptail macaques (Steklis et al. 1983), we concluded that, in this species as in others, hormonal factors interact with socioenvironmental variables in the expression of sociosexual behaviors. This is a conclusion also reached by Estep (1987) in a recent review of stumptail macaque sexual behavior. Specifically, Estep hypothesizes that cyclical variation in female sexual initiative may not be apparent in captive groups with restricted space, where the females may be unable to control sexual access to males. Alternatively, Estep suggests that even under natural conditions females may rarely demonstrate sexual initiative because they are overpowered by the more aggressive dominant males. Therefore, the present study examined cyclical variation in sexual behavior in a semi-free-ranging island setting that, unlike previous studies, allows greater opportunity for female control of sexual access to males. In this setting, the opportunities for social distancing and concealment provided by the natural terrain enable females to exercise a greater control over the initiation of sexual behavior than is possible in cages or enclosures, however large.

Methods

Subjects and Facilities

This study was carried out between January and August 1981 at the C. R. Carpenter Primate Center, a 0.70-hectare island facility in Bermuda (see Esser et al. 1979 for further details). Animals ranged freely on the island, which had trees, rocky outcrops, cliffs for shelter and refuge, and vegetation for foraging. The study group, which was established in 1978, comprised three adult males and nine adult females (table 16.1). At the beginning of this study, the age of the females ranged from 4.5 to 14.5 years, and that of the males from 4 to 13 years. All subjects, except for one adult male (no. 15) introduced in early December 1980, had been used in previous studies (O'Keefe et al. 1983; Steklis et al. 1983). All subjects had lived previously in social colonies. All males had been vasectomized, and all females had been drug-free for at least one year prior to the onset of this study. The cause of death of male number 15 is unknown.

Table 16.1.
Composition of the Colony, 1981

Subject No.	Sex	Origin	Comments
3	M	Captive	Oldest male
2	M	Captive	Youngest male
15	M	Captive	Died in 10th week of study
9	F	Feral	Mother of 10, 13, 14
14	F	Captive	Daughters of female 9 in order
10	F	Captive	of birth
13	F	Captive	
5	F	Feral	Lived in zoo cage with 3, 2 and 7
6	F	Feral	for 3 months
7	F	Captive	Youngest female
8	F	Feral	Oldest females
11	F	Feral	

Natural forage was supplemented daily with Purina Monkey Chow and fresh fruit. Water was freely available.

Menstrual Cycles

Menstrual cycles were monitored by detecting the onset of menses through daily vaginal swabbing, which in this species has proved to be a reliable procedure (Harvey 1983; Murray et al. 1985). Prior to the study's onset, females were trained (with food reward) to present their hindquarters at the observer's approach and permit the momentary insertion of a moistened cotton swab. This was successful in every case and afforded minimal interference with normal behavior. Following the criterion of Murray et al. (1985), only menstrual cycles ranging from twenty-five to thirty-four days in length were considered regular and were included in the analysis of phase-related behavior. Females with more than 50 percent irregular cycles were excluded from phase-related behavior analysis. This yielded a total of thirty-two regular cycles from six females, with an overall mean (±1 SE) cycle length of 29.0 ±0.37 days. Again following the procedure of Murray et al. (1985), cycles were divided, counting back from onset of menses, into follicular (days 20+), periovular (days 15-19), and luteal (days 14-1) phases.

Behavior Recording

All behavior observations were made by one observer, on an average of six days per week. Two primary methods of recording were used. One was a focal-male technique, consisting of 0.75 to 1.5 hours of observation per male per day, during which all male-female social and sexual interactions were recorded. This observation period was divided into three equal segments per male that were distributed over the course of the day. Males were observed in a random sequence. As a measure of male-female association independent of sexual behavior, at the beginning of each segment all females in proximity of the focal male were recorded. The focal-male procedure yielded a total of 450 hours of observation. In addition, all occurrences of copulation were recorded.

The second technique involved recording all occurrences of agonistic behavior interaction for all subjects during two half-hour blocks, one in the morning and one in the afternoon each day, for a total of 180 hours.

The following behaviors, based on Bertrand's (1969) ethogram for this species, were used in the present analysis.

Copulation: Mounting followed by intromission, pelvic thrusting, and ejaculation.

Sexual Inspection: Manual and/or nasal-oral inspection of female genitalia by the male.

Presenting: Spontaneous directing of the female's perineal region to the male. Presenting in response to male threat or physical contact was excluded.

Proximity: At rest within one meter of the focal male.

Male dominance rank was established by proportional directionality of aggressive and submissive interactions. Female dominance rank was determined according to the "dominance index" developed by Zumpe and Michael (1986), which yields ordinal ranks based on the direction of aggressive and submissive behaviors between all possible pairs of animals.

Data Analysis

All behavior data are expressed as rates per hour of observation. Rates of copulation were derived by dividing the frequency observed by the total hours of observation per day. For the analysis of phase-related behavior, a mean rate per phase day per female was calculated. These means were compared among the three phases of the menstrual cycle using a repeated-measures design, mixed-model univariate ANOVA procedure, with phase as the repeated measure. Where homogeneity of variance criteria were not met, data were log-transformed prior to analysis. In tests where variation among phases was significant, post hoc comparisons among phase means used the Wilcoxon statistic for related samples. All other group comparisons utilized the Mann-Whitney U test.

Results

Dominance Rank

The observed pattern of aggressive and submissive interactions among adult males consistently distinguished a dominant male from two nondominant males. One male (no. 3) directed aggression (rate per hour, 0.49) toward both of the other two males (nos. 2 and 15), whereas they directed no aggression toward him. The directionality of submissive behavior was similarly asymmetric, with number 3 submitting to numbers 2 and 15 at a rate per hour of 0.19 and receiving submission at a rate per hour of 1.3. Because of the short tenure of number 15 in the group, no attempt was made to rank the two nondominant males relative to each other.

The dominance index revealed a linear rank order for the nine females. The four related females were highest-ranking in the group as follows, in descending order of rank (dominance index in parentheses): number 14 (98), number 9 (83), number 13 (79), and number 10 (64). The remaining five females were ranked in order below these four as follows: number 8 (48), number 11 (39), number 5 (22), number 6 (16), and number 7 (1).

Dominance Rank and Behavior

The dominant male accounted for the majority of copulations of the group. Of a total of 268 copulations, male number 3 was responsible for 78 percent. Male number 15 was observed to engage in only five copulations during his ten weeks in the study.

There was a marginally significant relationship between mean female copulation rate and dominance rank (Spearman rank order correlation coefficient, $r = .52$, $p = .08$, one-tailed). However, it should be noted that female number 13 (third in dominance rank) accounted for 71 percent of the total copulations, all of which were with the dominant male, while female number 9, second in dominance rank, had the third-lowest rate of copulation.

To examine further differences between high- and low-ranking females, we divided the nine females into a high-ranking (nos. 14, 9, 13, and 10) and a

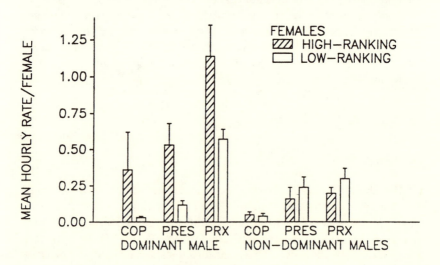

Figure 16.1
Mean (± 1 SE) hourly rate per female of copulation (cop) received from and presenting (pres) and proximity (prx) to the dominant and nondominant males by high- and low-ranking females.

low-ranking (nos. 8, 11, 5, 6, and 7) group. High-ranking females received higher mean rates (per hour per female) of total male-initiated sexual behavior (p = 0.3, Mann-Whitney U). However, this difference was accounted for largely by behavior involving the dominant male, in that the two groups differed significantly only on measures directed to and received from the dominant male (figure 16.1) — namely, copulation by the dominant male (p = .04, Mann-Whitney U, one-tailed) and presenting to the dominant male (p = .01, Mann-Whitney U). High-ranking females also received higher rates of sexual inspection from the dominant male, but this measure was not independent of copulation (Pearson's r = .96). These differences between high- and low-ranking females in sexual behavior were paralleled by differences in proximity to the dominant male, which was independent of copulation (Pearson's r = .29) (figure 16.1): High-ranking females were in proximity to the dominant male more often than were low-ranking females (p = .03, Mann-Whitney U).

Regularly vs. Irregularly Cycling Females

Six of the females (nos. 14, 9, 13, 10, 6, and 7) were considered as regularly cycling, and three (nos. 5, 8, and 11) as irregularly cycling. Total sexual interactions (i.e., both initiated and received) were higher for regularly than irregularly cycling females; mean rates per female (±1 SE) were 1.21 ±0.30 vs. 0.50 ±0.14, respectively (p = .04, df = 7, Mann-Whitney U). Since all subsequent analysis is concerned with the relationship of menstrual cycle phase to sexual behavior, irregularly cycling females are excluded.

Sexual Behavior and Cycle Phase

For the six regularly cycling females, ANOVA showed a significant phase effect for copulation with all males [F(2, 10) = 4.06, p = .05] and presenting to all males [F(2, 10) = 7.58, p = .01]. Periovular rates of copulation and presenting were higher than both follicular (copulation, p = .07; presenting, p = .03; Wilcoxon) and luteal rates (copulation, p = .07; presenting, p = .03; Wilcoxon). However, separate analysis for dominant vs. nondominant males revealed significant phase effects only for copulation with nondominant males [F(2, 10) = 4.89, p = .03] and presenting to the dominant male [F(2, 10) = 5.12, p = .03], with periovular phase rates consistently higher than either follicular rates (copulation, p = .07; presenting, p = .03; Wilcoxon) or luteal rates (copulation, p = .07; presenting, p = .03; Wilcoxon) (figures 16.2 and 16.3).

To examine the effect of female dominance rank on phase-related behavior, the six cycling females were divided into a high-ranking group

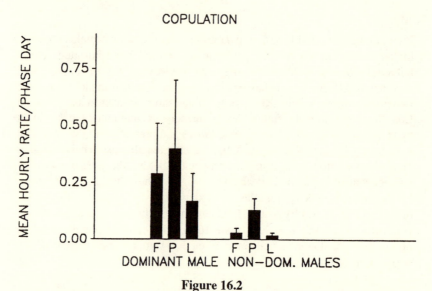

COPULATION

Figure 16.2

Mean (±1 SE) hourly rate per menstrual-cycle phase day of copulation initiated by the dominant and nondominant males during follicular (F), periovular (P), and luteal (L) phases.

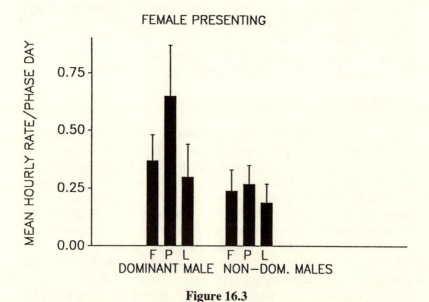

FEMALE PRESENTING

Figure 16.3

Mean (±1 SE) hourly rate per menstrual-cycle phase day of female presenting to the dominant and nondominant males during follicular (F), periovular (P), and luteal (L) phases.

(females nos. 14, 13, and 9) and a low-ranking group (females nos. 10, 6, and 7). Two-way ANOVA (phase x rank) did not produce any significant phase x rank interactions for any of the behavioral variables.

The rate per hour per day of "present" and "copulation" by phase for each female is shown in table 16.2. There was considerable variation among females in rate of sexual behavior. Thus, while there is an overall phase effect for "copulation with nondominant males," two females, numbers 13 and 7, had no sexual activity with the nondominant males. In the category "copulation with dominant male," female number 13 is disproportionately represented, again female number 7 had no copulations, and female number 9 had none during two of her phases. Only in the category "present to dominant male" was there consistent activity by all females in all phases, with a persistent trend toward a periovular peak. Overall, table 16.2 shows that the majority of sexual interactions involved the dominant male and the three sisters (nos. 14, 13, and 10).

Discussion

The main purpose of this study was to examine the influence of menstrual-cycle phase on male and female sexual behavior. Comparable to the results of a number of previous studies, male copulation and female presenting occurred more frequently during the periovular phase, although this pattern depended on male dominance rank.

Male Rank and Female Cyclicity

For the dominant male (no. 3), the pattern of copulation was one of a continuously high level throughout the menstrual cycle. While his mean rate of copulation did not vary significantly between phases, it tended to be higher at midcycle and lower during the luteal phase. For the nondominant males, on the other hand, there was a significant increase in copulation during the periovular phase. Nieuwenhuijsen et al. (1986) did not find a periovular copulation peak in their dominant male; however, their overall pattern of copulation by the dominant and nondominant males was comparable to the one found in this study. Our pattern of male copulation does not parallel the pattern found by Murray et al. (1985), which consisted of a significant periovular peak for dominant (N = 4) males only. However, because Murray et al. did not separate a single dominant male, their results are difficult to compare to ours or to those of Nieuwenhuijsen et al. (1986).

Studies of captive stumptail groups indicate that the alpha male monopolizes copulations regardless of the number of other males in the group (Estep et al. 1988). For example, Harvey (1983) reported that the alpha male

Female[a]	Dominant male			Nondominant males			Copulation Dominant male			Nondominant males		
	F	P	L	F	P	L	F	P	L	F	P	L
14	0.55 ±0.22 (39)	0.72 ±0.24 (27)	0.14 ±0.05 (66)	0.08 ±0.05	0.37 ±0.18	0.11 ±0.04	0.17 ±0.14	0.27 ±0.17	0.09 ±0.06	0.02 ±0.02	0.30 ±0.16	0.03 ±.02
9	0.26 ±0.08 (39)	0.38 ±0.17 (26)	0.36 ±0.09 (72)	0.12 ±0.05	0.08 ±0.06	0.10 ±0.04	0	0	0.06 ±0.04	0.05 ±0.04	0.08 ±0.04	0.02 ±0.02
13	0.77 ±0.20 (33)	1.53 ±0.37 (17)	0.96 ±0.21 (53)	0	0	0	1.37 ±0.46	1.88 ±0.77	0.78 ±0.23	0	0	0
10	0.46 ±0.22 (26)	0.97 ±0.41 (11)	0.18 ±0.11 (30)	0.46 ±0.18	0.24 ±0.10	0.38 ±0.16	0.20 ±0.14	0.12 ±0.12	0.04 ±0.04	0.10 ±0.06	0.18 ±0.13	0.04 ±0.03
6	0.06 ±0.04 (46)	0.18 ±0.13 (22)	0.08 ±0.06 (50)	0.27 ±0.08	0.42 ±0.17	0.05 ±0.03	0	0.12 ±0.12	0.04 ±0.04	0	0.24 ±0.13	0.04 ±0.03
7	0.12 ±0.06 (40)	0.14 ±0.10 (14)	0.08 ±0.04 (44)	0.52 ±0.16	0.52 ±0.29	0.51 ±0.12	0	0	0	0	0	0
Total	0.37 ±0.11	0.65[b] ±0.22	0.30 ±0.14	0.24 ±0.09	0.27 ±0.08	0.19 ±0.08	0.29 ±0.22	0.40 ±0.30	0.17 ±0.12	0.03 ±0.02	0.13[b] ±0.05	0.02 ±0.01

[a] Females are listed in descending order of dominance rank.
[b] Periovular (P) > follicular (F) and luteal (L) phases.

Table 16.2. Mean (±SE) Rate per Hour per Phase Day of "Present" and "Copulation" by Menstrual-Cycle Phase for Individual Females (Number of Phase Days in Parentheses)

accounted for 75 percent of copulations in a group of seven adult males. While she found a significant periovular peak for total male sexual activity, she did not analyze separately the phase-related behavior of the alpha male. In our study, combining all male copulations similarly yielded a significant periovular peak, but as in the study by Nieuwenhuijsen et al. (1986) with eighteen adult males, this peak was accounted for largely by the nondominant males.

Our results, as well as those of Nieuwenhuijsen et al. (1986), suggest rank-related reproductive strategies for stumptail males. A single dominant male, regardless of the number of males in the group, exhibits a pattern of continuous sexual activity across cycle phases. The nondominant males, on the other hand, having less access to females, copulate predominantly during the periovular phase, at a much lower overall rate of copulation. Either strategy would maximize the probability of inseminating females. The dominant male's strategy, however, could be seen as an expression of dominance in itself; i.e., he is able to copulate *ad libitum*, without regard to cycle phase.

Female Sexual Behavior

In the present study, female dominance rank was related to differences in mean rates of sexual behaviors initiated to and received from males, as well as in proximity to the dominant male. As a group, high-ranking females generally initiated and received more sexual behavior than low-ranking females. Nonetheless, there were pronounced individual differences. In particular, one female (no. 13) engaged in sexual activity exclusively with the dominant male (no. 3), and this pair's copulation accounted for 71 percent of the total. This is similar to the situation described by Harvey (1983), in which one female accounted for 61 percent of the completed copulations. In both our group and Harvey's, this highly preferred female was third in female dominance rank. In combination with the results on proximity, this suggests a pattern among stumptails of a mutual sociosexual preference between the dominant male and one of the higher-ranking females. This same pattern has been described for female rhesus monkeys by Zumpe and Michael (1987), who argue that preferential access of dominant females to males may be a form of mate competition.

Our results for overall female presenting agree with those of Harvey (1983), who found a clear midcycle peak in this behavior. However, in the present study, females showed a marked periovular peak in presenting only to the dominant male. Harvey (1983) did not examine phase-related presenting by females to males of different dominance rank. Her most dominant male accounted for 58 percent of all "presents" received, a figure comparable to the 55 percent of all presents received by our dominant male. It is therefore possible that the effect of phase on presenting in her study, as in ours, is dependent on male rank. Contrary to our findings on female presenting, Nieuwenhuijsen et al. (1986) and Murray et al. (1985) found no significant variation by phase for female-initiated sexual activity with either dominant or nondominant males. However, the results of Murray et al. (1985) are difficult to compare to ours, since their study did not report separately on female presenting and did not distinguish an alpha male from other males. The difference in the effect of phase on female presenting between our study and that of Nieuwenhuijsen et al. suggests that, in keeping with Estep's (1987) hypothesis, under more natural conditions females may have more control over sexual initiative.

Female Cyclicity, Rank, and Individual Differences

As in the study by Murray et al. (1985), irregularly cycling females engaged in significantly less total sexual activity than regularly cycling females. In a social group of *Macaca fascicularis*, Adams et al. (1985) found that low-ranking females had fewer fertile ovulatory cycles than high-ranking females. As Adams et al. used physiological measures to determine ovarian activity, our results do not lend themselves to direct comparison. Nevertheless, in our group there was an overall relationship between dominance rank and number of irregular cycles ($r = .45$), as defined by cycle length: high-ranking females had a lower percentage (range, 0-33 percent; mean, 19 percent; N = 4) of irregular cycles than low-ranking females (range, 29-100 percent; mean, 54 percent; N = 5).

Despite these differences that were found when females were grouped, not all regularly cycling females showed uniformly higher levels of sexual behavior than irregularly cycling females. Thus, two of the regularly cycling females engaged in levels of sexual activity as low as those of irregularly cycling females. Female number 9, the second-oldest female, while ranked second in dominance, had the third-lowest mean rate of copulation (table 16.2). Female number 7, the youngest in the group (and possibly related to male number 3), received no copulations. Since both these females presented to males at rates comparable to the other regularly cycling females (table 16.2), it may be that, in addition to dominance rank and reproductive condition, age (at either extreme) affects female attractiveness. The fact that three years previous to the onset of this study female number 9 had the second-highest rate of copulation with male number 3 (Steklis et al. 1983) is in keeping with the possibility that her increased age, despite her normal cycling, lowered her attractiveness.

These considerations lead us to conclude that a mechanical division of animals into "high-ranking" and "low-ranking," while producing statistical results, may mask considerable individual differences, which are determined by a constellation of factors other than rank. We have already seen that Murray et al. (1985), for example, divided their males this way (four high-ranking, four low-ranking), thus possibly masking disproportionate behavioral contributions of one dominant male like those found by us and by Nieuwenhuijsen et al. (1986). In our study, discrepancies are found between female rank and copulation rate (for females nos. 9 and 7, noted above), and dividing the six cycling females into high-ranking (nos. 14, 13, and 9) and low-ranking (nos. 10, 6, and 7) animals results in similar anomalies. Female number 9, in the high-ranking group, was relatively unsuccessful at copulations, while the low-ranking female number 10 evinces a sexual activity profile more like that of her two sisters, 14 and 13, than like that of either female number 9 or the other two low-ranking females.

Several factors, then, such as absolute and relative age, kinship, hormonal status, and reproductive status, interact with dominance rank. What is more, these variables change over time, as seen in the decline of female number 9 from a preferred copulatory position with the dominant male. In the 1978-79

Table 16.3.
Dominance Rank, Copulation Rank, Cycling and Age for
All Nine Females (1981 and 1979[a])

Female	Dominance rank 1981	(1979)	Regular cycling 1981	Age 1981	Copulation rank (all males) 1981	(1979)
9	2	(2)	Yes	12.5	7	(2)
14	1	(1)	Yes	8.0	2	(1)
13	3	(3)	Yes	6.2	1	(3)
10	4	(4)	Yes	7.2	3	(4)
8	5	(6)	No	14.5	8	(b)
11	6	(5)	No	14.5	6	(4)
5	7	(8)	No	6.0	4	(6)
6	8	(7)	Yes	7.0	5	(5
7	9	(9)	Yes	4.5	9	(c)

(a) From Steklis et al. 1983.
(b) Lactating in 1979.
(c) Sexually immature in 1979.

study, number 14 was the preferred female, with number 9 second and number 13 third (Steklis et al. 1983). Thus, the copulation rank changes over time, with aging obviously an important but not necessarily a determinative factor. Table 16.3 illustrates the most rational division of females in 1981, taking these diachronic factors into account.

Conclusions

Nieuwenhuijsen et al. (1986) concluded, from data very similar to ours, that sexual behavior in stumptails was "less hormone dependent" and "more dependent on social factors" than in other species. However, what our study and other studies seem to show is that in stumptails, as well as in other species of monkeys and apes, such behavior is more effectively explained, not by such stark dichotomies but in terms of the *interaction* between socioenvironmental factors and hormonal states, *with variable outcomes* (Steklis et al. 1983; Nadler et al. 1986; Eberhart 1988). Thus, in our colony of stumptail macaques, ovarian hormones do influence female attractivity and proceptivity, as indicated by periovular peaks in copulation and presenting; however, the expression of these phase-linked behaviors is dependent on dominance rank, as well as on female age and reproductive condition. Furthermore, the finding of this study and that by Murray et al. (1985), that irregularly cycling females engage in less sexual activity than regularly cycling females, indicates a significant influence of ovarian hormones on sexual behavior.

More importantly, as suggested by Estep (1987), environmental conditions do appear to influence the expression of sexual behavior in relation to hormonal conditions. Thus, we found a pattern of *male* behavior consistent with that reported by Nieuwenhuijsen et al. (1986) and a pattern of *female*-initiated behavior consistent with that found by Harvey (1983), both in enclosure studies. The more naturalistic setting of our study might well have allowed greater female initiative, while not suppressing what seems to be a basic pattern of stumptail male behavior, thus allowing us to reconcile seemingly incompatible findings.

Part Seven

Ideologies

Introduction to Part Seven

This is a little grab bag of items to round off the current encounters. All have their roots in previous encounters, like most things in this book. "Sumus Ergo Cogitamus," to start with. I thought this title was intelligible, but then my track record on intelligible titles isn't so hot, and I forget that we live in a de-Latinified culture (even if it is becoming more and more Latinofied). Descartes said "Cogito ergo sum," which is "I think therefore I am." I switched it to "We are, therefore we think." Thinking, in other words, is a product of our evolution as a species (hence the switch to the plural), just like everything else, and should be studied as such. This piece, which comes from the book *Neonate Cognition* already mentioned (itself a result of a conference at Rockefeller University that Jacques Mehler and I organized for the Harry Frank Guggenheim Foundation), could then have gone in part 5, except that its disquisition on the Western Intellectual Tradition's resistance to doctrines of the innate is also appropriately linked to the main theme of *The Search for Society* and so serves as a useful introduction to that line of thinking.

In *Encounter with Anthropology*, I put Marx (and Engels, of course) in the pantheon of the social science greats along with Darwin, Freud, and Lévi-Strauss, and while in *Red Lamp* I drew heavily on the last three, I went lightly on Marx. Recent events have had a dampening effect on Marxist scholarship, although the wits are saying that the only unreconstructed Marxists left in the world are on American campuses. But as I was moved here to suggest, we may be jumping the gun. What I do not go on to say, but what I said at the end of *Encounter with Anthropology* and still believe, is that the class struggle has moved on to the international scene, and that the showdown when it comes may be between the combined third and fourth worlds and the first (and perhaps second, now that it has so enthusiastically joined the first). The Gulf War may just be the first shot in that desperate conflict which is not going to go away while populations increase at their present rate (and there is no sign of their slowing down). One reason Marxist forecasts got derailed in the affluent world was that affluence bought off the proletariat, and continues to do so. But those huge "external proletariats" (to borrow a phrase from Toynbee) are sitting just outside the walls, hungry, desperate, and waiting to storm the gates. The United States has met the first wave — from Latin America, the Caribbean, and Asia. Europe is meeting its destiny now, and not liking it any better. For the moment the situation just holds because the influx helps make up for the declining birth rates in the affluent countries. But this won't be the case for long, and you can't put Great Walls around whole continents. (Why am I so vividly reminded of *Night of the Living Dead*?) I won't be around to see the results, and I derive no comfort from having said, "I told you so."

The piece provoked the expected responses from the expatriate anti-Marxist community, but I was most surprised by the resurgence of Leninism it brought to light. Many critics who didn't dispute my point about Marx nevertheless took mighty umbrage at my accusation that Lenin was the true father of Stalinist tyranny. I thought this was fairly obvious and uncontroversial, but not so. Apparently now that Marx (with Engels) has gone down for the count, there is a need to replace him with some other communist father figure who is still believable. Thus, Lenin must be absolved of any Stalinist connection. If only the Soviet Union had followed Lenin, and not been sidetracked by Stalin, the argument goes, there would have been no totalitarianism, no gulags, no KGB, no colonization of eastern Europe, etc. Maybe. I'm sceptical, but since it doesn't affect my argument one way or the other, I will leave it to the revisionists to hash out.

The Browning piece I put in because it was there, because it was left out of *Reproduction and Succession*, and because the reader deserves a change of pace. I have files crammed with pieces I have written for amusement and don't really know what to do with. So I snuck this one in. Enjoy. People ask me how, given my overall pessimism, I can possibly enjoy Browning, the spokesman of all that is optimistic. I think this is a very superficial view of Browning. His "official" philosophy might have been optimistic: as that dreadful Pollyanna-before-her-time Pippa warbles, "God's in his heaven/ All's right with the world" — or the harpist David carries on about "How good is man's life the mere living, how fit to employ/ All the heart and the soul and the senses forever in joy." But when it came to the examination of human nature, Browning saw it as basically weak or grotesque, and his "heroes" are always, after all, people who tried and failed, from Paracelsus through Sordello to Prince Hohenstiel-Schwangau (a thinly disguised Napoleon III). That our reach should exceed our grasp is the best we can hope for; that we should be the "high man" of the Grammarian's Funeral who aims for a million and misses a unit is a triumph! I don't find this a wildly optimistic picture of the human condition; but I do find it sympathetic. It was Kurt Vonnegut who had his own sad hero choose as his lapidary epitaph, "Here lies Kilgore Trout. He Tried."

The Teddy Bears' Picnic speaks up well enough for itself. It nicely rounds off my encounters with anthropology, and in taking us back to the theme of the prologue acts as an epilogue for the book, even managing to end on an up note (albeit seeing nothing but chaos and old night in the immediate future). But in case you think I am unduly alarmist about the state of things, let me relate a story I heard recently from a horrified mathematician. It happened, as these things do, in the extreme extension of a country of extremes — California — where anthropology textbooks on the American Indian were up for "adoption." Those being considered started with the obvious: that present evidence from archaeology suggests that the ancestors of the American Indians came across the Bering land bridge from Asia in a series of waves. There was evidently violent objection to this from the "multiculturalists," who insisted that this was a white male Eurocentric proposition and was at variance with the Native American accounts of their origins which had them here all the time — coming up through reeds from several underworlds, being pulled from the waters by earth diver, etc. Why, the objectors asked, since there are no objective canons of truth, should the eurocentricwhitemale version be "privileged" over that of the Natives? They won. The offending texts were disqualified. A motion was passed to admit in future only texts giving the Native version. (All rather silly since some Native Americans accept with pride an — albeit highly dubious — account of their trek across the continent from the Bering Straits: The *Walan Olum.*)

I'm not going to comment. This kind of thing is happening everywhere, not just in the lunatic extremes we have come almost affectionately to expect from California (as long as they are not exported). It goes along with things like "feminist science" — which never turns out to be anything but a series of complaints about male-centered metaphors in normal science and especially its popularization. (These people do not seem able to get the difference between bias in the *practice* of science, and the truth claims of scientific statements regardless of any bias in the practice.) It scares me a bit since it sounds — along with "black history" and such — shockingly like the Nazi insistence on separating "Jewish science" from "German/Aryan science" and

338 The Challenge of Anthropology

the like, with all its gory consequences. Science may be imperfect in its metaphors and its practice, but in the end there is no "Marxist science" as opposed to "bourgeois science" or any other ethnic or ideological sciences *as regards the truths of science itself.* The truth of the second law of thermodynamics (to borrow Lord Snow's famous example) does not depend on its racial or sexual provenance or the metaphors used to popularize it. If we lose our grasp of this, then we are truly lost as badly as the Nazis were lost, and we are in serious danger of picking up some of their bad habits.

Let me stress that I, no more than current philosophers, believe in an absolute truth "out there in the world," waiting to be discovered. "Truth" is the result of an interaction between the observer and the world; what matter are the rules for that interaction. The Teddy Bear piece will comment on all this. But I shudder for the coming generation, which will have to sort out this mess, if it gets a chance before the dissolution hitting the old communist empires sweeps across the West; a West which is not, as it seems to think, a triumphant observer, but part of the same phenomenon. Glasnost and perestroika started it over there, but they were simply an acceptance of what was already happening (in Poland, for example). Deconstruction, interpretationism, multiculturalism, feminism, diversity, critical theory, empowerment, postmodernism, and the rest, are simply names for the same kind of cultural dissolution that is taking place in the West. When a civilization loses its sense of itself, when its collective nerve fails, when it no longer knows what to teach its young, then disintegration is not far behind. This is bigger than anthropology, but anthropology has become part of the problem, when I wanted it to be part of the solution. Take it from here, next generation, and good luck.

There is one point where I perhaps need to back off a bit. My friend and very good critic, Dudley Young, thought I was too harsh on the literary critics, some of whom (from Mathew Arnold on, at least) offer us insight and even elevation. Absolutely agreed. It didn't occur to me that this would be an issue. To argue that Lit. Crit. has a constant crisis of authority which in turn leads some of its practitioners into weird behavior and ideas, does not mean that some literary criticism is not brilliant, insightful, enhancing, and sometimes even right. From reading Wilson Knight on Shakespeare as a teenager, through Francis Fergusson on theatre as a graduate student, to Camille Paglia on Decadence just last week (she likes Wilson Knight, too) I am very often truly transformed and see the world differently. This work of the literary critics may all be, when it comes down to it, "opinion." And this fact may provoke the crisis of authority I go on about. But it is truly (like Dudley Young on Yeats, for example — appeasement obvious here) very often superior and enlightened opinion, and we can all benefit from it. But at the same time I stick to my guns. It *is* opinion in the last analysis, and such authority as it has comes from its cogency and persuasiveness and scholarship and from nowhere else. And this is fine, until it gets delusions of epistemological grandeur and insists, illogically, that the only authority lies with those who deny any basis for authority — or something such.

I can't resist sticking in here my favorite aphorism, which appears in the postprologue of the second edition of *Encounter with Anthropology*. Once you've read Teddy Bears you will appreciate it. "If it looks like a duck, and walks like a duck, and quacks like a duck, it's a social construction of a duck." Think of this as an epigraph to the chapter.

17

Sumus Ergo Cogitamus: Cognitive Science and the Western Intellectual Tradition

The Harry Frank Guggenheim Foundation was instructed by its founder to pursue the scientific investigation of the relations among violence, aggression, and dominance — or "man's tendency to wish to dominate his fellows," as he put it. He saw this tendency, rather than more parochial causes, as lying behind man's proneness to violence, although he recognized that "dominance can serve many masters," and urged the examination of ideology — particularly religious ideology — in relation to man's violent tendencies.

In carrying out this mandate, the Foundation has not focused narrowly on studies of violence and dominance per se, but has sought to place these in their wider context. In examining human aggression and violence, for example, one cannot ignore the cognitive dimension. Animal studies can tell us a great deal about some of the mechanisms of aggression, for example, but in the case of human aggression it is the specifically human cognitive apparatus that is called into play to monitor and channel these mechanisms. Insofar as this apparatus has certain species-specific peculiarities, these must be examined. And it most surely has. If nothing else, language and self-awareness, the use of symbols, and the possibility of conscious reflection all affect the etiology and manifestation of violence. Perceptions and definitions of dominance also can be crucial variables. We have, therefore, encouraged studies of these interactions, but also studies of fundamental cognitive and neurobiological factors in themselves, insofar as we felt these were necessary to a general understanding of the role of cognition in behavior, and in particular to its role in understanding violence.

In doing this, we do not see ourselves as deviating from our view of man as the end product of evolution. On the contrary, the cognitive apparatus of man, although more complex than that of other animals, evolved by the same mechanisms of mutation and selection. Man's conscious and cultural abilities, the flexibility of his learning mechanisms, are ultimately the products of the same evolutionary process, the physical traces of which are the brain and central nervous system. The organism is the living memory of its evolution.

Investigation of these cognitive processes as evolutionary products has been hampered by a number of factors, not least the lack of information about the evolution of the body's soft parts. But it has also been retarded because of the intellectual hostility to the whole idea of the innate. In our work at the Foundation, we have tried to operationalize some of the issues raised by the question of innate abilities or propensities, but we are aware that this runs counter to intellectual fashion. The intellectual establishment does not want the issues operationalized; it does not even want them raised! Thus, this book, rather than being what it should be — a straightforward contribution to the examination of the cognitive abilities of newborns and infants — will be seen as a challenge to established "truth." No doubt in ten years this will be different, but in the meantime it deserves some examination, because it goes to the heart of the current debate on the future of the behavioral sciences.

The issue can be traced back, as can most things, to Greek philosophy, but it starts effectively at the Renaissance with the general claims of humanism versus religious dogma. By the time Bacon came to formulate the scientific method (essentially simple induction), the opposing parties were in place. On one side stood religion with its doctrine of original sin, and on the other stood science with its doctrine of the *tabula rasa*. It should be immediately noted that this was *not* a necessary opposition. One could oppose the doctrine of original sin by a doctrine of original-something-else, as Rousseau eventually did with his doctrine of innate goodness. But in the late seventeenth century, the battle lines became thus drawn because the inductive scientists wished to oppose not only sin as innate, but *ideas* as innate. And their reasons were not simply scientific. Locke, for example, insisted that the doctrine of innate ideas was grist for the tyrant's mill because he could always claim that, for example, deference to rulers was "innate" and so ineradicable. A tyrant could "claim for an innate principle that which would serve his purpose." The church could use "innate" or original sin in the same way: Inevitable sinners must be subject to church discipline. So it was that "science" became equated with induction and the opposition to "innate ideas," on the one hand, and with a liberal and democratic stance politically in opposition to monarchy and church.

As we have seen, it would have been just as possible to oppose one set of claimed innate ideas with another set, based on "scientific" investigation. But at the time this was not seen as an alternative. The church and reaction had claimed "the innate," so science, democracy, and progress had to embrace a rugged Empiricism. Particularly in British thought, these three were considered coterminous, and Empiricism dominated to the point of obliterating "subjectivism" as scientifically unthinkable. "There is nothing in the mind that was not first in the senses" became the first premise of science *and* politics, and the connection was seen as a necessary one.

It is usual to link Kant and Rousseau, since both represented a protest against this extreme position. Rousseau, as we have seen, certainly believed in innate features — namely, goodness and equality — that society had corrupted. Thus he showed how a *revolutionary* position could be derived from a doctrine of the innate. Kant, more subtly, showed that, whereas the *content* of ideas might be learned, the "categories of the understanding" — the mental schema that ordered these ideas — was not. Kant was thus the true beginning of the "interactionist" position that most sensible scientists now embrace. They ask not whether ideas or behavior are *either* innate *or* learned, but how the two aspects interact.

We have slipped in "behavior" here, but it should be noted that this came later. The original debate was about ideas. Even proponents of the *tabula rasa* had some, albeit hazy, notions of "human nature" — but these did not matter. Even if men were "by nature" lazy and greedy — as J. S. Mill believed, for example — as long as their *ideas* could be changed, then a radical reform of society was possible. Indeed, Mill most eloquently argued for the absolute necessity for "practical reformers" to embrace Empiricism and combat "intuitionism" — the doctrine of innate ideas. The stubbornness with which this connection is insisted upon persists to this day and for the same reasons, although latter-day proponents of the *tabula rasa* are rarely aware of their philosophical ancestry.

That it is not a necessary connection can be seen if we examine the arch-conservative Edmund Burke. Burke's conservatism was derived, in effect, from a violent *opposition* to doctrines of "human nature." In fact, Burke saw the proponents of human rights based on human nature (such as Rousseau) as truly dangerous revolutionaries, with the French Revolution as the awful outcome of their doctrines. For Burke, there was no human nature to appeal to; there were only social institutions developed by history that are *learned*, and that were our bastion *against* the vagaries of human nature. For this reason we could only ever overturn established social institutions at our peril. Thus, it made sense for Burke to attack the French Revolution, but to defend the American Revolution. The Americans, Burke argued, were defending liberties established by precedent against a ministry that was challenging these. The French, on the other hand, were arguing from abstract "human rights." Thus, the most famous advocate of conservatism was, logically, a convinced Empiricist; indeed, this conservatism derived logically *from* his Empiricism!

The notion, however, that a radical reformist position *required* an adherence to Empiricist doctrine persisted into the nineteenth century. Its most eloquent exponent was John Stuart Mill, who, as we have seen, insisted that a "practical reformer" *must* embrace an Empiricist position in epistemology. Whatever men's natures, "practical reform" for the Utilitarians could be achieved as long as men's *ideas* could be changed. With the decline of the enlightenment insistence on the primacy of ideas and reason under the impact of the Romantic movement, "emotions" came to be seen as ranking with reason or even superior to it. Thus, it was not only innate *ideas* that were seen as inimical to reform, but innate *feelings*.

This was the setting for the Darwinian revolution and its peculiar effect on the debate. But before that impact could be fully felt, Herbert Spencer had in fact offered an "evolutionary" solution to the epistemological problem that Kant had theoretically solved. For Spencer, the "environment" acting on organisms did indeed implant information, but this was, during the process of evolution, "accumulated by heredity," thus becoming part of the organism's innate endowment. What Darwin added was the argument that such accumulation would result from natural selection rather than the inheritance of acquired characteristics (although he vacillated on this point). The significance of Darwin's argument is that many scholars since Spencer have adopted the same position, which reconciles Empiricism and a priorism in a phylogenetic framework, but it has never crystallized into a dominant "school." Why the school never formed is a complex problem for intellectual history but can be attributed to two reasons:

1. The internal failures of Darwinism to produce a satisfactory theory; and

2. The eventual complete dominance of Environmentalism and Empiricism.

Darwinism initially was something of an ideological problem. At first it was seen as firmly in the "materialist" camp and thus a threat to faith and establishment. On the other hand, it was clearly a doctrine of the "innate." Its materialism attracted socialists and revolutionaries, but at the same time laissez-faire capitalist ideology seized upon some of its elements to produce so-called "Social Darwinism," stressing struggle and individualism. (This was, in fact, more a product of Spencer than Darwin.) Combined with the rise of eugenics and its stress on "racial health," Darwinism slid to the right, where, at least according to the epistemological myth, doctrines of the innate belonged. There was a relatively brief flourishing of "instinct psychology" under McDougall and others, but this too failed to produce much more than a thesaurus of human attributes.

The possibilities of a true "interactionist" epistemology were there. William James, for example, was brilliant on the subject of instinct. He wrote of instincts waxing and waning in strength. When an instinct was at its strongest, he said, then certain, specific *learning* could take place. He quoted the experiments of the Englishman Spaulding, who placed hoods on chicks, as evidence. In essence, he had discovered "imprinting" — later to be the mainstay of the ethologists' theory of "instinctual learning."

Despite these possibilities, however, the battle lines we have been following became strongly redrawn after World War I. "Instinct" declined as an explanatory principle and no Darwinian psychology emerged until much later. The more "scientific" Behaviorism came quickly to dominate. It had the virtue of experimentalism, and hence true "scientific" status, and its robust Empiricism enshrined in the very terms *conditioning* and *reinforcement* put it firmly in the "progressive" mainstream. Intellectual historians again will have to puzzle over how it came to be so firmly established in both capitalist USA and socialist USSR. But both were rapidly industrializing countries, so they had a lot in common. Each wanted to make man over in its own image, and Environmentalist doctrines stressing human malleability were bound to gain a foothold.

In the United States, there must have been relief in the "progressive radical" camp — usually referred to here as "liberal." True to the tradition of Locke, Mill, and the "practical reformers," they saw in instinct psychology and eugenics the old bête noir of "innatism" and reaction. Combined with quite explicit racism, this was too much. Boas in anthropology made the simple equation "genetic = race" and expanded the formula to "genetic = race ≠ culture." Thus the genetic (reactionary) versus culture (reformist) tradition was reasserted. Durkheim in Europe had similarly (in his ongoing intellectual quarrel with Spencer) equated the genetic with the individual, thus producing "genetic = individual ≠ society." This set up the same opposition and restored the ancient battle lines.

Freudian psychology was potentially an instinct psychology with the promise of an interesting interactionist position. But Freud's own vacillations on the one hand, and the persistent attempts, particularly in the United States, to redefine it in "operational" behaviorist terms (e.g., the Culture and Personality school of anthropology) blocked that possible development. It has found recent expression in the work of Bowlby — but that is to jump ahead. It is interesting, though, because, at least toward the end of Freud's life, ethology was making some impact, and he would surely have recognized its importance. However, because the ethological tradition was locked away in "naturalist" studies — or in Nazi Germany — not much could have emerged.

In the meantime, through the 1950s, Behaviorism, Environmentalism, and Culturalism dominated in all fields including linguistics (under Bloomfield), and in the USSR even agronomy (under Lysenko). Cognitive psychology, as such, is better dealt with by Mehler, but it was not at center stage, even in the discipline of psychology. Here the greatest hope lay in Piaget's work, which with all its problems was essentially an interactionist psychology. Even so, Lévi-Strauss felt it necessary to disavow Piaget because of the danger of reviving the notion of a specific "primitive mentality." He preferred to rest his psychology on the social learning theories of Susan Isaacs, now virtually forgotten.

But Lévi-Strauss had reintroduced (in 1949) the importance of the human "mind," which had, according to him, basic, built-in, irreducible "structures" — in fact, ideas or categories. He did not specify these as "innate"; indeed, his avoidance of Piaget was part of his adherence to the Durkheimian orthodoxy. On the other hand, "the mind" and its structures were returned to the center of discussion, and these were allowed to depend, ultimately, on structures of the brain. Thus a "cognitive" theory of behavior, resting on neurological foundations, found its way to the center of a lively discussion embracing anthropology, psychology, and — being French — literature and politics.

The 1950s saw a burst of activity that challenged the prevailing orthodoxy, producing a whirlwind of confusion, denunciation, and excitement that can only really be understood against the background of this long, deep-seated set of antagonisms we have been exploring. The discovery of the structure of DNA provided the greatest single breakthrough in genetics since Mendel (and possibly the discovery of mutations). Chomsky, in 1957, started a revolution in linguistics that totally reversed the Behaviorist dominance and argued for an innate "Language Acquisition Device." The work of the ethologists, which had been quietly going on this whole time, at last received widespread recognition, and a burst of activity in neuroscience and endocrinology put "brain and hormones" firmly back into the debate. Behavior genetics weighed in with experimental proof of quite specific gene effects. All this was aided and abetted by an upsurge of fossil finds confirming the antiquity of the human lineage, and a new wealth of data from primatology on the remarkable social lives and abilities of our nearest relatives, culminating in the "chimpanzee language" experiments. In the 1960s the original papers of Hamilton appeared, and eventually the brilliant work on population genetics of Fisher, Haldane, Sewall Wright, and Huxley, pioneered in the 1930s, was rediscovered, married to ethology, and transformed into the avowedly Darwinian "sociobiology." What this did was to provide the basis for a science of the evolution of social behavior that was "species-specific" and so ultimately shaped by the gene pool of the species — always, of course, in interaction with the environment. This coincided with the brilliant negative criticism of Behaviorist "laws" by John Garcia and colleagues — demonstrations that were at first rejected out of hand by the "official" psychological journals. ("I'll believe these results when I find birdshit in a cuckoo clock," one editor is reputed to have said. Well, the birdshit cometh.)

The cumulative effect of these developments was to shake the citadel of Environmentalism-Behaviorism-Empiricism. It no longer seemed self-evident that "scientific method" and "Empiricist epistemology" were synonymous. An empirical science of the innate was clearly a possibility. There were many false starts and much nonsense — to be expected given the confusion of ideas and relative suddenness of their rise — but the possibility was there.

However, as it has been the purpose of this short chapter to show, so entrenched in "liberal" thinking is the dichotomy "innate = reactionary : learned = progressive" that a virtually unthinking and hysterical opposition has been manifested to this cumulative onslaught on the progressivist ideology (in the marvelous colloquial American phrase, a "knee-jerk" reaction). The dust will have to clear and, with calmness of hindsight, intellectual historians will have to sort out the genuine intellectual objections to specific claims from the ideological outrage. But at least with this perspective we can understand the depth and nature of the outrage and seriousness of the challenge.

For what is being challenged is an orthodoxy so entrenched that it embraces the very notion of science itself and the very foundations of liberal progressive democracy. We can see now that these deep-rooted associations were not logically *necessary* connections; they arose out of historical circumstances. But they have been sufficiently periodically reinforced by racists and IQ fanatics to maintain, in the minds of decent liberal democratic scientists, at the very least an uneasy suspicion of innatist "science," even in its operationalized "interactive" version. No matter. The data continue to force our hand. In the field of sex difference, for example, a simple-minded cultural determinism is no longer even respectable, given the facts. We need not expand, however, on the nature of the ideological opposition to such a conclusion and the desperate attempts to avoid it. (All unnecessary. "Equal rights for women" has *never* depended on proving women are the same as men, but rather on insisting that they not be penalized because of differences!) That the rise of the "new innatism" coincided with a ferment of "radical" protest against militarism and racism, and with the rise of the latest version of feminism, did not help in giving it a dispassionate hearing.

Part and parcel of the demise of Behaviorism has been the rise of "cognitive science" — previously scorned as "subjective." And an essential component of this rise has been the study of neonate and infant cognition. James may have been right about instinct, but in characterizing the mind of the infant as a "blooming, buzzing confusion," he turns out to be way off the mark. To the Behaviorists, the infant was a little learning machine, and it was not until the work of Fantz and Bower that this view was effectively challenged. Married to the Chomskian view of language as acquired by an innate "device," the new view of infant cognition sees the newborn as equipped with a large repertoire of "outputs" and demands on the environment. As I wrote elsewhere, "instinct" in this context can be seen as the organism's demand for appropriate environmental input. This is the essence of the interactionist position, and the importance of neonate studies is that emphasis is shifted from the emotional system beloved of the ethologists to the cognitive system, so central to an understanding of human behavior.

Much of this revolution depends on innovations in technique, and much of this book is taken up with elaborate discussions of same. But, interestingly, few of the scientists here are concerned with technique for its own sake, which is a mercy for those of us who have undergone a lifetime of trial by methodology. The technique, however, is absolutely central. To those of us concerned with the "innate," one obvious source of information is the baby. What does it bring into the world? When I used to raise this question with students, they would usually counter with, Why not ask the baby? And of course the standard answer was: We can't. How wrong we were! How wrong was William James, and even Piaget in the late dates he set for the development of cognitive competencies.

I do not want to preempt anything from the book that follows — merely to place it in its intellectual and ideological setting. But its genesis was a conversation on a park bench in Paris, when I casually, and foolishly, suggested to Jacques Mehler that we, unfortunately, could not ask the baby. Several hours later, considerably dazed, I agreed that the world should know about what the baby knows. I emphasize "know" because it is *knowledge* that is explored here — cognition, knowing, understanding, awareness, competence. We are in the truly human realm — and should we have ever been surprised that this is built into the human organism? Perhaps not, and this all too brief history is a sad record of how our very human combination of knowledge and passion gets in the way of its own search for truth. But no one coming out of the other end of this book is ever likely to fall into that same trap. Despite all the internal debates (and the neuroscientists seem to be at odds with the psychologists, who seem equally to be unaware of the importance of evolution), the guidelines of the new cognitive science are there: *sumus ergo cogitamus*.

18

Are the Obituaries of Marxism Premature?

Has history ended? Is Communism dead and democracy triumphant? Is the future one of endless minor readjustments of an essentially capitalist economy and liberal democratic polity? Is Marxism discredited? We have been hearing variations on these themes ever since the Poles started the dominoes falling in eastern Europe and Gorbachev started on the road to perestroika and glasnost in the USSR.

But perhaps we should pause to ask just what has ended, what is dead, what is discredited? Our glee may be premature. What is happening may be the reverse of what we celebrate so cheerfully. What is happening may well be to the discredit of certain totalitarian regimes. But does the fall of Ceausescu mean the demise of Marxism as a theory of social change? Does the introduction of free-market elements into socialist economies mean the inevitable triumph of capitalism? Let us be cautious.

On the theoretical front, wnat is in disrepute is a theory often loosely labeled "Marxism" by careless commentators but always carefully noted as "Marxism-Leninism" by the pedants. And to the genuine Marxist it is the "Leninism" that is operative. Marx certainly called for a "revolutionary dictatorship of the proletariat" to ensure that the forces of capitalist reaction would not overturn the fragile revolution. But it was to be strictly a transitional stage to true Communism, not a permanent institutionalization of state power. Marx hated the state — any version — as vehemently as the

351

most dedicated laissez-faire capitalist. "Freedom consists in transforming the state from an organ dominating society into one completely subordinate to it" (*Critique of the Gotha Program* 1875). This slogan could have been proudly displayed on the banners in Poland and Romania.

Lenin, with the doctrine of "socialism in one country" began the process of totalitarian statism that ended in Stalin and his immediate successors. The true meaning of Marxism here was distorted as surely as the Christian church distorted the teachings of Christ. (Perhaps we should really call Christianity "Christism-Paulism" to push the analogy. Thus, what is happening now could even be seen as a kind of Reformation; but read on.) The total domination of a permanent state apparatus was anathema to Marx, and he would have rejoiced along with the rest of us to see it fall. That it was a "socialist" and not a "capitalist" state makes no difference. Marx held no particular brief for socialist states; this was Lenin's contribution.

What Marx did not foresee was that the overthrow of the capitalist state might not be a one-shot affair; it might have its ups and downs, its progressions and regressions. Many commentators have pointed out that one of the difficulties with his theory is that the revolution was not predicted for Russia or for eastern Europe (and certainly not for China) — notably undeveloped capitalist societies. And we must remember that the fiercest internal struggle in Russia was not between proletarians and capitalists at all, but between the Stalinist state and the recalcitrant peasantry. It can be (and has been) plausibly argued that what took place in Russia (and China) was not a genuine proletarian revolution against capitalism at all, and that certainly what followed was not a genuine dictatorship of the proletariat but the establishment of yet another oriental despotism. Djilas, in *The New Class*, represents one version of this criticism from within Marxism.

After World War II this form of statism was forced onto the only incipiently industrial-capitalist eastern European countries (with the connivance of the capitalist states). In addition, nailing "Marxism-Leninism" to their mastheads, various third-world "revolutionaries" proceeded to establish totalitarian states in tribal and peasant societies which had in most cases not even reached the incipient stage. Paul M. Sweezey (*The Nation* 250[8] [February 1990]) in trying to save something for "socialism" out of the current turmoil, refers to these states as being "inspired by the alternative principles of socialism that were given their classic formulation by Karl Marx in the nineteenth century." But while Marx certainly said that the temporary proletarian government should seize the means of production, distribution, and exchange from the capitalists, he said nothing about, and would have been horrified by, despotism, secret police, totalitarian repression, gulags, purges, genocide, and grandiose armament programs. These consequences of Leninism are what have brought about the downfall of "socialism" where it has occurred, along with the failure of the totalitarian system of production to raise living standards.

For Marx (and Engels is always understood here), the *only* route to true Communism was through the "internal contradictions of capitalism." These had to be fully developed and fully played out before a true proletariat endowed with true class-consciousness could emerge and make the transition to the next stage. This progression for Marx was governed by laws of history, and there was no way of cutting corners with the dialectic. One could never reach Communism via state despotisms imposed by external forces, or dictatorships established by charismatic tyrants in noncapitalist countries.

In this view, then, the past seventy years or so could be seen as an interruption of the basic process of social change, and one which a Marxist, as opposed to an apologist for Soviet-style tyranny (i.e., a Stalinist), would have predicted to be inherently unstable and doomed to failure. In the view of genuine Marxist theory, capitalism *must run its course*. There is no warrant for shortcuts. But because of the urge to believe that the millennium was coming in their lifetimes, many *soi disant* Marxists desperately went along with the Leninist model and rationalized the very un-Marxist consequences. Marx, who was not one to suffer fools gladly, would have scorned their simple-minded "unscientific" impatience.

What is now happening, then, could be seen as a massive vindication of Marxism, not the opposite. The east Europeans are reverting to capitalist modes of production and the liberal democratic state which is their necessary superstructure. The primitive oligarchic tyrannies that have held up the march of social change have been rightly swept away. Capitalism can now be allowed to run its course, and eventually the real revolution will occur. This may be longer delayed because what these countries will revert to is not a true laissez-faire economy but a compromise with "welfare socialism" where massive ameliorations of the workers' lot will stem the tide for a while. But insofar as the regimes are basically "capitalist" in the mode of production (like even Sweden — the new model society), then the contradictions will reassert themselves, and inflation, recession, unemployment, and maldistribution of wealth will accumulate to the inevitable breaking point.

Then, the Marxist could claim, the true revolution of the true proletariat will take place, and the transitional proletarian dominance will lead to the (hazy) utopia of true Communism: "From each according to his ability: to each according to his need." Of course, we are free to believe this will not happen. I am not a Marxist and I would like to think it won't. I think that certain primitive mechanisms like nationalism, religion, and nepotism will always upset the Marxist predictions based on class. But what we are not free to say is that it *cannot* happen because the events of the past year indicate a final and inevitable "triumph of capitalism and democracy" and the demise of

"Communism." The trouble with Communism is like the proverbial trouble with Christianity: it hasn't been tried. What has been tried is Leninism — the short-cut Marx would have repudiated. Now things are back to normal; history is back on course. Having burped up Leninism, it can now get back to trying to digest capitalism. The Marxist prediction, far from being discredited, is still open. And if we wish to prevent its realization, we had better recognize this fact before we become too complacent over the end of something that never in fact happened in the first place.

19

Browning and the Judges:
A Poet Looks at Law

People who have read my accounts of legal battles and complicated cases in *Reproduction and Succession* have often asked me, "Whence this fascination with the law?" Is it family background? (no, that was military); is it education? (not really, that was in sociology and philosophy); is it personal experience? (again no, apart from a couple of speeding tickets and divorces, I've steered clear of legal entanglements). Partly it's literary I think. I've always enjoyed, for example, courtroom dramas or plots where complicated legal issues were at stake. Naturally, *Witness for the Prosecution* was one of my favorite movies. As a student at the LSE, in the London of the 1950s, I was right in among the lawyers. The Royal Courts of Justice were around the corner, and many a meal of bangers and mash and a pint of bitter at a local off-Fleet Street pub was taken in the company of gowned and bewigged barristers during their mid-case luncheon. Lincoln's Inn Fields were our "campus," and we played endless games of tennis there and picnicked on the lawns. I used to wander a lot through Lincoln's Inn itself, admiring the chapel and dining hall and the neat quadrangles of this original "University of London" — which is what the Inns of Court were. I hobnobbed with law students and for a little while entertained a fantasy of becoming a barrister and sweeping in and out of courtrooms with gown billowing and wig askew like Rumpole of the Bailey.

I had a law student for a flatmate for awhile, and we argued the cases he had to study and various theories of jurisprudence through the night, in the way students used to do. We reveled in A. P. Herbert's crazy cases. I particularly remember the one where the Thames flooded the Embankment and a boat hit a bus. Each sued the other and the issue boiled down to whether the rule of the road or the law of the sea applied. I think in the end the judge decided that the Thames was a river wherever it happened to be flowing at the time, and therefore motor should have given way to sail and the bus was at fault. Something like that.

I used to go to law lectures (they were much more interesting to me than the compulsory statistics and demography), and so I suppose, more or less by osmosis rather than design, I picked up quite bit of stray information. I never did, of course, become a barrister — and indeed it was no more than a fantasy. Law and lawyers were interesting to study, but I would have felt as intellectually restricted being one as much as being stuck in any other job that did not allow complete intellectual freedom. But I continued to be fascinated for reasons only partly understood. One of the reasons I liked social anthropology, I think, was precisely the jurisprudential origins, language, and concepts that dominated it, and had done so from Maine and McLennan onwards. In starting to write a thesis (never finished) on "The Rational Ethic," I was drawn to the legal framework as a model for a rational ethical system; a legal framework to be imbued and informed with information from the behavioral sciences. I was concerned to break down the conceptual barrier between legal rules and moral imperatives, via a redefinition of moral argument as essentially a practical discussion of the application of rules to cases (casuistry, I suppose). The rules themselves were to be practically derived also, from a consideration of human needs. (Free will got in there somehow.) So in a way, with *Reproduction and Succession* I suppose I have come full circle and returned to the intellectual heartland just off Fleet Street and the Strand where it all started.

But as we all know, a fascination with the law penetrates all sectors of society. We are all touched by it, scared of it, sometimes glad of it, and always baffled by it. My favorite poet then (and I guess even now) was Robert Browning, whose *Ring and the Book* is perhaps one of the greatest tributes to a law case in verse (as well as the original of *Rashomon*, *The Bridge of San Luis Rey*, and all such of that genre). But in a much lesser known — in fact, virtually unread — long poem, he deals much more directly with what one might call the aesthetics of law: the logical charm of a judgement beautifully argued and delivered, the same element that attracts us in good music or good art. The poem with the unlikely title *Red Cotton Night-Cap Country* (actually unlikely in anyone but Browning; for him, it was par for the course) is a melodrama concerning a real court case in France that excited the poet's imagination. It was published by Smith Elder in London 1n 1873. Written in his unmistakable tumbling and cryptic blank verse, it takes 4,247 lines to tell the tale, and the law case comes right toward the end. Small wonder, perhaps, that no one seems to have paid much attention to it! But perverse as my taste may be, I can't get enough of Browning, so I read to the end and became fascinated with his fascination with the case and the judgement.

The odd title came from his friend Anne Thackeray, daughter of the novelist to whom the poem was dedicated (much to her later distress) and who is the person to whom the poet tells the story in the poem. She had a cottage in Normandy where the story is set, and she had whimsically described the area to him as "White Cotton Night-Cap Country" from the traditional sleeping headgear of the men there. (See her charming *Records of Tennyson, Ruskin and Browning* [London: Macmillan, 1892].) Browning changed the white to red, either because of the goryness of the tale he was to tell or, some suppose, because of Carlyle's insistence on the red cotton night-cap — worn by the sans culottes — as the true symbol of the Revolution. With typical Browning thoroughness, from lines 282 to 313, he goes through a list of great men who wore night-caps in the daytime, including Alexander Pope, Voltaire, Hogarth, William Cowper, and even Louis XVI when forced to by the mob at the Tuileries.

Browning was put on to the story while the events were in progress, in 1870, by a friend, Joseph Milsand, and he did his usual compulsive homework, reading all the transcripts, the will and legal documents, and the newspaper reports (mostly in the *Journal de Caen*), and visiting all the locales and interviewing the natives. The events of the story took place between 1867 and 1872, and since Browning was writing so soon after the case was decided on 9 July 1872 (he started the poem on 1 December 1872 and finished it on 23 January 1873), and since he took such a strong partisan stand, he and the publishers were worried about a possible libel suit. Two lawyers, including the attorney general, advised them to change all the names, including the place names, and this was done — a simple matter with a word processor, but a hell of a chore at the time. The poem was not well received. Browning's "obscurity" and his fascination with the grotesque came in for its share of Victorian distaste, and Miss Thackeray wished he had left her out of it. History has not been much kinder. But the story alone has its fascination by its very strangeness.

Most people evidently saw it as a case of "suicide while the balance of his mind was disturbed" on the part of the chief character Antoine Mellerio (Leonce Miranda in the poem), who died in a fall from a high tower on his Normandy estate. Browning chose to differ, and subtitled his poem "Turf and Towers" to stress his belief that the real theme was that of the conflict between the mundane and the sacred, and that the real motive for the "fall" was religious, and not, as opinion had it, remorse over unfillial behavior. Mellerio, born in 1827, was a jeweler by profession, and had led a "dissipated life," mostly in Paris, during which he attempted suicide and, in 1868, burned his hands off in a fit of religious remorse. He retired to Tailleville in Normandy with his mistress Anna de Beaupré (Clara Muhlhausen — née de Millefleurs — in the poem), who cared for him throughout. On 13 April 1870 he died in the fall from the high tower of his house. This was not suicide, Browning maintained, but literally a "leap of faith" undertaken by Mellerio, who was a devotee of the miraculous icon of Our Lady (La Delivrande — Browning's La Ravissante) at a nearby church. For Browning, the leap of faith to die by was an appropriate metaphor to live by.

Be this as it may — and the poet built a massive if speculative case for it — Mellerio's will left all his wealth to the church and a life interest to Anna (Clara). His relatives, whom Browning contemptuously refers to as "the Cousinry," contested the will on the grounds of his unsoundness of mind. The Franco-Prussian War of 1870 delayed the proceedings, but on 9 July 1872 a court at Caen upheld the will, an appeal being denied a year later (which meant the poem came out while the case was still under appeal, adding to the libel problems).

It is this 1872 "Miranda" judgement that Browning captures so neatly (lines 4161-64):

Here, issued with all regularity,
I hold the judgement — just, inevitable,
Nowise to be contested by what few
Can judge the judges; sum and substance thus:

The first issue was that of competency to make a will. Here the court was very subtle, for it did not say outright at this point that Miranda was definitely of sound mind, it simply pointed out the following (lines 4165-4173):

Inasmuch as we find, the Cousinry,
During that very period when they take
Monsieur Leonce Miranda for stark mad,
Considered him to be quite sane enough
For doing much important business with —
Nor showed suspicion of his competence
Until, by turning of the tables, loss
Instead of gain accrued to them thereby, —
Plea of incompetence we set aside.

Thus, if the Cousinry chose to treat him as sane when it suited them, they could not deem him insane when it did not. There is implied here that if they really were to have him condemned as insane, then all the business dealings with him from which they had profited might prove to be illegal. A pretty threat, if neatly veiled. Later, faced with the fact of his supposed suicide, the court concluded (lines 4201-4208):

> The minor accusations are dismissed;
> They prove mere freak and fancy, boyish mood
> In age mature of simple kindly man.
> Exuberant in generosities
> To all the world: no fact confirms the fear
> He meditated mischief to himself
> That morning when met the accident
> Which ended fatally.

What the Cousinry insisted was insanity the court insisted could just as well be seen as harmless, even generous, eccentricity in a kind old man. And indeed, he was not particularly unhappy during the time when he fell — or leaped — from the tower, a point Browning uses to establish that it was not remorse or depression that led to his leap but rather religious ecstasy. The court hadn't read Browning, of course, and reached the more mundane conclusion that it was most likely an accident and certainly no proof of insanity. Not only was Miranda not incompetent, but the court went on to hold (lines 4175-4184):

> The rather, that the dispositions, sought
> To be impugned, are natural and right,
> Nor jar with any reasonable claim
> Of kindred, friendship or acquaintance here.
> Nobody is despoiled, none overlooked;
> Since the testator leaves his property
> To just that person whom, of all the world,
> He counted he was most indebted to.
> In mere discharge, then, of conspicuous debt,
> Madame Mulhausen has priority,
> Enjoys the usufruct of Clairvaux.

Again the reasoning is beautiful. There are claims against the property, and these must be satisfied in order. The first claim on the estate is of course "conspicuous debt." This must be discharged before any other claims can be settled. The court finds here, then, that Miranda's bequest to Clara was not, as the Cousinry claimed, a crazy old man's indulgence of his mistress, but on the contrary, the discharge of his most conspicuous debt: that to the woman who had cared for him in his maimed condition. It did not even need to be considered a bequest; as a discharge of debt it had priority.

On the bequest to the church the court had an easy time in holding that this was both pious and regular, and, what is more, could scarcely be held as proof of insanity (lines 4181-4200):

Which disposition, being consonant
With a long series of such acts and deeds
Notorious in his lifetime, needs must stand,
Unprejudiced by eccentricity
Nowise amounting to distemper: since
In every instance signalized as such,
We recognize no overleaping bounds,
No straying out of the permissible:
Duty to the Religion of the Land, —
Neither excessive nor inordinate.

A man who, in his will, scrupulously discharges his conspicuous debts and leaves a generous bequest to the church can scarcely by accounted of unsound mind. One has the feeling that the court had its tongue a bit in its cheek here and was enjoying the solemn chiding of the greedy Cousinry a bit too much. After all, by the same token that Miranda can be shown to have been a pious son of the church, he can also be shown to have been a religious nut case, unless we want to overlook the burning off of his hands. But of course this is Browning's rendering of a legal decision in a French provincial court, and we do not know what liberties he took with the actual wording. (But what a marvelous Comp. Lit. master's thesis for someone who wants to spend time in the land of camembert and calvados!) However, the court did find in favor of the will, and we have no reason to think that the conscientious Browning did not follow its reasoning closely. The wording is too precise and legally clever, and Browning was not going to risk further legal action by misrepresenting the verdict. His original notes evidently do exist, so perhaps the clue lies there.

But for me this is immaterial. What matters is that the poet put into impeccable (if eccentric) blank verse the essentials of a legal judgement that clearly delighted him for its combination of nicety and compassion. The legal forms were used to see that decency prevailed, that justice was done, that greed did not triumph, and that love was rewarded. It remained for the poet to say that the protagonist's life was not a disaster that ended either in suicide or a ghastly accident, but was rather a spiritual search that ended in religious affirmation. Today we are not so concerned, I suppose, to have such a confirmation, and in consequence Browning's long and obscure poem is simply not read except by scholars and the occasional anthropologist who shares his Victorian love of melodrama, his quirky black humor, and his affinity for legal aesthetics.

20

Anthropology and the Teddy Bears' Picnic

When I was a mere tyke my favorite song was unquestionably "The Teddy Bears' Picnic," as much for the metaphysical questions it posed to a curious five-year-old as for the thumping good tune and the funny words. (From memory, so not necessarily 100 percent accurate.)

If you go down in the woods today
You'd better not go alone
It's lovely down in the woods today
But safer to stay at home
For every bear that ever there was
Is gathered there for certain because
Today's the day the Teddy Bears have their picnic.

"Why was it not safe? Why did one need protection, Mummy?"
"Because, silly, these are Bears."
"But they are *Teddy* Bears, Mummy. They're not dangerous."
"Be quiet, child, and listen."

Picnic time for Teddy Bears
The little Teddy Bears are
Having a lovely time today

363

See them, catch them unawares
They are so happy on their holiday
See them gaily gad about
They are so happy and free
They never have any cares
At six-o-clock their mummies and daddies
Will take them home to bed
Because they're tired little Teddy Bears.

"There. I told you so. They're not dangerous. They have mummies and daddies too who take them home to bed. So why is it dangerous?"

"Because they are Bears, silly child, and with Bears you never can tell. They may look a little like us, but they are really very, very different, so leave them alone."

And thus I learned. However much like us the Teddy Bears might appear to be, they were in fact the totally enigmatic Other. That they might live in nuclear families with mummies and daddies, have picnics, seem to enjoy themselves like us, go to bed at six-o-clock, etc. meant nothing. These superficialities only served to mask the unpenetrable Otherness of Beardom.

If you go down in the woods today
You're sure of a big surprise
It's lovely down in the woods today
But better go in disguise

And so on. I didn't sleep with my Teddy Bears that night. I only recovered my faith in bears after heavy injections of Winnie the Pooh some years later. But even then, there was indeed something strange about the friendly animals in the Hundred Acre Wood. They were, after all, pretty peculiar. None of them had parents, unlike the Bears — except for little Roo, of course. (But where was Kanga's husband? We are never told.) Pooh suffered from an eating disorder; Eeyore was a chronic depressive; Tigger was hyperactive to a fault; Owl was dyslexic; Piglet had an obvious anxiety neurosis. But Christopher Robin seemed at home with them and understood them despite their alienness. He was also not above affectionate value judgments: "Silly old bear!" Somehow, if the Teddy Bears' picnic had taken place in the Hundred Acre Wood, I reckoned I wouldn't have been afraid to intrude. Well, only a bit. This lesson learned in early childhood — and we all learn it — that those who are different, however much overlap between them and us there may appear to be, are dangerous and unfathomable at base, is almost impossible to unlearn later. However, there have always been Christopher Robins willing to suspend disbelief and try to join in the Teddy Bears' picnic, even to try to see it through the eyes of the bears themselves. Of course it's dangerous, if not physically then spiritually. Could anyone forget the arresting first "dream" in Kurosawa's stunning film *Dreams* where the little boy intrudes on the ritual dance of the Fox People? But they were "people" in that they were dancing and ritualizing, just as the Teddy Bears were holidaying and picnicking. There were points of contact, and they were points that joined us at the hip with the alien Others: family, ritual, leisure, dance, feasting, parental care, music, play, functional divisions of time, secrecy, and privacy; even hostility to strangers and the possibility of making amends for a wrong. Christopher Robin could read the emotions of his Others even if he could not share them: Pooh's greed and rationalizations, Eeyore's misery, Piglet's nervousness, Kanga's maternal solicitude, and so on. Of course, you will say, he was "projecting," and of course he was. But what he was projecting was not so far off the mark. If we were to draw up a litany of human emotions, we would find all of them represented in any human community, and any fantasy community for that matter, since we cannot invent fantasy communities without drawing on the list or they would not be intelligible. Even when science fiction tries to invent creatures lacking some of the human repertoire (Mr. Spock or Data, for example), it can only make them "work" by their obvious contrast with, and lack of, what we take to be basically human.

What is amazing about so much of what goes on in current anthropology and passes for the latest in "theory" — a word never more abused than currently — is its sheer intellectual wimpishness. Those preaching the incorrigible alienness of the Other lack the courage of little Christopher Robin. Of course understanding alien cultures is hard. This is the point of having anthropologists to do it. We take vows of poverty, like monks, go through awful initiation ceremonies to become members of the tribe, and then suffer hardships on the vision quest to bring back that Holy Grail of "understanding another culture." We may not even do it well. Some of our techniques may well be too culture bound to be helpful. We have to relearn category systems from scratch so as not to distort native meanings. Languages can seem impenetrable barriers. But no one ever said it was easy; they said it was the very devil. But no one equally, until very recently, said that it was *in principle* impossible. Such a statement would have seemed the height of racism to my generation, and it is odd that it is often promulgated by those most censorious of "racist" attitudes. We are all human beings. We share the same evolutionary heritage. Our brains are the same, and those extensions of our brains — our behavior and our cultures — are at bottom the same, however different they may look on the surface. It was precisely to delve below that surface that anthropologists existed in the first place. When our mummies and daddies told us that the Bears were dangerously different, we intrepid Christopher Robins said: No. We are going to live in the Hundred Acre Wood with these human-like animals, learn to speak to them, to understand them, and to enlighten you about them. Many things — not least our own cultural assumptions — will get in the way, so we have to work to overcome these. In the end we shall bring you a far-from-perfect picture of them and their lives and assumptions, but it will be a damn good try. (C. R. would have said a "jolly good try," but jollity in one's work is not exactly in fashion in these hyperprofessional days.)

And we could do it because we shared a faith in a common humanity, in the "psychic unity of mankind." It was, although not often expressed as such (except by such mavericks as Wissler), a biological faith: We are all of the same body; we evolved from the same stock; we are a single species evolved under common conditions; the physical differences between us are superficial; the mental differences between us are nil; the differences that are so obvious are the result of history, ecology, and even accident — in principle they can be understood. We resisted the nineteenth-century notion that differences were qualitative on a scale from "lowest savagery" to "advanced civilization." They were just different strategies adapted to different circumstances by people capable of managing any strategy from the most elementary to the most advanced.

We reduced the myriad kinship systems of the world to manageable order and even mathematical analyzability. We found the common and universal elements in myths and rituals. We "understood" nonmonetary economic systems as operating on principles of exchange and reciprocity. We interpreted the workings of political systems that had no sovereigns or central monopolies on force, but which did work. We invented "objective" phonetic systems for recording all the diversities of languages, and semantic analyses whereby we could compare them and even reconstruct their histories. We even found formulas that linked all these together as expressions of basic mental structures that we all shared. (Structuralism was shrugged off too early, and graph theory is taking up where it left off anyway.) What is more, we combined all this with the even more daring excursion into the other Other of the past and the very remote past. We literally dug up the ancient origins of our civilizations and their precursors — our Others in time, not just space. And this we related to our even more ancient origins in prehuman primate society to discover that common heritage from which we all sprang and which we all still carry within us as social and sociable beings. We know a lot about where we came from, how we got here, and what we are doing now. We even know a bit about why. There is a long way to go, but knowledge expands all the time, and even ten years ago we would not have predicted that we would have today the scientific tools we have to carry on these explorations into areas previously denied to our puny science. This is not a bad record for those intrepid Christopher Robins who refused to be put off by nursery fears of things that go bump in the jungle or the bush, but who tried to reach out to the Teddy Bears and draw them into the circle of the human family. How arrogant, say the critics, that we should assume that the folk categories of Christopher Robin have any validity over those of the Bears. Well, in an epistemologically perfect world, perhaps they would not. But the world we have is one in which this particular tradition of scientific enquiry — arising miraculously in one part of the world in one historical period — is all we have by way of a system of knowledge that will indeed transcend local cognitive boundaries. See how eagerly those who did not have it embrace it. And why? Because they are not stupid; they see it pays off. It can also backfire, as with the results of industrial pollution, etc. But it is capable of self-correction even here. The system can be used to discover flaws in itself. The ozone layer depletion and its causes were discovered by scientists, not magicians. No alternative cognitive system could have done it. Whether we like it or not, science with its objectivity (however this might be compromised in certain instances) and its openness to validation and refutation, remains the one international language capable of providing objective knowledge of the world. And it is a language that all can use, share in, and learn. It is also a language that can be improved; in particular, more thought can be put into its use and misuse. But it is not a language that can be abandoned in favor of a complete epistemological relativism that would decree all statements as of equal value. Those anthropologists preaching such relativism are way out of line with the people they think they are defending. The wretched of the earth want science and the benefits of science. To deny them this is another kind of racism. It will indeed have to be a different science from the buccaneering, technology-driven beast of the past, but this again is something anthropologists are well equipped to advise on — particularly the ecological brethren. What is not open to us is to abandon science altogether.

Yet that is currently what is being preached and drawing more than its fair share of attention in graduate schools across the nation. I doubt it will ultimately succeed. The silent majority of anthropologists is not heeding these siren calls; it is quietly getting on with the job. But graduate students seem relieved to be told that all knowledge is gender or class or culture relative (as though this were somehow a new idea!), and that science as we know it is a male white European enterprise and so tainted and of no more value than magical incantations. This appeals to the lazy, and graduate students seem to get lazier and lazier. It's far easier just to spout opinions (and any opinion is as good as any other) than to get down to the hard business of science.

Conversation between the ANGUISHED PUBLISHER (hereinafter AP) and the ANTHROPOLOGICAL AUTHOR (AA) as a result of the foregoing.

AP. You mean that there is still a large body of general anthropologists out there who will in fact buy your next book? I mean, it had better do better than the last one or we're all in trouble.

AA. No. I don't mean that. I said that the silent majority is getting on with the job, but I should have said with the "jobs" since very few even of the traditionalists see anthropology as a unified discipline anymore.

AP. You mean they don't buy the currently fashionable relativism, but they don't buy (I mean that literally as well as figuratively) the idea of unified science of man?

AA. Right. You see, they grew up with a heritage of relativism anyway. This was pretty much the anthropological orthodoxy from Boas on. It was primarily a value relativism ("each culture must be judged on its own terms") rather than a cognitive relativism ("one culture's categories are just as valid as another's"). But they confuse the two. In consequence, they find it hard to be too critical of cognitive relativism even though it hits at the heart of the scientific enterprise. They see the alternatives as "reductionism," "biologism," "genetic determinism" and all those bogeymen of value relativism. They have for eighty years or so been fighting to preserve the world for cultural relativism.

AP. But they didn't repudiate science?

AA. Absolutely not. On the contrary, they fought for scientific status. That was the only game in town worth playing. But in anthropology it was played on two fronts. The unification of the discipline was an artifact of its growing up in museums, where the archaeologists and cultural specialists were lumped together. And from working for the Department of the Interior, where they were put in charge, for example, of Amerindian languages. The famous "four fields" (cultural, archeological, physical, and linguistic) were never happily integrated from the start.

AP. But what about Darwin and evolution and all that?

AA. A common misconception. American anthropology was not born of a theoretical base in Darwinism at all. Morgan was not a Darwinist; Boas was if anything anti-Darwin. He made an early argument for the autonomy of culture from biology much as Durkheim had made for the social sciences in Europe.

AP. But the early textbooks (and the current ones for that matter) always had their sections on "early man" and even "the great apes" and definitely on fossils and races and all that.

AA. Absolutely. But this was largely lip service. Don't forget that a scramble was going on for bits of the world to monopolize in the burgeoning academic departments from the 1890s on. This is when the pattern got set. And anthropology, via the museum, got "early man" and "savages" as well as "evolution," even if it didn't really want them all. It had to maintain a distinction from psychology, sociology, history, and the like, and this combination certainly made it distinct. But early on, people began to specialize, and the "cultural" crowd split off in effect from the "physical." In fact, they rapidly developed a hostility to each other as the culturalists embraced Germanic-inspired relativism through Boas and rejected the identification of contemporary primitives with "early man" (which had sustained some unity of the subject in the nineteenth century with Morgan and the social evolutionists), and the physical crowd tended toward racial classification and eugenics — anathema to their cultural colleagues.

AP. So what you are saying is that there never was a unified "science of man" — it was always split against itself? If so, then why the continuation of the idea in departments and textbooks and graduate programs right up to the present?

AA. Something for the historians of ideas and institutions to chew on. There were those who really did believe in a unified anthropology. But mostly I suspect it was just academic inertia and territorialism, and the museums where they were all housed, of course. But by the 1940s the "requirements" in graduate programs had become almost token. If you were a social/cultural anthropologist, you took one compulsory course in each of the "four fields" and then forgot those not your specialty. When I was at Harvard in the 1950s, "social" candidates simply had to write a paper in "physical," and that was that. Linguistics was "in" then, so people were willing to take it. But archaeology was dropped altogether. Today, departments continue to pay lip service because sheer inertia has left them with the four fields' heritage. But there is no illusion about one unified field. They were given the chance, with neo-Darwinian theory, to try to integrate into one field, but the relativistic, cultural deterministic orthodoxy was too strong, and the chance was rejected.

AP. Isn't that where you come in though? Haven't you tried all these years to get them to reintegrate through neo-Darwinian theory? Has it all been a waste? Will we never sell these books?

AA. It's not perhaps as bad as even I have painted it, but it is bad. Our message was simple. "You missed your chance to become a unified discipline in the early twentieth century because of the shortcomings of Darwinism then plus the ingrained hostility of cultural determinism. Now you have a chance to recoup under the theoretical umbrella of the evolution of social behavior, comparative ethology, sociobiology, biosociology, or whatever you want to call it — basically, the neo-Darwinian synthesis as it applies to behavior. This will enable you to put together the primate and mammalian past with the archeological record and the ethnographic present under the aegis of evolutionary theory; a theory which will also link you into the expanding new knowledge of the biological sciences from molecular biology to neuroscience ..." and so on.

AP. It sounds like a grand invitation to weld together a unique and powerful science. But you say it was not heeded?

AA. It was heeded. Some people took it up — across a broad range of social sciences: political science, psychology, sociology, even law. But these were few — within anthropology very few. The prevailing cultural paradigm was too strong and too tempting to the lazy minded.

AP. Aren't you being a bit too hard on your colleagues?

AA. I don't think so. The vast majority of our colleagues are intellectually lazy. They "work" hard enough within their narrow confines, but having done their Ph.D.'s they really are mostly very unwilling to venture into new territory. Even within their "disciplines" they stay within narrow subject limits. The whole academic system fosters this. Your own list, with its categories of "subjects," fosters it. The world is divided up into set categories and subcategories, and no one wants to wander far afield.

AP. What about interdisciplinary research?

AA. Only with disciplines sufficiently like one's own not to cause too much effort. I remember a prominent cultural anthropologist, who must remain nameless, telling me that while he thought my ideas all very well in principle, he wasn't going to learn about "all those damned ancient ankle bones and those disgusting monkeys." And he was sympathetic. We live comfortable intellectual as well as social lives. We don't want them disturbed.

AP. I think you're being too cynical. People have genuine intellectual reservations.

AA. I agree. But I am cynical about how these intellectual reservations tend to make for a lazier intellectual life. The older cultural anthropologists clung to their cultural determinism for a mixture of ideological and personal reasons, not least among which was a reluctance at having to learn some real science. But they were open to debate at least on the grounds that they shared the desire for scientific status. The new humanistic bunch not only reject real science (through epistemological relativism) but reject scientific status for the cultural anthropology they want to do. This is a double rejection of science, and it amuses me how many cultural determinists who were most hostile to neo-Darwinism now see it as almost an ally in the battle against the antiscientism of the new *Wunderkinden*. At least "we" are all on the side of science.

AP. Good, then that means they will all buy your books.

AA. Not likely. I still think you'll get a better sale among interested laymen who are less likely to be caught up in all this ideological dueling.

AP. But surely these "new humanists" are still small in number?

AA. Yes. I said that before. But they are growing in influence, especially among graduate students always eager to be "up to date" no matter how non-sensical the latest lunacies from Paris and Frankfurt happen to be. And, as I said, they appeal to the lazy. It's much easier to abandon hope for understanding the Other and write self-reflexive poetry about the field experience — especially when the poetry in question is modernist free-verse drivel that requires no discipline either. Or to take up political attitudes and pass them off as analysis because, after all, knowledge is relative to political attitudes decided by gender, class, etc. So anything goes. I hear more of this daily.

AP. Well, it's true. At the publishing conferences and book fairs we are hearing more and more that what sell are books on minority studies, gender studies, "reflexivity," and "critical theory" — whatever they are. So this is not confined to anthropology.

AA. No. The academic world is riddled with it. It goes along with a new radical chic and, of all things, an insistence that modern *literary criticism* is the model for all cultural analysis! English literature departments are gleefully reconstituting themselves as "Cultural Studies" departments and trying to take over the intellectual world. It's a heady time for them and a scary time for science.

AP. Why literary criticism?

AA. It's a long story, but basically if you ditch science then what models have you got? You might say "history," but history itself is divided between the scientific and the narrative wings and has been since its invention as an academic discipline in the nineteenth century. My own interpretation is that lazy minds are happiest with the mere voicing of opinion, or with the easy task of dressing this up to make it look plausible. In modern literary criticism they have found the perfect model of this, along with a new philosophical doctrine of extreme relativism that says everything is only opinion anyway, to justify it. Thus the otherwise odd vision of thousands of social science children cavorting after the Pied Piper of Lit. Crit. and "discourse analysis."

AP. Cynical again?

AA. I've always been cynical about both Eng. Lit. as an enterprise and its partner in crime, Lit. Crit.

AP. What's the difference?

AA. Eng. Lit. is purely a university thing. Lit. Crit. is technically open to anyone. You don't need any qualifications, or even brains — simply an outlet. Eng. Lit. people do of course practice Lit. Crit., but rarely vice versa.

AP. When was the start? I mean, of Eng. Lit. as an enterprise?

AA. Quite. Lit. Crit. had always been there in the sense of commentaries on literature — usually politically or religiously motivated, and coming to a peak in the Grub Street Hacks of the eighteenth century who wrote for political factions, and their successors in the nineteenth-century Reviews. Eng. Lit. only came into existence with the agitation to get "English" as a "discipline" into the universities in the late nineteenth century. There was a surge of effort to take back English language from the philologists, marry it to literary history and criticism, and produce the monster called "English Language and Literature."

AP. You obviously regard this as a dubious venture. Why?

AA. Because no one really knew what it was, and they still don't. The passionate opposition at Oxford and Cambridge went something like this: Literature exists; we can study it linguistically, historically, or biographically; or we can express opinions about it. The first belongs to philology (linguistics, today), which exists anyway; the second to history; and the third to biography, both of which also exist. As to opinions, any educated persons can read Milton or Shakespeare and form their own — perhaps with some help from philology, history, and biography. And indeed they have been doing so for centuries without the help of departments of English. They have not needed and do not need a pointless academic discipline to form opinions for them. What reason have they to suppose that these "academic" opinions would be superior to their own, or even very useful?

AP. Who won?

AA. The Eng. Lit. crowd of course. Which meant the study of language became divorced from comparative philology to its detriment; literary history existed separately from history or sociology; literary biography in any case began to be shunned once the New Criticism took hold, and was and is largely done by amateurs; and Lit. Crit. became a matter of fads, fashions, schools, manifestoes, politics, and nonsense dressed up as scholarship (footnotes, bibliographies, etc.).

AP. So you think the original critics were right?

AA. Obviously. But even they didn't anticipate the ludicrous bloating of this enterprise in U.S. universities where, because of the need to teach undergraduates to read and write (unnecessary in Europe), English departments would become vastly inflated. And, because of the nature of the system, not inflated with remedial teachers of grammar, which was what was needed, but tens of thousands of aspiring Lit. Crit. types, all writing theses and clamoring for the publication necessary for promotion.

AP. But why is this a bad thing of necessity?

AA. As I said, right from the beginning, Lit. Crit. is opinion. You can make that opinion look scholarly with the appropriate ritual apparatus, but in the end it is just opinion. So Lit. Crit. is always frantically trying to justify itself — to give some reason why the academic Lit. Critic has more authority than any well-read person (and it's remarkable how ill read many academic Lit.

Critters are). I find when I discuss literature with them they often get angry. "Do you have a Ph.D. in English?" they demand — as though such a degree confers particular authority on their opinions, even if the thesis was on the use of the semicolon in seventeenth-century pastoral poetry, or something equally mind expanding.

AP. Then why on earth would the social sciences turn to this as a model?

AA. They suffer from a similar desperation. If you are, as many of them are, afraid of science and the scientific enterprise (too hard), you'll grasp at anything that justifies your desire not to be scientific. Hence the revival of the old natural science versus human science debate: that humans are not subject to scientific investigation because they have motives, intentions, and so on.

AP. This isn't a valid distinction?

AA. No. Because motives and intentions can themselves be subjected to scientific investigation. But it makes for a good excuse to dodge the rigors of science — the demand for verification and falsification — and promotes the relativism with which the social sciences have always sympathized.

AP. And Eng. Lit. panders to the relativism?

AA. It does, but that issue has been done to death.

AP. Look, I have to sell books. Educate me: what is the guts of it?

AA. The guts of it is that French Lit. Crit. — the heirs to Descartes (who ruined all subsequent French thinking) — hit on a way to achieve what all the other Lit. Critters, desperate for authority, never managed.

AP. Namely?

AA. The abolition of the author. They made the bold move by asserting that the author didn't matter (biography thrown out immediately) and that all there was was the text, the reader, and the commentary on the text. Since they were the commentators, they were all that stood between the reader and the text: reality became their opinions; it was the perfect solipsistic world. Some philosophers, equally desperate to figure out just what the French Lit. Critters were doing, went along with doctrines of extreme epistemological relativism to back it up.

AP. You really think this was revolutionary?

AA. In an essentially trivial way, yes. It really was a kind of Oedipal pique. In one stroke you killed off the father (author), took over the mother matrix (the text), and formed your own primal horde (critical commentators). The next logical move of course is to renounce the text. All that remains is a fraternal horde of Lit. Critters pronouncing with infinite regress on each other's opinions: This is hermeneutics. Only Kafka or Lewis Caroll could do it justice.

AP. How does this tie in with the supposed *radicalism* of "cultural studies" and the wave of political correctness that has swept some English departments?

AA. It's intertwined, though in a tortuous way which has to stem from the fact that these people *want* to be radicals to begin with. There is no logical reason why it should lead to "deconstruction" — which is to say, destruction — of all established categories and canons. Logically, the movement could just as easily be reactionary. But the essence is two premises: that there is no authority, except of course the authority of the critic; and that there is no value-free criticism. Since there is no "outside" authority (not even a canon), power determines which opinions prevail. Since those with power currently make their opinions prevail (dominate the discourse, etc.), the business of Lit. Crit., Cultural Studies, etc. is to reverse this, deconstruct the categories of the powerful, and speak for the powerless. And it doesn't much matter what they say — there are no canons of truth, don't forget — so long as they are effective. This is what "rhetoric" is about: winning the argument.

AP. But shouldn't someone speak up for the powerless, minorities, women, etc.? Hasn't social science traditionally done that?

AA. Yes, but from a seriously different perspective. Social science — even relativistic anthropology — worked from a Fabian-type hope that if it demonstrated enough of the truth about the world, this would of necessity help the weak and oppressed. The new relativistic radicals assert that there is no truth about the world, and hence, in a sense, you simply pick sides and slug it out. It's a kind of latter-day existentialism, I suppose. You use rhetoric to win the dialogue of power — and all that.

AP. Why does this appeal to Marxists — those few still around?

376 The Challenge of Anthropology

AA. There are a lot still around, not knowing what to do in the post-Marxist present and willing to rewrite the Marxist sociology of knowledge to fit the new wisdom. The old Marxist doctrine says: Knowledge is relative to one's class; the proletariat is the progressive class, so its knowledge is the truth. It sees the issue as truth all right; it just locates it in a particular social space, as it were. In the new radicalism, theoretically, truth is not an issue since there isn't any. I think a real Marxist should have trouble with this, but they seem ready to swallow any objections in the name of establishment bashing, with which it is easy to go along.

AP. So the issue is pure power?

AA. Yes. And via one of those periodic misreadings of de Saussure which continue to plague us, linguistic power, which in this world of "social construction" is real power because the world is not a *Ding-an-Sich* but only what we say it is. So who controls the say-so controls the reality. This also makes it a nice cozy game for academics to play since the real warfare has been taken from the streets and put into the discourse. So academics can put themselves on the line for the revolution without leaving the study. A few nifty deconstructions and the Bastille of linguistic power is stormed.

AP. From where do they get the independent action of power? Is this inherent in language or what?

AA. A direct hit! Power essentially is an extralinguistic part of this altogether messy paradigm; a piece of earthy reality that does not flow from the premises. Why should people not be *indifferent* to the social constructions of reality? To some extent, in some eastern religions for example, they are.

A.P. Is this the real Marxist component then?

AA. I believe so. I said that these people *wanted* to be radicals; it does not flow from their logic that they should be. They are the leftover, antisystem, left-liberal, chic-radical, campus rebels and lumpen Marxists of the 1960s and 1970s. Therefore if they are going to deny authority and enter into a power struggle — which they needn't logically; they could just retire and contemplate — then it's obvious which way they will go, dragging along the bewildered mass of well-meaning academic liberals in their wake, and a bunch of younger people who thought they were just going to get dull old academic jobs and suddenly find that they are in one or other "movement" and get to bully people. It's heady stuff.

AP. How do they justify the power thing?

AA. By and large they don't. It's an axiom. I have taxed them with this. "You must accept that we are a hierarchical and power-seeking animal," I insist, "or this whole movement would have no basis."

AP. Their answer?

AA. Mostly they just sulk. It's really all a kind of adolescent sulk. You must have noticed how adolescents turn all discussions of their behavior into an issue of "control." Often I can't understand at all what they are saying. Like all such movements, it develops a private language. Sometimes they admit it, just as Berger and Luckman (and Durkheim before them) had to admit that the human tendency to the social construction of reality was a given feature of the organism.

AP. But isn't this the thin end of the wedge for them?

AA. Absolutely. If you let power in as an extrasystemic variable, how can you keep out exchange, for example? It was the limitation of Structuralism that it emphasized exchange to the exclusion of power. It is the limitation of poststructuralism that it ignores exchange in favor of power. But the groups involved in "multiculturalism," "diversity," "pluralism," and so on exchange at least as much as they conflict. That would be hard to quantify, but I'll stand by it. Just take music and dance, or food and drink, for starters — to say nothing of humor, clothing, sports, theater, religion, and, in fact, the whole panoply of culture.

AP. Perhaps. Perhaps a book with that as a thesis would be nice and controversial and get onto the popular shelves? But back to poor fragmented anthropology and the problem of whom we sell the books to. Is anthropology going to go wholesale into the arms of postmodernism then?

AA. When I hear the word postmodern I reach for my gun. No. I don't think so. As I said, many are simply getting on with their ever more specialized jobs and ignoring it. What will happen when the wave of infected graduate students starts getting jobs I don't know, but I doubt they could make the situation worse.

AP. And there is no hope for reintegration through your precious neo-Darwinian synthesis?

AA. That has really ceased to be such. The stage has been seized by what I perhaps uncharitably call the New Improved Sociobiology, which is really a specialized branch of population genetics with a number of quick-fix formulae for explaining social behavior that are leading off into their own blind alley. They are as lazy over learning about human behavior as their opponents are about learning evolutionary biology. They have nailed down a few good issues to call their own, and may even rescue kinship from its present anthropological doldrums, but they tend to behave in the same sectarian manner as the rest of the "specializations." The molecular biologists, endocrinologists, and neurobehavioral specialists are all going their own ways too.

AP. So even physical anthropology is splitting apart?

AA. Pretty much. The primatologists are moving toward zoology proper; the paleontologists have split off from the molecular biologists; the ecologists are pretty much going it alone and have their own agenda. There is no overall unity of theory and purpose. And behind the Iron Curtain of the social/cultural camp things are no better. Just look at the way the American Anthropological Association has split up into forty different groups, each with its own membership on bases as far removed as geography (Anthropology of Europe), ideology (Feminist Anthropology, Humanistic Anthropology), status (Association of Senior Anthropologists, Student Anthropology), subject matter (Medical Anthropology, Education, Political and Legal, Biological, Nutritional, etc.), method (Visual Anthropology, Mathematical), academic location (Community Colleges), and on and on. There is a "General Anthropology" section and a "Cultural Anthropology" association, and someone has, irony of ironies, asked for a "Scientific Anthropology" section, and the Californians have an "Anthropology of Consciousness" which, among other things, studies paranormal phenomena. New cells burst from the mother body almost daily.

AP. Couldn't this be seen as a sign of intellectual ferment? Of change, development, and reshaping of the discipline?

AA. It would only be such if it were taking place within some overall design, some theoretical framework such as natural selection provides for biology. But this isn't ferment, it is the end game of a process of fragmentation that we have seen is inherent in anthropology anyway and has been exacerbated by the ridiculous growth of the subject in the 1970s and 1980s. There are too many anthropological mouths to fill, too many people scrambling for promotion, and consequently too much specialization and frenetic mindless activity devoted to ever more trivial and repetitive issues. Throw into this the routinization of indignation and the politicization of theory, and we have a mess, not a discipline.

AP. Then it really is hopeless? There really is no audience for anthropology books geared to a unified discipline? We really are condemned to a lifetime of gender studies and oppression studies and little specialized series?

AA. Calm. Calm. For now it is a mess. But if you want me to risk a sociological prediction I will say that the mess will sort itself out sooner or later. Anthropology, like a boil, is straining to bursting and will eventually burst. The fallout will be confusing, as the various bits and pieces run for cover under the shelter of related disciplines (much the same is happening in sociology); but that may be a good thing. In the reshuffle, a new leaner and meaner anthropology may reconstitute itself, and in doing so it will look to those who kept alive the torch of the synthesizing, wholistic science of mankind that is now just an echo in old memories. Truth will be back in fashion; evolution will remain the paradigm, as it must, because it is all there is in the end; science will have advanced on so many specialized fronts that the new anthropology will be able to pick up information beyond its wildest present dreams. It will be there because no other science offers a vision (and science must offer a vision to succeed) of a unified account of man in both time and space: evolution, history, ethnography. This has always been its claim to uniqueness and remains its only claim to distinction among the sciences. Yes it will have to be reconstituted from the present mess. But the madness will pass in time. What I can't predict is how long this will take. But fads and fashions have a short life in this modern world, and people seek eternal verities in the end. If they don't find them in a new science of man, then they will find them in new religions of either a parochial and nasty kind (the New Nationalism) or, preferably, of a global and benign vagueness (Divine Gaia is already a candidate — and see Fred Turner's marvelous epic poem *Genesis* for how that can turn nasty). Let us hope for the future of the species, to whose study we are devoted, that they choose to return to reason, science, and, above all, a rational science of humanity. For this goes beyond departments, disciplines, promotions, and grants to the heart of how we are to survive as a species in a world we are rapidly making uninhabitable for ourselves. The kind of anthropology I envisage will reconstitute itself, I believe (although it may be called something else — "Human Sciences" perhaps), because we have no real choice where our own survival is concerned.

AP. Then we should go ahead with the book?

AA. Definitely. There may not be much in it for us, but our great-grandchildren will thank us for it. After all, are we looking for prosperity or for posterity?

AP. With luck, both. But lay off the Christopher Robin stuff.

AA. Sure. I'm going to start with Goldilocks this time. Or perhaps, as they say, with something completely different. How about this little gem of relativism I came across recently:

> If relativism signifies contempt for fixed categories and men who claim to be bearers of an objective, immortal truth, then there is nothing more relativistic than (our) attitudes.
> ...
> From the fact that all ideologies are of equal value, the modern relativist infers that everybody has the right to create for himself his own ideology and to attempt to enforce it with all the energy of which he is capable.

AP. Who is that? Stanley Fish? Terry Eagleton? Betty Jean Craige? George Marcus? The MLA?

AA. Benito Mussolini. Ciao caro!

Notes and References

General Acknowledgments

Specific acknowledgments are contained in the notes to each chapter. Here I should first like to thank Irving Louis Horowitz and Mary Curtis, who talked me into this effort, thought up the title, and improved the format. Also thanks are due to Esther Luckett and all the editorial and production staff at Transaction Publishers, and especially, once again, to Arri Parker for her devoted editing, which has much improved the book. Tony Urgo has, also once again, proved himself an excellent and cooperative draftsman. I would also like to thank Adriana Greci Green, without whose valiant assistance the book would never have found a final shape.

The book is dedicated to an old friend and mentor, sorely missed, who changed my life for the better in innumerable ways. And this goes for his beloved Rutgers — as benign and supportive an institution as any academic could wish for.

Notes to Chapter 1

This chapter appeared originally as "Les conditions de l'évolution sexuelle," in *Sexualités Occidentales*, edited by Philippe Ariès and André Béjin, a special edition (no. 35) of the journal *Communications*, 1982. The whole edition appeared in English translation as *Western Sexuality*, published by Basil Blackwell (Oxford and New York, 1985). It is from this English translation that the present chapter is reprinted, with permission of the publishers.

The whole argument as presented here is spelled out in my *The Red Lamp of Incest* (New York: Dutton, 1980; 2nd ed. Notre Dame, IN: University of Notre Dame Press, 1983). The notes to chapter 2 of the present book contain many of the relevant references, but the reader might also want to consult Donald Symons, *The Evolution of Human Sexuality* (New York: Oxford University Press, 1979); M. Daly and M. Wilson, *Sex, Evolution and Behavior* (North Scituate, MA: Duxbury Press, 1978; 2nd ed. Boston: Willard Grant Press, 1983); and George C. Williams, *Sex and Evolution* (Monographs in Population Biology no. 8, Princeton, NJ: Princeton University Press, 1975). A good collection of essays on the topic is *Human Reproductive Behavior: A Darwinian Approach*, edited by Laura Betzig, Monique Borgerhoff Mulder, and Paul Turke (Cambridge: Cambridge University Press, 1988). Equally, Robert Trivers, *Social Evolution* (Menlo Park, CA: Cummings, 1985) is indispensable, especially on the subject of parental investment.

References for Chapter 2

Campbell, B. and Peterson, W. E. 1953. "Milk Let-Down and Orgasm in the Human Female." *Human Biology* 25: 165-68.
Gould, Stephen J. 1987. "Freudian Slip." *Natural History* February: 15-21.
Hrdy, Sarah. 1981. *The Woman That Never Evolved.* Cambridge: Harvard Univrsity Press.
Kinsey, A. C.; Pomeroy, W. B.; Martin, C. E.; Gebhard, P. H.; et al. 1953. *Sexual Behavior in the Human Female.* Philadelphia: W. B. Saunders.
Konner, M. 1990. *Why the Reckless Survive.* New York: Viking.
Masters, W. H. and Johnson, V. E. 1966. *Human Sexual Response.* Boston: Little Brown.
Morris, D. 1967. *The Naked Ape.* London: Constable.
Newton, N. 1973. "Interrelationships Between Sexual Responsiveness, Birth and Breast Feeding." In . J. Zubin and J. Money, eds.,*Contemporary Sexual Behavior: Critical Issues in the 1970's* (Baltimore: Johns Hopkins).
Rossi, A. 1977. "A Biosocial Perspective on Parenting." *Daedalus* 106: 1-33.
Tiger, L. 1992. *The Pursuit of Pleasure.* Boston: Little Brown.

Note to Chapter 3

This chapter was originally written for the *Enciclopedia delle Scienze Sociali* (Rome: Enciclopedia Italiana Treccani), and is reproduced with permission of the editors and publishers.

References for Chapter 3

Arens, W. 1986. *The Original Sin: Incest and Its Meaning*. New York: Oxford University Press.

Bateson, P. P. G., ed. 1983. *Mate Choice*. Cambridge: Cambridge University Press.

Bischof, N. 1975. "Comparative Ethology of Incest Avoidance." In R. Fox, ed., *Biosocial Anthropology* (London/New York: Malaby Press).

Bodmer, W. F. and Cavalli-Sforza, L. L. 1976. *Genetics, Evolution and Man*. San Francisco: W. H. Freeman.

Chance, M. R. A. 1962. "Nature and Special Features of the Instinctive Social Bond of Primates." In S. L. Wasburn, ed. *Social Life of Early Man* (London: Methuen).

Count, E. 1967. "The Lactation Complex: A Phylogenetic Consideration of the Mammalian Mother-Child Symbiosis, with Special Reference to Man." *Homo* 18(1): 38-54.

de Heusch, L. 1958. *Essais sur le symbolisme de l'inceste royal en Afrique*. Bruxelles: Université Libre De Bruxelles.

Fox, R. 1962. "Sibling Incest." *British Journal of Sociology* 13: 28-150.

Fox, R. 1967 *Kinship and Marriage: An Anthropological Perspective*. Harmondsworth: Penguin. 2nd ed.: New York: Cambridge University Press, 1983.

Fox, R. 1980. *The Red Lamp of Incest*. New York: Dutton. 2nd ed.: Notre Dame: University of Notre Dame Press, 1983.

Freud, S. 1913. *Totem und Tabu*. Vienna: Hugo Heller.

Freud, S. 1922. *Introductory Lectures on Psychoanalysis*. London: Allen and Unwin.

Goggin, J. M. and Sturtevant, W. C. 1964. "The Calusa, a Stratified, Nonagricultural Society (with notes on sibling marriage)." In W. T. Goodenough, ed., *Explorations in Cultural Anthropology* (New York: McGraw-Hill).

Gowen, J. W. 1964. *Heterosis*. New York: Hofner.

Hamilton, W. 1967. "Extraordinary Sex Ratios." *Science* 156: 477-88.

Hartung, J. 1985. Review of Shepher (1983). *American Journal of Physical Anthropology* 67(2): 169-171.

Herman, J. L. 1981. *Father-Daughter Incest*. Cambridge, MA: Harvard University Press.

Hopkins, K. 1980. "Brother-Sister Marriage in Roman Egypt." *Comparative Studies in Society and History* 22: 303-354.

Huth, A. H. 1877[1875]. *The Marriage of Near Kin: Considered with Respect to the Laws of Nations, the Results of Experience and the Teachings of Biology.* 2nd ed. London and New York: Longman's Green Co.

Lévi-Strauss, C. 1949. *Les structures élémentaires de la parenté.* Paris: Presses Universitaires de France.

Lindzey, G. 1967. "Some Remarks Concerning Incest, the Incest Taboo, and Psychoanalytic Theory." *American Psychologist* 22(12): 1051-59.

Livingstone, F. B. 1969. "Genetics, Ecology and the Origins of Incest and Exogamy." *Current Anthropology* 10: 45-61.

Middleton, R. 1962. "Brother-Sister and Father-Daughter Marriage in Ancient Egypt." *American Sociological Review* 27(5): 603-11.

Murdock, G. P. 1949. *Social Structure.* New York: Macmillan.

Pusey, A. E. 1980. "Inbreeding Avoidance in Chimpanzees." *Animal Behavior* 28: 543-52.

Sade, D. S. 1968. "Inhibition of Son-Mother Mating among Free-Ranging Rhesus Monkeys." *Science and Psychoanalysis* 12: 18-27.

Seemanova, E. 1971. "A Study of Children of Incestuous Matings." *Human Heredity* 21(1): 108-128.

Shepher, J. 1983. *Incest: A Biosocial View.* New York/London: Academic Press.

Shoumatoff, A. 1985. *The Mountain of Names.* New York: Simon and Schuster.

Slater, M. K. 1959. "Ecological Factors in the Origin of Incest." *American Anthropologist* 61: 1042-1059.

Weinberg, K. S. 1955. *Incest Behavior.* New York: Citadel Press.

Westermarck, E. 1926. *A Short History of Marriage.* New York: Macmillan.

Williams, G. C. 1975. *Sex and Evolution.* Princeton: Princeton University Press.

Wolf, A. and Huang, C. 1980. *Marriage and Adoption in China 1845-1945.* Stanford: Stanford University Press.

Note to Chapter 4

This chapter is the original manuscript that was used as a basis for several entries in Peter Marsh, ed., *Lifestyle: Your Surroundings and How They Affect You.* (London: Sidgwick and Jackson, 1990) (©1990, Andromeda Oxford Ltd.) and is reproduced by permission of the copyright owners.

References and Further Reading for Chapter 4

The following are either works referred to in the text or books that I have found particularly useful, or pleasurable, in understanding the history and ethnography of food and wine. The first two are both excellent histories of food and eating, and the best place to start.

Mennell, Stephen. 1985. *All Manners of Food*. Oxford: Blackwell.
Tannahill, Reay. 1988. *Food in History*. Rev. ed. Harmondsworth: Penguin.
Barr, Andrew. 1988. *Wine Snobbery: An Exposé*. New York: Simon and Schuster.
Beaton, Isabelle Mary. 1861. *The Book of Household Management*. London: S. O. Beeton.
Brillat-Savarin, Jean Anthelme. 1828. *Physiologie du goût, ou, Méditations de gastronomie transcendante: ouvrage théorique, historique et à l'ordre du jour, dédié aux gastronomes parisiens*. 2 vols. 2nd ed. Paris: A. Sautelet.
Douglass, Mary, ed. 1982. *Food in the Social Order: Studies of Food and Festivities in Three American Communities*. New York: Russell Sage.
Eaton, S. Boyd; Shostak, Marjorie; and Konner, Melvin. 1988. *The Paleolithic Prescription: A Program of Diet and Exercise and a Design for Living*. New York: Harper and Row.
Fussell, Betty. 1983. *Masters of American Cookery*. New York: Times Books.
Johnson, Hugh. 1989. *Vintage: The Story of Wine*. New York: Simon and Schuster.
Lévi-Strauss, Claude. 1969. *The Elementary Structures of Kinship*. Boston: Beacon Press.
Liebling, A. J. 1986. *Between Meals: An Appetite for Paris*. San Francisco: North Point Press.
Luard, Elizabeth. 1987. *The Old World Kitchen*. New York: Bantam Books
Remoff, Heather. 1984. *Female Sexual Choice*. New York: Dutton.
Strang, Jeanne. 1991. *Goose Fat and Garlic*. London: Kyle Kathie Ltd.
Tiger, Lionel. 1992. *The Pursuit of Pleasure*. Boston: Little Brown.
Wolf, Reinhart and Tiger, Lionel. 1976. *China's Food*. New York: Friendly Press.

Notes to Chapter 5

This chapter was originally written as a contribution to *Man and Beast Revisited*, edited by Michael Robinson and Lionel Tiger (Washington, DC:

Smithsonian Institution Press, 1991), and is reproduced by permission of the publishers.

Lionel Tiger made numerous useful suggestions for the improvement of this piece, and he and Michael Robinson encouraged me to try my arm and go well beyond what they originally intended.

Another version of it, intended more specifically to reconcile the conflict between the sinners and the perfectionists, will appear in a volume dedicated to Ashley Montagu and tentatively titled *Race and Other Misadventures: Essays in Honor of Ashley Montagu,* edited by Larry T. Reynolds and Leonard Lieberman (New York: General Hall Inc.).

Notes to Chapter 6

This chapter was originally a presentation for an MCM Research conference on "Alcohol and Public Disorder" at Oxford University in December 1990. It has been printed by MCM Research, but only for private circulation. It is here reproduced with their permission. I am very grateful to Peter Marsh and Kate Fox of MCM Research for their invitation, hospitality, and criticism. A fine example of their work can be found in Peter Marsh and Kate Fox Kibby, *Drinking and Public Disorder* (London: The Portman Group, 1992).

Still the best treatment of "escalation" in violence is Joseph L. Popp and Irven DeVore, "Aggressive Competition and Social Dominance Theory: Synopsis," in D. A. Hamburg and E. R. McCown, eds., *The Great Apes* (Menlo Park, CA: Benjamin Cummings Pub. Co., 1979). I am grateful to Irv DeVore for many useful conversations on this and most other topics. The latest on testosterone can be found in Theodore D. Kemper, *Social Structure and Testosterone* (New Brunswick, NJ: Rutgers University Press, 1990). See also J.-P. Ewart, *Neuroethology* (New York: Springer-Verlagh, 1980) and A. Gale and J. A. Edwards, eds., *Physiological Correlates of Human Behavior,* 3 vols. (New York: Academic Press, 1983).

Notes to Chapter 7

This chapter originally appeared as: "The Seville Declaration: Anthropology's Auto-da-fe" in *Academic Questions* 1(4) (1988): 35-47. It is reproduced here by permission of Transaction Publishers. I should like to thank Steven Balch and Caroll Iannone for their comments and help. It was later reprinted in the now defunct *Encounter* (73[3] [1989]: 58-64). I mourn the loss of this fine journal, and wish to thank its editors Mel Lasky and Anthony Hartley for giving me an outlet and encouragement over the years.

1. Two people wrote to the *Newsletter* protesting about the denigration of "a city and a nation" in the reference to Seville. This is puzzling. Do they mean there was no Inquisition; that it was not in Spain; that Seville was not its center there; that it was not sordid? No disrespect was meant to Spain or to Seville. But the Spanish Inquisition was a fact, and Seville was its sordid center.

2. *Harry Frank Guggenheim Foundation Newsletter* 4(1) (Fall 1987). The *Human Ethology Newsletter*, to its credit, printed this whole exchange in 5(5) (1988): 4. While this article was in press, *Psychology Today*, (22[6] [1988]: 35-38) printed an article by Alfie Kohn entitled "Make Love, Not War," devoted to promoting the views of the declaration by quotes from obvious supporters of the position and a printing of excerpts from the Statement. No contrary views were entertained, and there was no attempt at a critical assessment.

3. Peter Lengyel, *International Social Science: The Unesco Experience* (New Brunswick, NJ: Transaction Publishers, 1986).

4. This is what Hinde fails to grasp in his reply to Manson and Wrangham. The very reasoned and argued nature of his reply in effect belies the nature of the Declaration. If the arguments of the Declaration are to be countered or supported, then this must follow his model of countering the Manson-Wrangham arguments: reason and counterevidence — not majoritarian "resolutions" passed by bodies the majority of whose members have never engaged in relevant research and do not even know the basic published materials, but who are following an ideological line.

5. Robin Fox, "Aggression: Then and Now" in Michael Robinson and Lionel Tiger (eds.), *Man and Beast Revisited* (Washington, DC: Smithsonian Institution, 1991).

6. Hinde does not seem to see that what Wrangham and Manson fear is precisely what he naively denies: that the Declaration will have a damaging effect on aggression research if this research does not, in advance, fall into line with the Declaration's environmentalist ideology. It could not, for example, hope for much support from UNESCO or the professional bodies which have adopted the resolution.

7. See Kent G. Bailey, *Human Paleopsychology: Applications to Aggression and Pathological Processes* (Hillsdale, NJ: Lawrence Erlbaum, 1987); V. H. Mark and F. R. Ervin, *Violence and the Brain* (New York: Harper and Row, 1970).

8. Julian Huxley, *Soviet Genetics and World Science* (London: Chatto and Windus, 1949); David Joravsky, *The Lysenko Affair* (Cambridge, MA: Harvard University Press, 1970); Z. A. Medved, *The Rise and Fall of T. D. Lysenko* (New York: Columbia University Press, 1969).

Notes to Chapter 8

This was originally published as "Fatal Attraction: War and Human Nature" in *The National Interest* 30(Winter 1992/93):11-20, and is reproduced with the magazine's permission. I am grateful to Owen Harries and Michael Lind for their helpful comments. The subheadings are theirs. References are contained in the text.

John Mueller and I have had some correspondence over this issue, and I think we have agreed that we are not that far apart in our thinking. We both agree that war is a human construct. We differ in that I find such construction almost inevitable, while he thinks it is capable of deconstruction. I don't buy the analogies of dueling and slavery; he doesn't like mine of religion and prostitution — or at least thinks that both of these are equally dispensable human constructs. I don't think they are perfect analogies either, but am sceptical of their prospective demise (although I am using a much broader definition of "religion" than he: more like "ideology"). The difference ultimately is not so much in the analysis as in the conclusions drawn from it: mine are pessimistic, his optimistic. History will be the judge. At least we share a passion for the art of Fred Astaire — surely a sign of hope (see John Mueller, *Astaire Dancing* [New York: Wings Books, 1991]).

Notes to Chapter 9

This was originally published in *Belonging: Identity and Social Organization in British Rural Cultures*, edited by Anthony P. Cohen (Manchester: Manchester University Press, 1982), and is reproduced by permission of the press.

The work of mine on land tenure referred to is "Kinship and Land Tenure on Tory Island," *Ulster Folklife* LII (1967).

An excellent description of Gaelic on Tory is J. N. Hamilton, *A Phonetic Study of the Irish of Tory Island,* Studies in Irish Language and Literature, vol. 3 (Belfast: Institute of Irish Studies, The Queen's University of Belfast, 1974). Unfortunately this was not available to me during my fieldwork (1960-65), but I did meet Hamilton briefly on Tory and he gave me some valuable help at the time.

A good comparative survey of traditional European land tenure is *Family and Inheritance: Rural Society in Western Europe, 1200-1800*, edited by J. Goody, J. Thirsk, and E. P. Thompson (Cambridge: Cambridge University Press, 1976).

Full references to works mentioned here can be found in the notes to *The Tory Islanders* (Cambridge: Cambridge University Press, 1979).

Notes to Chapter 10

This was originally written for a memorial volume on the centenary of the publication of *The Golden Bough*, edited by H. Philsooph of Aberdeen University. The volume has not yet appeared, but may well do so. I should like to thank Dr. Philsooph for his excellent editing, and for saving me from a number of errors, and also Lowell Edmunds, Robert Fagles, Ashley Montagu, and Peter Kibby (who spotted Virgil's pun) for their helpful comments.

References are noted in the text, but the following bibliography will help those who want more exact source ascription. Dr. Philsooph recommended to me, as a good discussion of Frazer and classical sources, J. Z. Smith, "When the Bough Breaks," *History of Religions* 12(4) (1973): 342-371. An excellent biography of Frazer is Robert Ackerman, *J. G. Frazer: His Life and Work* (Cambridge: Cambridge University Press, 1987). A very good introduction to *The Golden Bough* for students and others who find the tomes daunting, is *The Illustrated Golden Bough*, abridged and illustrated by Sabine MacCormck and with an introduction by Mary Douglas (Garden City, NY: Doubleday, 1978). Popper's great *Logik der Forschung* was still untranslated when I was a student at LSE. My German was pathetic: picked up from my father's soldier version learned in handling prisoners in Holland post D-Day, plus my own direct contact with German prisoners in England during World War II, and augmented only by singing Bach and listening to Wagner. This would not do for Popper, and my knowledge of his critique of "Scientific Method" came from his lectures and classes on the subject, and from the passionate advocacy of his more avid fans. Of course, we all read *The Open Society and Its Enemies*, and eventually the translation of the *Logik — The Logic of Scientific Discovery* (London: Hutchinson, 1959). I have cited the facsimile edition of *The Waste Land* below since readers might like to see how the poem appeared before the lethal blue pencil of Ezra Pound did its job. At least he spared Eliot the embarrassment of calling the work "He Do the Police in Different Voices" (from Dickens).

The following is a rough literal translation of Lévi-Strauss's French in the passage quoted:

We must recognize that Frazer deserves the credit for being the first to call attention to the similarity in structure between marriage by exchange and marriage between cross cousins, and establishing the real connection which exists between the two institutions. The point of departure for his demonstration is the observation that in certain kinship systems permitting preferential marriage with only one of the cross cousins (usually the mother's brother's daughter) one finds nevertheless the double identification of mother's brother with father-in-law and father's sister with mother-in-law. This second identification cannot be understood, however, unless one hypothesizes marriage with the father's sister's daughter. This difficulty is cleared up, remarks Frazer, if we suppose that the two cross cousins are the same, that is if the mother's brother's daughter is at the same time the father's sister's daughter, a situation which automatically comes about in the case where the cross cousins are the issue of brothers who have exchanged their sisters.

The French is very easy, but there are subtleties that must be observed. Thus in his cotranslation, Rodney Needham renders "comportant" as "requiring" whereas I prefer the primary meaning of "permitting" or "allowing." It is hard to see how a system could "require" a form of marriage defined as "preferential." Those who remember the debate on "prescriptive" versus "preferential" marriage — one in which Lévi-Strauss took decided issue with his translator (see the sniping in the prefaces and introductions to the English translation) — will see that Needham is ever so slightly tipping the scales in his own — prescriptive — direction with this minor nicety. Lévi-Strauss refuses to read translations of his own works, or he might have caught it. (Oh how we pedants love these little points! I caught the great Arthur O. Lovejoy citing the wrong edition of Voltaire's *Philosophical Dictionary* in a quote in *The Great Chain of Being*. I was happy for a week. But one should never gloat. I've slipped up too many times myself.)

Works by Frazer Mentioned in the Text

Frazer, J. G. 1890. *The Golden Bough.* 2 vols., London: Macmillan. 2nd. ed., 3 vols., 1900; 3rd. ed., 12 vols., 1911-15; abridged ed., 1 vol., 1922.
———. 1910. *Totemism and Exogamy.* 4 vols. London: Macmillan.
———. 1918. *Folklore in the Old Testament.* 3 vols. London: Macmillan. Abridged ed., 1 vol., New York: Tudor Pub. Co., 1923.

Other Works Mentioned

Ayer, A, J. 1954[1936]. *Language, Truth and Logic.* London: Gollancz.
Eliot, T. S. 1971[1922]. *The Waste Land: A Facsimile and Transcript of the Original Drafts Including the Annotations of Ezra Pound.* Edited by Valerie Eliot. New York: Harcourt Brace Jovanovitch.
Evans-Pritchard, E. E. 1956. *Nuer Religion.* Oxford: Oxford University Press.
Gaster, T. H., ed. 1959. *The New Golden Bough.* Garden City, NY: Doubleday.

Kuper, A. 1988. *The Invention of Primitive Society*. London: Routledge.
Lévi-Strauss, C. 1949. *Les structures élémentaires de la parenté*. Paris: Presses Universitaires de France. English translation: *The Elementary Structures of Kinship*, by J. H. Bell, J. R. von Sturmer, and Rodney Needham, editor (Boston: Beacon Press, 1969).
Malinowski, B. 1922. *Argonauts of the Western Pacific*, with a preface by Sir J. G. Frazer. London: Routledge and Kegan Paul.
——. 1926. *Myth in Primitive Psychology*. London: Psyche Miniatures. Reprinted in *Magic Science and Religion and Other Essays*, with an introduction by Robert Redfield (New York: Doubleday, 1955).
——. 1948. *A Scientific Theory of Culture*. Chapel Hill, NC: University of North Carolina Press.
Murdock, G. P. 1934. *Our Primitive Contemporaries*. New York: Macmillan.
——. 1949. *Social Structure*. New York: Macmillan.
Namier, L. 1952. *Avenues of History*. London: Hamish Hamilton.
O'Rourke, P. J. 1991. *Parliament of Whores*. New York: Atlantic Monthly Press.
Radcliffe-Brown, A. R. 1952. *Structure and Function in Primitive Society*. London: Cohen and West.
Rice, Anne. 1985. *The Vampire Lestat: The Second Book in the Chronicles of the Vampires*. New York: Knopf.
Tylor, E. B. 1889. "On a Method of Investigating the Development of Institutions: Applied to the Laws of Marriage and Descent." *Journal of the [Royal] Anthropological Institute* 18:245-269.
Weston, Jesse L. 1920. *From Ritual to Romance*. Cambridge: Cambridge University Press.

References for Chapter 11

Allen, Ross. 1948. "The Big Circle Mounds." *Florida Archaeologist* 1(1-2): 17-21.
Campbell, Joseph. 1959. *The Masks of God: Primitive Mythology*. 4 vols. New York: Viking Press.
Crown, Patricia and Judge, James W., eds. 1990. *Chaco and Hohokam*. Santa Fe, NM: School of American Research.
Cushing, Frank H. 1897. "Exploration of Ancient Key-Dweller Remains on the Gulf Coast of Florida." *Proceedings of the American Philosophical Society* 35:153.
Densmore, Frances. 1956. *Seminole Music*. United States Bureau of American Ethnology Bulletin 161. Washington, DC: U.S. Government Printing Office.

Durkheim, Emile. 1893. *De la division du travail social: étude sur l'organisation des sociétés supérieures*. Paris: Alcan.

Eggan Fred, 1949. *The Social Organization of the Western Pueblos*. Chicago: Chicago University Press.

Fox, Robin. 1967a. *Kinship and Marriage: An Anthropological Perspective*. Harmondsworth: Penguin. 2nd ed. Cambridge: Cambridge University Press, 1982.

———. 1967b. *The Keresan Bridge: A Problem in Pueblo Ethnology*. London: Athlone Press; New York: Humanities Press.

———. 1975. "Primate Kin and Human Kinship." In R. Fox, ed., *Biosocial Anthropology* (New York: Malaby Press).

———. 1989. *The Search For Society: Quest for a Biosocial Science and Morality*. New Brunswick, NJ: Rutgers University Press.

Frazier, Kendrick. 1986. *People of Chaco: A Canyon and Its Culture*. New York: W. W. Norton.

Gellner, Ernest. 1990. *Plough, Sword and Book*. Chicago: University of Chicago Press.

Gilliland, Marion S. 1975. *The Material Culture of Key Marco, Florida*. Gainesville: University Presses of Florida.

———. 1989. *Key Marco's Buried Treasure*. Gainesville: University of Florida Press. Florida Museum of Natural History.

Goggin, John M. and Sturtevant, William T. 1964. "The Calusa: A Stratified Non-Agricultural Society (with Notes on Sibling Marriage)." In Ward Goodenough, ed., *Explorations in Cultural Anthropology: Essays in Honor of George Peter Murdock* (New York: McGraw-Hill).

Goody, Jack, ed. 1968. *Literacy in Traditional Societies*. Cambridge: Cambridge University Press.

Grant, Michael. 1990. *The Fall of the Roman Empire*. Rev. ed. London: Weidenfeld and Nicholson.

Hann, John. 1991. *Missions to the Calusa*. Gainesville: University Presses of Florida.

Havelock, Eric. 1963. *Preface to Plato*. Cambridge, MA: Harvard University Press.

Hayes, Alden C. 1981. "A Survey of Chaco Canyon Archaeology." In Alden C. Hayes, David M. Brugge, and W. James Judge, eds., *Archaeological Surveys of Chaco Canyon* (Washington, DC: National Park Service).

Lange, Charles H. 1959. *Cochiti: A New Mexico Pueblo Past and Present*. Austin: University of New Mexico Press.

Larsen, M. T. 1988. "Introduction: Literacy and Social Complexity." In J. Gledhill, B. Bender, and M. T. Larsen, eds., *State and Society: The Emer-*

gence and Development of Social Hierarchy and Political Centralization (London: Unwin Hyman).

Lekson, Stephen H. 1984. *Great Pueblo Architecture of Chaco Canyon, New Mexico*. Albuquerque, NM: National Park Service, U.S. Dept. of the Interior. Reprint: Albuquerque, NM: University of New Mexico Press, 1986.

Luer, George M. 1989. "Calusa Canals in Southwestern Florida: Routes of Tribute and Exchange." *The Florida Anthropologist* 42(3): 49-130.

Marquardt, William H. 1988. "Politics and Production among the Calusa of South Florida." In Tim Ingold, David Riches, and James Woodburn, eds. *Hunters and Gatherers 1: History, Evolution and Social Change* (Oxford: Berg; New York: St. Martin's Press).

Marquardt, William H., ed. 1991. *Culture and Environment in the Domain of the Calusa*. Monograph I, Institute of Archaeology and Paleoenvironmental Studies of the University of Florida. Gainesville: University of Florida.

Marshack, Alexander. 1972. *The Roots of Civilization: The Cognitive Beginnings of Man's First Art, Symbol and Notation*. New York: McGraw-Hill.

McGuire, Randall H. 1989. "The Greater Southwest as a Periphery of Mesoamerica." In T. C. Champion, ed.,*Centre and Periphery: Comparative Studies in Archaeology* (London: Unwin Hyman).

Mellart, J. 1966. "Excavations at Catal Huyuk, 1965: Fourth Preliminary Report." *Anatolian Studies: 1966.*

Mellart, J. 1967. *Catal Huyuk: A Neolithic Town in Anatolia*. New York: McGraw-Hill.

Ortiz, Alfonso. 1969. *The Tewa World*. Chicago: Chicago University Press.

Pfeiffer, John. 1982. *The Creative Explosion*. New York: Harper and Row.

Rowlands, Michael. 1989. "A Question of Complexity." In D. Miller, M. Rowlands, and C. Tilley, eds., *Domination and Resistance* (London: Unwin Hyman).

Spencer, Herbert. 1879. *The Principles of Sociology: Vol. 1*. London: Williams and Norgate.

Tainter, Joseph A. 1988. *The Collapse of Complex Societies*. New Studies in Archaeology. Cambridge: Cambridge University Press.

Tillion, Germaine. 1983[1966]. *The Republic of Cousins: Women's Oppression in Mediterranean Society,* translated by Quintin Hoare. London: Al Saqi Books. First published as *Harem et les cousins* (Paris: 1966).

Titiev, Mischa. 1944. *Old Oraibi: A Study of the Hopi Indians of Third Mesa.* Papers of the Peabody Museum, XXII:1. Cambridge, MA: Peabody Museum of American Archaeology and Ethnology.

Ucko, P. J. and Rosenfeld, A. 1967. *Palaeolithic Cave Art.* London: Weidenfeld and Nicholson.

White, Leslie A. 1962. *The Pueblo of Sia, New Mexico.* Bulletins of the Bureau of American Ethnology, Smithsonian Institution, no. 184. Washington, DC: U.S. Government Printing Office.

Widmer, Randolph J. 1988. *The Evolution of the Calusa: A Nonagricultural Chiefdom on the Southwest Florida Coast.* Tuscaloosa: University of Alabama Press.

Willey, Gordon R. 1949. *Excavations in Southeast Florida.* New Haven: Yale University Publications in Anthropology, no. 42.

Windes, Thomas C. 1984. "A New Look at Population in Chaco Canyon." In W. James Judge and John D. Schelberg, eds., *Recent Research on Chaco Prehistory* (Reports of the Chaco Center, no. 8. Albuquerque, NM: National Park Service, Division of Cultural Research).

Plate 11.2 and Map 2 are reproduced by the kind permission of the National Parks Service. I would like to thank Larry Nordby and the staff of the NPS Southwest Region for their help.

Notes to Chapter 12

Barnes, J. A. 1967. *Inquest on the Murngin.* London: Occasional Papers of the Royal Anthropological Institute, no. 26.

Fox, R. 1967. *Kinship and Marriage: An Anthropological Perspective.* Harmonsdsworth: Penguin. 2nd. ed.: New York: Cambridge University Press, 1983.

Fox, R. 1972. "Alliance and Constraint: Sexual Selection and the Evolution of Human Kinship Systems." In Bernard Campbell, ed., *Sexual Selection and the Descent of Man 1871-1971*(Chicago: Aldine).

Goodale, Jane. 1962. "Marriage Contracts Among the Tiwi." *Ethnology* 1: 452-465.

Hart, C. W. M. and Pilling, A. R. 1960. *The Tiwi of Northern Australia.* New York: Holt Rinehart and Winston.

Hiatt, L. R. 1965. *Kinship and Conflict: A Study of an Aboriginal Community in Northern Arnhem Land.* Canberra: Australian National University.

Lee, R. B. and DeVore, I., eds. 1968. *Man the Hunter.* Chicago: Aldine.

Meggitt, M. J. 1962. *Desert People: A Study of the Walbiri Aborigines of Central Australia.* Sidney: Angus and Robertson.

Rose, F. G. G. 1960. *Classification of Kin, Age-Structure and Marriage among the Groote Eylandt Aborigines: A Study in Method and Theory of Australian Kinship.* Berlin: Akademie-Verlag/ London: Pergamon Press.

Shapiro, W. 1968. "The Exchange of Sister's Daughter's Daughters in Northeast Arnhem Land." *Southwestern Journal of Anthropology* 24: 346-353.

————. 1981. *Miwuyt Marriage: The Cultural Anthropology of Affinity in Northeast Arnhem Land.* Philadelphia: Institute for the Study of Human Issues.

Notes to Chapter 13

One point worth explaining is that between publication of *The Keresan Bridge* in 1967 and of the article in 1972, I had come down firmly in favor of a definite Cochiti preference for marriage of a man into the clan of his mother's father, that is, with a real or classificatory MFZDD. (Marriage into one's own clan is of course forbidden — although in the large Oak clan there have been exceptions — and marriage into the father's clan is frowned on while not absolutely forbidden.) The other "available" grandparental clan, that of father's father, while not forbidden was not particularly encouraged either. I had noted in *Keresan Bridge* (pp. 130-31), under the heading of "sequential interclan marriages," the discussion of an "ideal" marriage. But at the time I missed the significance of its ideality. The reader can check that it was a marriage with an actual MFZDD (or one of two possible such relatives). This is why the elders were so excited about its possibility. I had simply taken it as a further marriage in the "sequence." In my notes, however, I had taken down several times the insistence that it was indeed a marriage into the boy's mother's father's clan. I had regarded this as incidental, whereas, of course, it was crucial.

An all-too-brief return visit to New Mexico in 1969 (a decade after my previous visit) enabled me to question several of the oldest Cochiti further on this preference. They made it clear to me that such a marriage was particularly auspicious and to be preferred. "In the old days" such a partner would be sought out and a marriage arranged. Today, of course, it was not the same since young people made their own choices, but when such a choice fell on a girl of the right clan, it was cause for great pleasure and celebration. It was, one of my friends told me laughingly, "what you would call a marriage made in heaven." (This was the irrepressible Joe Trujillo, ex-governor of the Pueblo, my "landlord" when I was there, and a very great gentleman indeed. He is now dead, as is my other main helper, Epifanio Pecos, ex-War Captain and chief linguistic cooperator.)

With the help of the marriage records, kindly supplied by the Franciscan fathers from the church at Peña Blanca, we tried to reconstruct the pattern as it might have appeared in marriages before World War II. After the war the preference was pretty much ignored and only cropped up occasionally, I was told. The problem was knowing the "grandparental" clans of the partners, and this got more and more difficult as the marriages receded in time, and when the preference would have been most likely to have been observed. Pueblo Indians do not keep, and are not interested in, deep genealogies. We did have Esther Goldfrank's genealogies from the 1920s and these helped enormously, but it was still difficult. Some of the marriages were easy to spot because they were within the forbidden degrees and required a dispensation (always given), while others were with classificatory rather than real second cross cousins and so escaped this particular sorting device. In other cases, I was told, "traditionalists" had simply avoided the Catholic marriage ceremony and gone with the Indian ceremony only. These were people most likely to observe the preference. It is more usual to have both weddings, but the truly conservative faction evidently often took the purely native route.

The upshot was a not very reliable count but one that was suggestive. In marriages where we could be sure of knowing the relevant clans, about one-fifth were into the mother's father's clan. No other clan came close, and the father's father's clan fared no better than unrelated clans in this respect. Why the system should have been skewed in this direction I do not know, except that the father's clan is regarded as "closest" to ego's own, which is of course his mother's, and hence the mother's father's clan is the next closest. These are the two clans that have married into ego's clan; or, looked at another way, these are the two clans that have taken women from ego's clan, or to whom ego's clan has given women — which is how the Cochiti would phrase it. They are thought of then as closely related to each other, and if ego cannot take a bride from his father's clan, the next choice will be the mother's father's. The father's father's clan is regarded as more or less "unrelated" in this sense. This is the sense of the matter I got from the older Cochiti.

Of course, going only by the symmetry of the clans, one should logically favor both mother's father's and father's father's clans, like the Cherokee. In either case, however, an "exchange" is involved if the rule is systematically followed; an exchange not unlike the Aranda system diagrammed in the previous chapter (12.3), but involving matrilines rather than patrilines (it makes no structural difference). For the interest of the kinship specialist, I have diagrammed below such a possible exchange system between four clans practicing systematic marriage into the mother's father's clan (MFZDD). I was loath to do this in the chapter itself since the discussion was already complicated enough.

Here we can see clearly the four matriclans involved: MM's, MF's, FM's, and FF's. An Aranda-like rule of marriage would produce marriage of a man with his MFZDD (who is also his MMBDD — the Aranda rule), but he could not marry his FFZDD, who would, however, have married into his father's (FM's) clan. His MBD and FZD would be identical, as in simple direct exchange, and they too would be unmarriageable. The structure is simple to understand, and the reader can juggle with it to see how to produce a system in which the MFZDD and the FFZDD are the same (the result of a systematizing of the Cherokee rule), or in which the MFZDD and the MMBDD are separated rather than equated. This, incidentally, would require six lines and may be the solution to the contentious Ambrym problem.

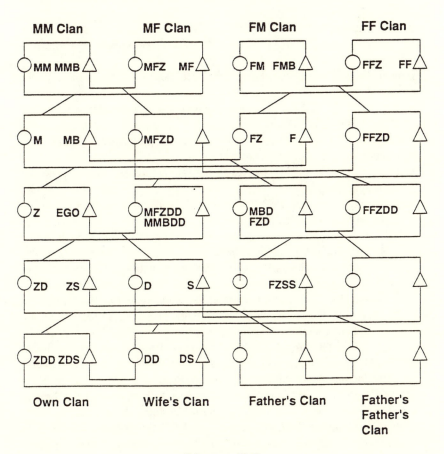

Diagram 13.8

Even more elaborate "solutions" are possible (some requiring sixteen-generation cycles, alternating FZD and MBD marriage, and the like), but they have only an interest insofar as it is always interesting to see what kinds of kinship systems we *could* come up with as opposed to those that actually occur. And we must always remember that such systems as the one above diagrammed will always, unlike the Australian systems, be immersed in a probabilistic flux, to use Lévi-Strauss's words. That is, they will never be "total" systems but represent tendencies inherent in what appear to be "Crow" or "Omaha" systems, like the "skewing" of the Cochiti system toward MFZDD marriage.

References to Chapter 13

Aberle, David F. 1961. "Navaho." In David M. Schneider and Kathleen Gough, eds., *Matrilineal Kinship* (Berkeley: University of California Press).

Benveniste, E. 1969. *Le vocabulaire des institutions indo-européenes.* 2 vols. Paris: Minuit.

Buchler, I. A and Selby, H. A. 1968. *Kinship and Social Organization.* New York: Macmillan.

Deacon, A. B. 1934. *Malekula: A Vanishing People in the New Hebrides.* London: George Routledge and Sons.

Dumont, Louis 1953. "The Dravidian Kinship System as an Expression of Marriage." *Man* o. s. 54.

Eggan, Fred. 1949. *Social Organization of the Western Pueblos.* Chicago: Chicago University Press.

———. 1966. *The American Indian.* London: Weidenfeld and Nicholson.

Fox, Robin. 1967a. *Kinship and Marriage: An Anthropological Perspective.* London: Penquin Books. 2nd ed.: New York: Cambridge University Press, 1983.

———. 1967b. *The Keresan Bridge: A Problem in Pueblo Ethnology.* London School of Economics Monographs in Social Anthropology, no. 35. London: Athlone Press.

———. 1972. "Some Unsolved Problems of Rio-Grande Pueblo Social Organization." In Alfonso Ortiz, ed., *New Perspectives on the Pueblos* (Albuquerque: University of New Mexico Press).

———. 1978. *The Tory Islanders.* Cambridge: Cambridge University Press.

Friedrich, Paul. 1966. "Proto-Indo-European Kinship." *Ethnology* 5: 1-36.

Gilbert, William H. 1937. "Eastern Cherokee Social Organization." In Sol Tax, ed., *Social Anthropology of the North American Tribes* (Chicago: Chicago University Press). 2nd ed.: 1955.

Hiatt, L. R. 1965. *Kinship and Conflict: A Study of an Aboriginal Community in Northern Arnhem Land.* Canberra: Australian National University.

Kaut, Charles R. 1957. *The Western Apache Clan System: Its Origins and Development.* Albuquerque: University of New Mexico Publications in Anthropology, no. 9.

Lévi-Strauss, Claude. 1949. *Les structures élémentaires de la parenté.* Paris: Presses Universitaires de France.

————. 1958. *Antropologie Structurale.* Paris: Plon.

————. 1965. "The Future of Kinship Studies." *Proceedings of the Royal Anthropological Institute 1965*, pp. 13-22.

————. 1969. *The Elementary Structures of Kinship.* Translated by J. H. Bell, J. R. von Sturmer, and R. Needham, editor. Boston: Beacon Press.

Lounsbury, F. G. 1964. "A Formal Account of the Crow- and Omaha-Type Kinship Terminologies." In W. H. Goodenough, ed., *Explorations in Cultural Anthropology* (New York: McGraw-Hill).

Morgan, L. H. 1871. *Systems of Consanguinity and Affinity of the Human Family.* Washington, D.C.: Smithsonian Institution.

Murdock, G. P. 1949. *Social Structure.* New York: Macmillan.

Needham, Rodney 1964. "The Mota Problem and Its Lessons." *Journal of the Polynesian Society* 73(3): 302-314.

Oliver, Douglas L. 1955. *A Soloman Island Society.* Cambridge: Harvard University Press.

Rubel, Paula G. and Rossman, Abraham. 1978. *Your Own Pigs You May Not Eat: A Comparative Study of New Guinea Societies.* Chicago: University of Chicago Press.

Service, E. R. 1962. *Primitive Social Organization: An Evolutionary Perspective.* New York: Random House.

Shapiro, Warren. 1970. "The Ethnography of Two-Section Systems." *Ethnology* 9:380-388.

Steward, Julian. H. 1938. *Basin-Plateau Aboriginal Sociopolitical Groups.* Washington, DC: Smithsonian Institution, Bureau of American Ethnology, bulletin 120.

White, Leslie A. 1939. "A Problem in Kinship Terminology." *American Anthopologist* 41: 569-70.

Diagram 13.7 is reproduced from the American Anthropologist 39(1): 37 by permission of the American Anthropological Association.

Note to Chapter 14

This chapter was first published as "Prejudice and the Unfinished Mind: A New Look at an Old Failing" in *Psychological Enquiry* 3(2) (1992): 137-152. It is reprinted here by permission of the publishers, Lawrence Erlbaum Associates.

Acknowledgments

This essay has been germinating for many years — ever since Ernest Gellner at the LSE in the 1950s made an otherwise lazy undergraduate read Hume closely in the original. Parts of it have been delivered as lectures over the past thirty years, but the opportunity to bring it all together was presented by Felix Browder and Renée Weber in the Rutgers Distinguished Lecture Series in the Spring of 1990. I should like to thank both of them for their comments and encouragement, and the audience at that lecture for its lively questions — which were largely concerned with my alleged misreading of Mr. Spock. Peter Klein and Bruce Wilshire made particularly pertinent comments (not about Spock). Michael Lewis, and Robert Storey, read the essay, and while disagreeing with me a good deal, nevertheless helped me to improve it. The readers for *Psychological Enquiry* made their valuable contributions. Since they were social psychologists, some of them wanted me to write what would have amounted largely to a survey article on "prejudice and stereotype" literature, which I have obviously resisted doing. The reasons will be obvious from the text, and in any case useful surveys have appeared over the years in various editions of the *Handbook of Social Psychology*. I of course exempt all commentators from any responsibility for errors and wrong conclusions, which are entirely, and no doubt perversely, my own. This is an essay which is almost designed for disagreement. I can only say I have benefited from the often tough criticism of the above-mentioned colleagues, while sticking to my guns on a number of contentious points.

Notes and References to Chapter 14

1. The original paper to which I refer was never, in its exact form, I think, published anywhere, but see D. Kahneman and A. Tversky, "Causal Schemata in Judgments under Uncertainty," in M. Fishbein, ed., *Progress in Social Psychology* (New York: Erlbaum, 1977), which came out shortly after. Excerpts from the papers at the conference (including my own on "Rational Ethics and Human Nature" — reprinted in its entirety in *The Search for Society*) were published in Melvin Kranzberg,

ed., *Ethics in an Age of Pervasive Technology* (Boulder, CO: Westview Press, 1980). It is from Kahneman's contribution, "Human Engineering of Decisions" (pp. 190-192), that the present quotations are taken. I should add in fairness that these conclusions have not gone unchallenged in psychology, and there is a lot of work showing that, as one commentator put it, while people may be imperfect at using logic, they are rarely completely out to lunch. Also, the ratios used by experimenters are more often of the order 7:3 than 9:1. At 7:3 I might be prepared to ditch "farmer" in favor of "librarian." Even so, I have used this example for nearly eighteen years now on highly sophisticated and intelligent people, and out of hundreds of respondents, only a negligible number have ever agreed to "farmer" (even at 9:1, or, if pushed, at 9.9:1!) without considerable and heated argument. One argument against the K and T position I have come across goes something like this: "This is not really stereotypical thinking since people are in fact in possession of "sociological" information about farmers, and what they are saying is, given this information, it is 90 percent probable that a person so described is not a farmer. One could only call it stereotypy if they had no — or very little — such information." This is a problem, because one never knows really how much real information about farmers people do have. In my experience, very little. And, as I keep repeating, it should not matter how unusual the farmer is. But in any case I am not here to defend K and T. They are for me *data*. I'm not concerned so much that they may be open to criticism, or that other work modifies their conclusions, and so on. I am concerened with the model of an "unfinished mind" desperately in need of "logical" mechanical adjuncts that they (or at least K) press upon us. The *degree* of "logicality" can be left for the cognitive and social psychologists to squabble over. (The ubiquity of Kissinger at this period is not without its relevance to Kahneman's fright at the prospect of unaided human fingers on the nuclear trigger. One reason I wanted sophisticated companions at that dinner was to try out Lionel Tiger's description of Kissinger as "the shopkeeper of nations," one of the better witticisms in an otherwise dry decade.)

2. These descriptions of Hume are taken from the "Biographical Note" in D. G. C. MacNabb, *David Hume: His Theory of Knowledge and Morality* (London: Hutchinson, 1951), pp. 9-12.

3. Willard van Orman Quine, *Quiddities: An Intermittently Philosophical Dictionary* (Cambridge: Harvard University Press, 1987), pp. 160-161. Robin Fox, *The Red Lamp of Incest: A Study in the Origins of Mind and Society* (Notre Dame: University of Notre Dame Press, 1983 [1980]).

4. Peter Strawson, "Freedom and Resentment," *Proceedings of the British Academy* 48 (1962): 1-25.

5. Robin Fox, *The Search for Society* (New Brunswick, NJ: Rutgers University Press, 1989), chap. 4.

6. See Kent G. Bailey, *Human Paleopsychology: Applications to Aggression and Pathological Processes* (Hillsdale, NJ: Erlbaum, 1987).

7. Notably, Richard D. Alexander, *The Biology of Moral Systems* (New York: Aldine, 1987); James Rachels, *Created from Animals* (Oxford: Oxford University Press, 1990); Malcolm Ruse, *Taking Darwin Seriously* (Oxford: Blackwell, 1986). The latter is the closest approach by another investigator to the position taken here. Ruse and I were obviously involved in parallel thinking on the subject of Hume, but there are subtle differences between our approaches. The title of his book, in fact, knowingly or unknowingly, echoes the final words of my *Encounter with Anthropology* published in 1973: "it [anthropology] should try, after a hundred years, to take Darwin seriously."

8. See part 3 (especially chaps. 14-16) of Gary Wills, *Inventing America: Jefferson's Declaration of Independence* (Garden City, NY: Doubleday, 1978).

9. Various recent attempts to rethink rationality suggest that this is not such an *outré* notion after all. See Patricia Churchland, *Neurophilosophy: Toward a Unified Theory of the Mind-Brain* (Cambridge, MA: MIT Press, 1986); Robert H. Frank, *Passions Within Reason: The Strategic Role of the Emotions* (New York: W. W. Norton, 1988); Herbert Simon, *Reason in Human Affairs* (Stanford, CA: Stanford University Press, 1983); L. Cosmides & J. Tooby, "From Evolution to Behavior: Evolutionary Psychology as the Missing Link," In: J. Dupré, ed., *The Latest on the Best: Essays on Evolution and Optimality* (Cambridge, MA: MIT Press, 1987); J. Tooby & L. Cosmides, "Evolutionary Psychology and the Generation of Culture, Part I: Theoretical Considerations" *Ethology and Sociobiology* 10(1989): 29-49.

10. George Lakoff, *Women, Fire and Dangerous Things: What Categories Reveal about the Mind* (Chicago: Chicago University Press, 1987).

11. D. Kahneman, P. Slovic, & A. Tversky, *Judgement under Uncertainty* (Cambridge: Cambridge University Press, 1982).

12. See Ralph L. Holloway, ed., *Primate Aggression, Territoriality and Xenophobia* (New York: Aacademic Press, 1974).

13. Still one of the best discussions of the origins and functions of these diacritics of group membership is Herbert Spencer's *Ceremonial Institutions,* part 4 of his *Principles of Sociology* (London: Williams and Norgate, 1879). Spencer concentrates more on their role in within-group

hierarchies, which is of course an important adjunct to their between-group discriminatory functions.
14. See discussion and references in chapter 8 ("The Passionate Mind") of Fox, *The Search for Society* (New Brunswick, NJ: Rutgers University Press, 1989).
15. Niko Tinbergen, *The Study of Instinct* (Oxford: Oxford University Press, 1951).
16. Henri Bergson, *The Two Sources of Morality and Religion*, translated by R. Ashley Audra & C. Brereton (London: Macmillan, 1935)[1932]).
17. For a wonderfully insightful and concise discussion of the whole issue of Lippmann and stereotypes, see Michael Curtis, "Walter Lippmann Reconsidered" *Society* 28(2) (1991): 23-31, and references therein.
18. Curtis points out that the social psychologists not caught up in the "prejudice" web, such as Mead and Cooley, came closer to a real understanding of what we now choose to describe as "the social construction of reality." One might add that neither of them would have probably been averse to the present interpretation, which lodges the basic processes involved in this construction firmly in the organism. Indeed, their insight that such constructions arise from the *interaction* of organisms is a basically "ethological" position. But I wouldn't want to push this. Curtis exempts Otto Klineberg and his intellectual heirs and successors from the accusation of too much negativity in looking at stereotypes. Klineberg suggested there was usually a "kernel of truth" in any stereotype. But the issue here is not whether stereotypes might be true or false; they can be either. To declare that they are often true, while at the same time seeing them as again only a by-product of thinking, is simply to make the inverse of the same basic mistake as Lippmann/Allport (Adorno/Fromm, etc.). Of all contemporary social psychological positions, perhaps the closest to the one being argued here lies in the work of Donald Campbell on evolutionary epistemology and ethnocentrism. For a popular but interestingly close-to-the-mark attempt to apply similar ideas to the "homophobic stereotype," see M. Kirk & H. Madsen, *After the Ball* (New York: Doubleday, 1989).
19. See S. Harnad, ed., *Categorical Perception: The Groundwork of Cognition* (Cambridge: Cambridge University Press, 1987), and particularly Harnad's own essay "Category Induction and Representation" therein.
20. This phenomenon was first noticed by Edward Sapir in "La réalité psychologique des phonèmes," in Pierre Janet & George Dumas, eds., *Psychologie du langage* (Paris: Alcan, 1933). Reprinted in English in David G. Mandelbaum, ed., *Selected Writings of Edward Sapir in*

Language, Culture and Personality (Berkeley: University of California Press, 1949).

21. Eleanor Rosch (Eleanor Heider), "Natural Categories," *Cognitive Psychology* 4(1973): 328-350. For an even stronger statement, which elevates color categories, facial expression, and geometric form to the level of "Platonic forms," see "Universals and Cultural Specifics in Human Categorization," in R. W. Brislin, S. Brochner, & W. J. Lonner, eds., *Cross-Cultural Perspectives on Learning* (New York: Wiley, 1975). For a more recent elegant statement, see "Prototype Classification and Logical Classification: The Two Systems," in E. K. Scholnick, ed., *New Trends in Conceptual Representation: Challenges to Piaget's Theory* (Hillsdale, NJ: Erlbaum, 1983).

22. Brent Berlin & Paul Kay, *Basic Color Terms: Their Universality and Evolution* (Berkeley: University of California Press, 1969).

23. Since I claim that the brain/mind is "pragmatic," am I not just reinventing Pragmatism? This has been urged, but I don't see it. Certainly in the Dewey-James-Pierce sense this is not Pragmatism. Theirs was a theory of truth or meaning. Mine is a suggestion of a theory of rationality rather than truth. For example, for Dewey "truth" resided in the interplay between organism and environment, and I have suggested the same thing for rationality. But my interplay is over millions of years of evolution, and its product is certain basic, innate modes of thought. For James and Dewey, the interplay was of *ideas with the world* in which, for various utilitarian reasons, some ideas won out over others. The winners were the "true" ideas. I am not talking about this kind of "truth" at all. The "pragmatism of the mind" here is an evolutionary product, not an evolutionary analogy. For the latter, the best modern example is in Richard Dawkins' *The Selfish Gene* (Oxford: Oxford University Press, 1976), with his notion of competing "memes" in a struggle for existence. Like James, he is inclined to find the "God meme" a prize example of an ideological survival of the fittest. He is perhaps reinventing Pragmatism; I am not. There is actually a great deal in the psychology of William James that is relevant to this argument — but the Pragmatic theory of *truth* is not it.

24. For one of the more sophisticated and up-to-date discussions of archetypes, which takes account of, for example, hemispheric lateralization theory, see Anthony Stevens, *Archetypes: A Natural History of the Self* (New York: Quill, 1983).

25. See James Twitchell, *Preposterous Violence* (Oxford: Oxford University Press, 1989).

26. The descriptions of Lamb are taken from "A Prefatory Memoir," in Charles Kent, ed., *The Works of Charles Lamb: Poetical and Dramatic Tales, Essays and Criticism* (London: George Routledge and Sons, 1889), pp. 3-26.

27. An excellent biography of Robeson is Martin Bauml Duberman, *Paul Robeson* (New York: Knopf, 1988). It is excellent in describing Robeson's primary value of *loyalty*. He would not, even though he was never a member, do anything to discredit the U.S. Communist Party — despite the terrible cost to himself. And this was because when the civil rights movement (as it later came to be called when it became a popular cause for well-heeled white liberals) was at its lowest ebb — when his people were at their most discouraged — it was only the Party and a few unions that stood by them unconditi onally. His loyalty to the USSR was of the same order. It was not ideological; it was something Kipling would have recognized and applauded. It was an expression of the almost superhuman humanity of this extraordinary human being.

Notes to Chapter 15

This was originally titled "Myth as Evidence of Psychological Processes" and written for Phillip Bock, ed., *Handbook of Psychological Anthropology* (Westport, CT: Greenwood Pub. Co., 1994). It is reproduced with permission. Cuts made for space reasons have been restored.

Aarne, A. and Thompson, S. 1961. *The Types of the Folktale*. Helsinki: Suamalainen Tiedeakatemia Academica Scientarum Fennica.

Bastian, Adolf. 1868. *Das Bestandige in den Menschenrassen und die Spielweite ihrer Veranderlichkeit*. Berlin: Rimmer.

Brewer, Derek. 1988. *Symbolic Stories*. London: Longman.

Brown, N. 1969. *Hermes the Thief: The Evolution of a Myth*. New York: Vintage.

Campbell, Joseph. 1949. *The Hero with a Thousand Faces*. Bollingen Series XVII. Princeton: Princeton University Press.

———. 1959. *The Masks of God*. 4 vols. New York: Viking.

———. 1990. *Transformations of Myth through Time*. New York: Harper and Row.

Carroll, Michael. 1986. *The Cult of the Virgin Mary*. Princeton: Princeton University Press.

Conrad, Peter. 1987. *A Song of Love and Death: The Meaning of Opera*. New York: Poseidon.

Crossley-Holland, Kevin. 1980. *The Norse Myths*. New York: Pantheon.

406   The Challenge of Anthropology

Durkheim, Emile. 1915. *The Elementary Forms of the Religious Life.* Translated by J. W. Swain. London: Allen and Unwin.
Eliade, Mircea. 1965. *Rites and Symbols of Initiation.* New York: Harper and Row.
Evans-Pritchard, E. E. 1937. *Witchcraft Oracles and Magic among the Azande.* Oxford: Clarendon.
Fox, R. 1980. *The Red Lamp of Incest.* New York: Dutton. 2nd. ed.: Notre Dame, IN: University of Notre Dame Press, 1983.
———. 1989. *The Search for Society.* New Brunswick, NJ: Rutgers University Press.
Frazer, James. 1891. *The Golden Bough.* London: Macmillan.
Freud, S. 1938. *The Basic Writings of Sigmund Freud.* Edited by A. A. Brill. New York: Random House.
———. 1952. *Totem and Taboo.* Translated by James Strachey. New York: W. W. Norton. First published 1913, Vienna.
———. 1957. *The Future of an Illusion.* Translated by W. D. Robson-Scott. Garden City, NY: Doubleday. First published 1943.
Friedrich, Paul. 1978. *The Meaning of Aphrodite.* Chicago: Chicago University Press.
Graves, Robert. 1946. *King Jesus.* New York: Farrar Strauss.
———. 1948. *The White Goddess: A Historical Grammar of Poetic Myth.* New York: Farrar Strauss.
Hughes, Ted. 1972. *Crow: From the Life and Songs of the Crow.* London: Faber.
Jung, C. J. 1971. *The Portable Jung.* Edited by Joseph Campbell. New York: Viking.
Leeming, David A. 1990. *The World of Myth.* New York: Oxford University Press.
Lévi-Strauss, Claude. 1958. *Anthropologie structurale.* Paris: Plon.
———. 1962. *Le totémisme aujourd'hui.* Paris: Presses Universitaires de France.
———. 1964a. *Mythologiques.* 4 vols. Paris: Plon. Other volumes 1967, 1968, 1971.
———. 1964b. *Le cru et le cuit.* Paris: Plon.
Malinowski, B. 1926. *Myth in Primitive Psychology.* London: Kegan Paul.
———. 1948. *Magic, Science and Religion, and Other Essays.* Glencoe, IL: Free Press.
Malotki, E. 1985. *Gullible Coyote/Una'ihu: A Bilingual Collection of Hopi Coyote Stories.* Tucson: University of Arizona Press.
Marshack, A. 1972. *The Roots of Civilization: The Cognitive Beginnings of Man's First Art, Symbol and Notation.* New York: McGraw-Hill.

Mullahy, Patrick. 1952. *Oedipus: Myth and Complex*. New York: Hermitage Press.

Radcliffe-Brown, A. R. 1952. *Structure and Function in Primitive Society*. London: Cohen and West.

Radin, Paul. 1956. *The Trickster: A Study in American Indian Mythology*. With commentaries by Karl Kerenyi and C. J. Jung. London: Routledge.

Raglan, Lord. 1936. *The Hero*. London: Methuen.

Santillana, G. de and Dechend, H. von. 1977. *Hamlet's Mill: An Essay on Myth and the Frame of Time*. Boston: Godine.

Smith, W. Robertson. 1956. *The Religion of the Semites*. New York: Meridian Books. First published 1889.

Stevens, A. 1982. *Archetypes*. London: Routledge.

Storey, Robert. 1978. *Pierrot: A Critical History of a Mask*. Princeton: Princeton University Press.

Tedlock, Dennis. 1972. *Finding the Center: Narrative Poetry of the Zuni Indians*. New York: Dial.

Trivers, Robert. 1985. *Social Evolution*. Menlo Park, CA: Benjamin/Cummings.

Turner, Frederick. 1991. *Tempest, Flute and Oz: Essays on the Future*. New York: Persea Books.

Turner, Victor. 1969. *The Ritual Process*. Chicago: Aldine.

Twitchell, James. 1985. *Dreadful Pleasures: An Anatomy of Modern Horror*. New York: Oxford University Press.

Ulansey, David. 1989. *The Origins of the Mithraic Mysteries: Cosmology and Salvation in the Ancient World*. New York: Oxford University Press.

Versnel, H. S. 1990. "What's Sauce for the Goose is Sauce for the Gander: Myth and Ritual Old and New." In Lowell Edmunds, ed., *Approaches to Greek Myth* (Baltimore: Johns Hopkins).

Waters, Frank. 1963. *The Book of the Hopi*. New York: Viking-Penguin.

Whiting, J. W. and Child, I. 1953. *Child Training and Personality*. New Haven: Yale University Press.

Winson, J. 1985. *Brain and Psyche: The Biology of the Unconscious*. New York: Doubleday.

Young, Dudley. 1991. *Origins of the Sacred: Ecstacies of Love and War*. New York: St. Martin's Press.

Notes to Chapter 16

This was originally published, with Horst D. Steklis, as "Menstrual-Cycle Phase and Sexual Behavior in Semi-Free-Ranging Stumptail Macaques (*Macaca arctoides*)," *International Journal of Primatology* 9(5): 443-456, and is reproduced by permission of the publishers, Plenum Publishing Co.

We would like to acknowledge the support of the Harry Frank Guggenheim foundation for the data-gathering phase, and Robert Azuma for his invaluable assistance. Rutgers University provided us with research assistance for the arduous task of putting the observational data on disk, and we would like to thank Cathy Greenberg and Cynthia Robin for their help. We are grateful for comments from Drs. R. Blumenschine, S. Cachel, M. McGuire, and M. Raleigh on early drafts of the manuscript. Errors of course are our own responsibility. One minor error has been corrected here and the wording of the conclusion and the set-up of table 16.3 have been minimally changed for clarity. Otherwise the article is reproduced exactly as in the journal.

References

Adams, M. R.; Kaplan, J. R.; and Koritnik, D. R. 1985. "Psychosocial Influences on Ovarian Endocrine and Ovulatory Function in *Macaca fascicularis*," *Physiol. Behav* 35:935-940.

Bertrand, M. 1969. *The Behavioral Repertoire of the Stumptail Macaque.* Bibliotheca Primatologica no. 11. Basel: S. Karger.

Eberhart, J. A. 1988. "Neural and Hormonal Correlates of Primate Sexual Behavior." In Steklis, H. D., and Erwin, J., eds., *Comparative Primate Biology*, vol. 4 (New York: A. R. Liss).

Esser, A. H.; Deutsch, R. D.; and Wolf, M. 1979. "Social Behavior Adaptations of Gibbons (*Hylobates lar*) in a Controlled Environment." *Primates* 20:95-108.

Estep, D. Q. 1987. "Sexual Initiation in Stumptail Macaques (*Macaca arctoides*)." *Primate Rep.* 16:27-33.

Estep, D. Q.; Nieuwenhuijsen, K.; Bruce, K. E. M.; De Neef, K. J.; Walters, P. A.; Baker, S. C.; and Slob, A. K. 1988. "Inhibition of Sexual Behavior among Subordinate Stumptail Macaques, (*Macaca arctoides*)." *Anim. Behav.* 36:854-864.

Harvey, N. C. 1983. "Social and Sexual Behaviors During the Menstrual Cycle in a Colony of Stumptail Macaques (*Macaca arctoides*)." In Steklis, H. D., and Kling, A. S., eds., *Hormones, Drugs and Social Behavior in Primates* (New York: Spectrum.

Murray, R. D.; Bour, E. S.; and Smith, E. O. 1985. "Female Menstrual Cyclicity and Sexual Behavior in Stumptail Macaques (*Macaca arctoides*)." *Int. J. Primatol.* 6:101-113.

Nadler, R. D.; Herndon, J. G.; and Wallis, J. 1986. "Adult Sexual Behavior: Hormones and Reproduction." In Mitchell, G., and Erwin, J., eds., *Comparative Primate Biology,* vol. 2, part a (New York: A. R. Liss).

Nieuwenhuijsen, K.; De Neef, K. J.; and Slob, A. K. 1986. "Sexual Behavior During Ovarian Cycles, Pregnancy and Lactation in Group-Living Stumptail Macaques *(Macaca arctoides)*." *Hum. Reprod.* 1:159-169.

O'Keeffe, R. T.; Lifshitz, K.; and Linn, G. 1983. "Relationship among Dominance, Interanimal Spatial Proximity and Affiliative Social Behavior in Stumptail Macaques *(Macaca arctoides)*." *Appl. Anim. Ethol.* 9:331-339.

Steklis, H. D.; Linn, G. S.; Howard, S. M.; Kling, A. S.; and Tiger, L. 1983. Effects of Medroxyprogesterone Acetate on Sociosexual Behavior of Stumptail Macaques." *Physiol. Behav.* 28:535-544.

Zumpe, D., and Michael, R. P. 1986. "Dominance Index: A Simple Measure of Relative Dominance Status in Primates." *Am. J. Primatol.* 10:291-300.

Zumpe, D., and Michael, R. P. 1987. "Relation between the Dominance Rank of Female Rhesus Monkeys and Their Access to Males." *Am. J. Primatol.* 13:155-169.

Note to Chapter 17

This was originally published in *Neonate Cognition: Beyond the Blooming Buzzing Confusion,* edited by Jacques Mehler and Robin Fox (Hillsdale, NJ: Erlbaum, 1985), and is reproduced with permission. It was the preliminary argument that formed the basis for much of my later *The Search for Society* (New Brunswick, NJ: Rutgers University Press, 1989). References to authors mentioned in the text can be found in the bibliographies of these two books.

Note to Chapter 18

This originally appeared in *The Nation* 250(19) (1990): 664-66 and is reproduced with permission. A belated acknowledgment is here given to the late Tom Bottomore, who taught basic Marx at the LSE in the 1950s — in fact, his class consisted of discussing his ongoing translations of the *Collected Works,* still wet from his pen as he circulated them to us. A fine teacher, affectionately remembered.

Notes to Chapter 19

The edition of Browning used here is *Robert Browning: The Poems*, vol. 2, edited by John Pettigrew, supplemented and completed by Thomas J. Collins (New Haven and London: Yale University Press, 1981). The notes are particularly valuable, as are, for the Browning fan, the collection of unpublished oddments at the end. Who can resist:

> She was fifteen — had great eyes
> Deep with dreams of paradise.

The second line sounds like Rossetti, but the first could be from Leonard Cohen or Bob Dylan. Or try his Latin poem on the safety valve, his limerick-like epigram on papal infallibility, or his "Terse Verse" to be contributed to a Scottish Anthology:

> Hail, ye hills and heaths of Ecclefechan!
> Hail, ye banks and braes of Craigenputtock!

Charles Lamb would have loved that one! I guess Browning's humor isn't for everyone. So much the worse for everyone. But you've got to love his "Rhyme for a Child Viewing a Naked Venus in a Painting of 'The Judgement of Paris'":

> He gazed and gazed and gazed and gazed
> Amazed, amazed, amazed, amazed.

And he could rhyme anything. When challenged to produce a rhyme for Rhinoceros, he managed:

> If ever you meet a rhinoceros
> And a tree be in sight,
> Climb quick! for his might
> Is a match for the gods: he could toss Eros!

And for "radishes":

> Give me bread and cheese and radishes —
> Even stalish bread and baddish cheese.

Not perfect. But could you do better?

Note to Chapter 20

Originally written for *Society* 30(1) (Special Thirtieth Anniversary Issue, 1992): 47-55. Reprinted with permission. I should like to thank Napoleon Chagnon, Melford Spiro, Dudley Young, Jonathan Benthall, and Norman Leavitt for comments.

Index

Acculturation, and kinship, 224, 238, 239
Adams, M., 330
Adams, David, and Seville Declaration Network, 95, 102, 103, 104, 108-10
Adaptation, debate on, 6, 21-23
Addiction, 62
Adrenaline, 90, 258
Affinal clans, 216, 235. *See also* Kinship
Affirmative Action, 272
Aggression: abolition of, 78; constructive function of, 80; culturalized, 80; distribution of aggressive individuals in a population, 76; and environmentalism, 75; and eugenicists, 74; and evolution, 69, 106; and external cause argument, 75, 81-82; and fascists, 74; frustration-aggression hypothesis, 88; genetic predisposition for, 106; and hormones, 90; inhibition of, 79, 86, 92; innate goodness and innate depravity, 69; and

instinct theory, 75; instinct versus learning, 69; internal mechanisms of, 78; linked with sex, 69; and Marxism, 74; nature versus nurture, 69; and neo-right conservatives, 74; as normal, 69, 70; and perfectionists, 74-80; and popular culture, 69; and ritual, 75, 79; and rules, 86; and sex, 69; scientific investigation of, 341, 342; and war, 119, 120-21
Aggression and Violence (Marsh and Campbell), 70
Aggressive potential, 75-76
Alcohol, 62; and inhibition of violence, 93
Allport, Gordon, 273
Alsop, Joe, 48, 49
Altruism, 39
American Anthropological Association, 95, 99
American Association for the Advancement of Science, 109
American Psychological Association, 109
Anansi, trickster myth of, 298

413

17; and human universals, 365, 366; and innate abilities, 342, 344; and kinship, 242; and logic, 257, 263, 269; and mind, 254, 256, 269, 270; and moral responsibility, 267; and myth, 285, 292, 294, 298, 308-9; and primatology, 314, 315; of sex, 4, 69; of social behavior, xii; and sociobiology, 346; and stereotypes, 257-58, 272, 275, 276; survival benefits of, 258, 262, 263, 276; and thought-action, 258; and war, 106. *See also* Hominid evolution

Evolutionary biology, xii, 3

Ewart, J. P., 386

Excalibur (film), 171

Excursion, The (Wordsworth), 268-69

Exogamy, 18, 30; motivations of, 33

Expression, and myth, 305

Eye of the Devil (film), 171

Falsification, 166

Fanaticism, 109; routinization of, 100; and war, 121-22

Fascists, 74

Fast food, 54

Father-daughter intercourse, 29, 35-36

Female, 10; orgasm, 23; primate congregating behavior, 11-12; reproductive strategies, 12-17

Feminist science, 337

Fergusson, Francis, 338

Fight sequence between conspecifics, 91

First-cousin marriage, 29

Fish, Stanley, 380

Fit, mind and world, 269, 273

Flandrin, Jean-Louis, 4

Focal ancestor, 139, 142

Focal ego, 200

Follicular phase, 316, 325

Food: and asceticism, 60; and courtship, 50, 51-52; and ethnicity, 41, 43; fast, 54; foreign, 47; and Freud, 59; and funeral feasts, 60; and gluttony, 60, 61; junk, 53; and love, 39; Meyer Fortes on, 59; and proper eating, 41; and public ritual of eating out, 53; and treats, 53; taboos, 40, 59. *See also* Cooking

Forde, Daryll, 130

Foucault, Michel, 4

Fox, Kate, 6, 386

Fragmentation of society, xi

Fraternities, 182

Frazer, George McDonald, 301

Frazer, Sir James: and *The Golden Bough*, 129, 153-56, 158-62, 164-73; and incest prohibitions, "inevitable evolutionary sequence" of knowledge, 118-19; and myth, 286, 287, 288; and science, 166-167; as translator, 162-63

Free love, and prostitution, 119

Free will: and determinism, 265; and responsibility, 265, 267

Freedman, Maurice, 4, 154, 163-64, 165

Freud, Sigmund: and behaviorism, 345-346; and dreams, 293; and food taboos, 59; and Frazer, 173; and incest prohibition, 33-34, 35, 36; and myth, 291, 292, 293

From Ritual to Romance (Weston), 155

Frustration-aggression hypothesis, 88

Functionalism, 153, 154

Funeral feasts, 60

Hormones, and aggressive
  encounters, 90
Horowitz, Irving Louis, x
Hospitality, 43
Household Management (Beeton), 44
Households, 149, 150, 151
Howard, John Eager, 48, 49
Hughes, Ted, 303
Human Ethology Newsletter, 96
Human evolution. *See* Evolution
Human nature, and Edmund Burke,
  343-44
Human sacrifice, 179-80
Hume, David: and cause and effect,
  259, 262, 273; and contiguity,
  259-60, 261-62; and custom, 262,
  267; and instincts, 273; and moral
  sense, 265; and nature, 263;
  philosophical therapy of, 261,
  264, 268; and reason, 260, 261,
  262-63, 271
Hustler, The (film), 301
Huxley, Julian, 104
Hyperaggressive: animals, 98, 106;
  people in small and large
  populations, 76
Hypothesis testing, 166

Iconotropy, 289
Ideology: and violence, 341; and
  war, 121, 126
Imagination: violent, 85; and war,
  119, 122
Imperfection of reason, 260, 261; as
  unfinished mind, 261
Imperial Animal, The, (Tiger and
  Fox), ix
*In Search of Human Nature: The
  Decline and Revival of Darwinism
  in American Social Thought*
  (Degler), 5
Inbuilt constraints of small groups, 76

Incest: avoidance motivations of,
  34-35; inhibition, 79; taboo, 4, 5
Indirect marital exchange, 206. *See
  also* Kinship
Inhibition of aggression: and
  evolution of brain, 79; rules of, 86;
  and yuppies, 92
Initiation systems, and sexual
  selection, 17-18
Innate, the: and Darwinism, 344-45;
  and emotions, 344; ethology of,
  346-47; genetics of, 346; goodness
  versus depravity, 69; and language
  acquisition device, 346; as
  learned, 342-43; and Lévi-Strauss,
  346; violence, 76, 77, 78
Instinct: and intelligence, 273; versus
  learning, 69; and stereotypes, 273;
  theory of, 75; and war, 103
Integration, and myth, 303-5
Intellectual autobiography, xvi
Intellectual crisis, xiii-xiv; and
  anthropology, xiv-xv
Intellectual wimpishness, 365
Interactionism, 343; and Piaget, 345;
  and neonate studies, 348
Intermoiety marriage, 208. *See also*
  Kinship
Internationalists, 115
Intuition, 256, 343; deserting reason
  for, 261; judgments by, 254; and
  reasoning, 255
Intuitive leaps, 270
Invention of Primitive Society, The
  (Kuper), 173
Irish, 131, 132; ritual fighting of, 92
Isaacs, Susan, 346
I've Seen the Best of It (Alsop), 48

James, William, 404*n23*; and
  interactionist epistemology, 345,
  348; and war, 119-20

422   The Challenge of Anthropology

female sexual behavior of, 329-330; male dominance among, 320, 323, 324, 325, 327, 329, 330, 331; menstrual cycles of, 316, 320, 322, 325, 327, 330; social behavior of, 322; and socioenvironmental variables, 320, 332; sociosexual behavior of, 320, 322, 329, 332
Suburbs, 63-65
Surrealist novel, 303
Sweets, 61-62
Sweezey, Paul M., 352
Symbolic activity and food, 39, 40, 60, 62
Symbolic intelligence, 120, 121
Symmetrical exchange: and asymmetrical exchange, 202, 205-6; and moieties, 200, 202
Systems of Consanguinity and Affinity of the Human Family (Morgan), 215

Tantric yoga, 24, 25
Tedlock, Dennis, 305
Teenager socialization, 64-65
Testosterone, 90
Thackeray, Anne, 357
"Theory" in anthropology, 365; wimpishness of, 365
Thinking: and categorical perception, 275; and certainty, 261; and contiguity, 259-60, 261-62; and custom, 261, 262; habitual, 261; as prejudice, 283; as reflex, 258. *See also* Stereotypical thinking
Thurber, James, 270
Tiger, Lionel, ix, 25, 54, 70
Tillion, Germaine, 176, 182
Tinbergen, Niko, 273, 403n15
Trade: large scale, 190-91; Pueblo, 190; specialists, 190

Transformations of Myth through Time (Campbell), 285
Transnational corporations and war, 114
Treatise of Human Nature (Hume), 259
Trickster: as author, xv; and "con man" theme, 301; and Dadaism, 303; history of, 297-301, 303; and innocent fool theme, 300, 301; and marginality, 301; modern forms of, 300, 301-3; splitting of, 301-2; Winnebago, 298
Triumph display, 90
Trobriand Islands, myths of, 287, 288
Tory Islanders: and ancestors, 136, 137, 139, 140; clanns of, 135-36, 137, 138, 139-40, 146, 148; degrees of relatedness among, 137, 138, 140-41, 147; focal ancestor, 139, 140; and genealogists, 134, 135, 136, 138, 139, 140, 148; genealogy of, 133-36, 138-412, 144; "Holy family", 149, 151; and households, 149, 150, 151; and kin recruitment on boats, 146-48, 151; kinship reckoning among, 137, 138, 139, 143-44, 148; and land inheritance, 141-42, 144, 149, 151; and marriage, 144-46, 148, 149-50, 151; and naming, 133, 137, 138, 139-40, 141; and nextness of kin, 144; and parents, 149, 150; and progeny, 134-35; residence rules of, 149, 150, 151
Tory Islanders, The: A People of the Celtic Fringe (Fox), xv, 129, 131
Totalitarian states, 352
Totemic myths, 291-92; and dream time, 304